ALTHUSSER REVISITED

PROBLEMATIC, SYMPTOMATIC READING, ISA
AND HISTORY OF MARXISM

A TEXTOLOGICAL READING

ALTHUSSER REVISITED

PROBLEMATIC, SYMPTOMATIC READING, ISA AND HISTORY OF MARXISM

A TEXTOLOGICAL READING

by Zhang Yibing

Translated by Yang Liu, Zhan Chongyang,
Yi Diandian, Wang Yan

CANUT INTERNATIONAL PUBLISHERS
Istanbul ▪ Berlin ▪ London ▪ Santiago

Published in 2003 by Central Compilation and Translation Press

The English version is published in cooperation with China Renmin University Press.
Original Chinese Copyright © 2003, First Chinese Edition
ISBN: 978-7-801-09646-3

Canut International Publishers
Published by Canut International Publishers
Canut Int. Turkey, Balipaşa Cad. 155a, Tel : +90-212-5124356, Istanbul, Turkey
Canut Int. Germany, Heerstr. 49, D-47053, Duisburg, Germany
Canut Int. UK, 12a Guernsay Road, London E11 4BJ, England
Web: http://www.leftreader.com
E-Mail: canut@leftreader.com

English Print edition: *Althusser Revisited. Problematic, Symptomatic Reading, ISA and History of Marxism. A Textological Reading*, March 2014

ISBN: 978-605-4923-01-4

English Digital Edition:

ISBN: 978-605-4923-00-7

Printed in England
Lightning Source UK Ltd.
Chapter House
Pitfield
Kiln Farm
Milton Keynes
MK11 3LW
United Kingdom

This book is dedicated to my teacher Sun Bokui

CONTENTS

PART TWO

RE-DIAGNOSE THE HISTORY OF MARX'S PHILOSOPHICAL THOUGHTS

CHAPTER VIII

NEW INTERPRETATION BY ALTHUSSER:
HIS INNOVATION ON THE METHODOLOGY OF RESEARCH
INTO MARX AND CRITIQUE

CHAPTER IX

THE NEW TEXTUAL RESEARCH INTO THE DEVELOPMENT
OF MARX'S PHILOSOPHICAL THOUGHTS

CHAPTER X

THE MOST IMPORTANT PRINCIPLE OF MARXISM

CHAPTER XI

MARXIST HISTORICAL SCIENCE

CONCLUSION:

RAIN OF DECONSTRUCTION:
THE END OF ALEATORY MATERIALISM

PUBLISHER'S NOTE

Althusser Revisited, this original textological analysis work reads the epoch making texts of outstanding Marxist philosopher, Althusser's *For Marx* (1965), *Reading Capital* (1965), *Lenin and Philosophy and other Essays* (1971) which includes his text *Ideology and Ideological State Apparatuses*; also the author delves into other texts of him to support the interpretation. Thus the first part of the book discusses the three core concepts of **problematic**, **epistemological rupture** and **ideology**, as well as **symptomatical reading** as raised by Althusser after remoulding Lacan. Zhang believes, problematic is the core theoretical paradigm of all of Althusser's philosophical methods, and without a clear understanding on this theory, we will inevitably miss the genuine and complete Althusser. The second part of the book deals with Althusser's theories on the history of Marxist philosophy and his ideas on how "scientific Marxism" was established. Althusser again and again becomes a major topic of discussion. Zhang suggests, behind him stood two others: the young, morbid Catholic one and the older, gloomy Pre-Modernity classical materialist one. Putting it more precisely, these existential figures are factual images that Althusser had, in the past, intentionally concealed. This neglect leads to an interpretative dramatization and an inexplicable mystery. A formerly dazzling yet fictive sage and a multi-faceted yet intentionally-concealed person both present themselves in the research realm. Therefore traditional academic circles were thrown into disorder and discomfiture when the accepted, singular conception of a "scientific Marxist" Althusser's original consistent image is destroyed, leaving only a mist that gradually dissipates. As Lacan put it, with the shedding of its coverings, the original vacancy further revealed itself. This is another victory of "the Other".

Nanjing's keen researcher Zhang Yibing, whom we know from his three other successful textological readings, published by our press, discovers Marxist Althusser shifting to an Althusser with four distinct facets. His reading suggests that the precondition of exploring his mystery is to demonstrate Althusser's complex, painful and obscure life and the mystery of his paradoxical thoughts. Although some other contemporary researchers became aware of the four different Althussers, we perceive that Zhang has indeed caught integrated research logic to demonstrate a complete Althusser interpretation, in which there still exists continuity between the four Althussers. Nanjing University is one of the brightest centres of international Marxism research centres in China, which actively promotes dialogues among world's Marxism researchers. We owe great thanks to Yang Liu and his team from the Institute of International Students for the English translation of the book. I should mention that without the help of our cooperation partner Renmin University Press's editors and support given by chief editor He Yaomin, it would be a very hard task to accomplish this complex English version. Besides we owe great thanks to Yang Liu and his team and proof-reader Lacey Bradley from the Institute of International Students for the English translation of the book.

Daivya Jindal
March 2014, Berlin

PREFACE

Althusser is no stranger to Chinese academia. His "Structural Marxism" is researched under Marxist philosophy and Lenin's philosophy, literature criticism, movie theories or aesthetic theories. The present European academia, which inhabits the post-modernist and post-Marxist era, increasingly appreciates Althusser's theories. We Chinese researchers are perplexed by this phenomenon and all our doubts boil down to one question: Have we misread Althusser? And my answer is: Perhaps. There might be two reasons for this: an important historical change and the cloak of a turbulence theory.

Firstly, the important historical change occurs during the 1990s when a stack of posthumous books are published and Althusser once again becomes a major topic of discussion.[1] Yet what is interesting is that behind the well-known Marxist philosopher Althusser stood two others: the young, morbid Catholic one and the older, gloomy Pre-Modernity classical materialist one. Putting it more precisely, these existential figures are factual images that Althusser had, in the past, intentionally concealed. This leads to an interpretative dramatization

---

1   After 1990, the following Althusser's works have been published: *The Future Lasts Forever: A Memoir* (1992); *On Philosophy* (1994); *The Specter of Hegel: Early Writings* (1997); *Machiavelli and Us* (1999).

and an inexplicable mystery. A formerly dazzling yet fictive sage and a multi-faceted yet intentionally-concealed person both present themselves in the research realm simultaneously.[2] The original consistent image is destroyed, leaving only a mist that gradually dissipates. As Lacan put it, with the shedding of its coverings, the original vacancy further revealed itself. This is another victory of "the Other".

The precondition of exploring this mystery is to demonstrate Althusser's complex, painful and obscure life and the mystery of his paradoxical thoughts. Before 1950, Althusser was a believer in the teachings of Catholicism. That is to say, Althusser I appeared first is a Christian, which is the real foundation of his thoughts. As such, the remnants of the divine can never be totally erased. In terms of theological logic, an individual's worldly being is a kind of Nothingness, and the absent but almighty God initiated the Critical Framework of Althusser I. It is of vital importance to remember this. The second theoretical position of the Young Althusser centres on Hegel. The path runs smoothly from the Hegelian logic, which negates the individual subject, to the structuralist theoretical framework **without individual subject**. Naturally, Althusser II would reject anything in humanistic form. At the beginning of the 1950s, Althusser decisively left Catholicism and turned to Marxism. This is the most dazzling scientific and Marxist Althusser III. What is interesting however is that Althusser, in his later years, suddenly returned to the "aleatory materialism" of ancient atomism when he made inquiries into the thoughts of Spinoza and Machiavelli. Thus people began to doubt the firmness of Althusser IV's Marxist position. This dense fog caused the different ruptures and separation of Althusser's thoughts into four distinct characterizations, and it is still an unanswered mystery in the contemporary research into Althusser. Contemporary researchers only make a distinction between the four different Althussers, but they fail to find an integrated research logic.

---

2   The Japanese scholar Hitoshi says that Althusser's works published during the 1990s display two Althussers to people: the public Althusser and the secret one. See: Hitoshi, Yimamura. *Althusser: Epistemological Rupture*. Trans. Niu Jianke. Hebei Education Press, 2001. p. 9.

Actually, according to my understanding, there still exists continuity between the four Althussers. This is an anti-teleological viewpoint of non-subject and pseudo-subject that takes the absence of individual subject as the core. Whether it is the God beyond the individual in Althusser I's Catholicism followed by the abstract framework in which Hegel criticized the passionate subject – a framework admired by Althusser II, or the invisible manipulation of problematic of Althusser III as a Marxist, or the implied meaning of the void in symptomatic reading and the social unconsciousness in Ideology, they all point to the elimination of the individual subject. The Marxian viewpoint that human essence is the sum of social relations becomes the Nothingness of the Subject, where Nothingness is used to construct Nothingness in the Lacanian context. The statement that the agent is an automaton in the invisible apparatus of social production is just a rewriting from the Lacanian mirror image and symbolic code to a combination of positive social relations. At this point, Althusser is undoubtedly an inversed Lacan. However, the inversion of Nothingness is still Nothingness. So when Althusser defines the essence of historical materialism as "a process without a subject," he is merely inheriting the work of others. If we describe the elderly Althusser's "aleatory materialism" as Althusser IV then he is, in reality, only a pessimistic shadow of Althusser III. In contrast to the positive liberalism of the Young Marx, Althusser no longer focuses on the dynamic deflection of Epicurus but seeks liberation of the real subject in the indefinite coupling of Democritus. The mode of production is the historical coupling of productive forces and relations, which is similar to the universality of *Geworfenheit* in Heidegger's *Ontologie*. Here humanistic poetics is rejected, and value-criticism is rewritten as the authenticity of historical reality. The moment when Althusser kills the other (his wife), he, having nothing, happily returns to the arms of God.

Since this book is a special subject study of Althusser's philosophical texts about Marxism, I do not intend to study his thoughts, in youth and in later years, one by one, but instead, solving this relational problem will be the incidental work of this book. I will use the newest literature and materials as an important foundation for interpreting Althusser.

Secondly, the veil of a turbulence theory is the primary way in which we misunderstand Althusser III. The Althusser, whom we discuss in this book (in the 1960s-1970s), is idolized and considered a Marxist "scientific" philosopher emerging as the time needs. Compared to other Marxist humanists, Althusser appears calm and rational. In his writings, there are no brand-new concepts or unique and systematic structures. He borrows structuralist and post-structuralist discourses from Bachelard, Lacan and Foucault to illustrate how to interpret Marxist doctrines scientifically.[3] Althusser explicitly proposes to differ from Marx's early Hegelian and Feuerbachian writings, as well as his later properly Marxist texts, and condemns the humanistic trend in Marxist theory (as represented by Georg Lukács, Erich Fromm and Henri Lefebvre). Althusser's re-reading indicates a historic theoretic backwash within Marxism.

In my opinion, we cannot simply characterize Althusser's thoughts as "structuralist Marxism" and denounce it. Althusser insists on his being a Marxist. Although there are various theoretical appropriations in his arguments and arbitrary concoctions in his re-interpretations, his academic standpoint is, without a doubt, Marxist in nature.[4] However, we maintain that Althusser did not break through the

---

3   Althusser's ideological context relies on Paris academia during the 1960s. The thoughts of Bachelard, J. Lacan and Foucault theoretically support Althusser's complex context. In terms of the relationship between Althusser and Foucault, some scholars comment that they both focus on the unconscious structure of human's subjective activities: the complicated form adopted by human's speech to differentiate from anthropological subjective philosophy. The relations between them influence one another. (Callinicos, Alex. *Althusser's Marxism*. Trans. Du Zhangzhi. Taipei: Long Stream Publications, 1990. p. 11.) In some sense, Althusser is closer to Foucault during the 70s. But afterwards Foucault's thoughts changed markedly, but Althusser remains unchanged. Althusser's theoretical background is more complex. Spinoza, Hobbes, Rousseau, Montesquieu, Machiavelli, and especially Hegel, represent his most important theoretical resources. See: Althusser, Louis. *Soutenance d'Amiens*. Cited from *Research Material on Marxism and Leninism*. People's Publishing Press, 1986. p. 292.
4   At this point, we clearly see that academia in the former Soviet Union was quite tolerant to the scientific trend in Western Marxism. In 1978, Soviet academics published a book of severe dogmatism called *Anti-Marxism under the Banner of "Neo-Marxism"* which thoroughly criticized "neo-Marxism". Almost all schools of anthropology in the ideological trend of Western Marxism were included in this book, except for the scholars who have a tendency towards scientism. (Beccohob, B. H. Anti-Marxism under the Banner of "Neo-Marxism". Beijing: China Renmin University Press, 1983.) However, the book *The Contemporary Philosophy of Marxism-Leninism* compiled by the Research Center of Philosophy of the former Soviet Union in 1984

shackles of the alternative logics of Western Marxism; he carried on too far when he correctly emphasized certain features of Marxism before turning to scientism – another extreme opposite of humanism. In some sense, he managed to misinterpret Marxism.

Althusser's Achilles' heel is not his so-called 'structural' metaphorical theories, but the ivory-tower nature of his theories. Althusser was only engaged in both theoretical research and struggles, which led to his theories' deviation from social development, especially that of labour movement. And it thus shared a fundamental emblem with the humanism of Western Marxism. Concerning this, "New Left" thinker Perry Anderson remarked quite pertinently: Theory became, for a whole historical period, an esoteric discipline whose highly technical idiom measured its distance from politics.[5] And this is the theoretical tendency of Western Marxism under pressure from capitalism. To some degree, Althusser is not as practical as Young Lukacs and Gramsci. However, when humanism was prevalent in Western Marxism, Althusser's beliefs were like fresh air, especially when many a western communist and left-winger felt disillusioned because of setbacks in the international communism movement and their own anti-war feelings. Some people comment that Althusser is the person who revives the basic concepts of Marxist philosophy from its endless dark nights.[6] Because of this, Althusser's philosophy is very important in the history of Western Marxism.

Nevertheless, among the introductions of Althusser made in China (in my opinion, people showed much interest in Althusser's theories yet it was not in-depth research), the focus is on the theoretical results that Althusser obtained under the control of a certain logic frame. This is mainly the reinterpretation of the ideological history of Marx, as well as the results of this reinterpretation, such as "theory of rupture," "anti-humanism in theory," "history is a process without

---

gives great consideration to Western Marxists. Though it criticizes some of Althusser and Della Volpe's views, these theorists generally belong to Marxist philosophy. See: *The Contemporary Philosophy of Marxism-Leninism*. Edited by A.G Myslivchenko and published by Beijing, Social Sciences Academic Press, 1986. Nevertheless, I have to point out that the ideological logic and theoretical analysis laid out in these books were extremely simple and shallow.

5   Anderson, Perry. *Considerations on Western Marxism*. London; New York: Verso, p. 53.
6   Erickson, Luke. Althusser and the Revival of Revolutionary Marxism. *Social Sciences Abroad*, 1983(11).p. 5.

a subject" and so on. In this context, what is neglected is exactly *the way of construction* that leads to the results. This will certainly cause a terrible weakness in interpretation: the real Althusser is veiled. In Althusser's words, we see things through the grid of the weak light of Reading I. This grid is still the traditional interpretation framework of philosophy. Why? Because Althusser's theoretical operation is typical imperialism of methodology that *hides and extinguishes the ontology*. In his eyes, *methodology is ontological logic, and the result is merely the concrete finished product*. If we can only see the result of the objectification of a theory and are unaware of the problematic as theoretical production mode, then we do not really understand it. Actually, up to now, we do not grasp the really wonderful things put forward by Althusser.[7]

Therefore, compared to the misinterpretation in the past, we have to first examine Althusser's methodological framework. Because of this I claim the book as a "textual interpretation." However, in contrast to my former two books, *Back to Marx* and *Atonal Dialectic Imagination*,[8] its analysis of the texts does not proceed according to the chronological order of writing, but rather it analyzes texts in the form of seminars. This book's interpretation of Althusser is mainly based on *For Marx, Reading Capital*, and *Ideology and Ideological State Apparatus*.[9] Among them, *For Marx*, published in 1965, is made up of eight essays he wrote from February of 1960 to March of 1965.[10] Besides the essays of Balibar, *Reading Capital* was also

---

7   Hitoshi points out accurately that the two main texts of Althusser in 1965 have two themes which are "what is authentic Marx" and "the method and position to obtain the truth" respectively. According to Hitoshi, most of our previous interpretations are about the first theme. See: Hitoshi, Yimamura. *Althusser: Epistemological Rupture*, p. 6.

8   *Back to Marx: The Philosophical Discourse in the in the Context of Economics*. Jiangsu People's Publishing House, 1999. English version, Back to Marx: The Change of Philosophical Discourse in the Context of Economics, was published by Göttingen University Press, in 2014. *Atonic Dialectic Imagination. The Textual Interpretation of Adorno's Negative Dialectics*. Joint Publishing, 2001.

9   I cannot agree with some foreign scholars. After a lot of Althusser's posthumous works are published, they refer to these texts as "tip of the iceberg" of Althusser's thoughts. However, in my eyes, these texts represent the most important and the most fundamental thoughts of Althusser's, which should be compared to "huge theoretical mountain".

10   In 1965, The Maspero Press in Paris published Althusser's *For Marx* and *Reading Capital* at the same time. *For Marx* has been printed a dozen times and was translated into many languages.

published in 1965 and it mainly includes Althusser's two long essays, *Introduction* and *Objects of Marx's Capital*. These are the lectures on *Capital* that Althusser made during the first few months at
École Normale Supérieure.[11] *For Marx* and *Reading Capital* can be
regarded as the summary of Althusser's most important thoughts in
1965 because his main theoretical constructions have been included
in these two texts. In my opinion, this is the only real theoretical
peak in Althusser's academic career. Hitoshi says exaggeratedly that
thoughts erupted like an earthquake in the year 1965.[12] Indeed, in
1965, Althusser did "make a gorgeous and shocking show," but unfortunately, it is the only one in his lifetime. In addition, *Ideology
and Ideological State Apparatus* was written between January and
April in 1969, and it included Althusser's new views after he was
influenced by Lacanian theories.

I created the introduction as the background for reading. Part I is then
given to the discussion of the Althusser's methodological Gestalt,
which is not familiar to Chinese academia. The reason for such a
design has to do with the fact that Althusser's structure of texts has
a significant deficiency, namely he does not explain his own problematic nor the many theories he borrowed from others. He assumes
that readers in different times and different contexts will understand
the theories of the French academia during the 1960s, which is probably the main reason why the interpretation of Althusser's texts goes
astray. It is no wonder that some claim that all of Althusser's theories
are based on himself.[13] Problematic and Symptomatic are discussed
respectively in Chapter 1 and 2. They are what I consider to be best
in the book. In Chapter 3 and 4, I "retrieve" Althusser's long-ignored
views concerning epistemology and specifically discuss the historical position of "Epistemological Rupture" in the history of ideology.
Then in Chapter 5 and 6, attention shifts to Althusser's most influen-
tial theory of ideology in the present age. Then in Part II, I examine
and analyze Althusser's interpretation on Marx. Chapter 7 focuses

---

11   In 1965, in the first edition of *Reading Capital*, there are essays of Ranciere besides those of Balibar. When the book was republished in 1968, only the essays of
Balibar are kept. In 2000 the Central Compilation and Translation Press chose the 1968
edition for translation.

12   Hitoshi, Yimamura. *Althusser: Epistemological Rupture*, p. 5.

13   Hirsch. The Ideological History of French New Leftists. *Research Material on
Marxism-Leninism*. Beijing: People's Publishing House,1983 (5).175.

on the discussion of the theoretical fluctuation in western academia in the specific historic context, i. e., the "de-Stalinization" after Twentieth Party Congress of USSR Communist Party. This leads to the recovery of the humanistic roots of Marx's thought. Althusser, however, opposed this trend and fought for Marx. Althusser is literally like a deflagrating torch in the Western left-wing circle. Chapter 8 comments on Althusser's views on traditional Marxist philosophical methodology, and though such "new hermeneutics" are important contents we tend to neglect them. The last three chapters examine and re-annotate Althusser's role in Marxist philosophical history; it is that here I have made breakthrough research on the subject.

In addition, it needs to be pointed out that my teacher Sun Bokui and I, because of our comprehension model toward the ideological history of Marxist philosophy, are sometimes mistaken as being analogical to Althusser. Thus this book also intends to help us make a clear theoretical distinction from Althusser.[14]

Zhang Yibing
Oct 30th, 2001

---

14   To put it bluntly, some scholars neither understand Althusser's thoughts nor comprehend our research method and arguments. They only obtain the same conclusion through a simple comparison of the two.

INTRODUCTION

NOTHINGNESS AND NIGHT:
PHILOSOPHICAL KEY WORDS OF YOUNG ALTHUSSER

As previously stated, Althusser is not a new subject of research within academia. Althusser, who was once considered the ideal Marxist philosopher – in some cases appearing almost "too good to be true" – has attracted the attention of the world once again thanks to the emergence of his many posthumous works during the 1990s. Behind the well-known Marxist philosopher hides a young Catholic, Hegel's follower and pre-modern philosopher who would, in his later years, advocate "aleatory materialism". It is surprising that both the formerly highly-regarded Althusser and the multi-faceted, yet intentionally concealed one, show up in the research realm at the same time. Truth and untruth coexist.

1 THE TRUE AND UNTRUE LIFE OF ALTHUSSER

Althusser was born in the small and quiet town of Birmendreïs near the suburb of Algiers on October 16, 1918. His birth seemed no different from many others. His paternal grandfather was a public servant in this French-colonized town, and his maternal grandfather was a local forest ranger. These two families had, for many years, maintained a close relationship. Interestingly, it was Althusser's uncle Louis who originally fell in love with and eventually became engaged to Althusser's mother, Luciana. However, Louis died in the cruel war, and Charles, Louis's brother, was lucky and survived. Shortly after his return, Charles proposed to poor Luciana, who had no choice but to agree to the marriage. The couple's rushed marriage exerted a profound influence upon their son Althusser's life, determining his tragic and inescapable fate from which only death would set him free. After her marriage, the young and lovesick Luciana was unable to forget Louis. She even named her unfortunate child Louis in memory of her beloved. Thus, in his mother's eyes, Althusser, from the very moment he was born, did not exist in this world as an independent Self but was projected and recalled as a dependent Other. For Althusser, the pronunciation of "LOUIS" should have belonged to him, but instead the word seemed quite hollow since it was conveyed his mother's love for her beloved, but not for him. Indeed, whenever his mother called his name he sensed not the least amount of love for himself. Without a doubt, it was the absence of motherly love that cast its long shadow over Althusser's entire life. He would later say:

I was named Louis the moment I was born. It was done out of my mother's will rather than my own. It is pronounced as another person's name, one who has stripped me of all of my individual characteristics. As an anonymous Other, "LOUIS" was being called and recalled at any time. But it refers to my uncle, the shadow standing behind me. "LOUIS" is Louis, the man my mother loved, not me.[1]

This remark conveyed both misery and clear rationality, laying bare the bitterness and desperation that had been trailing Althusser for decades. In the Lacanian sense, it is not the little other which deposes the ego at the mirror stage, but **an inverted Other (*utter*) instead of "I"**. Althusser's autobiography indicates that as a child, he already displayed the talent and keenness of a great thinker. He was even able to understand his mother's mind, realizing that what she truly cared about was only the name itself and not the physical presence it represented. The tender voice that passed softly from between his

---

1   Althusser, Louis *The Future Lasts Forever*, London, 1993. p. 39.

mother's lips was a call for her beloved long buried underground. She did not love Althusser, the corporeal substitute of her lover. For Luciana, human beings were a mass of **Nothingness** that had no substance; for Althusser, life was an endless and painful **Night** from the very beginning. It is the castration of motherly love and the splitting and inversion of the subject that would, in time, lead both to Althusser's structuralistic logic and to his schizophrenia.

Eventually, Althusser's father became a bank manager, making the young boy's life rather affluent and comfortable. However, this wealth could not alleviate the psychological depression and loneliness that so characterized the environment in which he existed. From 1924 to 1930, Althusser attended primary school in Algiers, and afterward his family returned to France where, in 1936, Althusser finished high school in Marseille. Althusser was also a practicing Catholic due in large part to the influence of his family. So it is not difficult to understand why his later anguish and unbearable loneliness made him harbor a pious reverence for God and Heaven. In 1936, Althusser moved to Lyon with his family and in that same year, he began studying foundation courses at the Ecole Normale Supérieure. Around 1937, Althusser began to take an active part in the movement of Young Christian Workers,[2] which brought together socialism and theology under the slogan of "combine religion with social reform". In this period, Jean Lacroix,[3] a scholar with a theological background, became Althusser's most important spiritual guide. During the German occupation, Lacroix was an active participant in the resistance movement. His courage and morale inspired Althusser's fighting will. Althusser soon became the leader of the Young Christian Workers movement at school. This experience would lay the foundation for Althusser's future Leftist career.

In July 1939, Althusser enrolled in the College of Arts at the Ecole Normale Supérieure with a sixth rank. But in September of that same year, his schooling was interrupted by the war, and Althusser left to join the army. When German troops occupied France in June 1940, he was jailed in German prison camp. His life in prison lasted for

2   The Young Christian Workers was founded in 1925 based on the principle of "participation of civil members in church hierarchy", and the idea of moving from traditional ceremonies to an active involvement in social life.
3   Jean Lacroix (1900-1986), a French Catholic philosopher.

five miserable years, and Althusser did not regain his freedom until the war ended. Unfortunately, the torment of his prison life would eventually be the catalyst for the first outbreak of his depressive disorder while its underlying cause was probably long-term psychological distress. The horrors of the war undoubtedly aggravated his mental breakdown, and Althusser would eventually suffer from nearly twenty different attacks of the disease. It was an illness that would haunt him for the rest of his life. According to Althusser's personal writings, it was actually the unique and complex circumstances of prison life that would allow him to temporarily rid himself of the long shadow of loneliness cast by his dismal childhood. The physical limitations imposed by his incarceration also helped him to capture the ephemeral spiritual and emotional freedom of the "endless dark night". More importantly, however, while he was in the prison camp Althusser met Pierre Courreges, a communist, who left a significant impact on Althusser's life and who first introduced Althusser to the beliefs of communism. In May 1945, Althusser finally returned to his family.

In December 1946, Althusser became acquainted with a Lithuanian-born Jewish girl named Heléne Rytman. She would later become his wife. Rytman was eight years older than Althusser, and at that time she was already a veteran communist, having been a member of the Party for over ten years. The courage she displayed in the resistance movement deeply affected Althusser. Moreover, the views they shared on love and life played a vital role in fully converting Althusser to Marxism. However, at the time Althusser did not realize this complicated love relationship would eventually bring him even greater pain and hardship.

That same year, Althusser entered the Ecole Normale Supérieure once again to study philosophy, supervised by the famous Professor Bachelard,[4] who was then teaching the intellectual history of

---

4   Gaston Bachelard (1884-1961), a French philosopher and science historian. He once studied natural science but then obtained a Doctorate in Literature in 1927. Starting in 1930 he began teaching as a professor at the University of Dijon, University of Paris, and the Ecole Normale Supérieure. In 1955, he took charge of the College of Science and History as an Honorary Professor and was elected as academician at the Academy of Ethics and Politics. In 1961 he won the National Prize of French Literature. His representative works include: *The New Scientific Spirit* (1934); *The Formation of Scientific Spirit* (1938); *The Psychoanalysis of Fire* (1938); *The Poetics of Illusion* (1961).

science. Bachelard attempted to reconcile reason with experience to create a kind of new rationalism without a subject. In his eyes, science is essentially a doctrine in which reason and experience keep an interactive relationship. New scientific spirit is generated after the "rupture épistémologique" of experience and common sense. Bachelard's philosophical thoughts have exerted far-reaching influences on both scientific philosophy and literary criticism in France. From Bachelard, Althusser learned about French epistemology, and like Foucault, Althusser's quasi-structuralism stemmed from a scientific framework and the epistemological rupture in Bachelard's intellectual history of science rather than that found in Saussure's linguistic structuralism. While Althusser was at the Ecole Normale Supérieure, his friend, Jacques Mattin, also had a significant impact on his philosophical thinking. Jacques Mattin was the first to reinterpret Problématic and helped Althusser to "pry into revolutionary theory of Marxist philosophy".[5] In 1948, Althusser finished writing his thesis entitled, "On Content in the Thought of G.W.F. Hegel", and from which we can clearly trace the theoretical path of Athusser I – a Catholic – transitioning towards Athusser II – a follower of Hegelian philosophy. In my opinion, through the discussion of Hegel's concepts of content, which are contained within this critical work, the young Althusser's unique philosophical theories, specifically those centering on emptiness, had already taken shape, which means that by that time he was already a good philosopher.

In October of 1948, Althusser was offered the position of director of studies (*agrégé répétiteur*) at the Ecole Normale Suprieure. While there, the noted philosopher, Hyppolite, became the director of the Ecole Normale Supérieure.[6] Unsurprisingly, Althusser became his assistant and eventually began to instruct senior students, including

---

5   According to Althusser, during the Nazi occupation period Mattin attended a seminar on Hegel's The Phenomenology of Spirit hosted by Hyppolite. See Althusser, Louis. The Correlation between Marx and Hegel; *The Specter of Hegel: Early Writings*. Trans. Tang Zhengdong. Nanjing: Nanjing University Press, 2005. p. 344.

6   Jean Hyppolite (1907-1968), a French philosopher. Together with Kojeve, they were the first to introduce Hegelian philosophy into French academic world, influencing an entire generation of French contemporary thinkers. In 1939, Hyppolite translated Hegel's *The Phenomenology of Spirit* into French. In 1954 he became the president of Ecole Normale Supérieure. His representative works include: *Research on Hegel's The Phenomenology of Spirit* (1947); *Logic and Existence* (1952).

those who would later become some of the most prominent French thinkers, such as Michel Foucault, Lucien Sève, and Pierre Bourdieu, among others.

Following his appointment, Althusser rarely left school except for everyday outings and travel. For Althusser, the Ecole Normale Supérieure turned into an invisible high wall that effectively isolated him from reality. In November, Althusser officially joined the French Communist Party. Thereafter, lecturing philosophy and endeavoring to become a communist became the two most important things in his life.

At the end of 1949, Althusser wrote to his former spiritual guide, Jean Lacroix, to both declare his Marxist stance and distance himself from Lacroix's theological teachings. In 1950, Althusser formally disavowed Catholicism and put an end to his attempts to reconcile both divinity and Marxism. In 1952, Derrida became a disciple of Althusser. Their friendship lasted a lifetime.[7] Although Althusser was Derrida's teacher, Derrida did not necessarily agree with Althusser's theories because the modern structuralistic logic used by Althusser to reinterpret Marx had been the object of Derrida's deconstruction. The significant theoretical differences between them, however, did not prevent them from maintaining a close friendship. Derrida would later say that while Althusser was suffering from episodes of his mental disorder he kept in communication with him, and at Althusser's funeral, Derrida even delivered an affectionate speech.[8]

---

7   J. Jacques Derrida (1930-2004), a French philosopher and the founder of Deconstruction. He was born in Algeria and when he was 19 years old, he went to study in France. From 1956 to 1957 he studied at Harvard University. In the 1960s, he became the core figure of the magazine *Tel Quel* but at the end of the 1960s, he split with the magazine. Then he had been teaching at the Ecole Normale Supérieure. He once worked as a visiting professor at both Johns Hopkins University and Yale University. Later on he became a researcher at the French Social Science Research Institute. His main works are: *Of Grammatology* (1967); *Speech and Phenomena* (1967); *Writing and Difference* (1967); *Dissemination* (1972); *Margins of Philosophy* (1972); *Positions* (1972); *The Ends of Man* (1980); *Spectres of Marx* (1993).

8   Derrida, Jacques. *Address at Louis Althusser's Funeral*; *Philosophy and Politics: Reading on Althusser*. Ed. Cheng Yue. Changchun: Jilin People's Press, 2003.

Around 1955, Canguilhem's thinking began to affect Althusser.[9] In 1956, after the Twentieth Congress of the CPSU, the French Communist Party began to follow Khrushchev and as a result, a serious disagreement emerged within the Party. Althusser wrote articles that criticized the humanistic trend that began to appear within the Party, confronting Garaudy who had taken charge of French Communist Party's ideological works.[10] In 1959, Althusser started reading Gramsci and taking note of Machiavelli, and he also published books on Montesquieu. Then in 1960, Althusser taught a seminar on the research of Young Marx's philosophy. Around this time, Étienne Balibar, J. Raneière, Pierre Macherey, and Michel Pêcheux all became Althusser's disciples.

In 1962, Althusser was promoted to associate professor. In the latter half of 1963, Althusser began to correspond with Lacan, and in December of that same year, these two thinkers met with each other

9   George Canguilhem (1904-1995) a French historian of science and philosophy and the successor of Bachelard's history of science and epistemological research. In 1924, he entered the Ecole Normale Supérieure and later studied medicine. In 1943, he obtained Doctorate of Medicine. He also served as the director in charge of research on history of science at the Sorbonne. In addition, he was Foucault's essay instructor. His most representative work is *Normal and Abnormal*,1943).

10   Roger Garaudy (1913-2012), a French humanistic philosopher and one of the representatives of "humanistic Marxism". He was born in Marseilles. During his youth, he studied at the College of Arts at the University of Paris and received a Doctorate of Philosophy. Later he took up teaching in University of Arbil (Algiers), University of Clermont Ferrand, and Poitiers University. Apart from teaching, he also took part in social and political activities. From 1946 to 1962, he served as Communist Party Congressman in the National Assembly, and for a time functioned as Vice Chair of the Assembly. From 1956 to 1970, he served a member of the Politburo of French Communist Party and took charge of ideological work. Additionally, he served as the director of Marxism Research Center. In the 1950s, he published a series of articles advocating Marxism. Politically, he was supportive of the CPSU, and achieved an Honorary Doctorate from Institute of Philosophy at the Soviet Academy of Science. After the Twentieth Congress of the CPSU, his belief in traditional Marxist theories began to sway. He gradually "merged" Marxism with abstract humanism. As a result, he had political conflict with the Central Committee of French Communist Party, and in 1970 he was expelled from the Party. After 1974, he began work as the editor of the magazine *Socialist Choice*, which publicized "non-dogmatic Marxist criticism". His representative works are: *Materialism Epistemology* (1953); *On Freedom* (1955); *Humanism of Marxism* (1957); *Man's Vision* (1959); *Karl Marx* (1964); *Marxism in the 20th Century* (1966); *Lenin* (1968); *Great Turning Point of Socialism* (1968); *Man's Discourse* (1976); *Calls from the Alive* (1979).

for the first time.[11] Shortly afterward, Althusser gave a seminar on Lacanian psychoanalysis at the Ecole Normale Supérieure. From then on, Lacan's thoughts began to have a profound influence on Althusser. Then in August, Althusser's friend, Jacques Mattin, committed suicide.

Starting in 1964, Althusser started a seminar on reading Marx's *Capital* at the Ecole Normale Supérieure. It was around that time that Althusser reached the peak of his intellectual career – he upheld the flag of Scientific Marxism within the tradition of Western Marxism. His *For Marx* and *Reading Capital*, published by Maspero Press in September and November 1965, respectively, used the key concepts of Problématic, Symptomatic Reading and Ideology to build up a unique theoretical framework, rendering Althusser a distinguished master of philosophy Althusser III. He was considered one of most celebrated French philosophers at that time. In January of 1966, the French Communist Party held a meeting attended by Party philosophers. In March, a Plenary Session was held. Both Althusser and Garaudy's theoretical orientations were discussed at the meetings, and Althusser was eventually forced to make a "self-criticism". In November 1966, Althusser gave a seminar on reading *The German Ideology*. In 1969, Althusser wrote the article *Ideology and Ideological State Apparatus*,[12] which began to move Althusser's thoughts closer towards Lacanian philosophy.

By 1968, Heléne Rytman and Althusser had begun to live together, and in 1976, they got married. However, the good times did not last long. Rytman's own mental troubles worsened, and as a result, she started psychotherapy. This incident created a crisis within the marriage. Meanwhile, Althusser's status as an already highly renowned thinker meant that he had to accept the fact that it would be increasingly difficult to make more breakthroughs in his intellectual career.

---

11   Jacques Marie Émile Lacan (1901-1981), a French contemporary post-structuralist, psychoanalyst and philosopher. Main works include: *On Paranoiac Psychosis in its Relations to the Personality-Dissertation* / Orig. *De la psychose paranoïaque dans ses rapports avec la personnalité* (1932); *Principles beyond Reality* (1936); *Function and Domain of Speech and Language in Psychoanalysis* (1953); *Seminar Report on "stolen letters"* (1955); *Positions of the Unconscious* (1958); *Collected Works of Lacan* (1966). Regarding Lacan's philosophy, the following work can be referenced: *The Impossible Truth of Being: Mirror of Lacan's Philosophy*. The Commercial Press. 2006.

12   Published in *Le Pensee* in 1970, a periodical journal attached to French Communist Party.

Indeed, the most splendid period in his life had faded away. In May 1968, the "Red Storm" took place in France. Although Althusser was confined to a psychiatric hospital, his silence during the events prompted his students, including his disciple Alain Badiou, to stand in opposition to him.[13] In spite of this, at the end of 1968, Nicos Poulantzas became a member of Althusser's research team.[14] After that Althusser published many essays about the philosophy of Hegel and Lenin, but did not exceed the bounds of his existing theoretical logic. Beginning in 1972 Althusser began to write articles of "self-criticism". In June 1975, he earned a National Doctorate at the Université de Picardie Jules Verne. Then in the *Soutenance d'Amiens* (later published with the title, *Is It Easy to Be a Marxist?*), Althusser began to express doubt about his original Marxist beliefs. In 1977, he delivered a public speech called the "Crisis of Marxism", demonstrating that Althusser's Marxist stance had been fundamentally shaken. Then, in October 1979, Poulantzas killed himself.

---

13   Alain Badiou (1937-), a French contemporary philosopher and post-marxist. Badiou was born in Rabat, Morocco. In 1956, he enrolled in the Ecole Normale Supérieure and became a teacher at Sorbonne in 1964. He is one of Althusser's most outstanding students. When he was at the Ecole Normale Supérieure, besides attending classes he also participated in Althusser's seminars. Like Balibar, Jacques Rancière, and Marchelier, he is also one of the writers for Althusser's *Reading Capital*. In 1967, Althusser invited Alain Badiou to take part in "Philosophy Classes of Scientists". During the May Movement in 1968, Badiou joined a revolutionary group that was Maoist in nature and when he was at the Universite Paris VIII, he joined a French Communist Coalition of Marxism-Leninism. He eventually broke with Althusser, and led the people rushing into Deleuze's class. At the end of the 70s, he turned to Lacan's philosophy. Currently, he is one of the most important post-marxists together with Jacques Rancière, Slavoj Zizek, and Giorgio Agamben. His representative works include: *The Concept of Model* (1972); *Contradiction Theory* (1970); *On Ideology* (1976); *Kernel of Hegelian Dialectics* (1978); *Theory of the Subject* (1982); *Being and Event* (1988); *Second Manifesto for Philosophy* (2009).
14   Nicos Poulantzas (1936-1979), a Greek Marxist philosopher. He was born in Athens on September 21, 1936. In 1953, as a result of his superior performance, he was admitted to the College of Law at University of Athens. In 1960 Poulantzas went to Paris and became an assistant teacher at the Sorbonne where he taught philosophy of law until 1964. Poulantzas maintained a close relationship with Jean Paul Sartre, Merleau Ponty, and Simone de Beauvoir. In the autumn of 1964, he became a member of the Editorial Board of the existentialist Marxist magazine *Modern Magazine*. One of his articles, which was published in *Modern Magazine*, attracted the attention of Althusser. Later, Poulantzas became a member of "Young Marxists". Poulantzas extended Althusser's method of structuralism into political analysis. His representative work is *Political Power and Social Classes* (1968).

On November 16, 1980, under the influence of his mental illness, Althusser killed his wife. Although immune from criminal prosecution, he was sent to the St. Ann Mental Hospital for treatment. In 1982, Althusser wrote an article entitled, *The Underground Current of Aleatory Materialism*, which signified the end of one theory and marked the beginning of another. In 1985, he wrote his autobiography, which he titled *The Future Lasts Forever*. Also in that year, Althusser's disciple, Michel Pêcheux, killed himself. Then in 1986, Althusser started writing about Machiavelli, but he never made any of these works public. For ten years he was silent on the European academic stage. Then on October 22, 1990, Althusser died of heart attack in Paris at the age of 72.

His main works, which were published during Althusser's lifetime, are as follows: *Montesquieu: Politics and History* (1959), *For Marx* (1965), *Reading Capital* (1965), *Lenin and Philosophy* (1968), *Philosophical Lectures for Philosophers* (1974), *Material for Self-criticism* (1974), and *Position* (1978). Althusser's posthumous works include: *The Future Lasts Forever* (autobiography, 1992), *Diaries in Prison from 1940 to 1945* (three volumes, 1992), *On Psychoanalysis: Freud and Lacan* (1993), *On Philosophy* (1994), *On Reproduction* (1995), *The Specter of Hegel: Early Writings* (1997), *Machiavelli and Us* (1999), *A Collection of Philosophy and Politics* (two volumes, 1999), and *Aleatory Philosophy: Later Works, 1978-1987* (2006).

How incredible it all appears! When Althusser was alive we were only aware of the existence of Althusser III – a man with a lofty and untarnished image. It was not until the publication of his posthumous works that we discovered the true nature of Althusser I and Althusser II – the two facets of himself, which he shielded on purpose – together with Althusser IV, the Althusser of "aleatory materialism".

2 THE FOUR-FACETED ALTHUSSER

Traditional academic circles were thrown into disorder and discomfiture when the accepted, singular conception of a scientific, Marxist Althusser suddenly shifted to an Althusser with four distinct facets. I contend that if we want to solve the puzzle of the multi-faceted Althusser, we should first dissect the complex and often bitter mystery of Althusser's existence and the contradictions and anguish embedded within his thoughts.

Before 1950, Althusser was a believer in the teachings of Catholicism. So it can be said that God is at the very core of his thinking. Indeed, we must accept that the remnants of the divine never disappeared from his heart. In Catholicism, an individual's worldly being is a kind of Nothingness. Compared to the divinity of God an individual is Nothingness, and divinity itself is in a state where people cannot possibly hope to reach. An individual with a body of flesh and blood can only communicate to almighty God through a medium. The world is a sea of bitterness, and as a result, an individual subject must undergo physical suffering as to redeem his original sin to the state of **"all is Nothingness"**, thus returning to the City of God empty-handed. In enlightenment discourse, God is the idolized **"Class"** (relation) of which human beings themselves are necessarily deprived. More specifically, God is the "Big Other", which is different from Plato's "idea-other". The central doctrine contained within the Protestant Reformation is to allow the individual subject a direct relationship with God. God is in my heart and let me be honest with God so that I may remove the mediated veil in Catholicism. After World War II, the young Althusser took part in upheavals within the church, such as the Young Christian Workers, which advocated social liberalization in the wake of the fear created by fascism and war threat. By linking divine favor with communism, this kind of practical theology also has direct relevance for the socialist liberation of human beings. **The Individual is Nothingness**. It is particularly important to remember that the absent almighty God had initiated the Critical Framework of Althusser I.

The young Althusser's second theoretical position focuses Hegel. Totally different from the Young Marx, the objection by Althusser II to feudal autocracy clearly highlights the type of self-awareness that is similar to personal-self in Hegelian philosophy. It is not simply a coincidence that the young Althusser chose the elderly Hegel who similarly ignores the individual passion of Catholics and instead advocates the absolute idea of **universality**. In his heart, human beings are still a dark Night. The core of his thesis "On Content in the Thought of G.W.F. Hegel", which he finished in 1947, is the concept of negative **void**. First of all, this void, on one hand, relates to the alienation criticism discussed by Hegel in *The Phenomenology of Spirit*. The being of reification reflects the negation of essence and emptiness of concept. On the other hand, it directly confirms the absence of the false individual Subject, namely God (Subject) in the context of enlightenment. Secondly, the young Althusser has seemingly uncovered the Kantian black hole that Hegel has filled. The void of ontological absence of the thing-in-itself is the reflection of truth. Finally, the change of the originally abstract concept to the historically concrete concept of Hegelian logic is the same as the evolution from the abstract void to the concrete void (based on reality of negative materiality). This is especially true when the idea is materialized and put into the historically metamorphic process of nature, society and individual awareness. The framework of absolute idea is the void of divinity. In fact, the path runs smoothly from the Hegelian logic, which negates the individual subject, to the structural theoretical framework **without individual subject**. Given that structuralism was flourishing in France during that time, it is not surprising that the young Althusser rebuffed humanism, including the humanistic alienation of the Young Marx, which he objected to from the beginning. Indeed, the theory of the pseudo-subject in Lacanian structural psychoanalysis became the most important spiritual drive of this transition.

During the early 1950s, the young Althusser abandoned Catholicism in favor of Marxism.[15] After ten years of silence, Althusser III showed up with a brand-new, more glamorous image. Supported by the French new scientific epistemology and Lacanian psychoanalysis, the method that Althusser used to reinterpret Marx immediately stood out. However, Althusser tactfully and successfully concealed his previous line of thinking, and in the process, made himself look like a master of scientific Marxism who suddenly appeared, as if falling out of the sky, without any origin or trace.[16] For a time, peo-

---

15   In 1950 Althusser wrote to his mentor Jean Lacroix and officially left Catholicism. See Althusser, Louis. *The Specter of Hegel: Early Writings*, p. 261.

16   At this point, Althusser consciously conceals something of his own. He once clearly said, "People are not supposed to make their manuscripts public, namely not publicize their own mistakes". He does not want others to see his dark side. All he wants to expose is the brightness.

ple only knew one Althusser – the scientific Marxist philosopher who, by his very nature, seemed to refuse humanistic logic.

The truth, however, would be disclosed sooner or later. Indeed, the pall of Althusser's identity would be removed concomitantly with the emergence of his posthumous works, and when this occurred, people were at a loss when suddenly faced with the true Althusser with multiple images. We remain in a trance while the images of Althusser as a sincere Catholic, a Hegel follower and a structural Marxist philosopher interlace and overlap right in front of our eyes. This is most evident when we see that late Althusser returned to the "aleatory materialism" (*Aleatory Materialism*, 1982-1986) of ancient atomic theory, and as a result, we are unable to recognize that formerly familiar Althusser. Some even began to question whether or not the final Althusser – Althusser IV – was still ultimately a Marxist, and some even went so far as to categorize him as an anti-Marxist. This ambiguity created the break and division of Althusser's thoughts that would later prove problematic in contemporary research on Althusser.

I do not intend to comprehensively probe into the internal logic of Althusserian philosophy at different historical stages in the introduction. I simply want to highlight two keywords in the exploration of Althusser II, which are the **subject of Nothingness** and the **human being as the Night**. In my view, this is the real theoretical thread that permeates to all of Althusser's philosophical thoughts. Perhaps, this is a key similar to the magic phrase: "Open Sesame".

3 NOTHINGNESS: THE ONTOLOGICAL LOGIC

As previously mentioned, the intellectual basis of Althusser II was Hegelian philosophy. the form What is interesting is that in 1948 Althusser still adhered tightly to Hegel even after learning of Marx and Engels' criticism of Hegel. Furthermore, Althusser's adherence to Hegel occurred within the milieu of a Hegel mediated by a French-specific context. And the magicians who carried out the mediating are the well-known Hyppolite and Alexander Kojeve. They both decoded Hegel in *The Phenomenology of Spirit* through the lens of the **the Master-slave dialectic** in Hegel's **falsification process of the spirit**. It is also the crucial intellectual context of

Althusser's voluminous 150,000-word book entitled, "On Content in the Thought of G.W.F. Hegel".

The point of departure in Althusser's logic is the concept of **content** in Hegelian philosophy. It is indeed a different and unique view. Certainly, the **content** here refers to the one **generated** as truth from a "historical perspective" rather than the one, which counters against form in the level of thinking. This is yet a capitalized **CONTENT**. The young Althusser wrote a powerful Hegelian phrase on the first page of his thesis: **Content is always young**. He agrees with Hegel on the point that **"philosophy is the thought about content"**. "For Hegel, thought must not remain on the threshold, but should rather step into the house; it has to dwell 'at home', *bei sich*, that is, in its object, its own content."[17] Actually, the content as a philosophical object is the internality of things and processes. This is obviously different from "a sort of internality from the bottom of one's heart" (*innerlich*) in the physical sense. The young Althusser believed that Hegel put forward a "philosophical view embedded in the life of its object" on the basis of rejecting Kantian transcendental cognition and Schelling's mechanic "reflectionism".

Then what exactly is Hegelian philosophy of content? In my opinion, the content, which "lives in the object", is the historical progress in which the idea behind the object develops in a fruitful way. More specifically, it is a ubiquitous God in the form of the Holy Spirit without physical body, according to Althusser I.

Therefore, the young Althusser sees that the content in Hegelian philosophy is manifested as "the given, reflection and the Self". Regarding the three forms, the content is the **Nothingness** of anti-materialization, formlessness, and the re-penetration of alienated forms. It is incorrect for Japanese scholar, Yimamura Hitoshi, to regard this sort of Nothingness as a "vacuum" or the void in the sense of Democritus.[18] Indeed, the Nothingness here does not have any suggestion of physical space. It is an ontological Nothingness; so it is a concept that is quite difficult to grasp.

---

17   Althusser, Louis. *The Specter of Hegel: Early Writings*. Trans. G. M. Goshgarian. London; New York: Verso, 1997. p. 61.
18   See: Yimamura Hitoshi: *Althusser: Epistemological Rupture*, pp. 43-44.

Hegel, in *The Phenomenology of Spirit*, found that the naïve consciousness is the reflection of the object. Rational intuition is based on what is given, but it cannot be perceived by the senses. However, the content in the form of the object is actually constitutive. Without the support of the subjective consciousness we are unable to constitute rational objects. Therefore, the given is really Nothingness. **Being is Nothing**. This is the first Nothingness – the Nothingness related to falsification. It resembles the emptiness or "dream" in Eastern Buddhism.

> *At this point we know only that the given is Nothingness. Not until the moment of reflection will we see the being of this Nothingness emerge; only then will the original void, experienced in the given, endow itself with its own content.*[19]

Althusser considers the sensible falsification, in the sense of phenomenology of perception, as the experience of empiricism. "The philosophical experience of the sudden deconstruction of the given was that of empiricism."[20] He deeply appreciates Hegel's rationalism and essentialism. In subsequent epistemological research, the young Althusser continually criticizes the directness of "seeing" in rational empiricism. The Phenomenology of Spirit is a history of consciousness falsification, which identifies that there is no rational form of the given. Of course, this kind of Nothingness identification tends to be the confirmation of real being, namely the being of idea. Hegel regards it as the spiritual logic of subject.

> *The Phenomenology too is its own undoing; it destroys itself qua form, and, after abolishing the difference between consciousness and its object, considers only its truth in its eternal content. This content is that of the Logic in which Spirit contemplates itself.*[21]

After eliminating the pseudo-existence of the form of the object, this logic begins anew. The **content** directly declares its presence. Logic itself is the initial and original content. The end of *The Phenomenology of Spirit* is the beginning of *Logic*. Logic is evidently an ontology, a sort of content purely established, and an origin of truth. The young Althusser even said, "*Logic* is the third Testament, from which we can not only read the words of God but also read

---

19   Althusser, Louis. *The Specter*, p. 68.
20   Ibid., p. 66.
21   Ibid., *The Specter*, p. 68.

his predictions, thoughts and manifestation".[22] Here, an extremely important theoretical connection subtly begins to occur: The Logic of Hegel *is* God, and this coincides with the divinity deeply hidden within Althusser I. In his sub-consciousness, the City of God is content, whereas the world is the pseudo-existence of dark forms of physical properties. In the presence of God, the helpless and lonely Althusser is still prostrating himself on the ground! Afterwards, the Logic evolved into the Problématique of Althusser III, the meaning of which is hidden beneath the surface of the Althusser's philosophical writings.

Logic is **the second Nothingness**. This Nothingness is an abstract beginning, namely negative "momentum". The young Althusser said, "The sphere of logic is abstract; it is not a given, but a primordial void that exists only by virtue of the content with which it endows itself."[23] The explanation of this Nothingness is target-oriented, which ruptures the idea of the traditional a priori (transcendental) or a posteriori idea of in-itself. Relative to the direct given object, the original Nothingness is the abstract idea and a sort of "pure Nothingness", **the Nothingness from which being originates**. This is a "pure hollow", just like Chia Pao-yu who has not yet been incarnated into the Grand View Garden in *A Dream of Red Mansion* – with uncontainable passion but without the realization of physical flesh.

> *The in-itself is not, for Hegel, a constituted whole: it is an original void which, through its own movement, constitutes itself as a whole. If one can speak of a totality here – and we shall see in what sense this is possible further on. Hence one may say that it is merely something hidden, a germ, something non-existent which will emerge as something existent, something immediate, something yet to come.*[24]

The Nothingness here refers to a subject that never existed and a pure spirit that has not been realized.

---

22   Hartmann, Nicolai. *German Idealist Philosophy*. Berlin-Leipzig, 1929, vol (2), p. 38.
23   Althusser, Louis. *The Specter*, p. 70.
24   Ibid., p. 71.

The second aspect is **the content as reflection**. At this level, the reflection of content is not epistemology. It presents as **reflexive** historical relations in an ontological sense. Specifically, if the pure logic of idea intends to be realized, it must show as an actual history of non-idea. The idea must become **the Other** if it wants to be realized. This is Fichte's non-ego and ego. The young Althusser uses the following key relational expression to illustrate this point: "The truth of the inside must be sought in the outside, the truth of the child in the grown man, the truth of the seed in the tree laden with fruit, the truth of Logic in Nature."[25] An idea has to be alienated from the history of nature and society before it can be generated, which is just like Adam and Eve who are banished from the Garden of Eden to the mortal world, or like Chia Pao-yu and the herb jelly that falls into Grand View Garden from the Great Dreamland, or like Faust who is unaware of the bet between God and the Devil. Althusser I, in darkness, will say, "Paradise lost is not a return to the chaos that preceded creation, nor is it the establishment of the reign of Nothingness on earth; it is the passage to the outside. In the intimacy of the beginnings, act and object coincided. Eve discovered the truth of this intimacy the moment she lost it: the truth of Paradise lies in the losing of it."[26] So in Althusser's content, the truth is no longer internal, but rather it is alienated between externality and materiality. Relative to externality, content becomes the Nothingness of being in history. This is **the third Nothingness**, the Nothingness of phenomenon in the sense of historical reality. Its direct meaning is engraved **behind** the revealed historical phenomenon. This Nothingness is actually the presence of **implicit** essence, the trick of idea.

> *From the standpoint of reflection, the content encounters its truth in the other, but does not realize that it is this other. Whence the relations which spring up on the basis of this misunderstanding: the content struggles amidst indifference,* **alteration** *and hostility, without understanding that it is merely struggling against itself. 'Destiny,' as Hegel profoundly says, 'is consciousness of oneself as an enemy.'*[27]

Yes, this is the famous Master-slave **Dialectic**!

---

25   Ibid., p. 72.
26   Ibid., p. 73.
27   Ibid., p. 76.

Man appears only after his physical body dies. As a result of the alienation of the given, content produces persons (subjects) who resist a natural existence through labor. Although Man, who lives inside his own skin, still exists in form of the physical body, his being starts from the Nothingness of the given. Thus, the young Althusser profoundly says, when we think about human beings, we discover that we are categorized as natural (physical body); however, as we contemplate nature, what we find is the opposite of human being. Nature is the being of the given, but human being is Nothingness. This is the beginning of **the fourth Nothingness**. Man is subject to thing. "But man was a king subject to the domination of dust."[28] Fortunately, Althusser sees himself in the negation of natural things and establishes himself through labor. Then, idea finally reaches its most important location: content is Self. "Now the content is not reflected in the other, but in itself; it no longer endures the servitude of externality, but is free, and henceforth has to do only with itself: it is **Self**."[29] These words contain much bitterness and hatred, but yet it is clear that young Althusser has great difficulty in expressing them! Indeed, the young Althusser still insists that Man is an empty Night. The fetters of loneliness, which he can never shake off, once again begin to torture him.

4 "MAN, THAT NIGHT"

In 1947, the young Althusser used this title to comment on an article about Hegel written by Kojéve.[30] Perhaps the use of the title reflects Althusser's stubborn opinion of Subjects, which he held throughout his miserable life. As previously mentioned, Althusser's own existence was extremely sad and painful. Starting from when his dead uncle replaced him as an individual Self to his later schizophrenia, Althusser was effectively excluded from society. For Althusser, the sea of loneliness was boundless. In life, he never sought to look for the shore. In his eyes, life was a web of dark Night without even the faintness light. Only the shimmering light of thoughts – the process of his theoretical exploration – could illuminate the darkness.

---

28   Ibid., p. 81.
29   Ibid., p. 84.
30   Ibid., pp. 226-229.

The Night is not simply without light. It also has a quality of light-ness that comes from its extreme Nothingness. *"Birds flock like the dark rain/fly from dusk to Night/Night with nothing to lose/why give me comfort?"* ("An Ode to Dark Night" by Bei Dao). The young Althusser once said that Hegel was passionate about the theme of romantic serenades because they express both tranquility and peace-fulness – qualities that can be found in Night. However, Night does not merely refer to the tranquility and peacefulness found in the darkness. In the theological sense, darkness is actually the birthplace of light. If there is no darkness, how can God say: "Let there be light"? Hence, the young Althusser insisted that the human being is an absurdity, a hollow being, "Nothingness" and "Night" at the level of nature. He agrees with Hegel when he says that we see the terrify-ing Night. Indeed, it is the darkness that we see when we are con-fronted by another human being. The birth of man means the death of nature. Man is born in the Nothingness of human beings. Without the discussion above, it may seem sudden to encounter these words. Yet, now we are able to understand that man is the death of nature, a Nothingness, and a Night. (This sentence can also be expressed in an inverted way. I often joke that social existence does not exist at Night).

> History is simply the triumph and recognition of man's Nothingness, secured by dint of labour or force of arms. For, through labour, man subjects nature to his will and makes it his place of abode; through struggle, he wins recognition from his fellows and builds himself a human abode.[31]

Man is Nothingness, which means that man's being is not based on the being of nature. The existence of man is characterized by his own labor and fighting. This existence of man is Nothingness rela-tive to the history of the direct existence of nature. More importantly, the Nothingness of man is achieved only after he is joined together with his spiritual idea. "For Hegel, the Spirit is Nothingness that has become being, or, in his romantic language, 'Night becomes day'. This Night is the universal *in actu* in man: 'the human being is this Night, this empty nothing', an empty nothing posited as not-being in its very being.' We see this Night when we look a human being

---

31   Ibid., p. 170.

in the eye."[32] The Spirit is history, and history is Nothingness. "The Nothingness by means of which history is engendered and then takes possession of itself as it evolves is in history. This Nothingness is man."[33] Spirit is Class, and spirit is universality. Universality is immortal (Class is eternal), and it can obtain itself only by individual death. The appearance of human beings mentioned by Hegel is the arrival of death, whose implied meaning lies in **individual death**. (It seems that we hear Heidegger's voice coming from a remote place, saying that the individual is *die Sterblichen*. For the individual, death is a universal motherland and human beings are a living death.

> *In this sense, history is a ruse that yields up its secret only at the end; it dupes the individuals who make it amidst toil and suffering. It is truly the triumph of Night and Death, for it is in the Night that men die comprehendingly. It would be pure deception if it were nothing more than this brutal, unrevealed totality, this self-contained, silent divinity, a blind galley human slaves propel only God knows where.*[34]

We cannot help exclaiming that the individual is pathetic. Man is that Night, while the individual is the fading cloud before Night falls. With the disappearance of light, the individual, who must vanish at Night, is the only bearer of Nothingness of the Spirit because it is only in history that the Spirit can get to know itself. Viewing it from this perspective, history is just the phenomenology of the Spirit, the development process in which the Spirit controls the form of its self-consciousness. (Now we can fully understand the context of **history is a process without a subject**, which Althusser embellished with Marxist words. The connection of idea never really ruptures and there exists no fundamental difference between four Althussers).

Since man is Night, then what might be the faint light at Night? The answer is very clear: when content turns into the Self, the spiritual idea experiences the essence of subjectivity in the dejected human subjects. Only by seeing through the falsehood of historical materiality can people find the light that penetrates the Night. Only by fully understanding alienation in social history can subjects return to the universality in idea.

---

32   Ibid., p. 94.
33   Ibid., p. 93.
34   Ibid., p. 96.

After abolishing the immediacy of the given in the otherness of reflection, the content realizes the truth of reflection in the Self, attaining peace and the totality. The Nothingness of the beginnings at last conquers the element of truth and actuality, the authentic unity in which the totality finally coalesces, in which it ceases to be divided against itself and to look beyond itself for its own truth. The Self is itself in the other; it exists in virtue of itself and the other simultaneously, and, overcoming contradiction, recognizes itself in its adversary. The contrary is no longer merely the flesh of its contrary, but flesh of its own flesh, and the battle, once ended, becomes the mediation of brotherhood. The necessity thus revealed is not, however, a new form of servitude, but the exercise of freedom: the content is its own content, it is everywhere, like God, and everywhere at home with itself, that is to say, free. Free of external alienation, free of internal alienation, the content is the Absolute.[35]

Thus, content is the Absolute, which is the absolute idea of self-realization by subjects rather than by God because only man is capable of recognizing and internalizing the spiritual essence of Self. Althusser is the first to label Hegelian philosophy **Conceptual Philosophy**.

Always circuitous, Concept is the Nothingness of directness. This is clearly relevant to the invisibility of God, which is expressed in the philosophy of Althusser I. "The universality attained without detour is a universality that brooks no appeal. Hence, the ambiguity of intuition, which turns the intransigent purity of man's gaze against him: the truth is literally blinding, like the sun when we look at it with open eyes. To philosophize with open eyes is to philosophize in the dark. Only the blind can look straight at the sun."[36] The Nothingness of Concept to a certain extent resembles the abstract beginning of logic. So it is similar to the "second childhood" of content because, this time, man will start from the empty abstract. Concept in man's hands is the death of the being of the object, the being of heterogeneity, and is finally killed by God (abstract Class). The generation of concept begins with Nothingness. This is **the fifth Nothingness**.

Meanwhile, concept is the new "Other" of content, while content changes into its truth, namely freedom. As Hegel defines concept as a kingdom of subjectivity, he also defines truth as substance turning into subject.

---

35 Ibid., p. 84.
36 Ibid., p. 85.

Not only is I an other, but, in the element of the concept, the other is I: the Self recognizes itself in the other. The content is *bei sich* (germ.), truth at last dwells in its own abode, God, descended from Heaven, dwells amongst men; this is no longer the Jewish God, whom his people do not recognize, "a stranger in his own land", but the truth become man in a human world that has become truth, a native land re-conquered, the profound unity of the Self and the totality.[37]

Finally, God, man and absolute idea are blended in a perfect way. We arrive at a splendid paradise – a kingdom of freedom.

5 CONCLUSION

After the mist fades way, in the depth of Night, the truth still stands. Surprisingly, there does not exist a simple rupture between the four different Althussers. After detailed questioning and analysis, it is not hard to find the continuity between them. In my view, the theoretical thread that connects these four Althussers is **the non-subject framework that centers on the absence of individual subject as well as the ontology of Nothingness**. No matter if it is the God beyond the individual in Althusser I's Catholicism followed by the abstract framework in which Hegel criticized the passionate subject – a framework admired by Althusser II, or the invisible manipulation of Problématique of Althusser III as a Marxist, or the implied meaning of the void in Lecture Symptomale and the social unconsciousness in Ideology, they all point to the elimination of the individual subject. The Marxian viewpoint that human essence is the sum of social relations becomes the Nothingness of the Subject, where Nothingness is used to construct Nothingness in the Lacanian context. The statement that the agent is an automaton in the invisible apparatus of social production is just a rewriting from the Lacanian mirror image and symbolic code to a combination of positive social relations. At this point, Althusser is undoubtedly an inversed Lacan. However, the inversion of Nothingness is still Nothingness. So when Althusser defines the essence of historical materialism as "a process without a subject", he is merely inheriting the work of others. If we describe the elderly Althusser's "aleatory materialism" as Althusser IV then he is, in reality, only a pessimistic shadow of Althusser III.

---

37   Ibid., p. 90.

In contrast to the positive liberalism of the Young Marx, Althusser no longer focuses on the dynamic deflection of Epicurus but seeks liberation of the real subject in the indefinite coupling of Democritus. The mode of production is the historical coupling of productive force and relations, which is similar to the universality of *Geworfenheit* in Heidegger's existence theory. Here humanistic poetics is rejected, and value-criticizing is rewritten as the authenticity of historical reality.

In my eyes, the moment Althusser kills the other (his wife), he has reached the other side. There, in the endless darkness, an Althusser having nothing returns happily to the arms of God. The rain of "aleatory materialism" flows like tears from the ruins of his deconstructed structuralism. At the end of this book, we will return to this miserable final point.

PART ONE
THE METHODOLOGICAL GESTALT OF ALTHUSSER'S PHILOSOPHY

CHAPTER I
ALTHUSSER AS A REVOLUTIONARY FIGHTER

CHAPTER II
PROBLEMATIC: ALTHUSSER'S THEORETICAL PARADIGM

CHAPTER III
ALTHUSSER'S SYMPTOMATIC READING

CHAPTER IV
MARXIST PHILOSOPHICAL REVOLUTION AND THE CRITIQUE OF THE EMPIRICIST CONCEPTION OF KNOWLEDGE

CHAPTER V
EPISTEMOLOGICAL RUPTURE: IDEOLOGY / SCIENCE DIVIDE

CHAPTER VI
IDEOLOGY: AN EVERLASTING FIELD IN IMAGINATION

CHAPTER VII
THEORY OF IDEOLOGY AND LACANIAN PSYCHOANALYSIS

CHAPTER I

ALTHUSSER AS A REVOLUTIONARY FIGHTER

During the 1950s and 1960s, as the influence of the humanistic theory of Marxism reached its peak in European leftist academia, the theoretical and ideological trend of **positivism** appeared in Western Marxism trend. The core of this trend was to reinterpret the classics of Marxist philosophy using the method of positivism, thus leading to a new way of thinking and differs from the dominant Western Marxist logic, which renders Marxist philosophy humanistic. The emergence of the theoretical conversion of Western Marxist philosophy is another one-sided theoretical logic that is complementary with the humanistic tendency of Western Marxist philosophy. The academic trends, which have arisen under the banner of Western Marxist positivism include Althusser in France, Della Volpe and Colette in Italy, as well as the analytical Marxism that appeared later in Britain and America. Althusser is the first one to explicitly proclaim the rallying slogan, "For Marx", from a scientific standpoint, and in the process he creates an epoch-making impact in the intellectual history of Western Marxism.

1 WHY ALTHUSSER DECIDES TO STEP OUT "FOR MARX"?

The emergence of scientific Marxism is a theoretical inversion of the humanistic western Marxist philosophy. Moreover, it should be said that the specific historical context in which this ideological trend was occurred when the Western European workers' movement fell into decline again after World War II, particularly the ideological trend of anti-communism and anti-socialism, which took place in the name of "anti-Stalinism" that took place after the Twentieth Congress of the Communist Party of the Soviet Union (CPSU). Scientific Marxism declares that the humanistic philosophy of Western Marxism is the fundamental intellectual basis of the ideological trends of anti-communism and anti-socialism. It is exactly these nonscientific rules that weaken Marxist philosophy into abstract humanity, totality and alienation and make Marxism itself lose its strong fighting will. Therefore, Althusser, Volpe, and Colette, among others, conclude that Marxist philosophy is facing a serious crisis, and it is important to step out in favor of "For Marx" to preserve the scientific nature of Marxist philosophy. As the pioneer of "For Marx", Althusser's contribution cannot be ignored.

I have stated that western Marxist philosophy is a humanistic ideological trend that emphasizes the subjectivity of human beings. Since the revolution of natural sciences, people's understanding of the disasters of war a new Western humanism expanded, becoming important during the 1930s and 1940s. At the same time, the philosophical mainstream of Western Marxism became a public rallying cry due to its reliance on humanistic Marxism. After World War II, new historical factors prompted the further expansion of Marxist humanism in both international communist and western Leftist circles.[1]

Both the end of World War II and the establishment of a strong socialist camp with its center in the Soviet Union were viewed in a positive light. However, the Soviets made critical mistakes in domestic and foreign policies, including the enforcement of unequal power politics within the socialist movement as well as advocating some dogmatic theories. The result was a series of negative outcomes. In

---

1   See: Zhang Yibing. *The Broken Wing of Reason.* Chapter 4. Nanjing: Nanjing University Press, 1990. pp.91-97.

Octobre 1947, an "Information Agency" (COMINFORM), which was headed by CPSU and comprised of communist parties from nine European countries, was founded. However, there were a number of problems associated with it. The Agency enforced policies and directions that did not match the reality of the Western European workers' movement, and pressured Western European communist parties to fight in a certain single mode. The result was massive discontent on the part of some Leftists and Western European communists, who had only recently ended their own wartime activities. Then in June of 1948, Yugoslavia, led by Josip Broz Tito, was expelled from the Information Agency because it attempted to rid itself of Soviet control and attempted to follow the new system of socialist autonomy. This event once again triggered people's deep resent against Stalinist hegemony. With great difficulty, some western European communist leaders even asked, "if there is no basic equality even among the communist parties, then what is the point of socialism?"

Theoretically, at the height of Stalinist dogmatism **political ideology was everything**. This not only happened within the Soviet Union, but it expanded to the entire international communist movement. It was during that time, in the philosophical circles of European communist parties, that some noted: "of the philosophers we were, without writings of our own, but making politics out of all writing, and slicing up the world with a single blade, arts, literatures, philosophies, sciences with the pitiless demarcation of class."[2] It is all either proletariat or bourgeoisie; either revolution or retroaction. "We had been made to treat science, a status claimed by every page of Marx, as merely the first-comer among ideologies."[3] This is a period with which we are all so familiar! As a theorist in the French communist party, Althusser uttered with acrimony: "under its imperative line, what then counted as philosophy could only choose between commentary and silence, between convictions, whether inspired or forced, and dumb embarrassment."[4] As a result of constant class struggle, our generation acts as sacrifices in terms of philosophy. This is similar to what our teachers often say nowadays: As

2   Althusser, Louis. *For Marx.* Trans. Ben Brewster. London: The Penguin Press, 1969. p.22.
3   Ibid., p. 22.
4   Ibid., p. 22.

long as he preaches and writes philosophy for the party, he can only parrot what others say and put forward some insignificant different opinions about well-known quotes within the party. We do not have audience in philosophical circle. This is exactly what Althusser lamented, and he was aiming directly at what was occurring during that time: philosophers do not have independent personalities and only mimic what others say using the same voice. This, however, is not reflective of true Marxism, and it certainly cannot win over an audience. Althusser identifies the dogmatic ideological framework as the first nonscientific "attack" to Marxist philosophy. Although he obviously does not agree with this dogmatic ideology, in truth Althusser does not actually break its tether.

I have noticed that, in contrast to traditional Western Marxism, Althusser was formerly situated in the traditional interpretative framework of Marxist philosophy and later turned objected to this ideological Gestalt. This is where Althusser is especially different from other western Marxists, (a similar case is Lukacs's zig-zag road).[5] Nevertheless, in Althusser's view, "to force their best opponents to pay them some attention, some Marxist philosophers were reduced, and by a natural movement which did not conceal a conscious tactic, to **disguising themselves** – disguising Marx as Husserl, Marx as Hegel, Marx as the ethical and humanist Young Marx – at the risk of some day taking the masks for the reality."[6] In French leftist circles of the time, the former is similar to that of Tran-Duc-Thaoc,[7] and the latter rely on Lefebvre and Fromm from Germany. Althusser's analysis is penetrating and right to the point. Later we will find that this is another form of ideology (I find that this is also happening in the research domain of Marxist philosophy in China).

In 1956, the situation quickly deteriorated. The Twentieth Congress of the CPSU criticized Stalin. Then the subsequent Polish and Hungarian incidents and the disintegration of the international communist movement altered the situation dramatically, prompting

---

5   See: Article of Zhang Yibin. An In-depth Interpretation: Western Marxism and Lukacs. *Development of Philosophy*. 1999(8).

6   Althusser, *For Marx*, p. 27.

7   Tran-Duc-Thaoc (1917-1993), a famous Vietnamese-French Marxist philosopher of phenomenology.

the emergence of widespread discontent on the part of Marxist adherents. At the Twentieth Congress of the CPSU, Khrushchev uncovered what people deemed were the "atrocities" of Stalin in the CPSU, particularly those made while handling the relationship with other communist parties. "Proletariat's great leader" had become a Fascist tyrant overnight. This nonscientific and simplified attitude towards Stalin quickly produced a tendency toward "non-Stalinization". Communist parties of other countries and Leftists felt amazed at this – a great Marxist immediately changed into a Hitler-like tyrant without any humanity. During this sudden and violent rupture, people not only mistrusted Stalin, but they also began to doubt Marxism. Quite abruptly, the beliefs of many adherents fell into disorder. People "impute all our disappointments, all our mistakes and all our disarray *in whatever domain*, to Stalin, along with his crimes and errors."[8] The key to this lies in the critique of Stalin and the CPSU in their specific historical context. More specifically, the critique was a mistaken humanistic, inversed interpretation that ascribed the errors of the Soviet Union to Marxist theory. Some regard the setback of the international communist movement as a direct result of the CPSU's revising of Marxism into "inhuman" scientific dogmatism. However, more people blamed Stalin for his cruelty towards humanity. Thus, people concluded that it was necessary to restore the humanistic essence of Marxism that had been lost. After writing the above, I recall the time when the Cultural Revolution ended. The novels of Shang Hen by Lu Xinhua and Ku Lian by Bai Hua demonstrated an emotionally charged situation centering on grievance and humiliation. The basic attributes of human beings ("In class society, nobody can avoid the stigma of class"), as once defined by Mao Zedong, started to change subtly. First, the naturalness of human beings, who coexist in different classes, is revealed. Then "the humanistic theory of landlord class and bourgeoisie" begins to gradually mirror the Marxist view of humanism. When people demonstrate that "Man, is the starting point of Marxism", then the **humanistic alienation theory** must make a timely appearance on stage. Deng Xiaoping terminated this metaphysical aesthetic just in time because he knew very well that China's prime need was the "inhuman" science and the real development of productive forces.

---

8   Althusser, Louis. *For Marx*, p. 30.

Undoubtedly, Althusser did not approve Stalinist dogmatism and economic determinism, but he was alert to the resurrection of humanism, which arrived by the overthrow of Stalinism.[9] Althusser refers to the death of Stalin and the Twentieth Congress of the CPSU as the "second attack" on Marxism. When "the empty proclamations are proved to be worthless in theory", the scientific theory itself will be abandoned. Then what follows will be "a practico-religious or positivist death of philosophy".[10] In order to offset their desperation, people "were only too eager and happy to rediscover our own burning passions in the ideological flame of his [Marx's] Early Works".[11] Academia passionately debates "human essence", "subject", "human philosophy", "philosophy of freedom", and "labor alienation". It attacks the inhuman reality with the same passion, finally diverting Marxism from scientific reason.[12] As a result of this, some people became enveloped in a kind of "mania", where they hastily referred to their feelings of liberation and their preference for freedom as philosophy. Both emotion and indignation act as the herald of reckless philosophy. The miserable living conditions of human beings are, thus, inversed and falsely established as a kind of humanistic "mania". This was due in large part to the use of ideology as a way to oppose another ideology. This was a common phenomenon in many socialist countries (including China) during the time of break with dogmatism.

For this, Althusser has a description of vital importance:

The critique of Stalinist dogmatism was generally considered as a kind of "liberation" by communist intellectuals. This "liberation" produces an ideological reaction with profound influence, namely the tendency of "liberalism" and "ethics". It spontaneously finds the obsolete philosophical topics of "freedom", "man", "man with humanity", and "alienation". The ideological tendency of Marx's early works does contain all philosophical arguments about man and the alienation and liberation of man. These circumstances altered the situation of Marxist philosophy in

---

9   Some accuse Althusser of being "neo Stalinist", which is not well founded. Hirsch. *Intellectual History of New French Leftists*. See: *Research Material on Marxism*. People's Publishing Press, 1983(5). p.182.

10   Althusser, Louis. *For Marx*, p. 29.

11   Ibid., p. 23.

12   Althusser, Louis. *Soutenance d'Amiens*. Cited from *Collections of Issue 3 and Issue 4, Serial Book of Research Material on Marxism and Leninism*. People's Publishing Press, 1986. pp.316-326.

a paradoxical way. More specifically, since the 1930s, petty-bourgeois intellectuals had taken advantage of Marx's early works as a way to combat Marxism. Step by step these works were later used as a new interpretation of Marxism. Today, however, many communist intellectuals, who were liberated from Stalinist "dogmatism" by the Twentieth Congress of the CPSU, are publicly developing this new interpretation. Both the propositions of "Marxist humanism" and the "humanistic" interpretation of Marx's works are gradually and irresistibly impacting contemporary Marxist philosophy.[13]

The above paragraph illustrates the specific social and historical context. Furthermore, Althusser's remarks can be counted as important supporting statements in favor of humanism. It was during this particular historical period that the humanistic Western Marxism began to win supporters. It would seem that the humanistic Marx really became the authentic form of Marxist philosophy, and socialism turned into a real practice that was inclined towards humanism. Althusser sharply pointed out that for those who are emancipated from semi-autocratic dogmatism: "it was not easy to resist the spread of contemporary 'humanist' ideology, and bourgeois ideology's other assaults on Marxism."[14] From shaking off the autocracy of dogmatism to indulging in humanistic indignation, this logical transition is quite similar to that of what has occurred in contemporary Chinese academia. Humanism is then generalized, and abstract humanism becomes a vast shadow, enveloping the international communist movement. This is directly related to the survival of Marxism. Scientific Marxism was in great peril! It was at this crucial moment that Althusser steps out and cries: **"For Marx"**. He later said that "if there was no the Twentieth Congress of the CPSU, the critique of Stalin by Khrushchev, and the subsequent liberalism, I would not write anything…Therefore, my targets are very clear, which are the nonsense of humanism, and those powerless arguments about freedom, labor or alienation."[15]

---

13   Althusser, Louis. *To My English Readers*. See: *Research Material on Marxism and Leninism*. 1983(5). p.153.
14   Althusser, Louis. *Lenin and Philosophy*. New York and London: Monthly Review Press, 1971.p.12.
15   *See*: Althusser, Louis. *Reading Capital*. Trans. Li Qiqing et al. Central Compilation & Translation Press, 2001. pp.IV-V.

Therefore, in his opinion, the paramount task of "For Marx" is to reject the humanization of Marxism. The interpretation of Marxist humanism at this time is actually the second magnificent reinvigoration of Marxism since the 1920s, while the first reinvigoration was the formation of Western Marxist humanism. Consequently, Althusser's theoretical sword must turn towards Western Marxist humanism. It should be noted that his philosophy has the serious drawback of ignoring the premise of philosophical ontology, as well lacks a broad theoretical view due to the specific theoretical context. In his eyes, this is a theoretical fight between humanism and anti-humanism, ideology and science. The confrontation and conflict between "ought" and "is" in philosophical ontology is everything.

2 "HUMANIST MARXISM" IN A SPECIFIC HISTORICAL CONTEXT

Althusser accurately sees that the Young Lukacs, Korsch, and Pannekoek were the first to criticize "Marxist science" in terms of "Leftism".[16] This refers to a specific era, namely the beginning of the 20th century when the Second International theorists prevented the age of revolution using the positivistic Marxism. Here, the word "Leftism" actually stems from Lenin (In 1920, Lenin accused Lukacs and Pannekoek of being "very Leftist and very detrimental").[17] In Althusser's view, "the historicist-humanist interpretation of Marxism came to birth in the portents and in the wake of the 1917 Revolution. Its significance then was that of a violent protest against the mechanicism and opportunism of the Second International. It appealed directly to the consciousness and will of men to reject the War, overthrow capitalism and make the revolution. It rejected absolutely anything, *even in theory*, which might defer or stifle this urgent appeal to the historical responsibility of the real men hurled into the revolution."[18] Moreover, Althusser declares explicitly that he does not approve the position of the Second International. He fully appreciates the "important significance" of the criticism aiming at the Second International mechanicism and economic determinism and

---

16   Althusser, Louis. *For Marx*. Trans. Gu Liang. The Commercial Press, 1984. p.226.
17   Althusser, Louis. *For Marx*, p. 30.
18   Althusser, Louis. *Reading Capital*. Trans. Ben Brewster. New York and London: Verso, 1970. p.140.

admits its "true historical merits." This historical illustration is essentially correct. Althusser then points out that "the reaction against the mechanicism and fatalism of the Second International necessarily took the form of an appeal to the consciousness and wills of men, to **make** the revolution at last which history had given them to make."[19] The philosophical ideas put forward by the young Lukacs and Gramsci were intended to awaken the materialized proletariat with righteous conscience and the subjective will of class.

Historical background of the occurrence of Western Marxism.
In the book, The Broken Wing of Reason, I once described the following historical context: Lukacs and Gramsci, the creators of western Marxism, believed that only Lenin really adhered to the dialectics of Marxism. They tried to move forward by following Lenin's theoretical road. After the October Revolution, Gramsci first published an article entitled, "Opposing the Victory of 'Capital'", saying that the economic determinism of the Second International, which claimed to have inherited the legacy of Marx, had in fact failed. Given that the October Revolution did not succeed in developed capitalist countries, Lenin overcame the capitalist theory of external determinism, which was polluted by the incrustation of positivism and naturalism, and smashed the "iron laws" with revolutionary will. Gramsci deemed that this was a case of "facts defeat ideas" because Marx's true thought was not actually economic determinism. Instead he argued: the main factor of history was not the rough economical one but social man, interactive man. The collective social will of these people (the proletariat) could make economical facts adapt to the need of their will until their will becomes the impetus of economical development. Having created objective reality, these impetuses live, move, and run like an active volcano, which can erupt at any time. Later, Lukacs and Korsch used basic philosophical theories to prove the above arguments. Although their viewpoints differed theoretically from Lenin's understanding; in essence, they shared the same goal in objecting to the positivism of the Second International, vulgar evolutionism and "economical materialism".[20]

---

19 Althusser, Louis. *Reading Capital.* Trans. Li Qiqing. Central Compilation & Translation Press, 2001. p. 120.
20 See: Zhang Yibing. *The Broken Wing of Reason,* pp.12-13. In textual discussion of this book, if relatively big theoretical supporting background needs to be provided, I will use a box to mark it out in order not to break the original context of discussion, hereinafter inclusive.

Althusser once specifically talked about the so-called "absolute humanism" of Gramsci. In his eyes, Gramsci, at first, cut off all the relations between Marxist philosophy and metaphysics. Then after "rejecting metaphysics", he rendered Marxist philosophy as ideologies in deed, "which are capable of penetrating deep into men's practical lives, and hence of inspiring and animating a whole historical epoch" through the concept of practice.[21] Here Gramsci exceeded the practice monism that contrasted idealism and materialism, transforming Marxist science into an **ethical protest of human beings**. Afterwards, Fromm, in his book Marx's Concept of Man, directly indicated that "Marxist philosophy is a kind of protest".[22] "The old resistance against the bookish Pharisee-ism still continues. Marxist theoretical science changed into a direct appeal to 'practice', to political action, to 'changing the world', without which Marxism would be no more than the prey of bookworms and passive political functionaries."[23] Undoubtedly, Gramsci's speech was quite impressive and full of genuine sentiment, but Althusser did not believe it was science.

Anderson holds that Althusser's comments on Gramsci were aimed at the wrong person.[24] In this respect, I cannot agree with Anderson's unfounded critique of Althusser, and I think Althusser's analysis is, for the most part, reasonable. In Althusser's opinion, Gramsci does not realize the distinction between Marxist science and ideology at all. "This 'break' between the old religions or ideologies, even the 'organic' ones, and Marxism was not really reflected by Gramsci, absorbed as he was by the necessity and the practical conditions for the penetration of the 'philosophy of praxis' into real history."[25] Thus, Gramsci inevitably neglected the heterogeneity between Marxism and all previous ideologies, as well as "the **scientific** nature of Marxist theories". Now, it is not very hard for us to understand why the "covert logic" behind Gramsci and others' practical philosophy

---

21   Althusser, Louis. *Reading Capital*, p.128.
22   See: Fromm, Erich. *Marx's Concept of Man*. Cited from *Discussion about Economical and Philosophical Manuscripts in 1844 by Western Scholars*. Shanghai: Fudan University Press, 1983. p.16.
23   Althusser, Louis. *Reading Capital*. Trans. Li Qiqing. Central Compilation & Translation Press, 2001. p.129.
24   Anderson, Perry. *Considerations on Western Marxism*, p.89.
25   Althusser, Louis. *Reading Capital*, p.131.

is the philosophical humanism that Marx had given up long ago. The main reason for this is because for those Western Marxists, such as Gramsci, Young Lukacs and Korsch, "…history has been introduced into human nature, making men the contemporaries of the historical effects whose subjects they are, but – and this is absolutely decisive – the relations of production, political and ideological social relations, have been reduced to historicized '*human relations,*' i.e., to inter-human, inter-subjective relations."[26] What really happens here is that the scientific historical materialism, created by Marx in 1845, was **regressing** into humanism. As Althusser points out as follows:

> *The proletariat is the site and missionary of the human essence. The historical role of freeing man from his 'alienation' was its destiny, through the negation of the human essence whose absolute victim it was. The alliance between the proletariat and philosophy announced in Marx's early texts was no longer seen as an alliance between two mutually exclusive components, The proletariat, the human essence in revolt against its radical negation, because the revolutionary affirmation of the human essence: the proletariat was thus philosophy in deed and its political practice philosophy itself. Marx's role was then reduced to having conferred on this philosophy which was acted and lived in its birth-place, the mere form of self-consciousness. That is why Marxism was proclaimed 'proletarian' 'science' or 'philosophy,' the direct expression, the direct production of the human essence by its sole historical author: the proletariat.* [27]

This is probably what Young Lukacs really wants to express in *History and Class Consciousness*. In the later works of Fromm and Lefebvre, humanistic logic is directly and adequately presented. It seems that Althusser resolutely opposes the humanistic reinterpretation of Marxism. He says that "the great advantage of Marxist humanism is to restore Marx to the stream of an ideology much older than himself, an ideology born in the eighteenth century; credit for the originality of a revolutionary theoretical rupture is taken from him."[28] This is a "felony conviction". In the eyes of scientific Marxists like Althusser, the core of humanistic Western Marxist philosophy consists of the following aspects:

---

26   Ibid., p.140.
27   Ibid., p.141.
28   Ibid., p.140.

Firstly, the philosophical basis of humanistic Marxism is an abstract ideology with an ethical tinge. Lukacs, Bloch and Lefebvre erroneously characterize Marx as a humanist. Using the early works of Young Marx, they turn to "real", "concrete", and "positive" humanism for help. In their opinions, this humanism is the theoretical base of Marx's thoughts.[29] They do not comprehend the great revolutionary meaning of the emergence of Marxist philosophy, also unable to see that Marxism is based on the humanistic logical negation of transcendental subjects such as "human essence" and "alienation". From then on, Marxism becomes a positive science, which penetrates into the essence of history from the perspective of the material conditions of real social life, as opposed to judging historical reality based on abstract humanity (the theory advocated as alienated labor in the *Economic and Philosophical Manuscripts of 1844*). Hence, it can be said that modifying Marxist philosophy into a humanistic ethical critique is both **theoretical self-deception and regression**. The reasoning behind why Marx leads the working class to revolt is unlikely to be based on thoughts such as "species being", "totality", and "freedom". Instead of being the realization of humanism in theory, socialism is the reality of history, as well as the objective and inevitable trend of the historical development of social life. Marxist philosophy is nothing more than the theoretical representation of this process. At this point, humanism is indeed completely wrong, and this is what Althusser endeavors to identify.

Secondly, the philosophical and methodological basis of humanistic Marxism is **nonscientific** metaphysics. In a later period, as Sartre, Fromm and others weaken Marxism into the new humanistic ideology of the 20th century, they naturally advocate a speculative discourse as being both subjective and non-positive. In their ostensible research on Marxism, the individual authentic state (potential or projected) becomes the pivot for their theoretical methods; whereas starting from an abstract, but not historical, individual necessarily results in an inclination toward subjectivism according to their logic of philosophical methodology. In this new humanistic ideological trend, the theoretical methods of Marxism are no longer a logical

---

29   Althusser, Louis. *Reading Capital*. Trans. Li Qiqing et al. Central Compilation & Translation Press, 2001. p.75.

presentation of objective dialectics, but rather, they are a speculative operation of individual subjective thoughts. The consequence of this methodological deviation is a degradation of Marxist science to metaphysical sophistry, as well as empty and unrealistic slogans. Thus, Althusser maintains that the premise for his exploring Marx is the establishment of **scientific methodology**.

Thirdly, the real foundation of humanistic Marxist philosophy is the deviation from the reality of the proletarian revolution. Due to the nonscientific understanding of Marxist philosophy adopted by humanism, Sartre and Fromm erroneously observe the reality of workers' movement and the practice of international communism through abstract humanism and metaphysical philosophic speculation. Both the Young Lukacs and H. Marcuse regard the reality of the proletariat as a confirmation of the philosophical and the ideological instead of regarding it as concrete and vivid experienced entity, or in terms of practical power as seen in actual history. They internalize practical class struggle as an intellectual operation rather than let theory serve for the proletarian revolution and make it the weapon of the revolutionary struggle. This is a total inversion of the relationship between theory and practice. Hence, Althusser firmly insists on historical **materialism**.

Nevertheless, it is exactly this humanistic Marxism, misrepresented as ideology that is turned into a remarkable subject by the non-Stalinist ideological trend among the European communist movement of the 1950s. People, suffering from mental disorders because of the emancipation of the mind, support the humanistic Marx, though in immense indignation. It is at this very moment that Althusser steps out and announces the world-astonishing slogan: **For Marx**.

3 AFTER THE DEATH OF DOGMATISM: IDEOLOGICAL MANIA OR RE-FIGURATION OF SCIENTIFIC THEORY?

Althusser claims that the spread of Western Marxist humanism in the European communist movement is merely an ideological "fever" that appears in a specific historical context. In this strong wave of humanism, the scientific position of Marxist philosophy is indeed "in danger", and it is "weakened" as a science. The humanistic discourse of "Marxist humanism", "practical philosophy", "subject philosophy", and "value philosophy" is attacking everything. "This ideology is threatening the 'understanding of positive things', surrounding science and distorting it beyond all recognition."[30] However, Althusser is firmly convinced that any "fevers sink as surely as stones".[31]

Althusser appears quite calm. He says that, in effect, the end of Stalinist dogmatism does not necessarily mean falling into the mire of ideology. Instead, it can make us face the thing itself with scientific theory, both truthfully and anew.

First, the deconstruction of dogmatism will indeed "enable research work to obtain true freedom" because we do not need to wear colored spectacles to perceive everything and to repeatedly demonstrate the ever "monotonous and ridiculous form". Only then is the premise for scientific research likely to be established. In the equal context of academic discussion, for the first time we gain freedom after deconstructing ideology.

Secondly, crossing beyond the shadow of dogmatism will certainly allow us to revalue ourselves and admit our merits and demerits honestly, engaging in research work in the true scientific sense. In previous theoretical discussions, there is no fault but "reaction". So academic research becomes a position, a choice, and a game of "lining up". What people worry about is not the fairness of science, but rather they are afraid of "standing in the wrong line". The dispersion of dogmatic ideology finally enables us to recognize the history of understanding on Marxist philosophy and reveals the reasons and results of why we had to make mistakes in the past. It is only under these circumstances that we possibly be able to obtain an underlying platform for scientific research.

Thirdly, negating the arbitrary self-conceit of dogmatism allows us to learn about and admit our achievements, both in the past and in the present. Meanwhile, it can make us realize how ignorant we are in understanding Marxism and thereby know ourselves in a true sense. In the traditional interpretative framework of philosophy, Marx's

---

30   Althusser, Louis. *For Marx*, p. 36.
31   Ibid., p. 30.

speech was equal to absolute truth, and anything else was fallacy. It would seem that the emergence of Marxism presages the finality of all intellectual histories. Only Marxism is incontrovertible truth, and human thoughts can only develop within the range of a Marxist context. This is a ridiculous and rash judgment put forward by non-Marxism. History is always surging forward, and the intellectual history of human beings does not stop after Marxism. Directly addressing the accomplishments of others can only make us stronger – not the other way around.

Finally, after breaking away from the rigid concepts of dogmatism, we are capable of fully recognizing that "Marx laid the foundation of Marxist philosophy by establishing his historical theories, but we still have a lot work to do." In other words, Marx does not finalize Marxist philosophy. To a great extent, "the Marxist philosophy still has "room" largely to be constituted".[32] No matter if it is in the past, in the present, or in the future, the situation will be the same. Otherwise, what is the point and need of the research being conducted by us so-called living Marxists?

These are the four scientific principles that exist as Althusser faces the dissolution of traditional ideology and simultaneously, strives to prevent the rebirth of humanism. In my eyes, these opinions are fundamentally correct and possess referential value.

Althusser says that "the **investigation** of Marx's **philosophical** thought, indispensable if we were to escape from the theoretical impasse in which history had put us",[33] suggests that the development of Marxism after Marx and Engels fatally concealed the truth of Marxist ideas. In the socialist practice seen in the Second and Third International, we always make biased exaggerations or highlight only one particular aspect or key point of Marxist scientific theories at the cost of Marxist basic principles and in order to satisfy immediate interests. We even call this illegitimate theoretical transgression "great development" and thus, derive from it a distorted practice. The act of "combining theory and practice" is undesirable in the beginning. Moreover, the repeated revision of wrong practice and political ideology is the act of replacing an old ideology with a new one. Althusser

---

32   Ibid., p. 31.
33   Ibid., p. 21.

deems that we are moving in the opposite direction and departing farther and farther from Marx in the historical haze of political ideology
and practice. Thus, the only way to really dispense with ideology and
restore the scientific nature of Marxism is to **return to history and
Marx**. There is no other option except for this, and this may also be
the magic weapon that we can use to break the cycle of ideology.

Certainly, Althusser's main theoretical purpose is to restore the scientific nature of Marxist philosophy, but the theoretical construction must be based on the principle of respecting history itself.
Specifically, the purpose is to gain a clear idea of the historical
process in which Marxist philosophy progresses by meticulously rereading and studying the literatures of intellectual histories.
"Philosophy meant retracing on our own account the Young Marx's
critical Odyssey, breaking through the layer of illusion that was hiding the real world from us, and arriving at last in our native land: the
land of history."[34] "Return to Marx to understand the thoughts sub-
merged by hardships of history."[35] This is an important theoretical
direction: **return to the initial horizon of history**. This theoretical
attitude totally differs from traditional ideology, which boasts about
the "new development" of Marxist philosophy.

Althusser names this historical reinterpretation research as "think with
Marx"[36] or "return to first principles".[37] He consciously shelves the
stereotypes of the traditional interpretative framework of philosophy
and chooses to confront Marx in a genuine way. In order to understand
what Marx has pondered over, we should at least return to Marx, and
think about what he has reflected on. This speaking style is really similar to the phenomenology of Husserl, by which Althusser intends to
present an **authentic Marx** to us. We know that the "authentic Marx"
in western Marxism logic is just the first dimension in understanding
Marx. As for the second dimension, Althusser sees the criticism of
capitalism as not being the basic requirement of theoretical logic. At
most, this criticism covertly exists in his critique of methodological
ideology. I assume this is most likely his "Achilles' heel".

---

34   Ibid., p. 29.
35   Althusser, Louis. *Soutenance d'Amiens*. Cited from *Research Material on Marxism
and Leninism*. People's Publishing Press, 1986.p. 297.
36   Althusser, Louis. *For Marx*, p. 21.
37   Ibid., p. 22.

4 PRE-PLACEMENT OF METHODOLOGY: THE SOLE APPROACH CONFRONTING AUTHENTIC MARX

We need to remind the readers that the logical development process in which Althusser returns to Marx and reproduces the historical horizon of Marxist philosophy is not based on a simple and direct interpretation. The thinking strategy, which his adopts, is the **pre-placement of methodology**. Without a brand new interpretative method, Marx cannot reappear historically. First and foremost, let us look at what road signs Althusser follows while returning to Marx.

Althusser does not rush to settle on a definition but instead he seeks to **raise a question** "irresistibly drawn from us even by our trials, failures and impotence: *What is Marxist philosophy? Has it any theoretical right to existence? And if it does exist in principle, how can its specificity be defined?*"[38] This is "the essential **question**". Please be mindful that the "question" here is unlike the inquiry which has an affirmative answer in the traditional philosophical principles, but rather, it is **an inquiry of thinking**. Furthermore, this inquiry leads us to several different questions: how can Marxist philosophy be possible as a theory? What is the boundary between Marxism and other theories? What is the most important thing that differentiates Marx from the "Hegelian and Feuerbachian philosophy that he once accepted but later abandoned?" In short, what is the "special difference" of Marxist philosophy?

This appears, at first glance, to be quite simple, but actually it is a complicated form of questioning. In traditional research into the history of Marxist philosophy, the theoretical core of Marxist philosophy is often said to be Hegelian dialectics that removes idealism and Feuerbach's materialism its mechanical-ness reformed. Thus the history of philosophy can be seen as a smooth transition and the essence of the intellectual revolution by Marxist philosophy will be a sort of artful addition. At best, Marx just ends the non-dialetics of idealism and old materialism of classical philosophy, but he is still the inheritor of traditional philosophy ("fundamental questions of philosophy"). It seems Althusser does not agree with this viewpoint. He clearly states that Marxist philosophy is an **overturning** and

---

38 Ibid., p. 31.

interruption of the traditional philosophical path. So "the question of the specific difference of Marxist philosophy thus assumed the form of the question as to whether or not there was an **epistemological break** in Marx's intellectual development, indicating the emergence of a new conception of philosophy – and the related question of the precise *location* of this break."[39] This is both an extraordinary affirmation and a statement of critical importance.

> *Examining the status of this declaration called for both a theory and a method – the Marxist theoretical concepts in which the reality of theoretical formations in general (philosophical ideologies and science) can be considered must be applied to Marx himself. Without a theory of the history of theoretical formations it would be impossible to grasp and indicate the specific difference that distinguishes two different theoretical formations. I thought it possible to borrow for this purpose the concept of a 'problematic' from Jacques Martin to designate the particular unity of a theoretical formation and hence, the location to be assigned to this specific difference, as well as the concept of an 'epistemological break' from Gaston Bachelard in order to designate the mutation in the theoretical problematic contemporary with the foundation of a scientific discipline.*[40]

"A sudden wind ripples the tranquil lake." Althusser's words here are like a gust of spring wind, making already commonly seen and un-dramatic issues of intellectual history complex, shaky and chaotic. One of the significant changes that he brought with him is that in traditional research the two red lines – as criteria in fundamental questions of philosophy, crossing materialism and the idealism duality in the intellectual history, as well as dialectics and metaphysics- were erased. **The methodological Gestalt of epistemology is everything**. Besides, the essence of this Gestalt is the difference between ideology and science. More specifically, Althusser greatly overstates the axiology ("ought") and view of facts ("is"). This is indeed an "original," but an extremely narrow vision. Later we will see that Althusser, with this pair of colored glasses, ignores the premise of heterogeneity between materialism and idealism, and he will pay a painful price for lacking any ontological dimension.

---

39   Ibid., p. 32.
40   Ibid., p. 32.

At first, a method (equal to **theory**) needs to be presupposed in order to understand Marx. "That this definition cannot be read directly in Marx's writings, that a complete prior critique is indispensable to an identification of the location of the real concepts of Marx's maturity."[41] This quotation points out that any understanding (reading) is not likely to be direct but rather it is the reading governed by a certain method. In his view, the previously direct reading of Marx's works in the traditional interpretative framework of philosophy is actually **based on illusion** (the ideological illusion of Young Marx or an illusion of some concept when Marx becomes mature). However, the premise of reading Marx's works is to possess the theory, which in nature is totally differentiated from all kinds of theoretical formations and their history. And this theory happens to be Marxist philosophy." Unlike the method of dialectics we once discussed, it is a **Gestalt of scientific concept**. Only by these means can we truly apply Marxist method to the research of Marx itself.

Secondly, the result of this new interpretation aims at interpreting the rupture of seemingly smooth intellectual history, namely the transition from a theoretical formation to another theoretical formation. Specific to the intellectual history of Marxist philosophy, it is the qualitative leap from Hegel and Feuerbach's formation of "philosophical ideology" to "scientific" formation of historical materialism. Althusser requires us to switch from focusing on the smooth intellectual history of ideas to the research of "history of theoretical formation" of various underlying theoretical Gestalts. This reminds us of Foucault's similar opinions in the *Archaeology of Knowledge*.[42]

A theory which enables us to see clearly in Marx, to distinguish science from ideology, to deal with the difference between them within the historical relation between and to deal with the discontinuity of the epistemological break within the continuity of a historical process, a theory which makes it possible to distinguish a word from a concept, to distinguish the existence or nonexistence of a concept behind a word, to discern the existence of a concept by a word's function in the theoretical discourse, to define the nature of a concept by its function in the problematic, and thus by the location it occupies in the system of the 'theory';

---

41   Ibid., p. 38.
42   Foucault, Michel. *Archaeology of Knowledge*. Trans. Xie Qiang et al. Joint Publishing Company, 1998. p.9.

> *this theory which alone makes possible an authentic reading of Marx's writings, a reading which is both epistemological and historical, this theory is in fact simply Marxist philosophy itself.*[43]

Althusser admits frankly that this is not a theoretical first, and he makes this breakthrough by double borrowing. The first one is the concept of problematic borrowed from Martin. The gist of this concept is to identify the special uniformity of certain theoretical configurations. Generally speaking, it is the particular position of intellectual history used by some thinkers to **question the world and construct their own unique theoretical vision**. Take Marx for example. He sets up the milestone in human intellectual history through the problematic of historical materialism. The second borrowing is the concept of rupture épisémologique from Bachelard, by which Althusser intends to start the overall reform of the deep Gestalt of problematic in the history of Marxist philosophy. He points out, in particular, that these two concepts are not "imposed on Marx arbitrarily or externally." Besides, they can be proved to both exist and move within Marx's scientific thoughts. If there is another new, important category that would be the concept of ideology, independently defined by Althusser. Frankly, this is no longer an easy theoretical borrowing; rather, it is a reinterpretation of popular words.[44]

The three core concepts of **problematic, epistemological rupture** and **ideology**, as well as **symptomatic reading**, as raised by Althusser after remolding Lacan, have constituted the main topics discussed in Part I of this book.

---

43   Althusser, Louis. *For Marx*, p. 39.
44   Althusser refers to the borrowing of other philosophical thoughts as "detour in other philosophies", which can make his own theories tenable. See: Althusser, Louis. *Soutenance d'Amiens*. Cited from *Collections of Issue 3 and Issue 4, Serial Book of Research Material on Marxism and Leninism.* People's Publishing Press, 1986. pp.291-327.

CHAPTER II

PROBLEMATIC: ALTHUSSER'S THEORETICAL PARADIGM

Problematic is the core theoretical paradigm of all of Althusser's philosophical methods. In the past, however, the profundity of content and the fundamental context surrounding this key word is veiled in research conducted both at home and abroad. In effect, problematic is the only path to Althusser's theoretical and logical "mansion." As stated in the introduction, people pay too much attention to the concrete theoretical result generated under the control of Althusser's logical framework (similar to the reinterpretation of Marx's intellectual history), but they ignore the constructive and the generative method, which produces the result. Therefore, misinterpretation is inevitable. I have said that Althusser's schematism is typical of Adorno's "methodological imperialism," so we must first face problematic – the implicit, methodological framework, towards which traditional research turns a blind eye, and we must also face the logical prototype of all Althusser's theories.

1 THE FUNDAMENTAL CONTEXT OF PROBLEMATIC

Althusser clearly stated that he "borrows for this purpose the concept of a **'problematic'** from Jacques Martin to designate the particular unity of a theoretical formation and hence the location to be assigned to this specific difference."[1] The general theoretical orientation is the particular unity of theoretical formation and its demarcation of heterogeneity. Since Martin is not a particularly important or distinguished person in French contemporary academic circles, the original context of his problematic is difficult to accurately ascertain. However, I am able to affirm that the mainstream, ideological trend of structuralism in European academic circles during the 1950s and 1960s can be regarded as the major supporting background of this theoretical concept.

The word **questionatic** is written as problematic in French. Yimamura Hitoshi says that Althusser's French concept of this word comes from *Questionatik* in German.[2] This word is usually translated into "problematic" in Chinese versions. There are also other scholars translating it into "questionatic structure",[3] "questionatic Gestalt",[4] "questionatic setting",[5] "doubts and suspicions",[6] or directly express it as "theoretical Gestalt."[7] I have noticed that Du Zhangzhi once paraphrased the problem presented in the text as "questionatic formulation."[8] This, indeed, approaches Althusser's

1   Althusser, Louis. *For Marx*, p. 32. Martin is Althusser's good friend. The book of *For Marx* is dedicated to him. Althusser even says, "if I am able to discover the scale of revolutionary theories of Marx's philosophical works, it is attributed to one of my closest friends-Jacques Martin". See: Althusser, Louis. *Lenin and Philosophy*. Trans. Du Zhangzhi. Taiwan: Long Stream Publications, 1990. p. 107.
2   Hitoshi says that Althusser "takes the German word *Questionatik* as the French translation of *questionatique*, transforming it into the theoretical concept of 'theoretical *Problématique*' that inteprets thoughts". See: Hitoshi, Yimamura. *Althusser: Epistemological Rupture*, p.118.
3   Hitoshi, Yimamura. *Althusser: Epistemological Rupture*, p. 287.
4   Yu Wujin. *Foreign Philosophical Schools of Marxism*. Shanghai: Fudan University Press, 1990. p. 463.
5   Althusser, Louis. *Althusser's Marxism*. Trans. Du Zhangzhi. Taipei: Long Stream Publications, 1990. p. 41.
6   Anderson, Perry. *Contemporary Western Marxism*. Trans. Yu Wenlie. Beijing: Oriental Press, 1989. p. 38.
7   Xu, Chongwen. *"Western Marxism"*. Tianjin People's Publishing House, 1982. p. 550.
8   Althusser, Louis. *Lenin and Philosophy*. Trans. Du Zhangzhi. Taiwan: Long Stream Publications, 1990. p. 42.

original meaning, but it sounds somewhat verbose. According to my own understanding, paraphrasing **questionatic into the production mode of theoretical questions** is more accurate and appropriate. On the one hand, what Althusser endeavors to confirm is, in essence, a theoretical production mode of how to inquire, which is obviously relevant to Marx's material production mode. The contextual meaning of problematic can be compared with the ideological trend of structuralism in Western linguistics during the 1960s and with the **productive theoretical Gestalt**, which had already emerged in the research of cognitive science. This includes Piaget's **constructive pattern**, Chomsky's deep **transformational framework of language function**, Simon's **cognitive production theory** and so forth. Distinct from the existing language system and scientific paradigm, which concerned scholars such as Saussure and Kuhn, people begin to pay more attention to the **productive mechanism** of these theoretical Gestalts. In terms of the content of discussion, Althusser is clearly closer to the latter theoretical group given the specific historical context. This is not unique. Foucault, Althusser's student, also uses the terminology of episteme with non-rigid structure.[9]

In terms of concrete textual context, Althusser's purpose in raising this concept is to object to the flighty learning style where people just focus on the surface words of texts and do not dig into the "printed problematic" of Marxist philosophy. "It arises because they do not succeed in conceiving what it is that constitutes the basic unity of a text, the internal essence of an ideological thought, that is, what its problematic is."[10] In Althusser's view, only the internal totality that does not remain on the surface of the text and the "nothingness" of internal Gestalt in visual inertia can "best grasp the facts." Meanwhile, Althusser makes a definite theoretical demarcation, namely fighting against the evasive ideal totality of Hegel.

---

9   Episteme is the kernel paradigm put forwarded by Foucault in his work *Les Mots et les Choses*. Its connotation restricts the epistemological Gestalts of basic concepts in different kinds of knowledge domains. In his view, the first important concept in European modern cultural history has a certain production conditions. Episteme refers to the invisible cognitive Gestalt that produces thoughts, a system layout of epistemological essentials in a certain era. Foucault weakened this paradigm after his The Archaeology of Knowledge.

10   Althusser, Louis. *For Marx*, p. 66.

*Indeed, to say that an ideology constitutes an (organic) totality is only valid **descriptively** – not **theoretically**. For this description, converted into a theory, exposes us to the danger of thinking nothing but the empty unity of the described whole, not a **determinate unitary structure**. In contrast, to think the unity of a determinate ideological unity (which presents itself explicitly as a whole, and which is explicitly or implicitly 'lived' as a whole or as an intention of 'totalization'), by means of the concept of its problematic, is to allow the **typical systematic structure** unifying all the elements of the thought to be brought to light, and therefore to discover in this unity a **determinate content**.[11]*

This means that although the traditional holism, represented by Hegel, has already underlined the internal organic totality, which differs from internal formal totality, it is a metaphysical general reference in nature. Even Hegel's organic ideal totality fails to identify a specific functional structure, which helps constitute the totality. Broadly speaking, Althusser's problematic refers to the specific structure inherent in totality and constructing total structure, namely the **typical systematic structure** that binds all of the elements of the thought. This seems to be the orthodox theoretical road of traditional structuralism. However, Althusser originally points out that a certain ideological content becomes a theoretical, ideological system because of **determinate inquiring means**.[12] Below, we will see that Derrida has also noticed this feature.

As the dominant "theoretical framework" (or cognitive structure) and the locus of research in modern scientific epistemology, Althusser's so-called problematic is a potentially constructive structure that enables a theory to raise and solve questions in a specific way. With respect to this, Callinicos states the following: For Althusser, the importance of science lie more in the approach to obtain results than in the specific results obtained. Not coming from theories like Newton's law of motion, scientificity derives from what Lakatos called the heuristic object, even if the discovery was the likely theoretical structure. This is not unfounded. At this point, Xu Chongwen's understanding is also right: Problematic is the "theoretical framework of a theory, whose basic concepts are located in the relations with each other. By the means of its position and function in the relations,

---

11   Ibid., p. 67.
12   Ibid., p. 67.

problematic decides the essence of every concept and gives special meaning to each one. It not only governs the solutions it can offer but also the questions proposed and the way how they are proposed."[13] The general idea presented here is basically true.

I think Althusser would agree with this explanation because he says that his own contribution is just "a question, which must therefore be posed in the terms of the theoretical problematic. In other words, the question of the **mode** of appropriation of the **real, specific** object of knowledge has to be posed."[14] We can detect a degree of humbleness here in Althusser's wording. His two most critical theoretical points are supposed to be set here: firstly, he emphasizes that a theoretical Gestalt produces specific ideas in the form of raising, analyzing, and solving questions. The theoretical structure refers to how questions are generated. "Problematic, the exceptionally strictly defined structure of thinking, makes possible not only the formal confirmation of various questions, but also the multiple answers to these questions."[15] Secondly, instead of generally referring to the overall Gestalt of a theorist's ideas, the trait of domination of the covert theoretical Gestalt, which seems to be **nothingness in the actual texts**, is the governing Gestalt that plays the key role in intellectual logic. To use the jargon of postmodernism, it is **right of discourse**. Storey once said that Althusser's problematic was the theoretical (and ideological) structure that made up and produced all interwoven and competing discourses.[16] This is undoubtedly an incorrect understanding.

Additionally, it is crucial to remember that while confirming problematic, Althusser clearly defines it as the **Subjective** production mode of theoretical understanding and does not intend to take it as the ontological basis that devours the world.

> *What actually distinguishes the concept of the problematic from the subjectivist concepts of an idealist interpretation of the development of ideologies is that it brings out within the thought the objective internal reference system of its particular themes,*

---

13   Xu, Chongwen. *"Western Marxism"*, p. 551.
14   Althusser, Louis. *Reading Capital*, p.55.
15   Hitoshi, Yimamura. *Althusser: Epistemological Rupture*, p.287.
16   Storey, John. *Cultural Theory and Popular Culture: An Introduction.* Pearson Longman, 2008. p. 72.

*the system of **questions** commanding the answers given by the ideology. If the meaning of an ideology's answers is to be understood at this internal level it must first be asked the **question of its questions**. But this problematic is itself an answer, no longer to its own internal questions – problems – but to the objective problems posed for ideology by its time. A comparison of the problems posed by the ideologue (his problematic) with the real problems posed for the ideologue by his time, makes possible a demonstration of the truly ideological element of the ideology; that is, what characterizes ideology as such, its deformation.[17]*

The context of the discussion seen here is that 'question' possesses two characters, namely the **objective** question (or **real** question) asked of the thinkers by the 'era' itself and the Subjective question proposed by thinkers. Developed from the specific social and historical environment, objective question is the real question presented by a particular era. Althusser opposes any idealistic behavior that furtively substitutes Subjective idea for objective question. This is the first point.

Secondly, every kind of thought is generated and constructed by a specific problematic. The problematic itself has been a detailed, **Subjective** answer to an objective question, and it is also the "problematic system," as manifested by a type of theoretical system.

Thirdly, there also exists a real/false distinction for problematic. After being applied to objective questions, the problematic that mirrors real social relations is "science," whereas the one that wraps reality with fantasy is ideology. This is the complex relationship Althusser genuinely wants to illustrate. Nevertheless, his thinking was not as clear as that. Rather, I have reconstructed this analysis myself.

Regarding domestic academic research into this issue, Hu Wanfu has noted Althusser's distinction between problematic and objective question.[18] However, he mistakably holds that objective question is "what thinkers receive from the era and transform into their own object of study and theoretical interest," precisely effacing the heterogeneity between idealism and materialism that Althusser endeavors

---

17   Althusser, Louis. *For Marx*, p. 67.
18   Hu Wanfu. *On the Young Marx*. Wuhan: Central China Normal University Press, 1988. pp. 74-75.

to distinguish. Hu Wanfu blames Althusser for confusing objective question and problematic, only talking about the latter, the solution to question and not facing the real objective question. I am afraid the one who errs is Hu, as he fails to carefully read the intricate context, as differentiated by Althusser, before drawing his conclusions.

Finally, Althusser imposes problematic, the new "dingus" in the modern context of Western philosophy, **on** Marx and Engels. Marx, Engels and Lenin put this forward – not me! Without a doubt it belongs to a **theoretical strategy of self-protection**, and it is proper for the occasion. The first evidence comes from Marx: "Marx never directly used it, but it constantly animates the ideological analyses of his maturity (particularly *The German Ideology*)."[19] Althusser cites the following words, written by Marx: "After all, the questions discussed by it (Powell-philosophical 'critique' of species, noted by the author of this book) are located in a certain philosophical system and engendered on the ground of Hegelian system. Mysticism is contained not only in its answers but in the questions put forward by it." Marx's words are not that easy to comprehend. Althusser must have taken great pains to completely decipher them.

Engels provides the second piece of evidence. The specific theoretical, interdependent relationship can be found in both *For Marx* and *Reading Capital*. In *For Marx*, Althusser says that "on this dual theme of the problematic and of the epistemological break (the break which indicates the transformation of a pre-scientific problematic into a scientific problematic), see the pages of extraordinary theoretical profundity in Engels's Preface to the Second Volume of *Capital* (English translation, Moscow 1961, pp. 14-18). I shall give a brief commentary on them in Lire le Capital, Vol. II."[20] But in *Reading Capital*, Althusser deliberately points out with an affirmative tone, "I am justified in putting forward this term **'theoretical problematic'** because in doing so I am **giving** a name (which is a concept) to what Engels says to us."[21] That Althusser names what Engels said is genuinely intriguing. Here, he takes the initiative.

---

19   Althusser, Louis. *For Marx*, p. 66.
20   Ibid., p. 32.
21   Althusser, Louis. *Reading Capital*, p.154.

Upon careful examination, I find that what Althusser quotes here is the foreword of Marx's *Capital*, written by Engels. Returning to the foreword, Engels is demarcating the fundamental heterogeneity between Marx and Classical Economics in the theory of surplus value. Marx expresses his opinion, **standing in direct contrast to all of his predecessors**. Predecessors to Marx believed that some questions already had answers to them, but Marx considered that that is exactly where the problems are located.[22]

He unearthed new questions in the places where his predecessors (Adam Smith and David Ricardo) already reached a conclusion. In Althusser's eyes, Engels offers the "theoretical rudiments of Rupture." Marx's economic thoughts focus on the rupture of traditional problematic in political economics. "The break is the mutation by which a new science is established in a new problematic, separated from the old ideological problematic."[23] The establishment of Marx's new philosophical vision is similar to this. Rather than Hegelian dialectics, or Feuerbach's materialism, or the transformation of old problematic, it is "a new systematic way of asking questions of the world, new principles and a new method" after thorough negation and rupture.[24] In the following section we will delve into a more detailed analysis.

2   HOW TO INQUIRE: THE PROBLEMATIC AS THE PRODUCTIVE BASIC-MODEL OF THINKING

First and foremost, Althusser redefines philosophy. He deems that the kernel of philosophical thinking is not conclusion but real inquiry. "In philosophy only the questions are indiscreet, as opposed to everyday life, where it is the answers."[25] His viewpoint is quite close to the **line of thinking** as proposed by Heidegger. Therefore, Althusser remarks that it is not answers, which make philosophy, but the question posed by philosophy that makes it so. Furthermore, it is in the question itself, that is, in the way it reflects the object (and not in the object itself) that ideological mystification (or in contrast, an

---

22   See: *The Complete Works of Marx and Engels*. Beijing: People's Publishing House, 1972. p. 21.
23   Althusser, Louis. *Reading Capital*, p.153.
24   Althusser, Louis. *For Marx*, p. 229.
25   Ibid., p. 72.

authentic relationship with the object) should be sought.[26] Beyond common sense, the source of philosophy is real inquiry. This naturally reminds us of the philosophical theoretical teachings that China has – not weakly – maintained until recently. More specifically, this includes pressuring students to study hard and retain information without reflection, and prohibiting them from thinking and inquiring more deeply beyond uniform standard answers. This is an ironic tragedy in the contemporary intellectual history of philosophy. There exists an enormous difference between the "kowtow" tradition that learns and memorizes ready-made knowledge (answer), and "inquiry" that bravely pursues new knowledge. In direct reference to this, Althusser divides respondent question (non-being) and questioning as inquiry of thinking (nothingness). This is also the relationship between **Vorhandenheit** and **Zuhandenheit** following Husserl and Heidegger's thought. At the same time, we can see Young Althusser's philosophical logic, which advocates "nothingness." In his early work of *On Content in the Thought of G.W.F. Hegel*, Althusser stated that the starting point of philosophy is a non-being, vacant state, and what fills the void, or absence, this is the very essence of philosophical thinking. The philosophical speculation of Nothingness is concretized to a productive, inquiring Gestalt. In fact, this context is fairly similar to Sartre's **Being and Nothingness**.

In addition, *Lenin and Philosophy*, written by Althusser in 1969, further defined this issue. In response to the academic criticism of the time, Althusser distinguished philosophy and science in a tangible way. Specifically, he maintained that **questions** trigger philosophy, and **Probleme** constructs science. He even thinks that "the approach of questions" cannot solve big questions and that the basis for questions lies in scientific problematic. Thus, he advocates that these problems and the philosophical issues, which are caused by the problems, must be pondered over in totally different ways and in the way of **Probleme**, namely in an objective and scientific way.[27]

As previously mentioned, in contrast to the type of questioning that has ready-made answers, problematic can produce new possibilities for thinking and inquiry. Althusser emphasized, "I am not posing the

26   Ibid., p. 66.
27   Althusser, Louis. *Lenin and Philosophy*, p. 42.

question I have posed in order to produce an answer fixed in advance by instances other than knowledge itself: it is not a question closed in advance by its answer. It is not a question of guarantees. On the contrary, it is an open question (it is the very field that it opens)."[28] This is very important. The purpose of intellectual inquiry does not lie in definite answers and conclusive affirmations. Real question never seeks the truth of a final answer. It encourages people to think independently and actively. Hence, it will not take any commitment or "guarantee" as the premise. The inconclusive "**open** question" is actually determined by an open structure of posing questions. That is to say, the root of a possible, open field for posing questions lies in the **"structure of openness"** in the process of thinking.[29]

Philosophical inquiry is not a firmly held torch that passes **ready** knowledge, but rather it is more akin to a fire that activates the occurrence of thinking, or an **open**, raging fire that sweeps in new intellectual fields and spreads across a wide intellectual plateau. In short, intellectual inquiry is the real **production**, **generation**, and **happening** of thoughts! This is in accordance with the essence of scientific cognition that Althusser identifies: **knowledge is production instead of reflection**.[30] We have to admit that Althusser's thinking on this point is immensely profound.

It is also important to point out that, distinct from Husserl and Heidegger, the questions that Althusser proposed are non-Subjective. In particular, he flatly opposed taking the individual Subject (Dasein) as the original inquirer. After God and absolute spirit are dispelled, any question is asked by Man. We can see this directly. However, simple things become complicated in terms of structuralism and post-structuralism. New questions emerge: Are you really asking by yourself? In other words, is it you who is speaking words, or **is it the words that are speaking you**? In structural linguistics,

---

28   Althusser, Louis. *Reading Capital*, p.55.

29   Ibid., p.55.

30   McLellan once said that Althusser stipulated philosophical task as creating concepts. The thought of productive concept contains "new Kantian emotions". I thought McLellan's vision is blurred because what Althusser stresses here is the happening of new questions. Moreover, it is also a construction of the *problematic*. This context has been Kuhn's norm-centered constructivism in the 1960s rather than the typical, metaphysical chaotic accounts of new Kantianism at the beginning of the century. See: McLellan, David. *Marxism after Marx*. Trans. Lin Chun et al. Beijing: Oriental Press, 1986. p. 322.

the independent subjectivity of an individual subject or a specific group is actually false. An individual or a specific group is always historically situated in certain language systems or discourse structures, and these actually govern the Subject's speech and inquiry. The truth is that language system and discourse structure are spoken through human beings. So the person who inquires (Subjectivity) is a pseudo image. The governing not of Subjective but of objective discourse structure results in the proposal of questions. Structuralism positively affirms the non-Subject, objective governing function of language structure, but questions become more mysterious for the post-structuralist Lacan. Lacan deems that individual is deprived of the master's existence by the Other in the mirror image and in the initial psychological construction. But in symbolic concepts, only the murdered Man and body of the thing are left. In the system of symbols, Subject never exists. Thus, in speech, Subject is an absent void. This statement is obviously quite to Althusser's taste. Certainly, in terms of value judgment, Althusser makes an inversion of Lacanian logic. Not considering the absence of individual Subject as a painful abnormality, instead he holds that Man is Nothingness in realistic existence. Thus, the idea of non-Subject naturally becomes Althusser's most important theoretical context. Later we will see that Althusser materializes this idea into the theoretical result of historical research, namely the well-known view of "history is a process without a Subject." In his opinion, "Man" is just the material load of objective relations of production or social function. Yet in the subsequent post-structural contexts of Bart, Foucault and Lacan, the non-Subject governing of structure turns into the object strictly questioned. Not only Man but also the rational structure itself, which Althusser defends, dies. This signals the beginning of post-modernity. The reason why Althusser is more "scientific" than Heidegger is because Althusser bases his inquiry on non-Subject, objective happening. Althusser says that the posing of a problem must be governed by imperative conditions: "definition of the field of (theoretical) knowledge in which the problem is posed (situated), of the exact location of its posing, and of the concepts required to pose it."[31] He does not mention the inquirer – Man has died on the beach of the Other.

---

31   Althusser, Louis. *For Marx*, pp. 164-165.

In the event of further classification and selection, then the key of the objective happening of questions is the inquiry method that prompts the generation of questions, which amounts to the systematic structure without a Subject, in structuralism. Actually, the so-called "into the questions" slogan that Althusser raises is to be aware of the inquiry method, namely how to inquire. This is somewhat similar to the relationship between "what to produce" and "how to produce," as said by Marx as he tried to determine the essence of history. It is known that a key aspect of Marx's historical materialism – exceeding old materialism – is breaking away from the emotional entity [being of object]. He discovers production activity in specific historical context from direct thing, and abstracts production mode "Nothingness") from the production activity. (change " direct thing" into "observable things")

On Marx's Material Production Mode

Marx believes that the real foundation of social history is production activity made up of both the certain individual and the certain mode. The key here is his abstracting a certain production mode from production activity. Marx writes, "The reason why humans have history is because they must produce their own lives, and proceed with a certain mode."[32] In other words, the particular ordered structure of how humans make up a certain production mode is the basis of "a certain" historical context, whereas Marx directly states: "the mode itself of common activity is 'Produktivkraft'!

In effect, when faced with production, Marx focuses on the internal structure of production and the functional realization of a dynamic pattern. He does not simply stay in the disordered totality of production because any production practice is concrete and ordered. This is the production mode defined as the essence of historical existence, namely the mode by which people produce the subsistence they need in social production activity, according to Marx. The production mode "firstly depends on the feature of subsistence which is currently attained by them and which needs to be reproduced. Meanwhile, it is also related to the 'reproduction of individual corporal existence.' More importantly and to a greater extent, the production mode is the mode of action of these individuals, a certain mode by which they display their lives, and

---

32   Marx, Karl & Engels, Friedrich. *On Feuerbach.* Beijing: People's Publishing House, 1988. pp. 10-11.

a certain mode of life of theirs. "[33] That is to say, on the one hand, the ordered structure of production is decided by the historical property of material subsistence, which is the historical premise. On the other hand, production mode exhibits the new ordered property of subject's activities when people create social history, which is the historical creativity of human existence.[34]

Finally, Marx determines a certain production mode in the production activity of social, historical life, while Althusser puts forwards a certain method of inquiry (functional structure) from intellectual inquiry (production). This is **the intellectual (theoretical) production mode that forms and governs the problem domain.**

3 APPERCEIVE THE LATENT FUNCTIONAL STRUCTURE OF THE PROBLEMATIC AND ITS OBJECT QUALITY

Althusser states, "In fact, its structure, its problems and the meaning of these problems are still haunted by **the same problematic.**"[35] Philosophy and theoretical thoughts are not self-sufficient but are, instead, being produced. Rather than a conceptual system of ready-made conclusions, thought is the realm of thinking constructed by specific problematic. Thus, "every **ideology** must be regarded as a real whole, internally unified by its own problematic, so that it is impossible to extract one element without altering its meaning".[36] This also means that the so-called problematic refers to a functional structure, governing the philosophical problem domain and its properties. In this sense, Althusser requires us to "ponder over a certain particular intellectual totality with the concept of **problematic.**"

First, Althusser specifically reminds people that, as an internal totality, problematic is the totality possessing a specific functional structure instead of the Hegelian vague "totality," that is, "empty totality without any content." At the same time, problematic is not the abstraction of total thoughts but rather it is a productive, **constructive system.** In Althusser's words, "problematic is not an abstraction

---

33   Marx, Karl & Engels, Friedrich. *On Feuerbach*, pp. 10-11.
34   See: *Back to Marx, The Change of Philosophical Discourse in the Context of Economics*. pp. 461-462; 470. English version published by Göttingen University Press, in 2014.
35   Althusser, Louis. *For Marx*, p. 73.
36   Ibid., p. 62.

for the thought as a totality, but the concrete determinate structure of a thought and of all the thoughts possible within this thought."[37] More importantly, Althusser maintains that unlike traditional theories, problematic does not focus on **concrete object**, such as human philosophy, practical philosophy or free thoughts. It neither easily answers what is human, what is practice or freedom, nor does it realize a philosophical, logical orientation by stressing the significance of human, practice and freedom (ontology, substance or **Wesenheit**). **"Wie," "sein"** and its development mode is the key of problematic. For instance, both the Young Marx and the Marx following the establishment of historical materialism talk about the identical theoretical object, the human beings. However, the crux here is not whether or not Marx speaks human, but rather how Marx speaks. Althusser asks that we should notice the heterogeneity between the two problematics of the Young Marx and the speaker of historical materialism. Therefore, "the concept of problematic brings out within the thought the objective internal reference system of its particular themes, the system of questions commanding the answers given by the ideology."[38] This is a particularly incisive statement.

Althusser adds, "if it is not so much the immediate content of the objects reflected as the way the problems are posed which constitutes the ultimate ideological essence of an ideology."[39] From this we can distinguish an extremely important theoretical boundary, and he has provided us with an example. Before Marx, people discussed both class and class struggles, but those discussions are all realized through the fundamental framework of bourgeois ideology. Marx's new contribution is not that he spoke of class and class struggles, but that he used a brand new problematic – historical materialism – to bring about **scientific** discussion. Apparently **different problematic** can accomplish a totally different, theoretical cognition of the **same object**. Besides, after erasing the remnants of established thoughts, **the same problematic** can run throughout the understanding of **different objects and different research domains**. A relevant and very typical example is as follows: The humanism of Feuerbach cannot only become religious problematic (*The Essence*

---

37   Ibid., p. 68.
38   Ibid., p. 67.
39   Ibid., p. 69.

of Christianity), but it can also turn into political problematic (*On the Issue of Jews*), and even historical and economic problematic (*Manuscripts of 1844*). Nevertheless, it is still the **humanistic problematic** although Feuerbach's "words" have been abandoned. With this example Althusser intends to demonstrate that the essential Gestalt of humanistic ideology is not altered even though new opinions emerged after the Young Marx had extended the humanistic problematic of Feuerbach to the fields of politics, law and economics. In principle, his viewpoint is correct.

Secondly, "it is not the material reflected on that characterizes and qualifies a reflection, but, at this level the modality of the reflection, the actual relation the reflection has with its objects, that is, the basic problematic that is the starting point for the reflection of the objects of the thought."[40] We see that new form of logic is implied here: **only the theoretical problematic determines the basic, theoretical property of cognitive object**. Naturally, **the change of theoretical problematic will lead to that of change in theoretical object**. Moreover, the theoretical or cognitive object, as described by Althusser, is absolutely not equivocal to the realistic object, which he subsequently endeavors to identify. While talking about the new economic, theoretical problematic established by Marx, Althusser, in *Reading Capital*, makes the following remarks:

> If it is true that the theory of a science, at a given moment in history, is no more than the **theoretical matrix of the type of questions** the science poses its object – if it is true that with a new basic theory a new organic way of putting questions to the object comes into the world, a new way of posing questions and in consequence of **producing new answers**. Speaking of the question, which Smith and Ricardo put to wages, Engels writes: "The question (die Frage) is indeed insoluble (unlöslich), if put in this form. It has been correctly (richtig) formulated by Marx and thereby been answered" (Vol. II, p. 17). This correct formulation of the problem is not a chance effect; on the contrary, it is the effect of a new theory, which is the system for posing problems in a correct form – the effect of a new problematic. Hence, every theory is in its essence a problematic, i.e., the theoretico-systematic matrix for posing every problem concerning the object of the theory.[41]

---

40   Ibid., p. 68.
41   Ibid., p.155.

When real **mutations** take place in the theoretical problematic, the **object** of the theory then suffers a corresponding mutation, which now does not only affect "aspects" of the object and details of its structure, but it also affects the structure itself. What is then made visible is a new structure of the object, often very different from the old. It is then legitimate to speak of a new object.[42] "You're on my voyage channel, I am in your field of vision." The object and the way of thinking about the **object** are interconnected and complementary.

What Althusser wants to express is that the Marxist economic thought revolution is the revolution of problematic, and the switch of problematic radically changes the theoretical object of traditional economic research.

Marx's discovery is not, therefore, a subjective problem (merely a way of interrogating a **given reality**, or a changed 'view-point', both **purely subjective**). In correlation with the transformation of the theoretical matrix for posing every problem concerning the object, it concerns the **reality of the object: its objective definition**. To cast doubt on the definition of the object is to pose the question of a differential definition regarding **the novelty of the object** aimed at by the new theoretical problematic. In the history scientific revolutions, every upheaval in the theoretical practice is correlated with a transformation in the definition of the object, and therefore, with a difference that can be assigned to the **object** of the theory itself.[43]

It is not that object which decides method but method determines object. Vividly speaking, what you can see depends on through what lenses you are looking. Along with the alteration of theoretical methods and the raining down of new thoughts like meteors, we are surprised to find "new aspects' that cannot be seen in the past," which is the new theoretical, cognitive ability that is achieved as a result of the brand new problematic. In Althusser's eyes, "this mutation in the **object**, like the mutation in the corresponding problematic, may become the object of a rigorous epistemological study. And as a single movement it constitutes both the new problematic and the new object, the study of this double mutation is in fact only a single study, belonging to the discipline which reflects on the history of

---

42   Ibid., p.156.
43   Ibid., p.155.

the forms of knowledge and on the mechanism of their production: philosophy."[44] Actually, after some equivocation, what Althusser really wants to say is that philosophy needs to study problematic.

Thirdly, the research of problematic is not that simple. Althusser raises an extremely important viewpoint: problematic, deciding theoretical totality and object, is not an overt, direct thing. Its existential state in theoretical totality is a kind of **functional structure that intrinsically plays a latent and conditioned role**. He says that a philosophy or a theory is no longer any simple unity, but rather it is **a structured, complex unity**. There is no longer any original simple unity (in any form whatsoever), but instead, there is the ever-pre-givenness of a structured complex unity.[45] This means that we will unconsciously fall into an existing, specific theoretical context after entering into the problematic. In most cases we are imperceptibly controlled by the concealed structure that functions like the "invisible hand." Accordingly, this determines that problematic can only be a **covert** system staying in concealment rather than a direct thing that can be perceived in both text and speech. Thus, Yimamura Hitoshi comments on Althusser's viewpoint in the following way: every thought has its unknown internal "mode of thinking." The mode not only decides the direction in which thinkers think in terms of depth of thoughts (namely unwittingly), but it even thoroughly stipulates the direction of its wording and conceptual meaning. This "mode of thinking" is called problematic,[46] which is a correct definition.

"So a problematic cannot generally be read like an open book, it must be dragged up from the depths of the ideology in which it is buried but active, and usually despite the ideology itself, its own statements and proclamations."[47] Not existing on the surface of human thoughts and texts, problematic always hides behind the overt thing. Relative to surface words and "being," problematic is the "nothingness" of the overt thing, but the "nothingness" in the "being" of words becomes the true lord that governs all real texts. It seems that we once again see God with the absence of Catholicism and the "Nothingness" of lofty Hegelian philosophical logic as transformed

---

44 Ibid., p.158.
45 Althusser, Louis. *For Marx*, p. 199.
46 See: Hitoshi, Yimamura. *Althusser: Epistemological Rupture*, p. 123.
47 Althusser, Louis. *For Marx*, p. 69.

by the Young Althusser based on his own understanding. He also deems that most people are not conscious of the problematic with which they are burdened. Now, we can better comprehend the following statement made by Althusser: "in general a philosopher **thinks in it rather than thinking of it**."[48] Especially in nonscientific, ideological problematic, people tend to be unconscious of their own theoretical problematic. Or the intentions of thinkers and the governing of problematic that really take place fight against each other. However, Althusser does not recognize the contradiction between problematic and ideas, either. For example, the Young Marx in 1844, whose political position had self-consciously switched to that of the proletariat, also objected to the social system of the bourgeois. However, his own implicit, theoretical problematic was still unable to break away from the logical Gestalt of humanism. Young Marx's who set correct revolutionary goals was based on transcendental logic, which was methodologically determined and caused by the Gestalt. The Young Marx was incapable of realizing that the decisive Gestalt, which restricted his thoughts, was nonscientific. As a result, Althusser says that on most occasions, "an ideology is already unconscious of its 'theoretical presuppositions', that is, the active but un-avowed problematic which fixes for it the meaning and movement of its **problems** and thereby of their solutions."[49] Some thinkers even believe they are self-conscious. This conceit is exactly the Other – the expression of ideology itself.

Fourthly, determining the theoretical object and its property, problematic also exhibits the theoretical vision of discussion and establishes the basic mechanism that governs thinking. Althusser raises this viewpoint in Reading Capital, which is a deepening of his discussion about problematic. By this time, his research has become far more penetrating.

Althusser thinks that problematic in terms of generating the theoretical vision is the source of light of vision that enables our "sighting". Please note that the "sighting" here is not simple vision or reading, but rather it is a kind of confronting in theoretical research. If taken further, it is even **an ontological confronting in our historical**

---

48   Ibid., p. 69.
49   Ibid., p. 69.

existence, which somewhat resembles the "standing out" of the "lighting" described by Heidegger. According to Althusser, **we are only able to see what we can see**. Any object or problem situated on the terrain and within the horizon, i.e., in the **definite structured field of the theoretical problematic of a given theoretical discipline**, is visible.[50] Structurally, problematic exhibits a certain vision, in which object and question are presented, such as the vision of scientific problematic. He wrote: "science can only pose problems on the terrain and within the horizon of a definite theoretical structure, its problematic, which constitutes its absolute and definite condition of possibility, and hence the absolute determination of the forms in which a problems must be posed, at any given moment in the science."[51] Scientific domain of discussion is the theoretical horizon presented by the scientific problematic. In the modernistic, arbitrary cognitive domain of Althusser, he is unaware that different scientific problematics engender distinct, legal scientific realms (from Kuhn's paradigm of incommensurability to Feyerabend's postmodern, scientific context). Similarly, ideological problematic is sure to produce or arouse a kind of intellectual fairyland, but this issue will be discussed in a more detailed way later on.

Rather than seeking ready-made answers, inquiring "sighting" is a constructive behavior. "The sighting is the act of its structural conditions, it is the relation of immanent reflection between the field of the problematic and its objects and its problems."[52] Meanwhile, the visual boundary, where problematic generates "sighting," also constructs the shielding wall, which hides things. In Althusser's view, "it is the field of the problematic that defines and structures the invisible as the defined **excluded**, excluded from the field of visibility and defined as excluded by the existence and peculiar structure of the field of the problematic."[53] In effect, the structural mechanism of problematic of the 1960s was universally accepted in the cognitive matching of **scientific epistemology**. This includes Piaget's schema recognition and acceptance, as well as the excluded, "mysterious remainder." Althusser makes a somewhat metaphysical comment on

---

50   Althusser, Louis. *Reading Capital*, p.25.
51   Ibid., p.25.
52   Ibid., p.25.
53   Ibid.,pp.25 -26.

this point: "the invisible is the theoretical problematic's non-vision of its non-objects, the invisible is the **darkness**, the blinded eye of the theoretical problematic's self-reflection when it scans its non-objects, its non-problems without seeing them, **in order not to look at them**."[54] In later discussions about Althusser's lecture symptomale in the Marxist economic thought revolution, we will develop this viewpoint further.

At this point, Storey has contributed what is almost a correct statement. He says, Althusser's "problematic consists of invisible content (what is unsaid and undone) and visible content (what is said and done)." But why is his explanation still incorrect? Let us take a closer look at Storey's specific illustration: one way in which a text's problematic is supposedly revealed is in the way in which a text may appear to answer questions that it has not formally posed. Such questions, it is argued, have been posed in the text's problematic.[55] In fact, what Storey is unable to perceive are two "invisible" things in Althusser's problematic. One is that problematic itself is the functional, deep Gestalt of questions rather than words on the surface and phenomenon on the external, theoretical forms and rules. In short, problematic is "invisible" in intuition. The other is that problematic determines particular domain of questions. It presents some questions, constructs a discourse, and demarcates a certain boundary, forming a visible blindness. The "invisible" things are not inborn in problematic but only emerge in the position of the Other, which Storey, in fact, confuses.[56] However, we have to admit that the relation between the problematic, which is identified by Storey, and the specific historical period is still of great importance.

At last, problematic is not a purely speculative issue. Its basis in reality is the real social historical environment. It is certainly a logical coupling of Western Marxism and Marx. At the same time, it is also a demarcation, by which Althusser distinguishes himself from common scientific, cognitive theory and structuralism. This explanation

---

54   Ibid., p.26.

55   Storey, John. *Cultural Theory and Popular Culture: An Introduction*, p. 72.

56   If I am not wrong, Storey's mistranslation comes from Jealous's similar viewpoints that are falsely quoted by him. Jealous, Norman. *Althusser's Marxism: Introduction and Criticism*. New Left Review. Western Marxism: Critical Reading. London, 1977. The Chinese Translation See: McLellan, David. *Marxism after Marx*, p. 322.

is seemingly much simpler. In the following section I will analyze it from two different aspects:

On the one hand, "it is not the interiority of the problematic which constitutes its essence but its relation to real problems: the problematic of an ideology cannot be demonstrated without **relating** and submitting it to the real problems to which its deformed enunciation gives a false answer."[57] Problematic is not abstract. Its functional existence is realized by every concrete inquiry. Otherwise, concrete questions will be mistakenly governed by problematic. Yimamura Hitoshi regards this as a vital concept in French new epistemology. "Distinct from 'cognitive philosophy' in philosophy, French scientific epistemology lays stress on the spot of scientific cognition, and the activity of scientific thinking in concrete historical reality, devoted to revealing the history of scientific cognition as well as the nature of society."[58]

Nevertheless, Althusser does not acknowledge Heidegger's "Dasein", which raises specific questions (the living state development process of individual subject). The specific questions refer to the particular content objectively generated in theoretical research. So on the other hand, we should learn to discover "the **typical systematic structure** unifying all the elements of the thought to be brought to light, and therefore to discover in this unity **a determinate content** which makes it possible both to conceive the meaning of the 'elements' of the ideology concerned – and to **relate this ideology to the problems left or posed to every thinker by the historical period in which he lives."**[59] A statement in the Marxist context is proposed here: namely, the true realistic foundation for problematic is social structure under certain historical conditions.

*The meaning of this whole, of a particular ideology (in this case, an individual's thought), depends not on its relation to a **truth** other than itself but on its relation to the existing **ideological field** and on the **social problems and social structure** that sustain the ideology and are reflected in it.*[60]

---

57   Althusser, Louis. *For Marx*, p. 67.
58   Hitoshi, Yimamura: *Althusser: Epistemological Rupture*, p. 19.
59   Althusser, Louis. *For Marx*, p. 67.
60   Ibid., p. 62.

The realistic foundation for specific problematic is a certain social, historical structure. Therefore, in order to fully understand the budding and blooming process of the flower of thinking, we must know the realities of the soil environment in which the flower of thinking grows, and we must reveal the internal totality of thinking, namely the intellectual problematic. In addition, the problematic must be linked to the real historical structure. It is the same case for Marx. To really decipher the bourgeois ideology Marx needed to comprehend the social, economic, and political structure of the capitalist society in which the theoretical problematic comes into being. Althusser's viewpoint in this context actually possesses a theoretical meaning from historical materialism.

APPENDIX

DECONSTRUCTION: JACQUES DERRIDA'S HISTORICAL DISSOLVING OF THE STRUCTURALIST DEEP SIGNIFICATION GESTALT

In September 2001, one of the most important contemporary thinkers, Derrida, was invited to Nanjing University for the celebration of its 100th anniversary, to give the first talk in the series of "Masters in Humanities." During our first conversation, after the translator had just finished translating my introductory words, Derrida immediately defended himself: "I am not a postmodernist. Neither am I a post-structuralist!" This was to my surprise. In later conversations, Derrida continuously emphasized that deconstruction is not only negation but also affirmation. This is obviously different from the Chinese academic understandings of his theoretical orientation, especially regarding contemporary Western academic interpretations of his work in postmodern discussions. Doctor Zhang Ning, who accompanied Derrida to Nanjing, told me that Habermas had recently apologized to Derrida for misinterpreting his theory of deconstruction. So what about Chinese academia? Apparently, this misinterpretation also led to the misunderstanding of Derrida.

In 1967, the earliest three works of Derrida, *Writing and Difference*, *Speech and Phenomena*, and *Of Grammatology*, were published two years after Althusser's *For Marx* and *Reading Capital*. As mentioned above, Althusser puts forward problematic, which grasps the deep logical structure of scientific theories in contrast to the speculative logic of humanism. Although this functional and productive problematic also rejects some sort of closeness, it still becomes Derrida's object of deconstruction. Here I intend to make an indirect and intertextual comparison by using the relatively independent appendix on the premise that the context of this book is not destroyed. I am only examining *Force and Signification* (written in 1963, two years earlier than the 'outbreak' of Althusser's thoughts), the first chapter of Writing and Difference, to see how Derrida regards Althusser's theoretical foundation-structuralism, especially the invisible structure of thinking.

As is well known, the beginning of the 1960s was the apex of structuralism in European and French academia, in particular. However, Derrida is different from Foucault and Bart. Wearing the beautiful "structural" clothes of colorful languages (notation) or cognition ("Episteme," "archives"), Bart and Foucault initially came upon the historical stage as a mainstay of the ideological trend of structuralism and later transformed themselves into post-structuralists by **revolting against structuralism**. Yet Althusser never moved toward post-structuralism, and the origin of Derrida's thinking is itself based on the critical query of structuralism. He was never a structuralist; so he has every reason to complain about the injustice of being misinterpreted: I am not a poststructuralist!

In *Force and Signification*, the first chapter of *Writing and Difference*, Derrida eagerly indicates that, using historical insight, structuralism's popularity will eventually **pass into history**. It was in 1963 that Derrida made this critical declaration. As measured by historical dialectics, structuralism is doomed to be lost to history similar to the way in which the sun fades into the west. At this point, Derrida's historical viewpoint clearly outweighs that of Althusser. Nevertheless, "if it recedes one day, leaving behind its works and signs on the shores of our civilization, the structuralist invasion might become a question for the historian of ideas, or perhaps even an object."[61] But what question? Derrida says that the appearance of structuralism signals a profound meaning. Being neither fashion icon nor an

---

61   Derrida, Jacques. *Writing and Difference*. Trans. Alan Bass. Routledge & Kegan Paul Ltd, 1978. p. 1.

object, it symbolizes "an adventure of vision, a conversion of the way of putting questions to any object posed before us."[62]

Derrida is aware that structuralism is a sort of newness of thinking, a change of the Dasein inquiring method. This is roughly equivalent to Althusser's problematic. He never denies the **profundity** of structuralism, but he still wants to make a further logical analysis.

For the convenience of expounding upon these points, here, I inverse Derrida's narrative logic in analyzing structuralism, namely through understanding his overall assessment of Western philosophy and then the location of structuralism in the logic of intellectual history. All of this happens to be the inverse in the narrative logic of Derrida's works. At the end of this chapter, Derrida comments that "the value of the entire western traditional metaphysics is established by a theoretical subject. Apparently, unless depending on light and non-light, presence and absence of consciousness, gain and loss of consciousness, otherwise it does not matter whether to gain or to lose."[63] This is his earlier identification on the logical Gestalt of arbitrary centrism in traditional philosophy, which is also widespread in subsequent interpretations of deconstruction. I am afraid this needs careful explanation.

First and foremost, Derrida says that in Western intellectual history, the rational subject constructs the origin of philosophy. Idea/Male/God is the sun, which is the light source/motive force illuminating the world. The essence ("one") will show up in "lighted" places. Light tramples darkness underfoot. Emotion/Female/Phenomenon/"Many" die in the "unlighted" places. Plato says that truth and being are just like the sunlight. Only when light shines on the object can humans see the object. In a knowable world, it is the idea of benevolence (God) that gives us light.[64] Certainly, those humans have climbed out of the cave and squarely confronted the sun after getting rid of the illusions of light. The darkness in the cave is the false appearance confronted by the "uneducated," while the sun (Apollo) represents the truth faced by those who obtain rational knowledge.

---

62   Ibid., p. 1.

63   Ibid., p. 32.

64   Plato. *Utopia*. Trans. Guo Binhe & Zhang Zhuming. Beijing: The Commercial Press, 1986. p. 266.

Light implies knowable, rational ability. Humans, in walking out of the darkness, underwent ups and downs, as well as shadow, reflection, object, moonlight and starlight. The last phase is confronting the sun. This is a leap from phenomenon to essence.[65] For this, Derrida pens a beautifully written paragraph:

> *Philosophy is the morning twilight of force. In sunny mornings, image, form and phenomena are speaking. Idea and divinity manifest themselves in the mornings. There the prominence of light quiets down. Its depth spreads in the light and stretches in level state.*[66]

After Eleatic school, philosophy turns into a revolving stage where motive force performs. From Plato and Aristotle to the Middle Ages, force is idea (spirit) and God. However, it does not come on stage directly but rather it illuminates the site where limited phenomenon, form and image spare no efforts in acting. For a time, the spotlight always focuses on some phenomena. They will shout both loudly and immediately, "I am God!" Yet as the light deviates slightly, they will fall into endless darkness. On the stage, only the lightened place is the center. Throwing our mind back to intellectual history, reason is the center of light. Derrida refers to **rational centrism** as the "metaphysics of heliocentric theory." This "means philosophical language that is based on light and metaphor. Light stands for truth, and darkness suggests error." Heliocentric theory is borrowed from Copernicus, though here it indicates Plato's centrism of rational light. As long as the center exists, there is arbitrary hierarchy. Lightened reason, male and essence are at an advantage, whereas dark emotion, female and phenomena at a disadvantage. "We would have to attempt a return to the metaphor of darkness and light (of self-revelation and self-concealment), the founding metaphor of Western philosophy as metaphysics. The founding metaphor not only because it is a photological one and in this respect the entire history of our philosophy is a photology, the name given to a history of, or treatise on, light-but because it is a metaphor."[67]

---

65   Ibid., pp. 272-274.
66   Derrida, *Writing and Difference*, p. 33.
67   Ibid., p. 33.

Secondly, metaphysics always hints at inextricable **phonetic centrism**. By comparison, the speech of the present subject is invariably the presence of a certain consciousness (direct trueness), but the absence of writing becomes the substitute for authentic voice. "That which is written is never identical to itself."[68] This is a more radical viewpoint than hermeneutics. A writer writes, or more precisely speaking, he **finishes writing** certain works. Because "the impossibility of its ever **being present**, of its ever being summarized by some absolute simultaneity or instantaneousness,"[69] the presence of subject consciousness is of a high grade, while present recording, which takes writing as the substitute, is of low grade. Evidently, this concept "always implies some privileged position of 'acoustics', such as attaching importance to phonetic expression mode that exists in life spoken language and distinguishing the accompanying, humble position of the silent work of 'force'. And the humble position is typically displayed in philosophical discussion of writing."[70]

Derrida holds that Plato initiates the system of hierarchical centrism, and his theory about "eidos" includes the two aspects mentioned above. In Plato's eyes, **"eidos"** refers to the conceptual form of motive force. The idea is what creates both light and the source of light in the visible world.[71] With light, we can see things. With idea, we can know the existence of truth in things. This is because rational knowledge is a sort of ability in our souls.[72] However, most of what we see and know is not the original sun and benevolence, but rather they are the outline of benevolent light given out by the sun, such as shadow, reflection, object, moonlight and so on. For instance, writing is a sort of "eidos" in which the speech closer to the rational motive force of subject is reproduced. However, it has become a recorded speech rather than present speech. Hence, Derrida says that "in metaphysical heliocentrism, the force losing to 'eidos' (namely the obvious form in metaphysical vision) has been separated from the original meaning of force, such as the feature of music that has been isolated from itself in acoustics." When the center of

---

68   Ibid., p. 29.
69   Ibid., p. 15.
70   Ibid., p. 33.
71   Plato. *Utopia*, p. 276.
72   Ibid., p. 277.

a stage is lightened, what we see has become phenomenon, namely the "eidos" of expressive force. So "when force is told, it has been phenomenon."[73] Taken the other way around, "Force is the Other of language. Without it, language will not be language."

In fact, Derrida is referring to the inversion of Platonic rational centrism by Nietzschean philosophy. As is known to all, Nietzschean philosophy is **the philosophy of force.** Yet Nietzsche believes that force is no longer universal reason or eternal, almighty God, but rather it is the will of **power** (primal impulse) of the limited, concrete individual. It no longer represents the rational Apollo spirit, but refers to a crazy Dionysus spirit (this is why he always tries to return to the time before Socrates and Plato). In Nietzsche's eyes, a rational, cultural history of human beings is actually the oppression of history, which causes people to lose their own authentic desire (will of power). Under the direction of reason and culture, people turn into hypocritical "chattel" and "moths" wearing masks.[74] In order to manipulate the object and the future, humans must learn to distinguish necessity and contingency, seek causal association, observe the present, predict the future, and handle the purpose and means from rational Gestalt. In this way, humans themselves can be evaluated.[75] Nietzsche decries how much blood and terror is hidden behind "good things," such as the knowledge and ethics of the past.[76] Thus he anxiously summons the appearance of the superman who possesses will of power and surpasses the conceptual "moth". **Philosophy is power!**

I think that Nietzsche, Bergson, Freud and Heidegger have rewritten the philosophy of force. The intellectuality of the rational concept is overturned as the limited existence of individual life. Subjects' original desire is endowed with supreme power above abstract ideas. Force is the existential power of the individual subject. This represents a significant change in philosophy during the first half of the 20th century. I often summarize it as the emergence of new humanism.

---

73   Derrida, Jacques. *Writing and Difference*. Trans. Alan Bass. Routledge & Kegan Paul Ltd, 1978. p. 32.
74   Nietzsche, Friedrich. *On the Genealogy of Morality*. Beijing: Joint Publishing, 1992. p. 26.
75   Ibid., p. 39.
76   Ibid., p. 42.

The readers must notice that the context in which Derrida discusses European structuralism happens to be the philosophical antithesis of the new humanism mentioned above. More simply, structuralism happens to oppose the humanistic philosophy of force, and it also dissolves subject philosophy. At this point, it is easier for us to understand Althusser. Next, I will go into a more detailed analysis.

First, Derrida deems that **the emergence of structure is an epiphenomenon of the failure of subject philosophy**. "When one no longer has the force to understand force from within itself That is, to create."[77] This is a typical French puzzle. The force here is the survival and creative power of an individual, namely the motive force of subject existence (like the "design" of Heidegger's Dasein). Later Giddens directly sets the contraposition between agency and structure.[78] This is because, for any subject, the 20th century is a miserable circumstance in which **Geworfenheit** tends to prevail in the existential state of subject. Kierkegaard's "single individual" and Heidegger's "Dasein" always face the strong world of ordinary people (fanatical masses) and the death of the "Auschwitz type". The individual rights (will of single person) of Stirner and Nietzsche are, in reality, distorted into Nazi devilry (relational structure). As the Force, the human subject always plays the role of the loser. So Derrida points out that "structure is perceived through the incidence of menace".[79] It can be seen that the presence of structuralism, in reality, implies miserable, black determinism. **The unlimited rise of structure is the entire failure of human beings**. In this sense, structuralism is bound to oppose humanism. Only when the death of humans is pronounced can the structure be dissipated. The heavy ontological basis of Man collapses and the structure turns into a slight methodology. However, "the structuralist solicitude and solicitation give themselves only the illusion of technical liberty when they become methodical. In truth, they reproduce, in the register of method (change it into: in the domain of methodology), a solicitude and solicitation of Being, a historico-metaphysical threatening of

---

77   Derrida, *Writing and Difference*, p. 3.
78   Giddens, Anthony. *Modernity: Interviews of Giddens*. Trans. Yin Hongyi. Beijing: Xinhua Publishing House, 2001. p. 51.
79   Derrida, *Writing and Difference*, p. 4.

foundations."[80] In this sense, Althusser makes an optimistic, positive rewriting of structuralism, essentially conquering the philosophy. Method is essence; non-subject is liberation.

In Derrida's view, this is "an era when history dislocates". Humans are expelled from subject (idea, Cogito, self-consciousness and Dascin) where they have resided for hundreds of years. Only when subject philosophy becomes academic "relics" can "the passion for structuralism characterized by experimental mania and modular reproduction" develop and expand on its own. How incisive historical insight is! In contrast to Althusser, Derrida discerns the failure of the new humanistic subject philosophy and the historical rise of structuralism, but he defines this historical substitute as the improper, opposite pole instead of viewing it as another absolute truth or the establishment of "scientific methods".

Derrida says that because structuralism is based on the debris remaining from the explosion of humanism, it turns into a pathological perspective and verifies the research of theoretical structure. "These analyses are possible only after a certain defeat of force and within the movement of diminished ardor. A reflection of the accomplished, the constituted, the constructed. Historical, eschatological, and crepuscular by its very situation."[81]

Therefore, it makes sense that Derrida likens the ideological trend of structuralism to "melancholy for Gide". If history is really the "process without a subject", as Althusser says, then structural life is destined to be miserable and wretched.

Secondly, if structure is a change of inquiring means, then it is a deeper signification, even a metaphor, but not a reference. More profoundly, Derrida senses the domain of meaning in structuralism. "To be a structuralist is first to concentrate on the organization of meaning, on the autonomy and idiosyncratic balance, the completion of each moment, each form."[82] However, structure in no longer the simply formalized Gestalt as a framework, but rather, it is unsubstantiated essence. Certainly, the essence is no longer something that

---

80   Ibid., p. 5.
81   Ibid., p. 3.
82   Ibid., p. 30.

is fixed: it is a productive and constructive invisible relation. More often than not, structural existence does not refer to the complex, but to a signification of deep system, a totality of "inquiring".

Simply put, this is a comment on Althusser's problematic. The linguistics of structuralism is not only a means of speech, but a semiotic system, an operation of discourse, a hidden, internal moving source, even Nothingness. The Nothingness is the absence of subject and force, but this does not hamper the interactive function in invisible, panoramic structure of meaning. "Preventing, but calling upon each other, provoking each other too, unforeseeably and as if despite oneself, in a kind of autonomousness over assemblage of meanings, a power of pure equivocality that makes the creativity of the classical God appear all too poor."[83]

To know why one says "structure" is to know why one no longer wishes to say eidos, "essence", form, Gestalt, "ensemble", "composition", "complex", "construction", "correlation", "totality", "Idea", "organism", "state", "system", etc.. One must understand not only why each of these words showed itself to be insufficient but also why the notion of structure continues to borrow some implicit signification from them and to be inhabited by them.[84]

The essence and absolute idea of subject is sublated. As the inner creative power of existence, "I" (individual subject), am suspended and as the existing internal force, am no longer related to individuals. The decisive factors have been neutralized into an objective construction of meaning totality beyond humans.[85] Thus, "the relief and design of structures appears more clearly when content, which is the living energy of meaning, is neutralized. Somewhat like the architecture of an uninhabited or deserted city, reduced to its skeleton by some catastrophe of nature or art. A city no longer inhabited, not simply left behind, but haunted by meaning and culture."[86]

God is still present. Structure, namely the signification, just turns into a **hidden God**. Here I have borrowed words from Goldmann. Structure is not that which is superficial; it is a deeper totality. So

83   Ibid., p. 8.
84   Ibid., p. 380.
85   Ibid., p. 4.
86   Ibid., p. 4.

Derrida thinks that "within structure there is not only form, relation, and configuration. There is also interdependency and a totality
which is always concrete". Or in other words, "structure is the formal unity of form and meaning."[87] Structure dissolves subject, but
by no means perishes the vitality of subject. "The liberty that this
critical (in all the senses of this word) disengagement assures us of,
therefore, is a solicitude for and an opening into totality."[88] Force,
neutralized once again, withdraws from individual subject and hides
as the total constructive power of structure.

So far, Derrida's intention regarding his criticism of structuralism
(also which contains the consistent doubt about Althusser's problematic) has become deliciously apparent. His questioning should
be: does structuralism really dissolve the subject? More importantly,
is the Logo-centrism since Plato indeed demoted in structuralism?
Derrida's answers are obviously negative. In his opinion, Logo-
centrism is actually further intensified. He draws an extremely important conclusion:

> The fact that modern structuralism grows up more or less by di-
> rectly or publicly relying on phenomenology is enough to bring
> it into the purest tradition of western philosophy. Exceeding its
> aversion from Platonism, the tradition leads Husserl back to
> Plato.[89]

By means of a reductive bracket of the Husserl type, structuralism
tries to dissolve and shelve the individual subject of new humanism,
but it guides our thoughts back to Plato. Structuralism **transforms**
what is negated by Husserl into the structural governing. Structure
is not an external form, but a unity of form and meaning. Thus,
structure is a non-subject and invisible force. Structure is first the
structure of an organic or artificial work, the internal unity of an **assemblage**, a construction; a work that is governed by a unifying principle, the architecture that is built and made visible in a **location**.[90]
False individual subject is excluded. Yet, the force does not really
disappear, but changes into **an internal totality, an isomorphism
and simultaneite (Fr.)**. The individual is absent but the objective,

---

87   Ibid., pp. 3-4.
88   Ibid., p. 5.
89   Ibid., p. 33.
90   Ibid., p. 17.

total governing power is present. According to Derrida, "this is only the phenomenon, the epidermis, the surface image of the essential truth of the universe as it is conceived and created by God. This truth is absolute **simultaneity**."[91] The force is not really gone but hides as structure, which is the absent God. In this viewpoint, the sun of Plato's ideas switches from shining directly to more deadly, invisible rays. For instance, in the context of structuralism, writing is no more the realization of subjects' (ordinary writers) creativity or imagination, but rather it shifts into a deep Gestalt manipulation where even the writers live in states of unconsciousness, such as Althusser's problematic. "No longer a method within the ordo cognescendi, no longer a relationship in the ordo essendi, but the very being of the work."[92] Surely, the work exists as structure, not the creativity of subjects. But the reading in the context of structuralism is the simultaneous confrontation with writing (deep structure):

> *In particular, a structuralist reading, by its own activity, always presupposes and appeals to the theological simultaneity of the book, and considers itself deprived of the essential when this simultaneity is not accessible. In both cases, simultaneity is the myth of a total reading or description, promoted to the status of a regulatory ideal.*[93]

For this, Derrida has made a fairly poetic analysis. Taking writing, for example, he reminds us that the writing of structuralism can be understood from the moment when human beings established pneumatology and interpreted pneuma, spiritus and logos as the three learnings of: God, angel and Man. Why? The writing history of metaphysics is also the writing history of us under holy light. Our writing is that the mighty and infinite creative power of Idea (God) realizes the dissemination of the Book through life (our passionate creation and imagination).

God did not know the anguish of choice between various possibilities: he conceived possible choices in action and disposed of them as such in his Understanding or Logos; and, in any event, the narrowness of a passageway that is Will favors the "best" choice. Each existence continues to "express" the totality of the Universe. There

---

91 Ibid., pp. 27-28.
92 Ibid., p. 17.
93 Ibid., pp. 28-29.

is, therefore, no tragedy of the book. There is only one Book, and this same Book is distributed throughout all books.[94]

Thus, our writing is just granted by *Vorsehung*. We are only **assigned** the conceptual Logos.

> *To write is not only to know that the Book does not exist and that forever there are books against which the meaning of a world not conceived by an absolute subject is shattered before it has even become a unique meaning; nor is it only to know that the non-written and the non-read cannot be relegated to the status of having no basis by the obliging the negativity of some dialectic, making us deplore the absence of the Book under the burden of "too many texts"! It is not only to have lost the theological certainty of seeing every page bind itself into the unique text of the truth, the "book of reason"...*[95]

To write is not only to know that through writing, through the extremities of style, the best will not necessarily transpire, as Leibniz thought it did in divine creation, nor will the transition to what transpires always be **willful**, nor will that which is **noted down** always infinitely express the universe, resembling and reassembling it."[96] "Rather, to write is also to know that what has not yet been produced within literality has no other dwelling place, does not await us as prescription in some topos ouranios, or some divine understanding. Meaning must await being said or written in order to inhabit itself, and in order to become, by differing from itself, what it is: meaning."[97]

To write is to know that what has not yet been produced within literality has no other dwelling place, does not await us as **prescription** in some topos ouranios, or some divine understanding. Meaning must await being said or written in order to inhabit itself, and in order to become, by differing from itself, what it is: meaning.

Writing as the origin of pure historicity, pure traditionality, is only the telos of a history of writing whose philosophy is always to come.[98]

---

94   Ibid., p. 9.
95   Ibid., p. 10.
96   Ibid., pp. 10-11.
97   Ibid., p. 11.
98   Ibid., p. 13.

Ah! Finally the parallelism has turned into a direct criticism of structuralism. It is structuralism that transforms the meaning totality (totality of meaning) from the ability of subject and individual into an objective element of Gestalt. The Gestalt comes from God and is the replacement for logos! The thing named structure or problematic (total meaning) is **waiting to be written out**. The structuralist writing is the book's **writing of me**. The speech of structuralism must be "word is speaking me!" Derrida remarks with irony: "if creation were not revelation, what would happen to the finitude of the writer and to the solitude of his hand abandoned by God? Divine creativity, in this case, would be re-appropriated by a hypocritical humanism."[99] Structure is still the light of reason though it becomes more piecemeal now. In the annihilation of the humanistic philosophy of force by structuralism, Platonic logo-centrism does not die, it is just hiding very well and obtaining legitimacy.

I admit that Derrida's observation is extremely insightful. In 1963, during the time when structuralism was thriving throughout France, Derrida still adhered to tradition and was not affected by fashion. The dissolving of structure starts the journey of Derrida's dialectics of deconstruction. Surely, Derrida cannot construct all his revolutionary, theoretical insights in this chapter alone, but he has found the most crucial passageway for liberation, which is **deconstruction**.

In this chapter of his, the word 'deconstruction' is not directly present, but the concept of deconstruction has been perfectly illustrated. This is most apparent in Derrida's dialectic comprehension of structure: in the context of structuralism, structure means the total happening of a meaning. Structure is always productive meaning. Its depth lies in that the identical, constant, reasonable logos of traditional subject philosophy is dissolved, and the external essentialism is replaced by historical total construction. Rather than the ontological dwelling of reasonable subject, meaning is historically constructed outside individual subject. Derrida says that the secret of structuralism lies in that "value and meaning are **reconstituted and reawakened** in their proper historicity and temporality."[100] Since the abstract metaphysics of subject is destroyed, the individual is bound to die eventually.

---

99   Ibid., p. 12.
100   Ibid., p. 15.

"That it can always fail is the mark of its pure finitude and its pure historicity."[101] So it is unable to really posses meaning and value. In case of structuralism, meaning is possessed by a certain functional, rational structure, and reconstructed in non-subject timeliness (Endlichkeit). "The truth of time is not temporal",[102] but rather it is the time of survivability in Heidegger's words. Meaning is invariably a present production of structure.

However, Derrida identifies that "if there are structures, they are possible only on the basis of the fundamental structure which permits totality to open and overflow itself such that it **takes on meaning** by anticipating a telos which here must be understood in its most indeterminate form. This opening is certainly that which liberates time and genesis (even coincides with them), but it is also that which risks enclosing progression toward the future-becoming-by giving it form."[103] Yes, structuralism eliminates the rational essentialism of subject philosophy, but does the structure that eternally possesses the totality of meaning not suggest teleology? Structuralists are unaware of whether every present construction of structure and historical generation of the totality of meaning are really the Structure. In this present, historical rewriting, structure becomes the overseer of individual subject, and the meaning of the meaning of historical generation. God is undoubtedly absent, but yet He reigns tacitly. This is still a defense of a metaphysical tyranny, still logos idealism! It is certainly a critique of Althusser's problematic. Derrida holds that the rational structure of the idealization of structuralism does not exist at all. The structure, rewritten every time, is never a duplication of prototype, but rather it is already **a surplus of non-structural meaning**. The fundamental reason here is that the rewriting of structural meaning is not present, and it is impossible for it to be present. Meaning is always masqueraded under a false name. Unlimited metaphors happen in the transition from signifier to signifier. The chain of the signifier is an **ontological parody** instead of a simple regression.

---

101   Ibid., p. 13.
102   Ibid., p. 27.
103   Ibid., p. 31.

And that the meaning of meaning (in the general sense of meaning and not in the sense of signalization) is infinite implication; the indefinite referral of signifier to signifier. And that its force is a certain pure and infinite equivocality which gives signified meaning no respite, no rest, but engages it in its own *economy* so that it always *signifies again and differs*.[104]

Thus, if the meaning totality always differs, then the absolute, holistic construction will be an illusion. In effect, the deep, rational Gestalt is self-dissolving. After striking down the subject, structure becomes responsible for its own death by hanging itself on the trestle of historical generation. Every construction of structure is deconstruction. Here we should inquire more cautiously: Is the great problematic of Althusser as solid as a rock or just an illusion, more akin to quicksand?

The important identification we make at last is Derrida's defense of himself, namely **deconstruction is not an absolute dissolution**, but it is also, simultaneously, a **construction**. Regarding Derrida's theory of deconstruction as a simple disassembly of structure is to misunderstand him. Derrida is not post-structuralism, which escapes from the tyranny of structure and appears as a release of force, such as Foucault's jailed power of madness (the second essay of *Writing and Difference* is about Foucault's madness), and Barthes' desire that flees from structure. Derrida is not "postmodernist" either. The ideological trend of postmodernism, a "game on the bottomless chessboard," is the fundamental deviation from modernistic system, such as Lyotard's irrational fragments, which casts off grand narrative, and Feyerabend's "anything goes" that breaks away from the autocracy of scientific reason. Derrida himself is the theory of deconstruction. At the beginning of 1967, he realized his double historical missions. On the one hand, he emphasized "the necessity of disintegrating metaphysics." On the other hand, he stressed the need not to negate philosophy. In other words, deconstruct philosophy, namely reflecting on some closeness of philosophy, but do not give up philosophy.[105] The philosophy identified here is not a general reference, but the theoretical logic (structure) of all traditional metaphysics in

104 Ibid., p. 29.
105 Ibid., p. 4.

Nietzsche and Heidegger's sense. **The philosophy of deconstruction does not desert it** as an integral, theoretical orientation. In a sense, deconstruction is some un-philosophical ideology of philosophy.[106] The point of departure really resembles that of Adorno, which is different from the postmodernism of absolute nihilism.[107] Derrida's theoretical, logical point is between "being and non-being". I tend to believe that the basic position of Derrida's theory of deconstruction is quite similar to Goldmann's logic.[108] When Derrida says "respect what we are deconstructing", he clearly differentiates himself from the scholars who only understand deconstruction as an explanation which emphasizes single-dimensional negation and dissolving.

No wonder Derrida is Derrida.

---

106   Ibid., p. 12.
107   Adorno advocates that reason cannot be abolished because of illness. Objecting to autocratic identity may only focus on the heterogeneity of identity, exhibit the conceptual nature that can't be grasped and still affirms the concepts about objects. See: *Atonalistic Dialectic Fantasy-Textual Interpretation of Adorno's Negative Dialectics.* Beijing: Joint Publishing, 2001.
108   In *The Hidden God*, Goldmann confirms an ontological logic of "being and non-being". Faced with industrial metal world, the present God is speechless. In later work *The Specters of Marx* by Derrida, from which the basic path of the presence and absence of Marx starts. See: Goldmann, Lucien. *The Hidden God.* Trans. Cai Hongbin. Tianjin: Baihua Literature and Art Press, 1998. Derrida, Jacques. *The Specters of Marx.* Trans. He Yi. Beijing: China Renmin University Press, 1999.

CHAPTER III

ALTHUSSER'S SYMPTOMATIC READING

If problematic is the main methodological and logical Gestalt of *For Marx*, then symptomatic reading can be considered the key concept in the cognitive framework of *Reading Capital*.[1] For Althusser, as problematic is an invisible theoretical framework; general research and reading are absolutely not effective if we want to pry them out of a thinker's mind and text. The only path is "symptomatic." I believe the so-called symptomatic is Althusser's textual hermeneutics. When going through all of Althusser's theoretical thoughts, the significance of symptomatic ranks only second to problematic.

---

1 *Symptomatic* can be translated literally into "症候" or "征候" in Chinese, meaning symptom or sign. But it refers to a reading or interpretation method in Althusser's discussion. Though he seldom use the phrase *symptomatic reading*, people generally translate *symptomatic* into "症候阅读" or "症候阅读法", meaning symptomatic reading method.

1 THE ORIGINAL SIN OF READING

Althusser expounds upon symptomatic reading in the long foreword of *Reading Capital*, "From Capital to Marx's philosophy". At first, he still interprets **the function of problematic in reading**. However, in this case he expresses – in a very literary fashion – **innocent reading** and **guilty reading**, which are apparently related to his discussion about the sighting of problematic and "darkness."

In reference to the idealized, **direct reading** based on everyday life, the innocent reading assumes that readers, unaffected by any external factor, they directly **"sight"** all what the author expresses while reading. But according to Althusser's theory of problematic, the pure reading can just be the innocence of **God's eye view**. In *On Content in the Thought of G.W.F. Hegel*, the Young Althusser once described the cognitive model of theological vision as: "it is based on direct "sighting". People regard cognition as the "eyes", and they believe that they will get a panoramic view of everything once they open their eyes. In reality, it is just theological fantasy because only the horizon of mighty God can reach the eternal, absolute truth, whereas human's "sighting" is given to different situations, ranging from looking back, or – with a smile – eagerly looking forward, to even a first-ever glimpse. "Together with Plato's 'mind's eye', concentrating on the horizon of eternal truth belongs to the pure and passive illusion, which are contemplative and reasonable ancient thoughts."[2] That is because anyone's reading is only the "sighting" with their own subjective feelings in the context of a certain knowledge background or life experiences. If elevated to a textual interpretation of theoretical research, it must be the interpretation governed by a certain problematic. Sighting is not only the vision of a perspective but a position, which is also the accumulation of theoretical culture. Only the results of knowledge that are generated under the control of a certain theoretical background are available to everyone. During the Chinese Cultural Revolution, Mao Zedong once asked general Xu Shiyou to read *A Dream in Red Mansions* and claimed "he would have no say if he did not read it five times". Xu Shiyou read it many times with the help of his secretary, but eventually he failed to see things beyond the romance and those who lived in the deep of the

---

2 Hitoshi, Yimamura. *Althusser: Epistemological Rupture*, p. 55.

Rong and Ning mansion. However, in A Dream in Red Mansions, what Mao had observed was the complicated network of social relations and the history of ups and downs seen in feudal families. This is the deep context produced and exhibited by Mao's theoretical background,' but Xu lacked the theoretical, supporting background to comprehend A Dream in Red Mansions. Therefore, Xu was blind to what has been observed by Mao. Althusser insists on cognition: "there is no reading that does not involve, at least implicitly, a theory which determines the character of the reading."[3] This somewhat resembles the scientific, philosophical domain of discussion after the theory-laden, (theory loaded) as proposed by Hanson.

Hanson's theory-laden is as follows: In 1958, Hanson, American scientist and philosopher, published the book, Patterns of Discovery, where he clearly objected to the demarcation made by traditional logical positivism of scientific languages, namely not depending on the difference between the theoretical observation language of neutrality and theoretical language. He immediately points out that scientific observation is not "sighting" in the visual sense, and people are never able to directly see observable objects in experiments. From the beginning, observation is influenced by different theories, interpretations or intellectual structures.[4] Take Thirupathi Gudi and Kepler, for example. While watching the sunrise in the east, they seem to be observing the same phenomenon. Why does one tell us the earth is fixed with the sun in orbit – not the earth, but yet the other reaches the opposite conclusion? Hanson believes that these two opposing statements stem from "subsequent explanations about what is seen" rather than "identical visual material." In fact, the truth is that previous knowledge of X constructs the observation of X. Thus, Hanson puts forward an important statement: The sighting act is a theory-laden thing.[5] Clearly, Gestalt psychology deeply influences this particular viewpoint. In 1958, Polanyi, the British philosopher of science, espoused similar opinions in Personal Knowledge, which laid the crucial, prescient foundation for Pope and Piaget's "theories prior to observations."[6]

---

3   Callinicos, Alex. Althusser's Marxism, p. 33.

4   Hanson, N.R. Patterns of Discovery. Trans. Jing Xinli & Zhou Peiyi. Beijing: China International Broadcasting Publishing House, 1988. p. 6.

5   Ibid., p. 22.

6   See: Zhang Yibing. Selected Works of Zhang Yibing. Guangxi: Guangxi Normal University Press, 1999. p. 93.

In this sense, Althusser clearly points out that all readings are sub-ject-laden **(the original sin of "theory-laden")**, and unlikely to be completely "innocent."[7] So Althusser thinks all readings are "guilty." This is the first context.

Althusser longs for the advent of an age marked by "the most dra-matic and difficult trial of all, the discovery of and training in the meaning of the 'simplest' acts of existence: seeing, listening, speak-ing, reading – the acts which relate men to their works, and to those works thrown in their faces, their 'absences of works'".[8] Grand nar-rative then collapses. Furthermore, this appears to be the age, which interprets the discourse of ordinary everyday life. The interpretation of everyday life will generate our new interpretations of the thinkers' texts. In Althusser's views, "only since Freud have we begun to sus-pect what listening, and hence what speaking (and keeping silent), **means** (veut dire); that this **'meaning'** (vouloir dire) of speaking and listening reveals beneath the innocence of speech and hearing the culpable depth of a second, quite different discourse, the discourse of the unconscious."[9] Freud once compared the entire spiritual life of humans to an iceberg in the sea. The peak part floating on the surface of sea is the realm of consciousness; the main part, immersed under the surface, is the more important part: unconsciousness of human spiritual life. He also declares that the phenomenon of conscious-ness is neither abnormal nor indifferent, but rather, it is the most significant factor that determines human spiritual psychology. This is because unconsciousness, the internal source of the individual hu-man's psychological activity and the switch touching the individual human's heart, owns original motivation (it already exists in your psychological activity). No matter whether the spiritual products are normal or abnormal, high-level or low-level, dynamic or material-ized, all psychological activities of an individual are the structures,

---

7   Hu Wanfu once commented that "Althusser is the first one to realize and system-atically analyze the boundary line between common subjective reading and objective reading". Actually, this explanation is inaccurate. In Althusser's eyes, there does not exist objective reading (namely "innocent reading" said by him) at all. All readings are subjective, and the difference only lies in whether self-consciousness (admitting guilt) or not. See: Hu Wanfu. *On the Young Marx*. Wu Han: Published by Central China Normal University Press, 1988. p. 42.

8   Althusser, Louis. *Reading Capital*, pp. 15-16.

9   Ibid., p. 16.

which are directly or indirectly affected by unconsciousness. This unconsciousness determines the essence, intention, approach and degree of an individual's psychological activity. Therefore, unconsciousness – not consciousness – is the better representative of the deep essence of human beings. Althusser wants to tell us that only since Freud have we begun to notice the extremely complex, true desire and fundamental motivation of unconsciousness suppressed behind innocent listening and speaking (or keeping silent). Humanity's belief in the directness and completeness of listening and speaking at the level of consciousness is actually illusory because both listening and speaking at a given time are, possibly, the suppressed Other-unconscious discourse. Later, Lacan rewrites it as: "unconsciousness is the discourse of the Other".

According to my judgments, the profound, theoretical background that Althusser describes here is Freud rather than that of the radical Lacan. Then Althusser changes figures and further states, "only since Marx have we had to begin to suspect what, in theory at least, **reading** and hence writing means."[10] This is a fair critical theoretical identification. Thus, the first context draws a deeper connotation, namely that the innocent, direct reading is manifested again as the **full presence** of **subject** and **essence (logos)** in writing and reading of theoretical texts. Althusser refers to it as "expressive" reading, which means undergoing a complicated and abstract, but direct, grasp of the essence of cognitive objects rather than the simple "sighting" mentioned above. This is another **cognitive directness**. In reading, people surmise that they directly and completely occupy essence. Althusser claims that in this reading model, "we have suspected the existence of the darkness of the religious phantasm of epiphanic transparency, and its privileged model of anchorage: the Logos and its Scriptures."[11] In his texts Althusser never fails to mention the Catholic, theological context of his own experience. At least while superficially criticizing, it is quite easy for him to enumerate logical Gestalt of theology and religious experiences to confirm the legitimacy of his thoughts.

---

10   Ibid., p. 16.
11   Ibid., p. 35.

What does this mean? Althusser gives an example here. In *Economic and Philosophical Manuscripts of 1844* (*Manuscripts of 1844* for short), the Young Marx once tried to **read** (in the true sense of the word) the "abstract" essence out of the "concrete" being of essence. If I understand this correctly, it means that in *Manuscripts of 1844* the Young Marx objected to the direct confirmation of economic phenomenon by classic economics. He attempted to directly penetrate into the alienated nature of workers' labor through philosophy in phenomenal, economic existence. Although covered by commodity relations, the alienated nature of labor can still be indirectly present by breaking through the obstacles (by sublating alienation and private ownership) via the critical power of ethical "ought." Althusser comments that the direct occupation of essence by Marx was obviously the remains of Hegel's absolute philosophy. "This immediate reading of essence in existence expresses the religious model of Hegel's Absolute Knowledge, that End of History in which the concept at last becomes fully visible, present among us in person, tangible in its sensory existence".[12] Through negation, abandonment of worldly life, and the stripping of phenomenology of mind, essence is **directly present** through objects, and God is **totally present** after discarding the vexation of worldly affairs. This is undoubtedly an innocent, theological fantasy.

> In Hegel, for the last time and on the terrain of history itself, assembled all the complementary religious myths relating to the voice (the Logos) speaking in the sequences of a discourse; of the Truth that inhabits its Scripture; – and of the ear that hears or the eye that reads this discourse, in order to discover in it (if they are pure) the speech of the Truth, which inhabits each of its Words in person.[13]

Althusser holds that truth is covered in such a fantasy and myth, and the direct reading in the second context is really an exaggeration. Althusser adds that Spinoza was the first one to question reading and writing in this sense (Marx was the first to question it theoretically) and "he was also the first man in the world to have proposed both a theory of history and a philosophy of the opacity of the immediate. With him, for the first time ever, a man had linked together in this

---

12   Ibid., p. 16.
13   Ibid., p. 17.

way the essence of reading and the essence of history in a theory of the difference between the imaginary and the true."[14] What does it mean? Althusser intends to state that, as a thinker, Spinoza moves toward materialism by means of nominalism; he rejects apriorism and idealism in any form, and opposes the precognition theory, which maintains that the whole world "belongs to me." In later years, Althusser wrote a very literary metaphor:

On the one hand, a materialist is a person who knows from which platform the train departs and at which destination it arrives. He is aware of this ahead of time. While getting on a train, he is aware of the destination because he is moving together with the train. On the other hand, when a materialist boards on the train, he knows neither the starting point nor the destination.[15]

Althusser points out that Spinoza's materialistic epistemology knows historicity and relativity, so he negates the primacy of truth. As Althusser has often mentioned, Spinoza influences virtually all his thoughts. According to Perry Anderson, "nearly all the novel concepts and accents of Althusser's Marxism, apart from those imported from contemporary disciplines, were in fact directly drawn from Spinoza."[16] In Althusser's eyes, Hegel, who confirms the historical truth, is still a servant to metaphysics because his historical ideas are constrained by absolute theodicy. In every logical, intellectual piece of the puzzle (historical happening), absolute idea is directly presented. "In the model **this** bread, **this** body, **this** face and **this** man are the Spirit itself."[17] God is eternally present.

But how can we eliminate the second illusion of direct reading? Althusser gives us the following recipe: "it was essential to turn to history to track down this myth of reading back to its lair."[18] That is because original works of authors and direct reading of readers never exist except in **the true history in thought**. "People discover that the truth of history cannot be read in its manifest discourse, because the text of history is not a text in which a voice (the Logos) speaks,

14   Ibid., pp. 16-17.
15   Althusser, Louis. *The Future Lasts Forever*, p. 215.
16   Anderson, Perry. *Considerations on Western Marxism*, p. 64.
17   Althusser, Louis. *Reading Capital*, p. 16.
18   Ibid., p. 17.

but the inaudible and illegible notation of the effects of a structure of structures."[19]

Indeed, this sentence is quite profound. It is not you that is writing, but rather the **objective function of historical structure is making you write and speak**. Unable to run away from the nets of historical structure, your speaking and writing can only stretch in narrow space. I am afraid this is the deepest theoretical statement of "word is speaking me" in poststructuralist theories of discourse. Apparently, we see here that Marx's principle of historical materialism is also embedded in textual writing and reading. At this point, the context of Althusser clearly overshadows those of Lacan and Bart. Althusser confidently states:

> *This explains to us why Marx could not possibly have become Marx except by founding a theory of history and a philosophy of the historical distinction between ideology and science, and why in his last analysis this foundation was consummated in the dissipation of the religious myth of reading. The Young Marx in **The Manuscripts of 1844** read the human essence at sight, immediately, in the transparency of its alienation. Capital, on the contrary, exactly measures a distance and an internal dislocation in the real.[20]*

In 1844, the Young Marx tended to equate the transcendental, logical setting with the essence of labor of which the workers were deprived. The free, autonomous and creative activities of humans became the purpose of communist revolutions. But in both in the writing and research of *Capital*, Marx has fully realized the distance between his theories and reality. This is also objective distance that **cannot be eliminated**. No longer overlapping with logic, revolutionary goals are based on concrete historical conditions. Althusser thinks that the distance between theoretical reading and distance is also the distance from true history, which will exist forever. Once this distance is neglected and erased, it will lead to the **fetishism of reading**. Althusser comments that "a distance and a dislocation such as to make their own effects themselves illegible, and the illusion of an immediate reading of them the ultimate apex of their effects: fetishism."[21] The essence of reading fetishism by Althusser is that you think you are

---

19   Ibid., p. 17.
20   Ibid., p. 17.
21   Ibid., p. 17.

innocent even if it is guilty reading. The distance between reading and historicity exists objectively, but you lose sight of the distance. So the innocence must be delusive. This is the nature of the ideology of reading. Faced with a classic work you tell yourself with a final sense of triumph after only one reading: "I am directly conversing with masters." If you fail to realize how little you understand of the book, you are engaging in self-deception.

It is only as a result of this that it becomes possible to understand what Althusser later says: "if there are no innocent readings, that is because every reading merely reflects in its lessons and rules which the real culprit: the conception of knowledge underlying the object of knowledge which makes knowledge what it is."[22] This identification is of vital importance. Any reading is under the governing of **theoretical standards** (epistemological concepts). Blank reading never exists, and **reading always bears the load of a certain theoretical Gestalt**, namely the **reading of problematic**. This is Althusser's "guilty." Actually, reading always has the preexistence of theory, which is the context for interpretation following Husserl.

After destroying the fantasy that innocent reading exists, Althusser says, "as there is no such thing as an innocent reading, we must say what reading we are guilty of."[23] For instance, when we are reading Marx's *Capital*, every reader will reach different conclusions through different problematic. "The studies that emerged from this project are no more than the various individual protocols of this reading: each having cut the peculiar oblique path that suited him through the immense forest of this Book."[24] Althusser clearly points out that his own reading of *Capital* is a guilty, **philosophical** reading.

> *Hence a philosophical reading of Capital is quite the opposite of an innocent reading. It is a guilty reading, but not one that absolves its crime by confessing it. On the contrary, it takes responsibility for its crime as a 'justified crime' and defends it by proving its necessity. It is therefore a special reading which exculpates itself by posing to every guilty **reading the very question** that unmasks its innocence, the mere question of its innocence: what is it to read?[25]*

---

22   Ibid., p. 34.
23   Ibid., p. 14.
24   Ibid., p. 14.
25   Ibid., p. 15.

Then Althusser makes a further analysis:

> ...*it is not possible to read Capital properly without the help of Marxist philosophy, which must itself be read, and simultaneously, in Capital itself. If this double reading and constant reference from the scientific reading to the philosophical reading, and from the philosophical reading to the scientific reading, are necessary and fruitful, we shall surely be able to recognize in them the peculiarity of the philosophical revolution carried in Marx's scientific discovery: a revolution which inaugurates an authentically new mode of philosophical thought.*[26]

So far, we have finally achieved an elementary understanding of "what is it to read" in Althusser's problematic.

2 SIGHTING AND PRODUCTION: THE EPISTEMOLOGICAL LABYRINTH OF DOUBLE READING

Althusser says "returning to Marx, we note it is not only in what he says but also in what he does that we can grasp the transition from an earlier idea and practice of **reading** to a new practice of reading and to a theory of history capable of providing us with a new theory of reading."[27] In the discussion above, we have obtained a preliminary understanding of the complexity of Althusser's theories of reading. Though I do not intend to scare the readers, I have to warn that this is only the entrance to the theoretical labyrinth. Althusser's reading of *Capital* is not simply about confronting the texts. While reading Marx, what we initially see is that Marx himself is **reading**. Thus, **we are reading another reading**. What an amazing saying! Besides, our reading of Marx, which is led by Althusser, is located in **double reading**. If wrapped by the word inter-textuality, which was put forward by J. Kristeva, Althusser's strategy can be called **inter-reading**. This is truly a daunting theoretical labyrinth.

In Althusser's eyes, the double reading of Marx reflects two totally different reading principles. The **first reading** of Marx (we can refer to it as Reading I) is the **reading through a grid**. In the first reading, Marx reads his predecessor's discourse (A. Smith's for instance) through his own discourse. The result of this reading through a grid

---

26   Ibid., pp. 75-76.
27   Ibid., p. 18.

in which Smith's text is seen through Marx's projection onto it and as a measure of it, is merely a summary of concordances and dis-cordances, the balance of what Smith had discovered and what he had missed, of his merits and failings, of his presences and absences. In fact, this reading is a retrospective theoretical reading.[28]

In simple terms, Marx uses his own vision to construct that of Smith in **Reading I**. Marx's vision is the "measure" and "grid." Yet in the same observation and analysis, Smith's vision has many blanks, such as his **incompleteness in theory** of value, labor and capital, or the **lapse** of mixing constant capital and variable capital. By means of his own reading Marx filled in the blanks of Smith's theories. Here, Althusser finds that Marx often uses the inattention – to be ex-act, the **disappearance** – of Smith to account for the blanks: Smith **loses sight of** things that have been clearly right in front of him, and he fails to seize what is at hand. Marx sees much more than Smith. This is perhaps the oft-employed method in our traditional research into the history of Marxism.

Althusser does not express too much agreement with Reading I, but argues that the formed linear channel of "vision" is not qualified to constitute the whole of Marx's reading methods. "This reduces every weakness in the system of concepts that make up knowledge to a psychological weakness of "vision". And if it is the absence of vision that explains these oversights, in the same way and by the same necessity, it is the presence and acuteness of "vision" that will explain these **"sightings"**: all knowledge recognized."[29] These are simultaneously both stunted and brilliant states of **"vision"**. Due to a weakness of vision (defective problematic), Smith **failed to see** it, but Marx **saw it** because of visual power. Since it fails to exceed the linear, direct logic of knowledge, Althusser criticizes that "we have relapsed into the mirror myth of knowledge as the vision of a given object or the reading of an established text, neither of which is ever anything but transparency itself – the sin of blindness belonging by right to vision as much as the virtue of clear-sightedness – to the eye of man."[30]

---

28   Ibid., p. 18.
29   Ibid., p. 19.
30   Ibid., p. 19.

Bachelard Against Visualism. It should be pointed out that the Althusser's analysis is permeated with the influence of his teacher, Bachelard. Bachelard objects to what he calls "visualism". In his opinion, the traditional phenomenology of "vision" sets the observation of object by subject. The combination of consciousness and intention, as exaggeratedly placed in the central position, turns into the starting point of all research. The subjects' vision becomes the center of the world. People focus on their shadows. So in the career of philosophy that regards eyes as the tool, people begin to realize the existence of shadows. Philosophers establish non-ego and ego.[31] Bachelard is strongly against this vision-centered philosophy of direct "sighting", against "reproduction", theory of reflection, as well as structures of presentation, surface and essence. However, he affirms practice and initiative, which is possibly the supporting background for Althusser's discussion. Thus, in the book On Content in the Thought of G.W.F. Hegel, Althusser discusses Bachelard's rejection of the view of direct vision. Althusser thinks that truth cannot be reached directly.

Hitoshi intervenes here: The direct vision theory rejects the mincing of words. It idealistically holds that people can arrive at the shore of truth without trudging, detouring, or encountering any setbacks. Truth is blind but is able to see the sun as soon as the eyes are opened. The philosophy of "opening eyes" is the philosophy of closing eyes. Only the blind are able to see the sun directly.[32] Therefore, the direct cognitive model of vision is the knowledge of "the blind." Hitoshi makes a wonderful comment that the opening of the eyes is equal to the closing of the eyes because deep theoretical structure cannot be analyzed with the direct mode of sighting.

Therefore, the difference between Marx and Smith when it comes to reading lay in whether the sighting was complete or not. "Marx thinks the theoretical difference that nevertheless separates him from Smith forever. And finally, we too are condemned to the same fate of vision – condemned to see in Marx only what he **saw**."[33] Evidently, the first reading is not symptomatic reading! Althusser's doubt about Reading I is as follows: Has Marx seen invisible things? Or can we see what Marx did not see?

---

31   Bachelard, Gaston. *On Land and Will*. See: Dagognet, Francois. *Reason and Passion: Biography of Gaston Bachelard*. Trans. Shang Heng. Beijing: Peking University Press, 1977. p. 37.

32   Hitoshi, Yimamura. *Althusser: Epistemological Rupture*, p.70.

33   Althusser, Louis. *Reading Capital*, p. 19.

Secondly, Althusser asks us to pay more attention to **Reading II, which is a second, and very different reading method** we can see in Marx's *Capital*. He says that in Reading I, only the "presence" and "absence" in the horizon, or direct sighting and oversight, are ascertained. However, Reading I loses sight of "the relationship between sighting and oversight." The reason why this problem is "absent" in direct horizon is because it can only be seen as an invisible thing, or what it involves is absolutely not given object. In the same visible horizon, the sighting and oversight of a given object are solely caused by the readers' eyesight, but the problem here is the necessary but **dormant relationship between visible and invisible fields**. The second type reading, which Althusser identifies, is to see the dormant thing in a **non-visual way**, which is really an overstatement and turns people's thoughts towards Kristeva's theory of double texts. In Kristeva's analysis of signification, she differentiates phéno-test from géno-text. The former is the phenomenon of the text and is the visible, concrete language as a product. The latter refers to the production process of preeminence in the vertical and productive sense.[34] These two different texts seem to be the heterogeneous objects of Althusser's different readings, visible reading and reading invisible. However, Storey – in an oversimplified way – identifies them as **"overt text"** and **"covert text"**.[35]

Compared with the grid of Reading I, what classical political economy does not see, is not what it does not see, it is **what it sees**; it is not what it lacks, on the contrary, it is **what it does not lack**; it is not what it misses, but on the contrary, it is **what it does not miss**. The problem of oversight does not lie in blind eyes but in ignorance even with eyes wide open. This is "oversight!" "The oversight is an oversight that concerns **vision**: non-vision is therefore inside vision, it is a form of **vision** and hence has a necessary relationship with vision."[36] Therefore, Reading II is not **the reading of direct vision**. Instead **it is the reading** of seeing what Smith and Ricardo do not see, Marx realizes through economics the essence of theoretical revolution, which is **the correct answer to a question that has just one failing: it was never posed.**[37]

---

34   Naoko, Nishikawa. *Kristeva*. Trans. Wang Qing & Chen Hu. Shijiazhuang: Hebei Education Pess, 2001. p. 44.
35   Storey, John. *Cultural Theory and Popular Culture: An Introduction*, p. 161.
36   Althusser, Louis. *Reading Capital*, p. 21.
37   Ibid., p. 22.

For this Althusser provides a famous example, namely the statement of classical economy about the value of labor. He says that in Marx's eyes, the answer of bourgeois economists can be expressed as: **the value of labor equals to maintaining and reproducing the necessary value of means of the livelihood, for living labor (worker).** In the answer there are two blanks. We are not entirely unfamiliar with them because they are the transformation of the nothingness of logic, as posed by the Young Althusser. In the eyes of the Young Althusser, "nothingness" is an appeal of Gestalt in the ontological sense. Yimamura Hitoshi comments that thinking is a spiritual activity that clearly sees a "vacuum" in a seemingly substantial place or continuum, makes the "vacuum" public, objectifies the **"vacuum"** that is like the dark abyss, and endeavors to fill it by reflection.[38] Discovering the nothingness of logic and absence plays an important role in theoretical research. According to Althusser, it is not Marx who intervenes to impose these two blanks, it is the classical text itself, which tells us that it is silent: it is silence is its own words.[39] Please note that the blank here is not the absence of being in the first type reading. It is not the simple "non-being," but rather it is the "nothingness" in being. Althusser refers to the blank as a peculiar "silence," namely "no comment." In this sense, Marx does not complete the incomplete definition of labor value in classical economics in the original problem, but he finds that the problem is its absence. Generally speaking, Marx has posed a problem that is **not expressed in classical economics**. Or in other words, what capitalist political economy does not see is the very thing that it is doing. It produces a new answer without reply and a new problem hidden in the new reply. While expressing the unexpressed concept in the blanks of the reply, Marx regards the blanks themselves as ones that exist and produces or expresses them. Thus, the concept of labor force and a brand new question come into being: what is the value of the labor force? By means of the symptoms (blanks and silences), which cannot be directly grasped in the text, the theoretical problematic behind words and common language are explored further. This is Marx's second reading, namely the **symptomatic reading**.

---

38   Hitoshi, Yimamura. *Althusser: Epistemological Rupture*, p. 42.
39   Althusser, Louis. *Reading Capital*, p. 22.

*Symptomatic Analysis and Psychoanalysis. In brief, Althusser borrows the jargon "symptom" directly from Lacan's semantics, and it can be traced back to Freud.[40] While analyzing the symbols in dreams and various unconscious speech errors, Freud argues for finding the **unconscious structure hidden deep down through the symptoms on the surface**. However, Lacan holds that "what is not revealed directly" is as important as the invisible, even more important than the phenomenon on the surface. Symptomatic analysis, pointing to deep structure of the other, has become a unique theoretical scenery in Lacanian philosophy. Certainly, the symptoms that Althusser uses here are neither the symptomatic rules elevated to the ontological level by Lacan in his later years (he comments that "human is a symptom"), nor the ideological and symptomatic concepts extended by Zizek.[41] Influenced by Lacan in his early years, Althusser extends symptomatic analysis to the reading of text, giving birth to the "symptomatic reading" that hes used as a unique method for the interpretation of Marx's works. He poses that while reading Marx's **Capital**, we should not only see Marx's written words, but also attach importance to the symptoms (blanks, nothingness and silence) in order to grasp the problematic (deep theoretical framework) of Marx; in other words, to seize the invisible discourse in the text.*

While illustrating the essence of the reading, Althusser raises his voice, "we must completely reorganize the ideas we have of knowledge; we must abandon the mirror myths of immediate vision and reading, and conceive knowledge as a **production**."[42] Knowledge

---

40   J. E. Lacan (1901-1981): a French psychoanalyst and philosopher. His representative works are: *On Paranoiac Psychosis in its Relations to the Personality* (1930), *The Mirror Stage as Formative of the Function of the I as Revealed in Psychoanalytic Experience* (1949), *Positions of the Unconscious* (1959), *Ecrits. A Selection* (1966).

41   According to Fukuhara Taihira, Lacan's theory of symptom is divided into three heterogeneous stages of development. At first, it served as the supplement to Freud's theory of symptoms, namely symptom taken for analysis by the unconscious. Then it was taken as the implicit symptom to be possibly interpreted. At last, it was the ontological symptom to supplement the Thing. Based on this, the symptom of Althusser should be the second context of Lacan's theory of symptom. With regard to the second context, Zizek once made the following statement: The symptoms are imagined as white spots, the imaginary factors of subject history with no signification. The process of analysis is that of signification, integrating the symptom into the subject's world of signs. The analysis will retrospectively provide meaning for what is initially showed as meaningless signs. See: Fukuhara Taihira. *Lacan: the Mirror Stage*. Trans. Wang Xiaofeng. Shijiazhuang: Hebei Education Press, 2002. p. 248. Zizek, Slavoj. *The Sublime Object of Ideology*. Trans. Ji Guangmao. Beijing: Central Compilation and Translation Press, 2001. p. 183.

42   Althusser, *Reading Capital*, p. 24.

(reading) is not a direct, linear reflection, but a production. In more classical words, it is a creative construction. Here we clearly sense the influences of *Tel Quel*,[43] the school of French structuralism. In the 1960s, Sollers, Barthes and Kristeva paid attention to the automatic "productivity" of the text. The text even became a mysterious, applied field of producing characters and words. Regarding this, Althusser makes a direct comment that knowledge is productive. Meanwhile, Goldmann's genetic structuralism of the 1970s and Macherey's literary production theory are both also reproduced on the basis of this. Without a doubt, the production here refers in particular to the production of knowledge in the reading activity and the displaying of the hidden. Concerning this, Geras makes an accurate comment: different from direct reading, "symptomatic reading" combines clear statements with blanks, white spots and silences to read. The latter is a somewhat unstated argument, referring to the many symptoms. Like all knowledge, the reading of correctly understanding and practicing is not imagination but the theoretical labor and production,[44] which is a quite precise and proper interpretation. Althusser even thinks that "to conceive Marx's philosophy in its specificity is therefore to conceive the essence of the very movement with which the knowledge of it is produced, or to conceive knowledge as production."[45] Undoubtedly, this has been a very precise theoretical orientation. If you still remember the discussion about the essence of problematic in the previous chapter, you will not think the production of knowledge is strange.

3 SYMPTOMATIC READING AND PROBLEMATIC

Next we need to focus on how the production of knowledge takes place in symptomatic reading. According to Althusser, the reason why bourgeois economists are so blind theoretically is "because their eyes are still **fixed on the old question**, and they continue to relate its new answer to its old question; because they are still

43   *Tel Quel*: the avant-garde magazine of literature chiefly edited by Philippe Sollers. Roland Barthes often published articles in it.
44   Geras, Norman. *Althusser's Marxism: Introduction and Criticism*. New Left Review. Western Marxism: Critical Reading. London, 1977. The Chinese Translation See: McLellan, David. *Marxism after Marx*. Trans. Lin Chun et al. Beijing: Oriental Press, 1986. p. 322.
45   Althusser, *Reading Capital*, p. 34.

concentrating on the old **'horizon'** within which the new problem 'is **not visible.**'"[46] Eventually Althusser finds the key point, which differs from linear reading: symptomatic reading exerts **stress on problematic**. In truth, **the so-called productive reading is merely the emergence of horizon in new problematic**. The Marxist revolution of economic theories is **the revolution of capitalist economy and theoretical problematic**. Althusser has expounded on the relationship between problematic and the theoretical horizon, which is the third point in my discussion of problematic.

I have pointed out that the research into the problematic in this book has gone a step further compared with that of *For Marx*. Together with a relevant and detailed discussion, the symptomatic reading identified by Althusser has displayed Smith and Ricardo's theoretical horizon, which are totally different from Marx even in the same problem domain. In effect, the objects or problems like the "value of labor force" are **necessarily invisible** in the field of the existing theory "because they are not objects of this theory because **they are forbidden** by it – they are objects and problems necessarily without any necessary relations with the field of the visible as defined by this problematic. They are invisible because they are rejected in principle, repressed from the field of the visible: and that is why their fleeting presence in the field when it does occur (in very peculiar and symptomatic circumstances) goes unperceived, and **becomes literally an imperceptible absence** – since the whole function of the field is not to see them, to forbid any sighting of them."[47] This is the application of the viewpoint that the problematic determines theoretical object.

According to Althusser:

> *It is literally no longer the eye (the mind's eye) of a subject which sees what exists in the field defined by a theoretical problematic: it is this field itself which sees itself in the objects or problems it defines –* **sighting being merely the necessary reflection of the field on its objects**. *(This no doubt explains a 'substitution' in the classical philosophies of vision, which is very embarrassed by having to say both that the light of vision comes from the eye, and that it comes from the object.)*[48]

---

46   Althusser, *Reading Capital*, p. 24.
47   Ibid., p. 26.
48   Ibid., p. 25.

I notice that for the first time Althusser directly quotes from Foucault's *The History of Madness (Madness and Civilization)*, claiming that the problematic (called "Episteme" by Foucault) decides a certain theoretical horizon. First, it means that the theoretical presence or absence is not something external, which can be explained by the spatial metaphor. "The invisible is not therefore simply what is outside the visible (to return to the spatial metaphor), the outer darkness of exclusion – but the **inner darkness of exclusion**, inside the visible itself because defined by its structure."[49] Hitoshi says that although the "sighting" is a visual metaphor created by Althusser, it has been used to illustrate the "thinking." When based on the problematic, the "sighting" is no longer the behavior of humans, but just the opposite. "Sighting" is the "thinking," the problematic itself, and **the "sighting" of structure**. The subjective thoughts of people are only the bearer of the structural function. The traditional structure of thinking is completely inversed: the structure (problematic) thinks by taking subject (human) as an instrument. Problems, able to see something or unable to see anything, are not those defined by the sensitivity of subjects' vision or the openness of their horizons. Visible and invisible things can be distinguished only through the problematic that is equal to the structure of thinking and can be regarded as a "switch." The "head" of subjects is "tied up."[50] Despite its clumsiness, the metaphor is right to the point. So the "structure that sees something" is the problematic in reading, which broadens the vision and stipulates what is seen and unseen by readers (thinkers). However, the presence and absence of the specific horizon are not like the difference between light and darkness. In Heidegger's words, the **light is simultaneously darkness**, which is referred to as **"internal darkness"** inherent in Althusser's visible horizon. Moreover, Althusser adds that on some specific occasions, the development of problems engendered by the problematic will also **lead to the instant appearance of unseen aspects** in visible horizon, and the instant appearance itself is invisible. Taking classical economics for example, from time to time the representatives of classic economics stop for a while but leave eventually, only one step between them and the truth. In their domain of discussion, the truth shows up every now and then, but it is always overlooked.

---

49   Ibid., p. 26.
50   Hitoshi, Yimamura. *Althusser: Epistemological Rupture*, pp. 158-159.

Horizon is a gap in the overgrown jungle of knowledge. Thanks to the blanks, the exuberant world lets all knowledge restructure itself and define its positions. Nevertheless, when Smith and Ricardo used the light of vision offered by the old problematic to "sweep past" the problem domain of the value of labor force, they did not make careful reflections. Referring to the value of labor force, Althusser wrote: "this invisible thus disappears as a theoretical lapse, absence, lack of symptom. It manifests itself exactly as it is: invisible to theory – and that is why Smith made his 'oversight'."[51] Here Althusser does not directly point out that the "invisibility" of classic economists is decided by the problematic of bourgeois ideology.

To see the invisible, to see these "oversights", to identify the lacunae in the fullness of this discourse, the blanks in the crowded text, we need something quite different from an acute or attentive gaze; we need an **informed gaze**, a new gaze, itself produced by a reflection of the "change of terrain" on the exercise of vision, in which Marx pictures the transformation of the problematic.[52]

Here I will cite a paragraph of Geras' comments on Althusser's viewpoint: While determining what to include, problematic also determines what to exclude. Thus, together with the concepts and questions already posed, the concepts excluded (gaps and blanks), and the questions not fully posed (half-silences and analytical gaps) or the questions not posed at all (silences) constitute a part of the problematic. Because of this, it is very hard to grasp the correct argument in the original text simply by using a literal understanding and intuitive reading. In order to grasp it, symptomatic reading must be used to combine the correct argument with those gaps, blanks and silences. The latter is another "unspoken argument", which is a number of symptoms hidden in the original text and unrealized by people. Like all knowledge, the reading of both understanding and practicing the reading correctly is theoretical labor and production rather than imagination.[53]

---

51   Althusser, Louis. *Reading Capital*, p. 27.
52   Ibid., p. 27.
53   Geras, Norman. Althusser's Marxism: Explanation and Evaluation, *Western Marxism: Critical Readings*. London: 1977, p. 244. The Chinese translation: McLellan, David. *Marxism after Marx*, p. 322.

Here Althusser reiterates an important view, namely the **non-subjectivity** of the problematic that we have already discussed. Instead of the autonomous change of the cognitive subject's gaze (eyesight), the "change of terrain", caused by the reform of problematic, is an objective mechanism, which is a brand new gaze, produced by objective theoretical structure. The cognitive subject and the brand new gaze are re-made, and Althusser refers to them as the idealism of anti-epistemology.

> *The fact that this "change of terrain" 'which produces as its effect this metamorphosis in the gaze, was itself only produced in very specific, complex and often dramatic conditions; that it is absolutely irreducible to the idealist myth of a mental decision to change "view-points"; that it brings into play a whole process that the subject's sighting, far from producing, merely reflects in its own place; that in this process of real transformation of the means of production of knowledge, the claims of a "constitutive subject" are as vain as the claims of the subject of vision in the production of the visible; that the whole process takes place in the dialectical crisis of the mutation of a theoretical structure in which the "subject" plays, not the part it believes it is playing, but the part which is assigned to it by the mechanism of the process.*[54]

I am afraid this is the most significant epistemological essence in symptomatic reading, which is also the confirmation of **non-subject process** in epistemology. In France at that time, **pseudo subject** had become a major consensus. The free and independent writers have died in Bart and Kristeva's inter-textuality. Rational subject died on the boat of punishment, which Foucault steered from Renaissance to the beach of modernity. As the basis of individual existence, the psychological subject also died before the mirror of Lacan's other. Subject is absent in the whole Symbolic. In the requiem for the subject's death, Althusser's notes signaled the fading of cognitive and historical subjects.

---

54 Althusser, Louis. *Reading Capital*, p. 27.

4 SYMPTOMATIC READING AND UNDERSTANDING MARX

According to Althusser, symptomatic reading divulges the un-divulged event in the text which it reads, and in the same movement relates it to **a different text**.[55] The first reading by sighting is the reference of two texts, but it is still the reading through a grid and concerns **how much** has been sighted. In symptomatic reading, **the second text** is articulated with the lapses in the first text. The lapse is the inevitable, theoretical silence of the problematic that cannot be presented in the grid of Reading I.

We already know that only the objective terrain of a theoretical problematic can produce the same objective, brand new inquiry and result. The brand new inquiry is not direct "sighting", but unearths its silence from different kinds of symptoms of the first text through internal reflection. At certain moments, in certain symptomatic points, this silence emerges as such in the discourse and forces it against its will to produce real theoretical lapses, in brief blank flashes, invisible in the light of proof.[56] However, what are the symptoms that Althusser is discussing? In my opinion, the symptoms here refer to the **nothingness of deep language** caused by the governing of the problematic, or they may even refer to the silence of words. This is a kind of **theoretical unconsciousness**. Absence and presence are always misplaced. In the case of the absence of unconsciousness, the problematic is yet presented to reflection. A. Callinicos states that this is because "the problematic of a theory is complex and contradictory, involving dislocations between different levels. These contradictions are reflected on the text's surface, as symptoms of a complex structure, in gaps, lapses, silences, absences."[57] Aiming at this, Yimamura Hitoshi has a wonderful explanation: Language has the time of emptiness. The empty terrain is called the "symptom". Symptomatic reading is able to understand the symptoms. It destroys the continuity of languages to expose the symptom of nothingness. Then the symptomatic reading diagnoses and interprets the

---

55   Ibid., p. 28.
56   Ibid., p. 86.
57   Callinicos, Alex. *Althusser's Marxism*. London: Pluto Press Limited, 1976. p. 35.

symptoms of nothingness and emptiness.[58] Though not perceptible on the surface, the theoretical silences and blanks can still be symptomatically found in the new problematic. Please notice that symptomatic reading does not break the nothingness directly but instead, it uses a certain theoretical symptom as the entrance into the problematic. Theoretical traces (gaps, blanks, vacuum, absences, etc) are interpreted as secret signals.[59] In this sense, the concept of problematic is symptom theory and trace theory. It analyzes the given apparent speech (theme) in specific cases, and liberates the invisible, potential theme (speech) contained in it, as well as the new problematic it reflects.[60] Hitoshi even considers the interpretation of Derrida's deconstruction as the development of the symptomatic reading of trace theory,[61] which is a fairly interesting viewpoint.

Now let us look at Althusser's own illustration:

> *All that a simple literal reading sees in the arguments is the continuity of the text. A "symptomatic" reading is necessary to make these lacunae perceptible, and to identify behind the spoken words the discourse of the silence, which, emerging in the verbal discourse, induces these blanks in it, blanks which are failures in its rigour, or the outer limits of its effort.*[62]

The limit mentioned here refers to the function of the problematic on its elements of inquiry, which is the final border of a given theoretical horizon. It bears resemblance to the last tension of normal operation in the scientific, theoretical structure of Kuhn and Lakatos, or the last level of productivity in a given production mode posed by Marx. This is a duel between the old and new discourse. In a brand new horizon, the change of terrain caused by the revolution of problematic reveals and divulges incompetent and incarcerate silences in the original problematic. New discourse emerges in the cracks of the old discourse, which is also the rupture of the continuity of discourse. Unfortunately, Althusser fails to make a detailed analysis of the symptoms themselves, which is quite troublesome given the elaborate analysis of the problematic.

---

58   Hitoshi, *Althusser: Epistemological Rupture*, p.292.
59   Ibid., p.164.
60   Ibid., p.165.
61   Ibid., p.165.
62   Althusser, Louis. *Reading Capital*, p. 86.

Althusser requires us to "try to apply to Marx's reading the **'symp-tomatic' reading** with which Marx managed to read the illegible in Smith, by measuring the problematic initially visible in his writings against the invisible problematic contained in the paradox of **an an-swer which does not correspond to any question posed.**"[63] Our question therefore demands more than a mere literal reading, even an attentive one: it demands a truly critical reading, one which ap-plies to Marx's text precisely the principles of the Marxist philoso-phy which is, however, **what we are looking for in** *Capital*.[64]

This is a very important theoretical purpose, which was correctly posited by Althusser but not practiced carefully (My book *Back to Marx: The Philosophical Discourse in the Economic Context* en-deavors to achieve this theoretical purpose).

On the one hand, Althusser proposes "a **'symptomatic' reading** of the works of Marx and works of Marxism, **reading** one with an-other, i.e., the progressive and systematic production of a reflection of the problematic on its objects such as to make them **visible**, and the disinterment, the production of the deepest-lying problematic which will allow us to **see** what could otherwise only have existed allusively or practically."[65]

This is an in-depth interpretation. With regard to this, Hirsch com-ments that Althusser adopts the technology of "supervisor" in struc-tural linguistics to "reinterpret" the text and employs the new theo-retical framework unconsciously to interpret the true meaning of the text, which was used by Marx in his scientific, historical discovery to "interpret" the true meaning of the text.[66] Marx once used the new theoretical framework in his scientific and historical discovery. In my view, if we say Althusser realizes Marx's unconscious logic in his some texts and thoughts (in some texts and thoughts of Marx's), then it will be right to say that through symptomatic reading Althusser has realized Marx's unconscious logic in some texts and thoughts of Marx. However, if we say Marx is unaware of the theoretical Gestalt that he himself discovered, it will not be quite right.

---

63   Ibid., p. 28.
64   Ibid., p. 74.
65   Ibid., p. 32.
66   Hirsch. *The Intellectual History of New French Leftists.* See: *Research Material on Marxism-Leninism*, 1983(5), p. 174.

On the other hand, owing to the limitations of history itself, there also exists the inevitable **absence** of theory in Marx's thoughts. In that era Marx did not master a concept that would enable him to deliberate his own results, namely **the concept of the effectivity of a structure on its elements**, such as the new concept of problematic. Without doubt, Althusser is identifying and improving himself. Thus, the poor Marx tended to "parade" the formula of Hegel's dialectics in his texts, putting on a "**real drama**". "In this drama, old concepts desperately play the part of something absent which is nameless, in order to call it onto the stage in person – whereas they only 'produce' its presence in their failures, in the dislocation between the characters and their roles."[67] **In the context of later generations, this piecemeal realization** of Althusser's identification manifests into his perspicacious views.

Actually, Althusser wants to express the desire to produce what Marx fails to produce. The conclusive affirmation reached is that science relies less for its life on what it knows than on what it **does not know**. The essence of scientific knowledge is to produce what it **does not know**, which absolutely differentiates it from the empirical epistemology that regards the essence of knowledge as what has been present and been directly seen. Obviously, Althusser advocates the innovation of scientific theories. If a conceptual omission has not been divulged, but on the contrary, consecrated as a non-omission, and proclaimed as complete, it may, in certain circumstances, seriously hinder the development of a science or of some of its branches. This point is, indeed, prescient and sagacious. Althusser reminds us that instead of concentrating on the success and accuracy of science, scientific research focuses on "what it contains that is fragile despite its apparently unquestionable 'obviousness', certain silences in its discourse, certain conceptual omissions and lapses in its rigour, in brief, everything in it that 'sounds hollow' to an attentive ear, despite its fullness."[68] This is the only possible path for us to take in order to arrive at the shore of scientific development.

---

67 Althusser, Louis. *Reading Capital*, p. 29.
68 Ibid., p. 30.

Likewise, "some part of the life of the Marxist theory of history perhaps depends on this precise point where Marx shows us in a thousand ways the presence of a concept essential to his thought, but absent from his discourse."[69] This really puts Marx's successors into difficulties.

On Reading, by Barthes — A Theoretical Reversal of Althusser

The first chapter discussed Althusser's reading theory, which I believe is analyzed both fully and thoroughly. However, Althusser's, lecture on essentialism, which still belongs to modernity (who still discusses the modern essentialism), is faced with a crisis in postmodern era. I admit that Althusser's opinions about reading in the last century can still benefit contemporary academic research in China, but to some extent they are merely strategic signs of suggestions. Therefore, the postmodern rupture is necessary. This is like a person who is lost in a movie but then suddenly 'wakes up' into a cruel reality when he turns around and sees the projector. This is called "reversal" in the jargon of movie studies. Besides, three years after Althusser finishes the three texts about reading, his compatriot Barthes[70] also wrote a paragraph of textual writing in S/Z. At this time, Barthes had reinvented himself as a post-structuralist. Now let us compare his theory of reading with Althusser's modern reading theories.

---

69   Ibid., p. 30.
70   Roland Barthes (1915-1980): a French literary critic, a literatus, a semiologist and a postmodern philosopher. On November 12th in 1915 he was born in Cherbourg. From 1935 to 1939 he studied at Sorbonne and obtained the degree of classical Greek literature. In 1952 he entered National Center for Scientific Research to engage in the study of lexicology and sociology. At the beginning of the 60s, he did research work in Academy of Social Science. Barthes travelled to Japan and America in the late 60s, and delivered a speech at Johns Hopkins University. In 1967, he published his most famous paper *The Death of Writer* that signaled his farewell to structuralism. Then Barthes continued to publish articles on the Avant-garde literary magazine of *Tel Quel* whose editor in chief was Philippe Sollers. The magazine highly appreciated and supported other theories stemming from the works of Barthes. Later he was elected as the chairman of literature and semiotics at College de France. On February 25th in 1980, he was injured by a truck when returning from a banquet hosted by President Mitterrand. On March 26th, one month after the accident, he died at the age of 64. His representative works include: *Writing Degree Zero* (1953); *Mythologies* (1957); *S/Z* (1970) and *Camera Lucida* (1977).

S/Z is Barthes's recording of two seminars held in 1968 and 1969, which Barthes intended to use to interpret Balzac's short story, Sarrasine. By that time, Barthes had turned to post-structuralism. The book has altogether ninety-three chapters in which the first nine chapters focus on how Barthes understands the (postmodern) reading.

Speaking of reading, the object of reading (text), the producer of the text (writer) and the subject of reading (reader) are all indispensable. In contrast to classic reading (theological hermeneutics), in the modern reading theory of Althusser, reading theory is carried forward. God is no longer simultaneously present in every word of the Scriptures, and the explanation for the text is no longer singular. Certainly, if in the context of postmodernism, the modern reading also implies the basic logic of the first philosophy: while reading, **who writes** outweighs anything else. The writer is undoubtedly the **first** spokesman of the text. Although not being God, he is the "Big Brother" in charge of the interpretation for the text. Furthermore, while the writer composes the text, the text becomes the object that breaks away from the writer. The aim of reading is to explore the writer's essence of writing by interpreting the text, which is naturally the objective and **supreme noumenon** owned by the writer. Moreover, no matter how intelligent the reader is, his task is only to find within the text, to find the meaning that approaches the truth. In ways that are entirely different from the theory of classic reading, the writer is emancipated from divinity and transforms into the individual subject. There, interpretation of the text may lead to different results, but the results are orderly and vectorial. More specifically, it is **the logic of hierarchy** progressing from the superficial appearance to profound essence. Evidently, Althusser's symptomatic reading simply refines and polishes the modern reading theory.

However, Barthes' postmodern reading is entirely different from this. Let us look at the poetic reading that he put forward. From time to time, you stop reading, not because of a loss of interest. On the contrary, you stop due to the advent of inspiration, excitement and association. Has this ever happened to you? In other words, have you ever **looked up occasionally and then continued reading**?[71]

---

71 Barthes, Roland. *S/Z*. Trans. Tu Youxiang. Shanghai: Shanghai People's Publishing House, 2000. p. 50.

According to Barthes, the journey of reading is not to interpret the authenticity of the text. For the readers' joy and association, the journey picks up the verses that accidentally fall along the road, and it encounters lines long forgotten. This is a Copernican turn in the theory of reading. In past centuries, we have shown too much interest in writers, and paid little attention to readers. The writer is regarded as the permanent owner of his works, while his readers can only use them.[72] First, the writer is God. As the insignificant hollow man, we hurry to find deities and Gospel in the Scriptures (such as when Althusser asks us to desperately seek the problematic and blanks). Then, as the first subject, the text writer is the master whereas the reader is the inessential user (consumer) of the text. In the logic described below, the writer is considered as the **center** of the text:

The writer, having precedent over the readers, forces them to accept certain specific **meanings** in his works. This is certainly the correct and the true meaning. Thus a critique in the sense of rights is engendered. Flaw occurs when critical ethics is created with "misunderstanding" and "anti-significance": people only care about what the **writer signifies**, rather than what the **reader understands**.[73]

Even in Althusser's symptomatic reading, finding the **authentic** meaning exhibited by the invisible problematic in the text is the only purpose of our reading. Barthes wants to tell us that this reading involves unconscious **enslaving and power**. In his opinion, the reader, in reading, is the obedient slave, who devoutly admires the writer, regards the text as the first subject, and passively devours the leftover of meaning in the text. The purpose of reading is to keep the writer's intention **in harmony with** the context of texts, whereas our interest and thoughts, as inferior readers, are completely ignored. We constantly prevent ourselves from being authentic in the text and constantly press ourselves to be practical in the text. Under these circumstances, the reader sinks into an idle place, never mixing with objects and always putting forward the impression of **sérieux**. By not displaying his own ability, the reader cannot fully experience the ecstasy of the significance, as well as the delight in the writing. The reader only has the freedom to either accept or refuse the text.[74]

---

72 Ibid., p. 51.
73 Ibid., p. 51.
74 Ibid., p. 56.

Resisting the modern age reading, Barthes calls on readers to raise their heads and to read as masters. In his eyes, reading is merely for the readers, for our joyful and active thinking. Then what is Barthes's *S/Z*? In simple words, it is a text. While we look up, the text is being written down in our heads. This is really interesting.

In modern reading, the dominant part, the writer's subjectivity is exposed. "Subjectivity is a total imagination."[75] "Subjectivity is totally an imagination." This bears a resemblance to Althusser's viewpoint regarding the writer's subjectivity. Later in the book we will see that "Subjectivity is totally an imagination" is Lacan's opinion. Actually, by the time we come to Gadamer and Jauss, modern reading theory has gradually weakened the freezing shell of center and the hierarchy, which advocates "writer first, text first" through its introduction of historical relativity. Through the bi-directional fusing of vision and the receptive context of readers, the identical, violent reading has gradually been softened. The writer's narrative discourse with subjective intention is also negated. In the past, people always assumed the subjective mightiness of the writer and that he purposefully composed the text to resemble a monologue. The specific model of every story is extracted, and the grand narrative structure (for examination), which involves everything, is produced by a multiplicity of models. Afterwards, the grand structure is applied to any narrative.[76] Thus the text is a manipulated sitcom. Once divorced from the writer, it is hardened into a fixed objectivity. In front of readers, the text is an external, objective thing that is a self-sufficient, identical whole and has spontaneously formed narrative structure and rigid logic. However, objectivity is a filling of the same type.[77]

Certainly, Barthes does not agree with the theory of modern text. The new text is plural in his eyes, and the features of the plural are of vital importance. The most essential element of the plural is refusing to admit that the text is created exclusively by the writer. This view stems from Bakhtin's theory of polyphony, which was introduced by J. Kristeva, and later become the famous post-structural text of intertextuality.[78] Barthes calls for the text to be saved from

---

75   Ibid., p. 69.
76   Ibid., p. 55.
77   Ibid., p. 69.
78   Naoko, Nishikawa. *Kristeva*, pp. 50-52.

its both externality and totality. It is impossible for plural texts to have the structure, grammar, or logic of the narrative.[79] The narrative structure of totality is an imaginary mythology. The plurality of the text (no matter how economical it is), rather than its authenticity (the deep structure of the text that is of vital importance to the whole situation), is ascertained. The units of significance (the implicit signifier) fall grain by grain according to every reading unit. They are scattered and no longer aggregated. And the méta-sens, the final structure we give to the units of significance, can no longer be obtained.[80] The authenticity of the text, which is of vital importance to the whole situation, is the very theoretical structure (problematic) of the text that Althusser has taken great pains to unearth. However, Barthes abandoned it. In the text, by no means does there exist the final structure of significance that the writer has created, by himself. The constitution of significance lies in its plurality. The construction of the text does not exist. Everything is signification. Nevertheless, the representation right is not transferred to the ensemble, the ultimate structure.[81] Meanwhile, the writer's original right to speak is also false, and the text is always the intertextual fabric. The existence of thought, discourse or text, which is created by the writer, is impossible. It is in this sense that Barthes shouted the stupendous slogan: the writer is dead!

> The author is dead: his civil status, his biographical person have disappeared; dispossessed, they no longer exercise beyond his work the formidable paternity whose account literary history, teaching, and public opinion had the responsibility of establishing and renewing.[82]

That which is dead is, of course, the false, monological subject writer, which bears a resemblance to Althusser's own understanding of the matter. The death of the writer does not mean nothingness, but refers to the writer dissolving into the text. "The subject unmakes himself, like a spider dissolving in the constructive secretions of its web."[83]

---

79   Barthes, *S/Z*, p. 63.
80   Ibid., p. 75.
81   Ibid., p. 72.
82   Barthes, Roland. *The Pleasure of the Text*. Trans. Richard Miller. New York: Hill and Wang, 1975. p. 27.
83   Ibid., p. 64.

Therefore, the text in Barthes's eyes is not the dead object, but rather it is a context newly generated through open eagerness and calling. No longer being simply a monologue, reading begins to demonstrate a tacit agreement with the reader; it glances back and smiles; there is an exchange of call and reply, an understanding of performance and applause, and a resonance like that of a valley and its echo. On most occasions, the "text" does not refer to a finished woven product. What Barthes emphasizes is the continuous process of producing and weaving. The text keeps weaving and introducing. Not only does the text weave, it also continuously introduces.[84] It should be noted here that this is also Derrida's viewpoint.[85] In contrast to traditional theories of text, the text, as described here, is neither the way to absoluteness, God and truth, nor the deserted corpse of used thoughts. The text exists in a living intellectual state!

The uniqueness of text does not lie at the entrance of *un Modèle*, but in the ubiquitous reticular entrances. The text aims at distant goals, and observes perspectives (from other texts, fragments of codes and voice) rather than *une structure légale* that coincides with or deviates from conventions, and patterns of narrative or poetry. Then *le point de fuite* is mysteriously presented. Every (unique) text is the theory of *le point de fuite* and the difference that continuously reappears and *revient*, but not *sans se conformer*.[86]

Nevertheless, in contrast to Althusser, Barthes does not seek "definitive structure" and "pattern", or a permanent "shaped" goal. The text itself is a **living production and reproduction**. This is productivity, and the text is a productive force.[87] Barthes says that the text could guide people to write. Its model belongs to the production type instead of the reappearance type.[88] Laclau notes that Zizek's *The Sublime Object of Ideology* is the "writerly text".[89] It appears

---

84   Ibid., p. 76.
85   Derrida points out that we can possibly sketch by means of some interpretative conture. Besides dotted lines we do not show anything else, meanwhile locating or abandoning the blanks any text can't lack. If the text means tissue, then all these essays have stubbornly defined it as loose stitching (faufilure). See: Derrida, Jacques. *Writing and Difference*, p. 537.
86   Barthes, *S/Z*, pp. 72-73.
87   Ibid., p. 92.
88   Ibid., p. 61.
89   Zizek, Slavoj. *The Sublime Object of Ideology*. Trans. Ji Guangmao. Beijing: Central Compilation and Translation Press, 2001. p. 6.

that opposing to the re-appearance type and advocating the production type are the same as we see in Althusser's theory. After careful reflection, however, we will find that there is a difference because what Althusser says is the productivity of knowledge, while Barthes claims that the text is productive. Furthermore, Althusser confirms the productivity of textual interpretation on the premise that he admits the established structure of writer-text. However, Barthes denies the established meaning of text and is ignorant of the imaginary writer. The text is what can guide people to write, and **it is we who are writing.**[90] **We are the text!** An overturning logic is included here. The hierarchy where the writer and text take the upper position is, at once, broken. We readers are no longer menial and obedient slaves. The text is merely the stage where our thoughts dance. So:

> To rewrite the text that can guide people to write is to separate and break the text, which takes place in infinite and discrepant area. The text, which guides people to write, is a fiction without fiction, verse without verse, argumentation without argumentation, writing without style, production without products and tectonic activities without structure. In the ideal text, network systems can be seen everywhere. They interact with each other and there is no ranking between them. The text is the galaxy of signifier instead of the structure signified. Reversible and without source, the paths are crisscrossed and can be walked on at any point or place. The texts depend on each other and cannot exist on their own. The circulating codes spread and abound and are impossible to determine. The systems can receive the absolute plural text but the number of plural texts will never be settled because the languages on which it relies are innumerable.[91]

No longer being the source of suffering that segregates us from the writer's arbitrary and eccentric ideas, the text becomes the sky for the free flight of our thoughts. The text is (it should be) the uninhibited one![92] Everything goes. Besides, Barthes proposes an extremely important opinion that he does not intend to let "us" and "me" take the upper position in solipsism.

---

90   Barthes, *S/Z*, p. 62.
91   Ibid., pp. 61-62.
92   Ibid., p. 64.

The more plurality the text has, the less it is written prior to my reading it. I do not perform a predicate operation on it, and because of the existence of text the operation is called lecture. Moreover, rather than a pure subject, **je** does not exist ahead of the text and does not treat the text as what is to be disintegrated and occupied. The je that explores the text has turned into *pluralité* of other texts and *infinis codes*.[93]

In fact, like the writer's subjectivity, the reader does not possess the ideal, self-sufficient subjectivity, either. We are a plural. This is a total revolution. "On the stage of the text, no footlights: there is not, behind the text, someone active (the writer) and out front someone passive (the reader); there is not a subject and an object."[94]

With such an understanding, let us reexamine Barthes's reading theory, which has undoubtedly become the sub-cynicism that can be guessed. The title of the reading theory is "I read the text."[95] This is a corrected logic: plural and non-subjective readers are confronted with intertextual texts. Also, reading does not respect the text since it dissects the text, and reading shows infatuation for the text and restores the text in order to absorb nutrition. What I am trying to dispel is such reading.[96] The encounter of vision and text are like two crushed leaves blown together by chance. In this kind of reading, respect for the text has disappeared. We arbitrarily cut the texts apart into the fragments that we wish. I want what I wish. Text resembles a flowing river, and reading is like a moving lake. This reading mode, breaking rigidity and absolutenesss, keeps extending outwards. Once separated from the ideology of *totalité* then the focus of reading would be on wounding and dissecting the text.[97]

Opening a text and locating it in the system of reading need not only to show that it can be freely understood but that it can also particularly and thoroughly lead to confirmation: there does not exist an objective and subjective truth of reading but rather the truth of the game. Besides, the game cannot be understood as a pastime, and it

93   Ibid., p. 69.
94   Barthes, Roland. *The Pleasure of the Text*, p. 16.
95   Barthes, *S/Z*, p. 69.
96   Ibid., p. 50.
97   Ibid., p. 76.

should be regarded as a job in which the hardships of labor vanish. Reading activates our bodies (on the basis of psychoanalysis we understand that the body goes well beyond our memory and consciousness). Under the direction of textual symbols and all languages, the language crosses the body back and forth, becoming a glistening abyss of sentences.[98]

Reading is no longer the laborious effort which implies autocracy. Instead, it becomes the game that can bring true exultation, like fish jumping happily across the shimmering water.

Barthes clearly states that the fundamental evaluation of all texts is unlikely to come from science because science never evaluates. It is also unlikely to derive from ideology since the ideological value of a text, such as morality, aesthetics, politics, and truth, is a representation rather than production of value (ideology reflects but not creates).[99] Reading is neither a scientific experiment nor a valuable critique. Sometimes reading is even a pornographic infatuation.

We try to make the text split like a star, dispersing the whole piece of signification (reading only understands its smooth surface, which is caused by the coherence of sentences), the flowing words in the process of narrating, and the strong naturalness of daily language. Immense in size, the text resembles the infinite sky, or the bottomless abyss, without boundary and signs. Sketching an imaginary rectangle with the point of the stick, the prophet follows a given rule to witness the flight of birds. The reviewer is no exception. He follows the reading section sketched by the text to explore the motion of meaning, the appearance of codes and the passing of quotes. The unit of reading is just the cladding of a semantic scroll, the ridge of plural texts, like the dike of potential meaning below the river of discourse (but systematic reading has controlled and possessed the potential meaning). The units of reading and their connection have formed a polyhedron, whose every plane is covered with words, word groups, sentences, paragraphs, or languages (language is its "natural" excipient).[100]

---

98   Ibid., p. 53.
99   Ibid., p. 56.
100   Ibid., pp. 74-75.

It is not reading but writing poetry! This is the characteristic of Barthes: our reading is inscribing a certain attitude on the text and as a result, it is full of vigor.[101] Reading is a beautiful dance, from which the truth of free thoughts emerges and turns into butterflies. So the reading is "unconcerned with the integrity of the text; our very avidity for knowledge impels us to skim or to skip certain passages (anticipated as "boring") in order to get more quickly to the warmer parts of the anecdote (which are always its articulations)."[102] Thus, "what I enjoy in a narrative is not directly its content or even its structure, but rather the abrasions I impose on the fine surface; I read on, I skip, I look up, I dip in again."[103] Reading, together with happiness and joyfulness, is even an unutterable ecstasy.

Strictly speaking, reading is neither a parasitic behavior, nor the *complément* of a writing that we consider to have all the charms of creativity and *antériorité*. Reading is a job that is similar to that of topology. So it would be better to refer to reading as the behavior of *léxéologique*, or even *léxéographique*, because I write my own reading. I am not hiding in the text, but just wandering through it. My task is to move and vary the systems whose viewpoints end with neither the text nor "me". From the perspective of utility, the meaning that I discover is not ascertained by "me" or otherness, but by systematic signs. The prevue of reading is only the trait and durability of *systématique*, or in other words, only its operation.[104] In the sense of topology, reading is a creative behavior, giving rise to novel thoughts through the process of moving and changing. This is a marked deviation from Althusser, though he is also talking about the productivity of reading.

In order to make sure the productivity of classical texts, we need to move step by step. The text is merely the decomposition of reading. It can also be called a slow-motion process, not presenting the complete picture and not making a comprehensive image analysis. The *commentaire* is a digression that is hard to integrate into the discourse of knowledge. Then we can observe the reversibility of structures that weave the text.[105]

---

101   Ibid., p. 53.
102   Barthes, *The Pleasure of the Text*, p. 11.
103   Ibid., pp. 11-12.
104   Barthes, *S/Z*, p. 70.
105   Ibid., p. 73.

According to Barthes, reading is to find the meaning, to name meaning. However, the already named meaning spreads into another name. All the names call to each other and then rejoin. Then the group asks for further naming. I name, I remove the naming, and I name again. In this way, the text extends forward: it is a naming in production process, an approach of diligence, and a metonymic labor.[106] Although they both intend to find the meaning, Althusser's traditional reading theories try to discover the final meaning, whereas Barthes stresses the continuous production and naming of textual meaning rather than the theological, permanent meaning.[107] Reading connects systems, which is based on the plurality of systems rather than the limited number of them. Reading never stops.

Therefore, in contrast to Heidegger, Barthes is sure to strike up a discordant tune. He says that "I forget, therefore I read."[108] Reading must negate and abandon all bases, all essences, and all homelands! How can you see the sun if you do not dispel the clouds?

Finally, reading must be **relecture (re-reading)**. The *relecture* proposed by Barthes deviates from the reading habits of commercial and ideological reading habits of our society. According to Barthes, the stories (works) will be abandoned once consumed ("gobbled"). The readers will search for other stories and buy new books. Only the readers such as children, the elderly and professors can bear *relecture*. Barthes thinks that relecture rearranges the internal order of texts (this happens before or after that), reproduces the time of *mythique* (no "before" or "after"). The initial reading has features of original shape, simplicity, and phenomenon. It seems that the origin of reading exists and everything has never been read. *Relecture* **is a game instead of consumption**. This is certainly not Althusser's science.

---

106   Ibid., p. 70.
107   Ibid., p. 70.
108   Ibid., p. 71.

CHAPTER IV

MARX'S PHILOSOPHICAL REVOLUTION AND THE CRITIQUE OF THE EMPIRICIST CONCEPTION OF KNOWLEDGE

We are more clearly aware that, in *Reading Capital*, Althusser attempts to read Marxist **philosophy** through symptomatic reading rather than through a discovery of the scientific content of economics in it. He presents to us "the infinite extent contained within its minute space: the extent of Marx's *philosophy*".[1] Historically, Marx always exists as Dasein. Although his text is narrow and concrete, his philosophical thinking is boundless. However, interpreting the text is not the purpose; the key lies in whether or not we can detect Althusser's way of thinking. I am afraid that, when we interpret Althusser, this is also the right goal. Actually, Althusser intends to further discuss the revolution of epistemological methodology and its historical process in a broader theoretical scope. Epistemology accounts for a significant proportion of Althusser's philosophical Gestalt, but in many previous researches, it has been hidden.

---

1 Althusser, Louis. *Reading Capital*. Trans. Ben Brewster. London; New York: Verso, 1970. p. 9.

1 PSEUDO-DUALISTIC COGNITIVE GESTALT: "VIEW ESSENCE THROUGH PHENOMENON"

According to Althusser, our reading of *Capital* was, in the past, can be best characterized as Reading I – or, the reading through a grid. More specifically, Reading I is to discover **what Marx had said** compared to Smith. Without a doubt, this kind of reading is unlikely to uncover Marx's true philosophy, as expressed in *Capital*. In Althusser's opinion, Marxist philosophy does not seem to exist in the traditional philosophical texts on which people tend to concentrate. Indeed, this view of him makes sense to some degree, but it is also a little too arbitrary. It is more appropriate to say that Marxist philosophy does not merely exist in his philosophical texts. Althusser states that this is because "the protocols of *The German Ideology*'s philosophical rupture do not give us it in person. Nor do the earlier *Theses on Feuerbach*, those few lightning flashes which break the night of philosophical anthropology."[2]

I must here point out that Althusser's understanding of Marx's texts is actually very abstract. Indeed, he is good at keeping a high profile regarding the method of interpretation, but he never reads Marx, Engels, and Lenin's books carefully. The grandiloquent way in which Althusser studied the texts was sure to lead to arbitrariness, gaps and even retardation in his interpretation of Marx. I will expand upon this issue later.

In Althusser's view, *The German Ideology*, the first monograph on Marxist philosophy co-authored by Marx and Engels, does not present us real Marxist philosophy. And *Theses on Feuerbach*, which is the summary of new worldviews, only briefly lightens the new vision. In my opinion, Althusser does not think that there are no philosophical thoughts in either *The German Ideology* or the *Theses on Feuerbach*. Instead, he holds that these two texts contain too many remnants of the humanistic ideological discourse- even after its "death" and he evaluates with reference to the non-subject Gestalt of historical materialism. In addition, *Anti-Dühring*, which is the basis of the interpretative framework in traditional philosophy, follows Dühring and enters the domain of philosophical ideology or

---

2   Ibid., p. 9.

the worldview that appears in the form of "system." This kind of po-
lemical argument, which includes Lenin's *Materialism and Empirio-
criticism*, cannot possibly be Marx's true philosophical discourse.
Althusser maintains that the place where we can **read** Marx's true
philosophy is *Capital*. He also asserts that it is only in *Capital* where
we find the "living water, which has not yet flowed away," or the
true representative of Marxist philosophy.

In Althusser's opinion, the philosophical reading of *Capital* can only
be carried out by applying Marxist philosophy and that should exactly be the object of our research. This forms an inevitable logical
cycle.

It is not possible to read *Capital* properly without the help of Marxist
philosophy, which must itself be read simultaneously, in *Capital*. If
this double reading and constant reference from the scientific reading to the philosophical reading and from the philosophical reading
to the scientific reading, are both necessary and fruitful, we shall
surely be able to recognize in them the peculiarity of the philosophical revolution embodied in Marx's scientific discovery: a revolution
which inaugurates a genuinely new mode of philosophical thought.[3]

Please note that the theory of textual reading, which we have discussed above, will be extended to a wider theoretical platform
where the philosophical revolution is equaled to the **epistemological** revolution.

So what is the essence of the Marxist philosophical (epistemological) revolution? Althusser thinks that it is the revolution of a brand
new mode of philosophical thinking based on the critique of **the empiricist conception of knowledge**. Starting from this, Althusser sets
about guiding a debate over the revolution of macro epistemological
methodology starting from the narrow discussion of symptomatic
reading. The focus of the debate is **the essence of knowledge**.

In Althusser's eyes, **epistemology is the theory of the conditions and forms of scientific practice and theory of its history
in the concrete sciences**.[4] The essence of knowledge is not the

---

3   Ibid., p. 76.
4   Althusser, Louis. *For Marx*. Trans. Gu Liang. Beijing: The Commercial Press,
1984. p. 235.

direct reflection of a mirror, but a **productive inquiry** governed by the "**conception of knowledge**" (paradigm). The "Conception of knowledge" is a much broader idea about/on epistemology, which is based on problematic. However, if we are to clarify the essence of Marxist philosophical conception of knowledge, the empiricist conception of knowledge must first be elucidated upon. Regarding it as the "worldly variant" of religious reading, Althusser claims that "the empiricist conception of knowledge resurrects the myth we have encountered, in a very special form. To understand this correctly, we must define the essential principles of the theoretical problematic which underlies it".[5] Regarding our understanding of different stages of intellectual history, the theological Gestalt indeed revives in the cognitive structure of reason and modernity, of which Hegelian absolute ontology is a typical example.

Apparently, the empiricist conception of knowledge illustrated here is not the empiricism represented in common intellectual history. This is because it embraces a rationalist empiricism as well as a sensualist empiricism. More specifically, this refers to the dualistic epistemological problematic of the **confrontation between subject and object**. The dualistic problematic here "presents a process that takes place between a given object and a given subject" in cognitive activities.[6] Firstly, the subjects of knowledge (psychological subject, historical subject, etc.) and the objects of knowledge (constant or inconstant, mobile or fixed) must be determined in this kind of problematic. The dual confrontation exists before knowledge occurs. Knowledge, or the **relation** between subject and object, is usually determined by real object. Secondly, "the whole empiricist process of knowledge lies in fact in an operation of the subject called **abstraction**. To know is to abstract from the real object its essence, the possession of which by the subject is then called knowledge".[7] According to Althusser, the abstraction probably comes in many forms, but it keeps an invariant structure: **subject abstracts the essence of phenomena from object**. Empiricist abstraction, or abstracting its essence from the given **real** object, is a **real abstraction** that leaves the subject in possession of the **real** essence. Real

---

5   Althusser, Louis. *Reading Capital*, p. 10.

6   Ibid., p. 35.

7   Ibid., pp. 35-36.

abstraction extracts the essence from reality. In the problematic of empiricist conception of knowledge, "knowledge is an abstraction, in the strict sense, i.e., an extraction of the essence from the real, which contains it, a separation of the essence from the real which contains it and keeps it in hiding".[8]

Here an ontological split appears, namely the dual separation between the essence of real existence and the "crust" covering the essence. "**The real**: it is structured as a dross of earth containing inside it a grain of pure gold, i.e., it is made of two real essences, the pure essence and the impure essence, the gold and the dross."[9] Or, generally speaking, the objects which are faced by subjects are made up of two different things: the essential and inessential. Correspondingly, knowledge becomes the simple process of seizing the essential and eliminating the inessential.

"**Knowledge**: its sole function is to separate, in the object, the two parts which exist in it, the essential and the inessential – by special procedures whose aim is to **eliminate the inessential real** (by a whole series of sortings, sievings, scrapings and rubbings), and to leave the knowing subject only the second part of the real which is its essence, itself real. This gives us a second result: the abstraction operation and all its scouring procedures are merely procedures to purge and eliminate **one part of the real in order to isolate the other**."[10]

This is the basic structure of traditional epistemology. When observing essence through phenomena, the main task of cognitive activities is stripping phenomenon from real object and extracting the essence from behind phenomena. The key, regarding this epistemological structure, is still vision. This is probably the main reason why Althusser attributes all of them to "empiricism". Certainly, the vision illustrated here is no longer the visual sighting of feelings, rather it includes reasonable vision, which is the visible and invisible relationship between **inside and outside, direct and indirect** in the subject's cognition. Vision is based on light, and the difference between brightness and darkness exists because of light. More specifically,

8   Ibid., p. 36.
9   Ibid., p. 36.
10   Ibid., p. 36.

brightness is the essence displayed in the lightened place, and darkness is the covered object. This can also be described as the visual metaphysical history of Derrida. Additionally, Heidegger's profundity lies in his posing "brightness is also darkness-" the opinion that opposes the divided phenomenon of subject and object. According to Althusser:

> *The inessential part occupies the whole of the **outside** of the object, its **visible surface**; while the essential part occupies the **inside** part of the real object, its **invisible** kernel. The relation between the visible and the invisible is therefore identical to the relation between the outside and the inside, between the dross and the kernel. If the essence is not immediately **visible**, it is because it is concealed, in the strong sense, i.e., entirely covered and enveloped by the dross of the **inessential**.[11]*

Callinicos explains that, according to the epistemology criticized by Althusser, "the real is immediately present in the phenomena accessible to our observation. To grasp the real requires only a properly informed gaze, a gaze, which can distinguish between the essence and its phenomena. This ability is guaranteed by an underlying complicity between subject and object. The structure of the object of knowledge is such as to render possible the penetration of the subject's gaze through the contingent to the real."[12] In the past, our epistemological logic was perhaps very close to this. Knowledge is the exposed essence after outside phenomena are uncovered. It is akin to unpacking something, breaking the shell of an almond, peeling fruit, or unveiling a maiden, truth, God and a statue." Nonetheless, in Althusser's eyes, all of this is self-satisfaction, which reflects the philosophy of vision as mirror-images.

So far we have found that Althusser is illustrating a cognitive Gestalt, which advocates Reading I. He claims that the problematic of the empiricist conception of knowledge and the religious problematic, – whose essence can be seen in transparent existence– , are twin brothers! The only difference between them is that God or the absolute idea does not exist transparently, but rather it is veiled by the exterior. As long as the exterior is uncovered, the real essence will be obtained. So knowledge becomes the simple "vision" of

---

11   Ibid., p. 37.
12   Callinicos, Alex. *Althusser's Marxism*, p. 32.

essence. This is the **epistemology of representation and mirror image**. Following Bachelard, objecting to the epistemology of representation has become a consensus in French academia. Foucault once particularly criticized it, while he illustrated the theory of episteme. Barthes also had a similar opinion, and Lacan elevated it to an ontological sense and depressed the relationship of mirror image and symbol to the borderline of alienation logic.

2 KNOWLEDGE = REALITY?

Althusser holds that the "structure" of empiricist knowledge can be expressed as an inference that our **knowledge** of real objects is directly identified as the **real parts of real objects**. Accordingly, the unearthed (abstract) essence is hidden and invisible, but it is the truest thing in reality. The theory's most central truth is that subject's knowledge is the result of an active subject's cognition. Though the process of knowledge is finished "outside the object", it is declared as a part of real objects. Althusser ironically says that it "adds to the real existing object a new existence."[13] This is similar to the strange assumption that Adam had a navel. The subjective result of knowledge is directly identified as the objective structure of objects. Isn't the subjective result imposed on objects? This is the first meaning. Althusser's criticism reminds me that the "materialistic dialectics," as described in our own textbooks on dialectical materialism, is also the same. The three "laws" and categories theoretically **stipulated** by materialistic dialectics are obviously the result of our (the writers of textbooks) **limited, historical, and subjective** knowledge of the outside world, but they are arbitrarily equaled to the real law and essence in the objective existence. I once blamed myself as having "implicit idealism."[14]

Another theoretical point is that knowledge exists in real object. This is similar to the ridiculous logic of using a sieve to get milk. When people set the results of knowledge as real objects, an absolute and homogeneous logic naturally occurs, namely the **homogeneity** of knowledge and object. The result of this as the falsity of falsity is

---

13   Althusser, Louis. *Reading Capital*, p. 38.
14   See: *The Selected Works of Zhang Yibing*. Guangxi Normal University Press, 1999. p. 2.

as follows:

> *The existence of its knowledge is completely **inscribed in the***
> ***structure of the real object**, in the form of the difference between*
> *the inessential and the essence, between surface and depth, be-*
> *tween outside and inside! Knowledge is therefore already **really***
> *present in the real object it has to know, in the form of the respec-*
> *tive dispositions of its two real parts!*[15]

Knowledge is object, and object is knowledge. "The whole of knowledge is thus invested **in the real**, and knowledge never arises except as **a relation inside its real object between the really distinct parts of that real object**."[16] The conclusion seems to make sense, but in all traditional research on epistemology, it is almost a self-evident premise.

Althusser points out that **"this investment of knowledge, conceived as a real part of the real object, in the real structure of the real object, is what constitutes the specific problematic of the empiricist conception of knowledge"**.[17] To the point, this generalization is both crucial and profound. He believes that the empiricist conception of knowledge is the core of the problematic of Western classical philosophy. The significance of Althusser's affirmation cannot be understated, so we need to explore this point further.

In Althusser's opinion, the empiricist conception of knowledge, "the problematic **avowed** by the eighteenth century, from Locke to Condillac, is profoundly present in Hegelian philosophy".[18] This statement sounds a little strange. The former part is the ancestor of empiricism, and the latter is the master of rationalism. Although it seems irrelevant, after careful thought, it is not difficult to see that Althusser's identification makes sense. The cognitive structure of modern empiricism is the doctrine of correspondence, and knowledge reflects emotional objects. However, they fail to find that empiricists mistake the results of knowledge for emotional objects and regard what derives from experience as the reflection of real objects. This is the cognitive schema of empiricism. By contrast, theorists (the earliest are Eleatic school and Plato) like Hegel are more direct.

---

15 Althusser, Louis. *Reading Capital*, p. 38.
16 Ibid., p. 39.
17 Ibid., p. 38.
18 Ibid., p. 38.

They have discovered that things like "essence" result from the governing of concepts, so they directly identify concepts as the real! Thus, the order of the process of knowledge is inverted as follows: identifying the falsity of empirical objects ("the arrow of paradox", "allegory of the cave", and "the phenomenology of spirit") to, once again, present the hidden essence (God and absoluteness). This runs counter to empiricism. As we noted above, Althusser's discussion of the empiricist conception of knowledge has double meanings, namely the true meaning of the double logic of emotionalism and rationalism. Meanwhile, Althusser points out that the empiricist conception of knowledge is also the real theoretical foundation of modern empiricism. Without a doubt, the theoretical configuration recognizes itself as "the innocent form of a theory *of* models".[19] Nevertheless, it cannot run away from the "web" of **ideology of knowledge.**[20]

In addition, Althusser states: "in its variants of problematic, including the mute variants and their denigrations, can give a projected history of philosophy an essential principle for the construction of its concept during this period".[21]

Certainly, the empiricist conception of knowledge, as discussed by Althusser, is the logic permeating through the whole of European classical philosophy, but he also reveals another meaning, namely that the forms of problematic in intellectual history are diversified. Sometimes the same problematic is even shared by the opposite forms. We note this is really crucial to understand the intellectual history of knowledge.

Althusser comments that the empiricist conception of knowledge is incompatible with Marx. This is both a theoretical demarcation and defense. Yet, he frankly admits that on most occasions "Marx, **had to use it** to think the lack of a concept whose effects he had produced nevertheless, to formulate the (absent) question".[22] The young Althusser's philosophical logic of "nothingness" emerges at a deeper level. The old problematic cannot solve new problems, thus making the new problems shown as "nothingness" in the old problematic.

---

19   Ibid., p. 39.
20   Ibid., p. 39.
21   Ibid., p. 38.
22   Ibid., p. 38.

The focusing and magnifying of the nothingness of absence will deconstruct the original problematic to become the nothingness of the structure of dominant power discourse. For example, in his eyes, it appears in Feuerbach's works and Marx's *Theses on Feuerbach* and *The German Ideology*. In these scenarios, Marx is still using the problematic of classical philosophy (binary Gestalt of empiricism) to think over the new and absent problem. Marx does not give the reply to the absent problem (new conception of knowledge) until *Capital*. Although Marx still uses the concepts of old problematic in *Capital*, like essence and phenomenon, surface motion and real motion, the inside and outside, he has, in fact, changed the problematic. Certainly, Althusser does not conceal the fact that this problematic still exists after Marx. He writes: "We find it at work in many passages of Engels and Lenin, who found a motive for its use in the ideological battles."[23] Althusser's explanation for this evaluates Engels and Lenin slipping into the enemy-occupied area (of Dühring and Bogdanov) and fight back against them with a combination of arguments and concepts of ideology. As one of the main theorist of the French Communist Party, Althusser does not want to point the sword of criticism directly at the textbooks of traditional philosophy*. This is probably a well-meaning sophistry.

3 DIFFERENCE BETWEEN OBJECTS OF KNOWLEDGE AND REAL OBJECTS

Based on the above discussion, we have been able to infer that the core of Althusser's objection to the empiricist conception of knowledge centers on his objection to equating the objects of knowledge with real objects. I think further clarification needs to be made: The problem here is not the simple difference between objectivity and subjectivity, material and consciousness. The mixing of theories, as pointed out by Althusser, is a deep-rooted **theoretical unconsciousness**.)

The old materialism mistakes the material concepts that were the result of knowledge (the subjective image of objects under certain historical conditions, the "water" of Thales, the "fire" of Heraclitus,

---

23   Ibid., p. 38.

*)   Ed.: Soviet origin philosophy text (educative) books.

the "pneuma" in ancient Chinese philosophy, the "atom" in atomic materialism) for the objective "material" itself, regarding these concepts as the reflection of the "material". Nonetheless, all idealism erroneously recognizes objective reality as idea or the internal production of mental imagery. The "material" that the old materialism relies on is eliminated. This is also the meaning elucidated by the phenomenology of perception seen in all idealism. So carefully marking out the difference between objects of knowledge and reality becomes the next important theoretical task. Althusser comments that this symbolizes our stepping out onto the road which is opened up by Spinoza and Marx. According to Perry Anderson's analysis, "the categorical distinction between 'objects of knowledge' and 'real objects' made by Althusser was taken straight from Spinoza's famous separation of idea and ideatum".[24] I am afraid this is well-founded.

First of all, objects of knowledge and real objects are completely different. Althusser says that "against what should really be called the latent dogmatic empiricism of Cartesian idealism, Spinoza warned us that the **object** of knowledge or essence was in itself absolutely distinct and different from the **real object**".[25] These are two totally different things, namely the idea of the circle as the **object** of knowledge and the circle as the **real object**. But Marx makes a distinction here after negating Hegel's idealistic mistake of mixing real objects with objects of knowledge, real process with process of knowledge. Althusser points out that in *The Preface to the Critique of Political Economy* Marx "defends the **distinction** between the **real object** (the real-concrete the real totality, which **survives in its independence, after as before, outside the head**) and the **object of knowledge**".[26] This is because the objects of knowledge are the production of thoughts and they are produced as things "absolutely different" from real objects.

24   Anderson, Perry. *Considerations on Western Marxism*, p. 64.
25   Althusser, Louis. *Reading Capital*, p. 40.
26   Ibid., p. 41.

At this point, Althusser admits that he takes the word "production" from Spinoza and Marx.[27] Compared with the real production process of objective materials, this is a totally different production process of producing thoughts. Besides, the former, the real and historical production, is completed according to the order of stages in the **historical** development process, whereas the latter is realized through another subjective, "logical order" in the process of knowledge.

Secondly, objects of knowledge come into being because of a unique thinking mode. Althusser wants to illustrate the following issue: in traditional philosophy, regarding the results of knowledge as the real Gestalt of identity is incorrect because it fails to see **the unique production mode and process** of the results of knowledge, which are distinct from the production of real objects. The production process of knowledge is carried out in **thought**. The thought is neither a faculty of a transcendental subject or absolute consciousness, nor a faculty of a psychological subject, although human individuals are its agents. The thought posed by Althusser is **an objective structure of knowledge which is outside individual subjects**, namely "the historically constituted system of an **apparatus of thought**, founded on and articulated to natural and social reality".[28] Therefore, thought is the specific mode of production of knowledge under certain real conditions of social history, which is a theoretical identification of Consciousness. In the above discussion of problematic, Althusser has made a preliminary identification of the final point in the discussion of his concept: the problematic.

> *The thought in itself is constituted by a structure, which combines the type of object (raw material) on which it labours, the theoretical means of production available (its theory, its method and its technique, experimental or otherwise) and the historical relations (both theoretical, ideological and social) in which it produces.[29]*

Thought is constructed by a structure, which is the typical discourse of structuralism. The structure is the governing structure that takes place objectively outside individual subjects. According

27   Althusser, Louis. *Soutenance d'Amiens*. Cited from *Research Material on Marxism and Leninism*. Beijing: People's Publishing Press, 1986, p. 311.
28   Althusser, Louis. *Reading Capital*, p. 41.
29   Ibid., p. 41.

to Althusser's explanation, as described above, it is an extremely complicated systematic structure, and the summation of relations is constructed around absent subjects, which includes both objects of thought, certain subjective data, and tools of processing objects. Althusser uses the word "theoretical production mode," but this actually refers to problematic. Outside, it refers to the system of social relations which can enable thoughts function, on the other side the Gestalt of theoretical relevance and ideology, especially the real social structure that determines the nature of these relations. In this large systematic structure, the thought operates initiatively with the false appearance of **autonomous subject**.

In Althusser's eyes, this system of theoretical production is both objective and subjective because it is produced and formed on the basis of practice of existing economy, politics and ideology. The real practice provides "raw material" for the system of theoretical production, making the production mode of knowledge possess the determinate objective reality. Afterward, the cognitive structure of the determinate objective reality becomes the individual subjects' premise of thinking. In this sense, Althusser says:

> *Far from being an essence opposed to the material world, the faculty of a "pure" transcendental subject or "absolute consciousness", i.e., the myth that idealism produces as a myth in which to recognize and establish itself, thought is a peculiar real system, established on and articulated to the real world of a given historical society which maintains determinate relations with nature, a **specific** system, defined by the conditions of its existence and practice, i.e., by a **peculiar structure**.* [30]

Finally, the process of knowledge, which is mixed up with the empiricist conception of knowledge, is clarified to some extent as follows: "Therefore knowledge never, as empiricism desperately demands it should, confront a **pure object** which is then identical to the **real object** of which knowledge aimed to produce precisely the knowledge. Knowledge working on its 'object', then, does not work on the **real** object but on the peculiar raw material, which constitutes, in the strict sense of the term, **its 'object' (of knowledge)**, and which, even in the most rudimentary forms of knowledge, is distinct from the

---

30   Ibid., p. 42.

real object."[31] Objects of knowledge are not equal to real objects. Regarding the process of knowledge, what people are directly faced with is never a pure sensuous intuition or representation, but rather, they are faced with an already complex raw material, a structure of intuition or representation, combining together sensuous, technical and ideological elements. Thus, objects of knowledge stem from practice. The complex structure (sensuous, technical ideological structure) strongly works on the material and as a consequence, changes its form. It is the Gestalt of Knowledge, which transforms raw material into objects of knowledge.

In sum, this epistemological analysis, which is heavily based on Spinoza, makes much more sense. This is particularly true when compared with the epistemology in the interpretative framework of traditional philosophy, and as such, we can experience it in a deeper context. However, Althusser's discussion cannot get rid of its absolute and metaphysical shackles. While correcting a misconception about idealism, his research on epistemology is inevitably drawn toward another sort of one-sidedness, and this is exactly what we should pay attention to in our research. Goldmann thinks that Althusser's borrowing from Spinoza is closer to mechanical materialism. At most, however, it is an exquisite, contemporary transformation.[32]

---

31 Ibid., p. 43.
32 Goldmann, Lucien. *Marxism and Humanities*, p. 161.

CHAPTER V

EPISTEMOLOGICAL RUPTURE: IDEOLOGY/SCIENCE DIVIDE

When we embarked upon our research into Althusser, we found that Western epistemology and the history of epistemological theory were areas that were of great concern to him, but were remarkably overlooked by scholars. From discussions in the last chapter, we can see that a number of his important theoretical paradigms are established and extended in the context of epistemological study. Indeed, Althusser discussed a few epistemological issues, which turned out to be significant in the post-modern context. For instance, he holds out against the dualistic cognitive framework and ideological illusions with the sense of utility value. He calls for the transformation of practical ideology into theoretical ideology in order to keep up with scientific development following the breakup of ideology. Because of these original and thought-provoking ideas, research fields in epistemology and scientific methodology, which have not been studied in a systematic manner, are brought to people's attention.[1] Thus, we can see this as a noteworthy theoretical contribution.

---

1 As a matter of fact, since Lukacs and Korsch in their youth, epistemology has remained to be the field that the western Marxism is concerned about. Adorno and Schmidt have written much about it too. But it is the first time that researchers like Althusser studied epistemology from the perspective of the history of thoughts.

1 THE VICIOUS CIRCLE IN THE IDEOLOGICAL AND COGNITIVE THEORY

Althusser asserts that the modern history of Western philosophy is a history of **ideological** philosophy (we have been introduced to ideology many times and will discuss it in the next chapter, but for the time being we take it as "unscientific" regularity). This is, naturally, rather alarming to those who research Western philosophy. As Althusser sees it, the focus of this kind of ideological philosophy is the so-called "epistemological issue" or "epistemology" in the dualistic framework. It is a theoretical tradition that originates from Descartes and reaches Husserl, via Kant. "This posing the 'problem' of knowledge is **ideological** insofar as this problem has been formulated on the basis of its 'answer,' as the exact **reflection** of that answer."[2] If I am not wrong, this has something to do with the empirical concept of knowledge, which Althusser assumed to be both dualist and mirror-like. This means that the theoretical logic of the theory of knowledge presumes the predetermined sameness of the object of knowledge and the subjective result of the subject. The 'answer' he refers to is the unconscious presupposition of the subjective result as the realistic object, which we have already discussed, and that people's false 'answer' is knowledge. Therefore, the process of knowing is in fact the ideological representation of this relationship. Accordingly, the problem of knowledge is not a real problem in the real world, but rather it is a **false** problem of ideology. More specifically, it is a kind of problem that needs to be proposed so that **ideology** may be seen as the key to the problem.

In this sense, all contemporary and modern Western philosophies are controlled by variations of "problems of knowledge," such as the reflection of a material reality or the introspection of human beings' existence or original intuition, etc. The "material reality", "existence," and "original and direct viewing," which are regarded as the **authentic** object in the vision of knowledge, are actually subjective results of the determinate activity of thinking, though they are used as real objects. As a matter of fact, the dualist framework of knowledge is predominated by the problematic, which has been

---

2   Althusser: *Reading Capital*, translated by Li Qiqing et.al., Central Compilation & Translation Press, 2001, p. 51.

constructed based upon "produced terms" and "theoretical basis." In other words, the answer has already been determined and imposed before the problem is raised. Therefore, knowledge becomes a mirror-like reflection, which is of course a framework of ideology. Althusser notes:

> *(The) terms and on a theoretical basis (are) produced (whether consciously, as by some, or unconsciously as with others, is not important here) in order to make possible the theoretico-practical effects expected of this **mirror recognition**. In other words, the whole history of Western philosophy is dominated not by the 'problem of knowledge', but by the ideological **solution**, i.e., the solution imposed in advance by practical, religious, ethical and political 'interests' foreign to the reality of the knowledge, which this 'problem' **had to** receive.*[3]

Althusser's observation is fairly reasonable. He points out that "we must walk out of the ideological space, which is determined by the problem of ideology; we must walk out of this **must-be closed** space (because this is one of the important results of the structure of **re-considering** which is the characteristic of the productive modes of ideological theories: a must-be closed circle). We would also see that this circle metaphor is rather crucial. He mentions that Lacan named this structure of knowledge "**dual mirror relation**."[4] This relationship supposes that the object is produced subjectively but then is re-determined as the real object of knowledge. Hence, knowing can only be a circular **self-referring** process (like Hegel's self-awareness). Thus, the whole history of the 'theory of knowledge' in Western philosophy form the famous 'Cartesian circle'. The circle of the Hegelian or Husserlian teleology of Reason **shows us that** this 'problem of knowledge' is a closed space, i.e., a vicious circle (the vicious circle of the mirror relation of ideological recognition).[5]

Althusser also admits that Husserl's phenomenology rejects the Vorhandenheit in the dualistic framework, which has reached the "ultimate height of consciousness and integrity", but Husserl has not truly stepped out of the closed circle in his phenomenology. Indeed, the self-referring **vicious circle** still exists in the logic of consciousness

---

3   Ibid., p. 51.
4   Ibid., p. 52.
5   Ibid., p. 52. The Chinese version has been modified.

research, which is meticulously made by phenomenology. Therefore
Husserl has not been unshackled from ideology. Heidegger made
another similar theoretical effort. He consciously broke from this
dualist framework to enable the Being-in-the-World in the historical time-span to become isomorphic, and he did this by dissolving
the fossilized Seiendes. However, as long as Heidegger attempts to
call for a return, with the ethics of conscience, to the originality in
the alienated and materialized world, he falls back into the 'closed
ciecle' again. Hence, Heidegger has not wandered out of the circle.
He tried to consider this 'closed' in the 'openness' (which is rather
the unclosed ideology being closed off), that is, the absolute conditions for the possible 'repetition' of the closed history in the Western
metaphysics. This is a magic circle from which no one can escape.

Althusser further notes that the core of the dualistic ideology of
knowledge is the **Subject** and the **Object**. He wrote: in the epistemology, "the theoretical characters cast in this ideological scenario
are the philosophical Subject (the philosophizing consciousness),
the scientific Subject (the knowing consciousness) and the empirical
Subject (the perceiving consciousness) on the one hand; and, on the
other, the Object which confronts these three Subjects, the transcendental Object, the pure principles of science and the pure forms of
perception."[6] The former three are the three layers of the essence
of the Subject of knowing and the latter three correspond to Hegel,
Lacan and Husserl respectively, as the objective Object.

> ...that this parallel distribution of attributes disposed Subject
> and Object face to face; that this conjures away the difference
> in status between the object of knowledge and the real object on
> the Object side, and the difference in status between the philoso-
> phizing Subject and the knowing subject, on the one hand, and
> between the knowing subject and the empirical subject on the
> other, on the Subject side. That thereby the only relation which is
> thought is a relation of interiority and contemporaneity between
> a mythical Subject and Object, required to **take in charge**, if need
> be by falsifying them, the real conditions, i.e., the real mechanism
> of the history of the production of knowledges, in order to subject
> them to religious, ethical and political ends (the preservation of
> the 'faith', of 'morality' or of 'freedom', i.e., social values).[7]

6 Ibid., p. 54.
7 Ibid., p. 54.

Althusser would naturally affirm breaking from the vicious circle of ideology in the epistemology. He plainly asks for an **open** structure of knowledge. "I am not posing the question I have posed in order to produce an answer fixed in advance by instances other than knowledge itself: it is not a question closed in advance by its answer. It is not a question of **guarantees**. On the contrary, it is an open question (it is the very field that it opens)."[8] We are already aware of this particular view thanks to our previous discussion of the problematic. In contrast to the closed vicious circle of ideology, which is contained by the present answers, the "secret agreement of ideology" that is made between the ideological roles of the subject and the object is not acknowledged in the scientific epistemology. In other words, the opening scientific process of knowing sees no pre-made promise or guarantee, nor does it see the agreement or correspondence between the knowledge and the object, or the identity, which is a rather original point. Its problematic requires the creation of an "open question". Our previous discussions show that such openness refers to the essence of scientific knowledge as being **productive**, that is, the characteristics of creativeness that is non-identity in the epistemology. Althusser argues that "(it) must therefore be posed in the field and in the terms of the theoretical problematic which demands this structure of openness. In other words, the question of the **mode** of appropriation of the **real, specific** object of the knowledge has to be posed."[9] This is the problematic of scientific knowledge.

Therefore, and firstly, the problematic of scientific knowledge must "exclude any recourse to the ideological solution contained in the ideological characters Subject and Object, or to the mutual mirror-recognition structure, in the closed circle in which they move."[10] The approach to opposing the "secret agreement" of ideological identity among the subject and the object, thought and the being, and consciousness and matter is that the scientific knowledge must break from the vicious circle of identity in the epistemology, whether it be through the theory of reflection of materialism or through the mode of self-reflection of idealism. Such an argument against identity can immediately be related to Adorno. Secondly, we must use the "terms

---

8   Ibid., p. 54-55. The Chinese version has been modified.
9   Ibid., p. 55.
10   Ibid., p. 55.

which form the concept of the knowledge structure, an open specific structure, and which, at the same time, are the concept of the
question knowledge posed itself – which implies that the place and
function of this question be thought even in posing the question."[11]
In contrast to the closed ideological circle, the logic of knowledge,
which is directed by the scientific problematic, is to be opened. This
will always elicit, analyze and solve new questions. It is the real
thinking, and the best way to achieve this is to emancipate theory
from the utility of practice.

2 TOWARDS THEORY: PRACTICE AND IDEOLOGY

Readers, who are familiar with Marxist philosophy, may be harbor-
ing a question. That is, can the ideological paradox of epistemology,
that Althusser uncovers, be resolved by practical means, as this is
the basis of the Marxist epistemology? It is a shame, however, that
Althusser instantly blocks all the gaps and takes a clear stand against
any approach, and substitutes the basis of knowledge with practice.
He even defies traditionalists by using practice as the criteria of
knowing. Indeed, this runs counter to traditional understandings of
Marxist philosophy.

In Althusser's eyes, it is possible that taking practice (social practice)
as the intermediary has certain effects, but they must be the products
of the struggle that takes place within the ideological realm: "for it
is an **ideological** answer, one which is situated precisely on the opponent's ideological terrain."[12] The **practice field** only yields the
ideological spirit of practice. This is, in fact, the field of discussion
for Kant's practical reason, but it is not a field for the discussion of
Marx. When Engels enters the ideological terrain of Dühring, he
writes *Anti-Dühring*; when Lenin enters the ideological domain of
Mach et al, he writes *Materialism and Empirio-critism*. Those endeavors could only give rise to the products of the practice of ideology rather than of scientific theory. "One is obliged or forced to fight
on the terrain of the ideological opponent, when it has proved impossible to draw him onto one's own terrain, if he is not ready to pitch

---

11   Ibid., p. 55.
12   Ibid., p. 56.

his tents there, or if it is necessary to descend onto his terrain."[13] This kind of struggle is a practice in the ideological sense. Althusser firmly believes that "this kind of **pragmatist** answer leaves us hungry as far as our theoretical question is concerned."[14]

Rather, answers of this kind would cause a negative impact on subsequent theoretical development. Here, Althusser hints at the negative effect that the interpretations of Marxist ideology in the context of successful practice might have on the socialist movement. For him, Lenin made these interpretations during the October Revolution and Mao Zedong made them during the Chinese revolution. If I remember correctly, Adorno also made similar claims. Please note that the term "theory" is not used in the common sense here. Rather, it is a specific use, which refers to Althusser's **scientific philosophy** and is different from the ideological status. It is from this context that Althusser also develops his idea that, theoretically, Marxist philosophy objects to humanism.

Before we continue talking about this issue, let us take a look at a particular parameter that Althusser lay down regarding practice and theory. This particular statement is made in his book *For Marx* (the specific discussion about the statement is in a chapter entitled, "On the Materialist Dialectic"). In the "To My English Readers" chapter, Althusser directly announces that the word **Theory** refers to Marxist philosophy (dialectic materialism), while the word **Philosophy** is saved for ideological philosophy. Theory is the scientific philosophy established by Marx, and he considers that all traditional philosophies should be classified as ideology (that is, the "vicious circle" of dualistic recognition that we have seen previously).

Marx sees the significance of **theoretical problems and practical answers** in a quite different way compared to Althusser. At first glance, Althusser takes it that theory is always related to science, while practice is always associated with the immaturity of theory and of the **practical state**, which is often ideological. It is important that we should clarify the conflict here. As a matter of fact, Althusser's concept of practice does not originate from the Marxist

---

13   Ibid., p. 57.
14   Ibid., p. 55. The Chinese version has been modified. The translator has mistaken pragmatism for "activism", which differs much from the original text.

tradition but rather, it originates from Freud, especially the practical process that Freud uses to analyze and treat his subjects. Althusser once quoted Lacan in that Freud has constructed a science (a science of unconsciousness), which is both a **theory** and a practice. This practice that corresponds to the theory is mainly the process of analysis and treatment. Hence, Althusser forms his own opinions accordingly: as for science, "practice is not the absolute condition of science, it is only a link affiliated to theory."[15] He is very much aware of the attitude that he argues on theory and practice. In order to further clarify this complex idea, we need to take a look at how he specifically discusses the issue.

First, Althusser agrees with Marx on the general understanding of practice:

> *By practice in general I shall mean any process of transformation of determinate given raw material into a determinate product, a transformation effected by a determinate human labour, using determinate means (of 'production'). In any practice thus conceived, the determinant moment (or element) is neither the raw material nor the product, but the practice in the narrow sense: the moment of the labour of transformation itself, which sets to work, in a specific structure, men, means and a technical method of utilizing the means.[16]*

It is very accurate to use the word "determinate" here to indicate historical limitations. This demonstrates that Althusser was well versed in the Marxist concept of historical practice. However, Marx's general definition must be considered as being in the social realm, because the concrete practice is not the same. "This complex unity of 'social practice' is structured, we shall soon see how, in such a way that in the last resort the determinant practice in it is the practice of transformation of a given nature (raw material) into useful products by the activity of living men working through the **methodically organized** employment of determinate **means of production** within the framework of determinate relations of production."[17] More importantly, besides the production practice that Marx stresses, social

15 Althusser: *Lenin and Philosophy*, translated by Du Zhangzhi, Yuan-Liou Publishing Co., Ltd.(Taiwan) ,1990, p.217.
16 Althusser: *For Marx*, translated by Gu Liang, the Commercial Press, 1984, p.139.
17 Ibid., p.139.

practice should also include other "basic practices:" like the political practice which "processes determinate social relations as raw materials into determinate products (new social relations);" the ideological practice which processes varied "ideological objects;" the theoretical practice which develops in the direction of determinate science recognition, etc. Those understandings of Althusser have already started to blur the boundary that Marx has drawn for material practice.

Second, theory is a specific form of practice. This has been inverted. For him, theory is a form of practice, but surely, it must be a very specific form of practice.

> *By theory, in this respect, I shall mean a specific form of practice, itself belonging to the complex unity of the "social practice" of a determinate human society. Theoretical practice falls within the general definition of practice. It works on a raw material (representations, concepts, facts), which it is given by other practices, whether "empirical", "technical" or "ideological". In its most general form theoretical practice does not only include scientific theoretical practice, but also pre-scientific theoretical practice, that is, "ideological" theoretical practice (the forms of "knowledge" that make up the prehistory of a science, and their "philosophies").[18]*

The theory produces determinate products of thought in determinate means. Therefore, it is a form of practical activity. It is a confusing to think that theory is one of the forms of practice. However, the scientific theoretical practice differs from the theoretical practice in the ideological period before history. Althusser's primary theory refers to the scientific period that follows ideology. He states that people describe all theoretical practices, which are scientific **Theory**, and take the specific **theoretical system** (its basic concept is both contradictory and unified in a determinate phase), which is authentic and scientific, as "theory". **Theory** is scientific in general, while "theory" means the concrete scientific theory. This is the major theoretical context that Althusser uses as opposed to practice.

> *In its "theory" any determinate science reflects within the complex unity of its concepts (a unity which, I should add, is more or less problematic) the results, which will henceforth be the*

---

18   Ibid., p.140.

conditions and means, of its own theoretical practice. I shall call
Theory *(with a capital T), general theory, that is, the **Theory** of*
practice in general, itself elaborated on the basis of the Theory of
existing theoretical practices (of the sciences), which transforms
into "knowledges" (scientific truths) the ideological product of
existing "empirical" practices (the concrete activity of men).[19]

Another complex definition!

Of course, Althusser is aware that science cannot be clearly separated from ideology, and that both theory and practice are closely
interwoven. "For we know that there is no **pure** theoretical practice,
no perfectly transparent science which throughout its history as a
science will always be preserved, by I know not what Grace, from
the threats and taints of idealism, that is, of the **ideologies** which be-
siege it; we know that a 'pure' science only exists on condition that
it continually frees itself from the ideology which occupies it, haunts
it, or lies in wait for it."[20] This is nothing less than a dialectic relation. Science cannot stand-alone; it always goes hand in hand with
the struggles and redefining efforts of ideology. But Althusser does
not analyze clearly enough whether or not the interweaving between
theory and practice, which he defines, only refers to the pre-science
historical period.

> *So a practice of theory does exist; theory is a specific prac-*
> *tice, which acts on its own object and ends in its own product:*
> *a knowledge. Considered in itself, any theoretical work presup-*
> *poses a given raw material and some "means of production" (the*
> *concepts of the 'theory' and the way they are used: the method).*
> *The raw material worked by theoretical labour may be very "ide-*
> *ological" if the science is just coming into being; where an al-*
> *ready constituted and developed science is concerned, it may be*
> *material that has already been elaborated theoretically, concepts*
> *which have already been formed.[21]*

Knowledge is a theoretical product, and this is an issue that gets more
and more confusing. The following idea of him is more understand-
able: "The moment of the Theory of **theoretical practice**, that is, the
moment in which a 'theory' feels the need for the **Theory** of its own
practice – the moment of the Theory of method in the general sense

---

19   Ibid., p.140.
20   Ibid., p.143.
21   Ibid., p.145.

– always occurs *post festum*."[22] The specific method that is distilled from theoretical practices does not show up until the latter phase of the theoretical practice. In a classical case, Marxist dialectics exist in *On Capital*, "(**but**) that [they] (**only**) exists in the practical state."[23] However, Marx does not spare more time to discuss the present but invisible dialectics; he only leaves us behind the dialectical practice in *On Capital*, leaving no time for dialectical theory.

In *For Marx*, Althusser makes a rather famous proposition about the operation of theoretical practice, that is, the logical advancement of the "3 Gs". More specifically, Althusser adduces Marx's phrase "from the abstract to the concrete" and formulates the process of theoretical practice into three kinds of Generalities with their complex relations and specific operations. Generality I (G I) refers to the "object processed by science" or theoretical materials. The object here is not reality, "it is always the 'general being' which science processes", even if it appears in the form of "fact," it remains a concept.

Generality II (G II) is the "production material" or tool used by science to produce, and is a "concept group" of "which the contradictory unit constitutes the 'theory' of science in the specific historical period." As a matter of fact, it is the problematic that Althusser proposes.

Generality III (G III) means knowing the concrete, that is, the result of the theoretical practice.[24] Althusser notes "theoretical practice produces Generalities III by the work of Generality II on Generality I."[25]

Callinicos later explains it in a more explicit way. He says that G I is the starting point of theoretical practice, that the material is not the objective matter in the world, but rather it is the concept. Therefore, the theoretical practice always starts **from the abstract**; G II is the problematic, which makes the scientific theory and it is also logic; G III is the "concrete thoughts", the "knowledge produced by G II working on G I, or the concept which the problematic that the appointed

22   Ibid., p.146.
23   Ibid., p.146.
24   Althusser: *Soutenance d'Amiens*, compiled in *Research Material of Marxism and Leninism, from Issue 3-4* (combined issue). Beijing: People's Press, 1986, p.311.
25   Althusser, Louis. *For Marx*, p.139.

science defines."[26] This is the well known theoretical process of "from the abstract to the concrete" observed by Hegel and Marx.

Above all, in contrast to Marx's practical ideas, Althusser almost relegates practice to a pre-science state, which is quite close to ideology, as we have seen his highly personalized grouping of theory and practice. In this way by him, the dismal status of practice is predetermined in the discussion of ideology. We may also understand, in this particular context, why Althusser disagreed with taking practice as the basis for knowing and with "fooling with the standards of practice." As he sees it, the "pragmatism (which is preconditioned by practice) does nothing but set out, like the ideology of the idealist 'theory of knowledge', on a hunt for **guarantees**"[27] Unlike the classical idealism, "pragmatism sets out on a hunt for **real** guarantees: the **success** of practice, which therefore always becomes the sole content of the so-called 'standard of practice.'" In Althusser's eyes, it provides us with an ideological answer, and at the same time a "mechanism," except only that this time it is not guaranteed by the accordance of recognition and object but by the fact (utility) of the practice. This is still an ideological "vicious circle!" Althusser indicates that if this practice is a "cunning trick" from the very start, what should we do? He says that the sin of class-based human society is, "proof by repetition for hundreds or thousands of years of the social practice of humanity (that night in which all the practices are grey)! So what!"[28] It is not unlike the "resurrection of Christ", the "Virginity of Mary", all the truths of religion and all the prejudices of human impulsiveness, which have been repeatedly proved as the accomplished "facts" during the long night of feudal autocracy that has lasted for thousands of years? In essence it is the ideological trick that the ruling class plays to enslave the masses, "the common rule which permits this action is in fact the question of the **guarantees** of the harmony between knowledge (or Subject) and its real object (or Object), i.e., **the ideological** question as such."[29] In other words, Althusser describes the negative side of practice as extremely serious, and this tends to appall readers.

---

26   Callinicos: *Althusser's Marxism*, p.70.
27   Althusser, Louis. *Reading Capital*, p. 57.
28   Ibid., p. 57.
29   Ibid., p. 58.

He says that the meaning of the word practice in its pragmatic sense is just a reflection in the mirror or a concept opposite to theory, and this dichotomy is merely an ideological myth, according to which, the interest reflected by the 'theory of knowledge' is utterly different from the rational interest, or the interest of the division of social labor. This makes some sense. Of course, Althusser is not against practice. What he opposes is original and **abstract** practice in general and he rejects it in its ontological sense. He notes, "we are affirmative about the **primacy of practice** in theory," but this original status is at most the final measure of decisiveness amongst his multi-determinants (Ed.: The author discusses this issue later) This does not mean that practice is turned into an "origin" in its ontological sense. It is just like in the ideological theory of knowledge, or like the reversion to the originality of consciousness in Husserl's philosophy, or like the expectation of facing the "original ground" of "nature land" in Heidegger's philosophy. I can say it is also similar to the ideological recognition mechanism of Christianity where human beings simply live in original sin, and there is "**an original knowledge effect**"[30] predetermined by God.

The mortal human individual could only reach the truth through various intermediaries that are presupposed as origins. Althusser claims that in this ideological epistemology, human beings need to turn to the myth of **origin**, to the primitive and unified myth (they have the same origin, therefore the knowledge would occur at the same time), which is inseparable between the subject and the object, the reality and the knowledge of reality, and to the myth that has taken place; this is the **intermediate** myth that is both **abstract** and indispensable. Very likely, "the function of the concept of origin, as in original sin, is to summarize in one word what has not to be thought in order to be able to think what one wants to think."[31] See? Is it not the vicious circle of the ideological epistemology?!

Althusser asserts that even practice cannot be placed at the basic position of ontology. As an origin, practice remains ideological. "Instead of the ideological myth of a philosophy of origins and its organic concepts, Marxism establishes in principle the recognition

---

30   Ibid., p.64.
31   Ibid., p.65.

of the givenness of the complex structure of any concrete 'object', a structure which governs both the development of the object and the development of the theoretical practice which produces the knowledge of it."[32] Obviously, Althusser attaches more importance to practice, that is, the operation of science itself. And this theoretical practice of science will appear only after the epistemological rupture of the ideological practice.

3 "EPISTEMOLOGICAL RUPTURE" AND THEORETICAL HISTORY OF KNOWLEDGE

After meticulous discussion and examination, we are about to reach the crux of the argument: Althusser's famous "epistemological rupture." There is a specific context associated with this: that is, the extended background of the history of the development of knowledge. Althusser says:

> [It is just the] theory of the history of knowledge or theory of the history of theoretical practice [that] enables us to understand **how** human knowledges are produced in the history of the succession of different modes of production, first in the form of ideology, then in the form of science. It makes us spectators of the emergence of knowledges, their development, their diversification, the theoretical ruptures and upheavals within the problematic that governs their production, and of the progressive erection, in their domain, of a division between ideological knowledges and scientific knowledges, etc.[33]

This implies that the demonstration of the ruling abilities in the framework of cognition in the epistemological field does not suffice to illustrate the history of scientific recognition, especially the particular process of knowing for a determinate discipline. Therefore, Althusser proposes to study the theoretical history of knowledge, namely to analyze the evolution of the history of the cognitive structure of different disciplines in different areas. This logic follows in the tradition of Bachelard's and Canguilhem's research into the history of scientific recognition. Althusser states:

> I propose to call this history the history of the theoretical as such, or the history of the production (and transformation) of what at a given moment in the history of knowledge constitutes the

---

32   Althusser, Louis. *For Marx*, p.170.
33   Althusser, Louis. *Reading Capital*, pp. 62-63.

theoretical problematic to which are related all the existing vali-
dating criteria, and hence the forms required to give the order of
theoretical discourse the force and value of a proof.[34]

This is a deepening of his abstract discussion of epistemology with historical views—and it is a likely proposition, especially given Althusser's statement that historical knowledge of this kind is mainly focused on the theoretical history of the problematic revolution. As such, this proposition appears to be even more critical.

To go beyond the merely formal concept of the structure of theo-
retical practice, i.e., of the production of knowledges, we must
work out the concept of the history of knowledge, the concepts
of the different modes of theoretical production (most important
the concepts of the theoretical modes of production of ideology
and science), and the peculiar concepts of the different branches
of theoretical production and of their relations (the different sci-
ences and their specific types of dependence, independence and
articulation).[35]

The two quotes are, in many ways, similar. It is not enough to merely understand the ruling power that the structure of cognition exerts upon the knowing process. We need to break through the mist to know the real history of how such a structure operates. Furthermore, we will better comprehend the essence of knowing only in the differences between the various modes of theoretical production and the relations and influences of varied structures of cognition. Additionally, the most important matter at hand is the difference between the modes of production, which define science, and also the modes of ideological production. It is also because of this that Althusser begins to resolve another crucial pair of theoretical concepts, that is, the historical relationship between ideology and science. According to his own explanation, it seems Althusser learned the scopes of science and ideology from Canguilhem.[36] He later says, "it is materialism and its critical power that brings out my interest in philosophy: to approve of scientific knowledge, and to oppose all the deliberate mystification of the **ideological** 'knowledge'"[37] Based

---

34   Ibid., pp. 46-47. The Chinese version has been modified.
35   Ibid., p. 40.
36   Althusser: *L'Avenir Dure Longtemps (The Future Lasts Forever).* London, 1993, pp. 184-185. Georges Canguilhem (1904-1995), French modern philosopher.
37   Althusser, Louis. *Lenin and Philosophy,* 1990, p.19.

on his previous theoretical logic, this is the relation between two utterly different theoretical problematics. Althusser has repeatedly used this pair of scopes in his For Marx, where it seems that he wishes to elaborate on them in a more systematic and theoretical manner.

Firstly, Althusser calls our attention to the traditional research of scientific history by saying that this tradition "is still seared by the philosophical ideology from the Renaissance, that is, the rationalistic brand of theology or idealism." What does this imply? Althusser holds that the history of science is regarded as a history, which developed consecutively and linearly according to the traditional views of the history of science. And this kind of history becomes a process in which the sense (the God variant) realizes and recognizes itself continuously. This is similar to Hegel's absolute views, which has been in existence since the starting point of history, and it is recognized and proposed again and again in the form of a rational history. Althusser evidently rejects this **linear scientific view, which progresses quantitatively**. He goes for a brand new idea of scientific history: "a theory which enables us…, to distinguish science from ideology, to deal with the difference between them within the historical relation between them and to deal with the discontinuity of the epistemological break within the continuity of a historical process;"[38] that is to say, to care about the **discontinuities** of history development. I should say this is both a surging and earthshaking view of history.

> *We are beginning to conceive this history as a history punctuated by radical discontinuities (e.g., when a new science detaches itself from the background of earlier ideological formations), profound re-organizations which, if they respect the continuity of the existence of regions of knowledge (and even this is not always the case), nevertheless inaugurate with their rupture the reign of a new logic, which, far from being a mere development, the "truth" or "inversion" of the old one, **literally takes its place**.[39]*

This view must be related to the "shift of locations" brought by the alteration of problematics. But what is involved here is not only the framework of cognition in the space of reading, but the revolution of the general problematic in the course of the development of

---

38   Althusser, Louis. *For Marx*, p.20.
39   Althusser, Louis. *Reading Capital*, p. 41.

scientific theory during the entire history of ideas. Here, Althusser proposes two important notions: one is the rupture from the history of ideas of cognition, and the other is that this kind of rupture is represented as the historical break-up between science and ideology.

In order to understand these two theoretical points, we have to temporarily abandon this train of thought and look at the background of Althusser's problem domain, that is, his teacher Bachelard's view of science and the so called "new epistemology".

Althusser declares that he "borrow(s) … the concept of an **'epistemological break'** from Gaston Bachelard to designate the mutation in the theoretical problematic contemporary with the foundation of a scientific discipline."[40]

This alleged epistemological break is an important part of Bachelard's view of science and the so- called "new epistemology".

As a scientist who has rich knowledge of the history of science, Bachelard thinks that there is no simple question of evolution in science. Science is reconstructed continuously though sudden breaks brought on by repetitive revolutions. Using numerous scientific facts, he displays and proves the creativity of scientific theory and its many imposing and splendid fissures of qualitative changes. Bachelard says, "even in the historical evolution of another single problem, we cannot conceal those real ruptures and sudden changes. This is enough to overthrow the idea that the cognitive development is a continual process."[41] Regarding the logic of philosophical ontology, Bachelard opposes the doctrine of duration of the inner life of which Bergson approves, and emphasizes the appearance of interrupting. He views that Bergson's duration (continual entity) is in effect a false image: "Duration is composed of interrupted moments." This is a kind of **new moment in the making**. The existence of life is a kind of discontinuity of growth rather than a continuum.

---

40 Althusser, Louis. *For Marx*, p.13. The Chinese version has been modified.
41 Bachelard: Sur les Connaissances Similaires, Vrin, Paris, 1927, p.270. Quoted from Dagognet: *Gaston Bachelard: sa vie, son œuvre*, avec un exposé de sa philosophie, translated by Shang Heng, p. 9.

Bachelard's comment is exceptional: "Time no longer passes. It is an **outburst.**"[42] And it is here that Schmidt makes an incisive comment, "Bachelard takes the entire scientific development as a continuum of disconnected items. As he sees it, he departs from Bergson."[43] Bachelard argues that rupture means qualitative changes, and this refers to the overall revolution of scientific theory in scientific epistemology. "This rupture affects the theoretical methods as well as its objects, and it also indicates the appearance of a new issue and a new level."[44] As for ontology, however, this rupture is the creation and production of existence.

In his historical view of science, Bachelard describes two kinds of epistemological breaks: One is the theoretical leap from pre-science to science, which Schmidt discusses: "we always need to separate ourselves from a remaining problematic to reach a scientific level. This problematic is ideological within the scope where other concepts function with the reflections and myths which unconsciously exert influence."[45] The other is the general argument regarding the advances produced when one scientific and theoretical state breaks with another new state (like the sudden appearance of the new physics of the 20th century). In the history of thoughts, Bachelard's view is always criticized as the continuity and discontinuity of the history of science. Clearly, Althusser has stressed the first aspect of this kind of discontinuity and has made special requirements for the historical relation (rupture) between ideology and science.[46]

As a matter of fact, the then French academic circles had reached an agreement regarding the research of epistemology, that is, to make difference between science and common sense. In effect, Bachelard's follower Canguilhem utterly negates the view of accumulative

42 Bachelard: L'Intuition de l'instant, quoted from *Biographie de Bachelard*, translated by Gu Jiachen and Du Xiaozhen, Beijing: People's Press, 2000, p.79.
43 Schmidt: *History and Structure*, translated by Zhang Wei, Chongqing Press, 1993, p.104.
44 Ibid., p.100.
45 Ibid., p.106.
46 Imamura Hitoshi has an incorrect understanding of this. He does notice that Althusser has adopted the first layer of meaning regarding Bachelard's "theory of rupture", that is, the special break between science and ideology, but not the transformation of the problematic in general. Imamura Hitoshi: *Althusser: Epistemological Rupture*, translated by Niu Jianke, Shijiazhuang: Hebei Education Press, 2001, p.118.

scientific progress, and he is strongly against Hegel's argument of the rational objective. This view had a profound influence on both Foucault and Althusser. Canguilhem regards the development of scientific knowledge as a contingency-led continuous reconstruction, and scientific thoughts are able to stand out of experience and common sense due to their different modes of construction. Science is always established upon its rupture with common sense. The break itself is a kind of conquering of the so-called "obstacles of epistemology" and a way of reconstructing the scientific problematic upon a brand new theoretical platform.[47] To observe and emphasize the silent historical discontinuity is a crucial theoretical point in the shift from structuralism to post-structuralism. This includes Foucault's historical ideas regarding the historical disruption noted in the preface of his book *The Archaeology of Knowledge*.[48]

In this theoretical climate, Althusser comes to confirm that the epistemology in the understanding of philosophical ideology of the Renaissance was false, and its biggest fault was its not being able to realize the theoretically consequential and practical difference between science and ideology. "Therefore, this historical view of epistemology could really ... learn ... to treat the ideology which constitutes the prehistory of a science, for example, as a real history with its own laws and as the real prehistory whose real confrontation with other technical practices and other ideological or scientific acquisitions was capable, in a specific theoretical conjuncture, of producing the arrival of a science, not as its goal, but as its surprise."[49] Hence, "there is a beginning for all sciences," and the beginning of science has a pre-history, which shares a similar realistic experience, that is, the history of ideology, and the scientific history is "reborn" out of the rupture with ideology. "The universally acknowledged science is always reborn from its pre-historical period, and while it is forsaking the pre-history as a fault, it is being reshaped repeatedly from the pre-history (it co-exists with science as the **Other** of science in the

47 Edited by A.G. Myslivchenko, *Contemporary Foreign Marxist and Leninist Philosophies*, translated by the research office of Central Compilation and Translation Bureau, published by Social Sciences Academic Press in 1986, Volume II, p.456.
48 Foucault: *The Archaeology of Knowledge*, translated by Xie Qiang et.al., SDX Joint Publishing Company,1998, p. 9.
49 Althusser: *Reading Capital*, p. 42.

pre-historical period; this reshaping is what Bachelard claims is the '**rupture** of epistemology')."[50]

Althusser says, "we have to propose the conditions for initiating the Rupture épisémologique (epistemological rupture) for all sciences." This quote is from Bachelard, and is fettered to indicate that is has a special meaning. "…The break: (is) the mutation by which a new science is established in a new problematic, separated from the old ideological problematic."[51] Althusser evidently regarded all scientific happenings as a kind of historical dissolution of a determinate ideology:

> *When a new science is born – when it detaches itself from the field of the ideology from which it breaks at its birth: this theoretical 'uncoupling' always and inevitably induces a revolutionary change in the theoretical problematic, and just as radical a modification of the **object** of theory. In this case, it is strictly correct to speak of a **revolution**, of a qualitative leap, of a modification affecting the **very structure of the object**.*[52]

In his *For Marx*, Althusser says, "science (which apprehends reality) constitutes **in its very meaning a rupture** with ideology and that it sets itself up in **another terrain**, that it constitutes itself **on the basis of new questions**, that it raises **other questions** about reality than ideology, or what comes to the same thing, it **defines its object** differently from ideology."[53]

History suggests that science is always produced in its absolute separation from ideology when radical "shift of locations" simultaneously occurs for both theoretical problematic and theoretical objects. "A science is obtained … by abandoning its ideological problematic (the organic presupposition of its basic concepts, and with this system, the majority of these concepts as well) and going on to establish the activity of the new theory 'in another element', in the field of a new, scientific, problematic."[54]

---

50 Althusser, Louis. *For Marx*, pp. 225-226. In his own terms, he borrows Bachelard's concept in order to "make it more explicit", and uses it as the "central field of his early essays". He has another interpretation which Spinoza has realized the "rupture of epistemology" before Bachelard. See Althusser: *Soutenance d'Amiens*, compiled in the Journal of *Research Data of Marxism and Leninism*, from Issue 3-4(combined issue) of the year 1986, p. 312, People's Press of China, 1986.

51 Althusser, Louis. *Reading Capital*, p. 176.

52 Ibid., p. 181.

53 Althusser, Louis. *For Marx*, p.58, Note 2.

54 Ibid., p.164.

Althusser also notes, "we have to think (in a completely novel way) the relation between a science and the ideology. The ideology gives rise to science and continues to accompany it silently more or less throughout its history."[55] I think what he wants to express here is that when ideology loses its sovereignty after the rupture, it does not disappear all together; instead, it will, in many forms, follow and lead scientific development. Therefore, Althusser does not indicate that what he means is the history of science; but instead he does, in other situations, make an explicit announcement about what he calls the "three new scientific continents."

He believes that on the atlas of the history of science, there are three new continents, "before Marx, there have been two such continents which open their gates to scientific knowledge: the continent of math and the continent of physics. The former is opened by Greeks (Thales), and the latter is by Galileo. Marx has explored the third one which leads to scientific knowledge: the one of history."[56] This is the pre-history of ideology before those continents are discovered. When the prehistory of ideology concludes, a whole new scientific continent emerges where the rupture occurs.

> The advent of the "breaks"... establishes a science by detach-ing it from the ideology of its past and by revealing this past as ideological."[57] To take the epistemological rupture in Marxist theory as an example, "... a historical break ..., not only in the history of the science of history, but also in the history of philoso-phy, to be precise, in the history of the **Theoretical**; this break (which enables us to resolve a periodization problem in the his-tory of science) coincides with a **theoretical event**, the revolu-tion in the science of history and in philosophy constituted by the problematic introduced by Marx.[58]

However, this is an abstract comparison, and it is over simplified. Althusser's views are different in some ways from Bachelard's ideas on the scientific history of discontinuity, as the former determines that every discipline (since ideology) is the historical beginning of science, while Bachelard often mentions the discontinuity of differ-ent phases of scientific theories in the scientific progress – the break

55 Althusser, Louis. *Reading Capital*, p. 42.
56 Althusser, Louis. *Lenin and Philosophy*, pp.22-23.
57 Althusser, Louis. *For Marx*, p.140.
58 Althusser, Louis. *Reading Capital*, p. 177.

between quantum mechanics and classical mechanics. I suppose that Althusser's arbitrary conclusion on this point cannot withstand the textual research of scientific facts. In the following discussion, we are going to expound upon his many errors regarding the history of Marxist ideas.

Of course, Althusser admits that when science appears after the ideological break, it still exits in the continual development of renewal, He writes: "Marxism did not stop at Marx any more than physics stopped at Galileo. Like any other scientific discipline, Marxism developed even during Marx's own lifetime. New discoveries were made possible by Marx's basic discovery. It would be very rash to believe that everything has been said."[59]

I can say, may be, science does not simply develop in the form of breaks. Callinicos says that Althusser "transforms science into something that surpasses the historical process."[60] This is fairly reasonable, because Althusser's science is no longer natural science in its narrow sense, but rather it is the **scientific theory** which is elevated to the logic of meta-theory in the entire process of the history of thoughts; in the same sense, the ideology that he confronts is not the immature period of science in pre-history, but an unscientific and general phantom of ideology. The generality of ideology is what we are going to talk about in the following.

---

59   Althusser, Louis. *For Marx*, p.43.
60   Callinicos. *Althusser's Marxism*, p.135.

CHAPTER VI

IDEOLOGY: AN EVERLASTING FIELD IN IMAGINATION

Well, here is the issue that we are unable to avoid: that is, what does Althusser mean by ideology and science? Although he has not set down boundaries for science in his discussions, it does seem that he agrees with what academia sees science in general. Above all, he is fully convinced that the theoretical concept of science produced by the various natural sciences, at the position where common-sensical ideology breaks off, lies in the deliberate redefinition of Marxism as a new science of history after the rupture from humanistic ideology. However, what we would like to clarify is the ideology, which opposes science. It is fair to say that the theory of ideology weighs quite heavily in Althusser's philosophical research, and his influence upon post-modern culture is the primary issue of this research of mine. Indeed, ideology is a fairyland where humans coexist. It has no history; rather, it lasts forever. The uncommon theoretical concept of ideology, which Althusser defines, is different from that of Marx and Mannheim defines. Therefore, his influence still reverberates in the current post-modern discourse. Indeed, Althusser's theory of ideology is the most notable component of his entire archive of thoughts.

1 BACKGROUND OF ALTHUSSER'S THEORY OF IDEOLOGY

It is worth mentioning that, quite early on, Althusser uses the field of ideology within the intellectual history of Western Marxism, and it is Althusser, who for the first time, appoints this concept as the core field in the philosophic logic of Marxism. Before Althusser, the history of Marxist ideas only evaluates the issue of ideology approached from specific perspectives: that of Lukács' Materialized Consciousness Theory and Gramsci's Hegemony.

Post-anthropology is also an individual case of ideology, as the Frankfurt School uses their Dialectics of Enlightenment as a turn in the middle of the development of this school. I believe that there are at least two directly related backgrounds for Althusser as he establishes his theory in the then historical context: One is the historical themes of discussion regarding Marx, and the other is the ideology of Mannheim. Judging from the methods of discussion in the strictest sense, we can argue that the ideology of Western humanistic Marxism did not directly influence Althusser's academic background.

As we know, the word ideology was first coined by French thinker Destutt de Tracy (1754-1836), who used the word, in his book *Eléments d'idéologie* (1810-1815), to establish a theory of "ideas". In fact, the original context of the word does not disapprove of this concept. Of course, the pre-history of the theory of ideology includes Plato's Idols of the Cave, and Bacon's "doctrine of four idols." After Tracy, Hegel proposes numerous illusions of things as the representations of a spiritual phenomenon, and Feuerbach inverts the alienating fantasy of religious theology. However, Marx undoubtedly establishes the modern context of ideology. In his book *The German Ideology*, which is written in 1845-1846, Marx employs the term, "ideology," in the form of ideas in general and in the broadest sense of the word, but Marx, for the first time, establishes an important semantic metonymy in accordance with the nature of the history of the system of ideas in the process of all social existence. He points out that the nature of the system of ideas, as exists in a class-based society, is that it can only be represented by the will of the ruling class, even if it is shown in the form of **society in general**. Like the religious theology, the Enlightenment thinking of the bourgeois, the God that cares for all and the common nature of equal rights among all people, these are always the embodiment of the will of the ruling class under certain historical condition. While, as the ruling class wishes to visibly or subtly secure their interests, these **determinate ideas are discreetly transposed into the ideas of society in general**. The conversion from the specific to the general represents the logical core of Marxist ideology theory. Therefore, these ideologies are inevitably the illusions of real social relations hidden by the unreal relation of ideas. Thus, Marx, for the first time, explicitly inaugurates the significance of ideology in its **critical** sense in the history of thought.

As I see it, the most important theoretical contribution that Marx makes in his *The German Ideology* does not lie in his proposition on the false nature of ideology; rather, it is his assertion on the **historical unconsciousness** of the ideology. It would be wrong if someone thinks that the medieval churches and clergymen, identified by Marx, voluntarily followed the order of the feudal kings, or that Adam Smith and David Ricardo, out of their own free will, were assisting capitalists in their pursuit of wealth. The nature of ideology is that it is class unconscious, and in the course of history, it is inevitable. Regarding Marx's criticism against German ideology the false idea of such unconsciousness not only refers to the idealistic philosophy of Hegel, but it also encompasses the young Hegelian School (Bauer, Feuerbach and Stirner) that readily finds fault with German feudalism. Furthermore false idea of such unconsciousness also reaches out to Young Marx's alienated historical view related to labor But we see that in *Manuscripts of 1844* the standpoint of the Young Marx's alienated historical view related to labor changes to the alienation of the proletariats, although it was still governed by the humanistic philosophical discourse and tainted by the then prevalent "true socialism"[1] thought trend in Europe.

---

1   See, Chapter III of Zhang Yibing: *Back to Marx: The Change of Philosophical Discourse in the Context of Economics*. English version published by Göttingen University Press, in 2013.

We should also point out that after the turning point of solid establishment of historical materialism by Marx, criticisms of the **value** of Marxist philosophical ideology have been directly transformed into the historical and scientific criticism of all the bourgeois fetishism in economic research.[2] However, it is a shame that after the Second International, the critical content of the Marxist theory of ideology was largely weakened in our traditional Marxist research. Ideology was altered into a number of positive descriptions, which are agreeable to the oneness of class consciousness in order to meet the needs of the state's ideological governance. This kind of descriptions includes the ideology that is interpreted as social consciousness in traditional historical materialism textbooks. Hence, Marx's field of ideology becomes a strange concept in this traditional research mode.

In the 1930s, Mannheim publishes *Ideologie und Utopie* (1929), which enriches Marx's theory of ideology. **Eagleton holds that Lukacs had influenced Mannheim.**[3] Mannheim, the bourgeois scholar, specifies the scope of ideology in the discussion of his self-acclaimed sociology of knowledge. Besides, Mannheim's theory of ideology is obviously **non-critical**. We can tell that the theoretical foundation of this discussion is the idea of **collective unconsciousness** at the social psychological level. This is rather close to the class unconsciousness of Marx.

Firstly, Mannheim quotes Marx to argue that ideology is always associated with the interest of a certain social group, but ideology is no "conscious language" or self-deception, which voluntarily or involuntarily "cheats others." Instead, "it refers to the false field of which, its very nature is psychological; it is unlike some intentioned deception and is not produced with intentions, but instead it is some necessary and unconscious result with certain cause and effect relations."[4] Mannheim concurs with Marx regarding the belief in the interest-oriented nature of ideology, but he also stresses that

---

2   Zhang Yibing: *Subjective Dimension of Marxist Historical Dialectics*, published by Canut Publishers in 2011, London Section IV, Chapter III.
3   Edited by Zizek: *Illustrations Ideology*, translated by Fang Jie, Nanjing: Nanjing University Press, 2002, p.252.
4   Mannheim: *Ideologie und Utopie*, translated by Li Ming, Li Shuchong, the Commercial Press, 2000, p. 62.

ideology is **unwilled**. Ideology is not a lie which is intentionally made up nor is it an illusion: "only when we no longer take the opinions of our adversary as concocted lies, only when we feel untrusting in the entire course of his action, we would start to regard his ideas as ideology." Objectively speaking, this is a profound and crystal clear understanding of the issue.

Secondly, the historical origin of ideology can be classified as any context of ideas related to a certain social environment. "The meaning of our world is forever an ever-developing structure which is determined by history." Judging from this view, we can say Mannheim is evidently affected by historicism. This is an assertion. When the "social situation changes, the pre-formed system of rules is no longer compatible." Under this condition, if people see the special opinions, which form in the determinate historical background as the absolute truth and value, which are everlasting and **transcendent**, then ideology occurs involuntarily. "When knowledge cannot be used to explain the emerging realities which evolve with time, or when it knowledge to contemplate these realities with inappropriate ways of thinking and even attempts to cover them up, knowledge becomes something contorted or ideological."[5] This judgment is acceptable. I believe that although Mannheim has specified that the new meaning of his concept of ideology has nothing to do with Marxism, the "familial resemblance" can hardly be erased. The following section, which examines the research of the theory of ideology, will focus on Althusser.

2 SYSTEM OF UNCONSCIOUS REAPPEARANCE: GENERAL DEFINITION OF IDEOLOGY

Althusser basically acknowledges the theoretical background outlined above, although he does not mention Mannheim on purpose. He notes in his "Ideology and Ideological State Apparatuses" in 1969 that:

> The notion "ideology" is created by Cabanis, Destutt de Tracy and their friends, who regard the theory of (the origin of) ideas as the object in the study of ideology. Fifty years later when Marx employs this word, he understands it quite differently, even in his

---

5   Mannheim: *Ideologie und Utopie*, p. 98.

early works. Here, ideology has become a system of ideas and
their representations which suppresses a man's spirit or a social
group.[6]

However, Althusser thinks that Marx has not specifically discussed
the **theory** of ideology. As he sees it, although Marx does talk about
the criticism of ideology in the book *The German Ideology*, "this
theory is not a Marxist theory"; Althusser also mentions the various
ideologies of capitalist economics in his *On Capital*, but they are not
shown as a finished theory. That is to say, this is a task that Althusser
still has to accomplish. Besides, Althusser would undoubtedly object
to traditional Marxism's (the one after the Second International) attempts to transform Marx's negative context of ideology into positive language. Additionally, Althusser purposefully stays away from
the humanistic Marxist approach, in fact which has revived the concept of ideology.

I find that although Althusser has frequently used the concept of ideology in the majority of his articles in the early chapters of the book
For Marx, he seldom carries out any concentrated or systematic discussion about it. Only in the last article "Marxism and Humanism"
does he explain ideology in detail.

First of all, Althusser thinks that "an ideology is a system (with its
own logic and rigour) of representations (images, myths, ideas or
concepts, depending on the case) endowed with a historical existence and role within a given society."[7] Neither Marx nor Mannheim
has probed deeply or meticulously enough into the inner structure
and mechanism of ideology. Althusser, however, has done this.
Ideology seems always related to something erroneous. Yet this is no
simple fallacy because it is not some random incorrect knowledge
of a human object or lie, which exists at the conscious level. Rather
it is an objective **system of the representation** of consciousness,
which has its own inner structure and mechanism in a determinate
social environment. We know that the original meaning of Tracy's
ideology is the system of ideas; while Marx sees it as a logical system of fallacious thoughts which unconsciously occur; Althusser,

---

6   Althusser: *Lenin and Philosophy*, pp.176-177.
7   Althusser: *For Marx*, translated by Gu Liang, published by the Commercial Press,
1984, p.201. The Chinese version has been modified.

however, points out that ideology is a "system of representations," which is supported by its own "special logic and rules." This unoriginal, second-hand representation is the nature of the problematic of ideology. His critique against the logic of representation is part of the original achievements that Althusser acquired in his efforts to absorb the ideas of Bachelard.

> *The truth of ideological history is neither in its principle (its source) nor in its end (its goal). It is in the **facts** themselves, in that nodal constitution of ideological meanings, themes and objects, against the deceptive backcloth of their problematic, itself evolving against the backcloth of an "anchylose" and unstable ideological world, itself in the sway of real history.*[8]

Ideology is not self-sustained; therefore, it is a highly critical theoretical consideration to reproduce the historical realities and present a world of ideological relations within a particular problematic of ideology.

But what is the essence of the reproduced system? As Althusser sees it, there is no abstract human entity; the "subject" of history is the particular human society. In this sense, human subjects are merely a substitution for the views of social realities. We are not unfamiliar with the idea that human subjects are nothing, but it seems that Althusser aims to point out that the hollowness of this quasi-subject is filled up by ideology. Please note that the **emptiness of the quasi-subject** is different from the **absence of individual subjects** in the theory of ideological interpellation. Social realities are always represented in a collective manner, but the collection of real beings is not **solitary** nor does it share **the same origin**. It is, however, constructed in a **complex and coordinated** manner. Without the relation to economic activities and political organizations, ideology becomes **a system of ideas (or relations) of similar origins** and an "organic component of the society". Gramsci once likened ideology to the "cement," which binds bricks together to form a social skyscraper, and it is also in this sense that Poulantzas, Althusser's student, explains that "ideology is related to the world that human beings live in, the relationship between human beings and nature, and various relations of activities (including economic and political activities) where

---

8   Ibid., p.50.

human beings, the society and others are involved."[9] Certainly, this is a system of **existent and non-existent** relations reproduced by a conglomerate of ideas, but if there is no imaginary bonding of ideology, human society could not exist. It is important in the same way that air is to human beings. In the sense of realism, ideology is only the **emptiness** in the imagination, but this imaginative relation of reflection, which is all illusionary, is an indispensable condition for the stable existence and consistent development of a society. This may be an important when it comes to the ruling classes' maintenance of ideological illusions. Since Althusser, academia has further expanded the realm of ideology. Zizek says: "Now 'ideology' can refer to anything, from the dependent and passive attitude towards the misunderstanding of the social reality, to a whole set of beliefs that guide the actions; from the indispensable media with which the individual maintains his relation with the social structure, to the wrong ideas that offer legality to the dominating political power."[10]

Here, Althusser is rather certain that there will never be a "**non-ideological** society."

This reminds us of the notion which argues that ideology (though not some historical forms of ideology) will ultimately be replaced by science and disappear all together from the planet, or argues that the ethics of ideology, which is ideological, will be replaced by science or change into some pure science. Those are downright illusions. So even if people understand the nature of ideology, they cannot exterminate it. Besides, Althusser also hypocritically quotes Marx:

Marx never believed that an ideology might be dissipated by a knowledge of it: for the knowledge of this ideology, as the knowledge of its conditions of possibility, of its structure, of its specific logic and of its practical role, within a given society, is simultaneously knowledge of the conditions of its necessity.[11]

For instance, Marx negates the idea that humanism is theoretical, but he does not deny the necessity of regarding it as an ideological and historical being. Therefore, "ideology is not an aberration or a

9   Poulantzas: *Political Power*, p. 225.
10   Edited by Zizek: *Illustrations Ideology*, p.4.
11   Althusser, Althusser. *For Marx*, p.200.

contingent excrescence of History: it is a structure essential to the historical life of societies. Further, only the existence and the recognition of its necessity enable us to act on ideology and transform ideology into an instrument of deliberate action on history."[12]

Here we can be sure that Althusser's corroboration of ideology is evidently different from Marx's critical context. Ideology is a basic structure of a social life, and this understanding perpetuates its existence; while Marx holds that ideology will vanish when the ruling-ruled structure of society ceases to exist. Thus, Althusser proposes that ideology will always exist and function within its determinate structure, even in a communist society. This is a very original remark. I can certify that Marx never intended to argue for the perpetuation of ideology. Here, Althusser, purposefully, tries to conceal his difference from Marx. Now we must expose this trick.

Although ideology belongs to the field of ideas, its existence is **involuntary**. This is the issue that both Marx and Mannheim have touched upon, but Althusser highlights that the ideological problematic itself is involuntary: **"its own problematic is not conscious of itself."**[13] This is interesting, is it not?

> *Ideology is indeed a system of representations, but in the majority of cases these representations have nothing to do with "consciousness": they are usually images and occasionally concepts, but it is above all as structures that they impose on the vast majority of men, not via their "consciousness".*[14]

Ideology is always imposed on people as a structure and as such, it subtly rules everything. Comparatively speaking, this is the area where Althusser has probed more deeply than Marx and Mannheim, as he has started to study the mechanism of the self-involuntariness of ideology. Ideology has often been regarded as an illusionary idea of the real world, but the reality is far more complex. Poulantzas has made a blunter statement about ideology: "Ideology spreads all over a relatively harmonious entirety of system, which forms a realistic relation and a **fantasized relation** as well: it means that people's realistic relations are the living conditions for their imaginary relations. It also means that ideology is related to life experiences

---

12   Ibid., p.202.
13   Ibid., p.49.
14   Ibid., pp.202-203. The Chinese version has been modified.

after all, and it cannot be degraded as an issue between subjects and ideas."[15] Here, Althusser also notes that ideology is not a form of ideas, but an object of the human "world;" it is the human world itself. Here some interpretation is needed.

Given that Althusser says ideology is both a subject and the human world itself, he wants to differentiate ideology from the item that is simply independent from the object in the dualistic cognition, as ideology does not reflect the relationship between human beings and their living conditions, but the **ways** in which they experience this relationship. Ideology is the complex result of those ways. This is the "relation of all relations;" the "relation on the second tier". However, when this complicated relation of relations in the social life is mistakably referred to as an easy relationship of reflection and is imposed upon people in the way of voluntary ideas, it becomes an inversion.

Here is the hint: the other important context of Althusser's theory of ideology stems from the Lacanian structural psychoanalysis, especially from the theory of the mirror – symbolizing the other. But according to my findings, Althusser is prone to confuse Lacan's critical context and then probably stretches his own theory as: **the mirror of social ideology**. We will further discuss this issue.

Althusser explains that the relation of experiencing between human beings and the human world "only appears in the form of 'ideas' when it is involuntary." As a matter of fact, this relationship has already differentiated itself from the ideology of object-in-itself. In Zima's words, "most individuals (not scientists) could sense the natural ideology, which is the component of their social environment. They are inclined to view the value of ideologies which lead them to action as present, humane, and common, but they seldom try to understand the historic significance, distinctiveness and contingency of those ideologies."[16] This is a classic statement. Althusser observes that for an ideology, the real relations are unavoidably incorporated in the imaginary relations, which are represented as a will (conservative, obedient, reformed or revolutionary), or even as a hope or as a nostalgic feeling, not the description of the reality. This also implies

---

15 Poulantzas: *Political Power*, p.225.
16 Zima, *Manuel de sociocritique*, translated by Wu Yuetian, Guilin: Guangxi Normal University Press, 1993, p.15.

that when the complex relation of experiencing between human beings and the human world is treated as a simple relation in an ideology, there are real relations and relationships of 'experiencing' and "imaginations". Therefore, "Ideology, is the expression of the relation between men and their 'world', that is, the (overdetermined) unity of the real relation and the imaginary relation between them and their real conditions of existence."[17] "Overdetermined" is a concept which Althusser borrowed from Freud. It refers to the result of multiple factors, and he uses this concept against the simple linear relationship. Later, we will deal with this concept in detail.

It is also because of the relationship between numerous decisions that ideology is equipped with certain special dynamic functions: Ideology reinforces or alters the attachment of human beings to their living conditions in imaginary relations. Generally, "the men who would use an ideology purely as a means of action, as a tool, find that they have been caught by it, implicated by it, just when they are using it and believe themselves to be absolute masters of it."[18]

This is Lacan's theory magnified into the social and historical philosophy. I thought I am the owner of my personality; actually I am unknowingly enslaved by the ideology. This is probably a common phenomenon in the majority of human societies throughout history. Zizek expresses his views in a more radical manner: "Ideology happens to pop up when we are trying to dispense it, but it does not appear where people thought it would be."[19] Or perhaps: it happens when people attempt to "**step out of the ways in which we are controlled by ideology (or everything that we have experienced as ideology)**."[20] This is a rather alarming declaration.

Thirdly, in contrast to the real and conscious scientific understanding of the reality, "the reason that ideology as a representative system differs from science lies in the fact that within an ideology, the practical and social functions of it overwhelm the theoretical function (or cognitive function)."[21] In fact, the practical and social functions represent a certain social **interest relationship**. Althusser later

---

17   Althusser, Louis. *For Marx*, p203.
18   Althusser: *For Marx*, p204.
19   Edited by Zizek: *Illustrations Ideology*, p.4.
20   Ibid., p.20.
21   Althusser: *For Marx*, p.201.

points out that "it is a peculiarity of every **ideological** conception...
that it is governed by 'interests' beyond the necessity of knowledge
alone."[22]

It is also because of the practical field in which the interest is pri-
oritized that ideology must give prominence to something that sup-
ports the determinate interest, and that it hides something else, especially the real, but often the antagonistic social contradictions.
Therefore, in contrast to the cognitive system of science, ideology
can never tolerate any contradictions within itself, and it always
seeks to solve those problems by excluding them. As Poulantzas
notes: "**Everything contributes to the fact that the ideological
center which holds the ruling status has never been a place for
authentic understanding; it appears to execute its concealing
function by adapting its position, that is, by distorting the subject of scientific researches.**"[23] This helps to consolidate and further
illustrate similar ideas put forward by Marx.

> *Unlike scientific researches, the patent role of ideology is to cov-
> er up real contradictions, and re-establish relatively harmonious
> discussions from a fairly rosy perspective, fixing it as the expe-
> rience of agents; by molding them into the images of realistic
> relations, ideology incorporates them in the integrated whole of
> a social relation. This is Gramsci's considerations for employing
> the rather obscuring metaphor of "cement" to denote the social
> function of ideology.[24]*

In a class-based society, ideology serves as the necessary "relay baton
and tracks" for the ruling class to adjust the relationship between the
oppressed people and their living conditions, according to their own
interests. This is what Marx means by "ideology is a representation
of the will of the ruling class." "Within a social structure, ideology is
governed by the totality of elements, like performance, norms, wills
and beliefs, which contribute to the political stability which lasts for
a long time. In other words, this type of social formation can be controlled by the ideology of the group distinguished as the ruling class."[25]

---

22   Althusser: *Reading Capital*, translated by Li Qiqing et.al., Central Compilation &
Translation Press, 2001, p.162.
23   Poulantzas: *Political Power*, p.231.
24   Ibid., p.226.
25   Ibid., p.229.

As Althusser understands it, in a classless society, ideology is also an indispensable condition for an individual to experience the surviving process according to his own interest. In a communist society, the ideology, which exhibits people's interest relationships, still exists, but the functioning of ideology is not embodied in any kind of a simple way. In a class-based society, the ruling class does not agree that it is their own class which is exerting the ruling ideology that is a reflection of their own will, and they do not "maintain ... an external and lucid relation of pure utility and cunning,"[26] such as the liberal ideology of the bourgeois; but this kind of liberalism always attempts to interpret the bourgeois, as "it gave its own demands the form of universality, since it hoped thereby to enroll at its side, by their education to this end, the very men it would liberate only for their exploitation."[27] The bourgeois emancipate the slaves from their farm in order to have and employ free laborers. Therefore, for the bourgeoisie, the emancipation of human beings is firstly an economic issue. However, **"the capabilities of ideology are not simply hiding away the decisive economic factors, but they are concealing the factors that take the charge and the fact of their ruling status."[28]** How do all of these things happen?

Althusser confirms that the bourgeoisie humanism and the liberal ideology, which conceal the ruling class, these ideologies do not aim to deceive, but rather they aim to produce countless fanciful "magic shows".

In reality, the bourgeoisie has to believe in its own myth before it can convince others, and not only so as to convince others, since what it lives in its ideology is the very relation between it and its real conditions of existence which allows it simultaneously to act on itself (provide itself with a legal and ethical consciousness, and the legal and ethical conditions of economic liberalism) and on others (those it exploits and is going to exploit in the future: the "free laborers") so as to take up, occupy and maintain its historical role as a ruling class. Thus, in a very exact sense, the bourgeoisie lives in the ideology of freedom the relation between it and its conditions of existence: that is, its real relation (the law of a liberal capitalist economy) but invested in an imaginary

---

26   Althusser, Louis. *For Marx*, p.204.
27   Ibid., p.204.
28   Poulantzas: *Political Power*, p.230.

relation (all men are free, including the free laborers). Its ide-
ology consists of this play on the word freedom, which betrays
the bourgeois wish to mystify those ("free men"!) it exploits,
blackmailing them with freedom so as to keep them in harness,
as much as the bourgeoisie's need to live its own class rule as the
freedom of those it is exploiting.[29]

The quote above has two implications: one is that ideology assists
the "evil". It helps the ruling class to govern the exploited class,
which is the major function of all of the imaginary relationships of
ideology. In this way, the ruled people tend to believe that the legality of governance is the password and key to ruling; the other is that
"the ruling class serves ... in its own constitution of itself as the ruling class, by making it accept the lived relation between itself and
the world as real and justified."[30] This is the self-mirror recognition
and self-deception that the ruling class harbor regarding ideology,
and it is what Lacan means by the magnification of the self in society. This analysis is both profound and succinct.

The last connotation is the mode of the occurrence in the ideological problematic. It is not until he reads *Capital* with an exhaustive
contemplation effort that, Althusser obviously proposes the mode of
historic occurrence of the ideological problematic.

In the theoretical mode of production of ideology (which is utter-
ly different from the theoretical mode of production of science in
*this respect), the formulation of a **problem** is merely the theoreti-*
*cal expression of the conditions which allow a **solution** already*
produced outside the process of knowledge because imposed by
extra-theoretical instances and exigencies (by religious, ethical,
*political or other "interests") to **recognize** itself in an artificial*
problem...[31]

In contrast to the scientific problematic, which is inclined to be open-
ended, ideology always accommodates **preexistent** answers, which
are not theoretical results attained in understanding the reality, but
rather they are coerced by a "super-theory" of the determinate interest relationships of a society. The ideological problematic is simply
an involuntary representation of this requirement. As any interest
relationship is a product which is yielded under determinate social

---

29   Althusser: *For Marx*, p.204.
30   Ibid., p.205.
31   Althusser, Louis. *Reading Capital*, p.51.

and historical conditions, the conviction of ideology is congealing, and it is determined to overstep its authority. As regional interests are generalized as a whole, and the historically limited item is made perpetual, the nature of the ideological problematic is doomed to be temporal under certain historical conditions. And, Eagleton made the following criticism: "the concept of ideology came into being when the system of ideas initially realizes its one-sidedness; when those ideas are forced to come up against the different voices or other forms, the moment comes along."[32]

Althusser notes:

> ...*it moves, but with an immobile motion which maintains it **where** it is, in its place and its ideological role. It is the immobile motion which, as Hegel said of philosophy itself, reflects and expresses what happens in history without ever running ahead of its own time, since it is merely that time **caught** in the trap of a mirror reflection, precisely so that men will be caught in it too.*[33]

I should say, the essence of this above statement owes a debt to Mannheim, but it is actually more accurate and profound when compared. It is true that "an ideology is both theoretically closed; and politically supple and adaptable. It bends to the interests of the times, but without any apparent movement, being content to **reflect** the historical changes which it is its mission to assimilate and master by some imperceptible modification of its peculiar internal relations."[34] This is the embodiment of a certain flexibility that ideology exhibits in defending its interests.

Bennett, the British scholar, has described Althusser's concept of ideology like this: "Ideology, in Althusser's eyes, is a practice of processing the materials of social relations with the tools for producing ideas provided by the kernel structure of the subject. Within this process, ideology transforms the social relations, and then presents them in front of the public as 'imaginary' ones; these 'imaginary' relations formulate the status of 'life' of the relationship between us and the circumstances of social existence, and lures us to 'mistakably approach' this social existence."[35] I think that Bennett's

---

32   Edited by Zizek: *Illustrations Ideology*, p.251.
33   Althusser, Louis. *Reading Capital*, p.163.
34   Ibid., pp.162-163.
35   Bennet: "Science, Literature and Ideology: Louis Althusser's Literary Theories", *Journal of Liaoning University*, 1994, Vol. 4, p. 39.

summary is basically correct, but this is again related to Althusser's 1969 re-discussion, and associated with the appended content of the theory of ideology.

3 IDEOLOGY AND IDEOLOGICAL STATE APPARATUSES

In 1969, Althusser once again returns to the issue and writes his famous essay "Ideology and Ideological State Apparatuses", which is a collection of his reading notes. For the first time, this essay allows Althusser's theory to surpass that of Western Marxism.

Zizek's Evaluation on Three Modes of Ideology:

Here I would like to illustrate that, according to Zizek,[36] Althusser's theory of ideology encounters a change.. Zizek names Althusser's previous theory of ideology as the theory-in-itself. The first kind of ideology is the ideology as the complex of ideas (theory, belief, faith and process of argumentation). The mode of existence for this kind of ideology is the "interior ideological concept of the complex of a dogma, an idea, a faith, or a notion. It aims to convince us to believe its 'truth', and it is actuallyin in the service of some unsaid special interest or power. And the mode of critical ideology that struggles against it is symptomatic reading: The criticisms are made to uncover the hidden biases through ruptures, blankness and faults of the official texts."[37]

---

36   Slavoj Zizek, born in in Ljubljana, Slovenia on March 21, 1949. Ljubljiana was then a northwestern city in the former Yugoslavia. He received a Bachelor of Arts in Philosophy and Sociology at the Department of Philosophy, College of Literature, University of Ljubljana in 1971, and a Master of Arts in Philosophy in 1975 and a Doctorate in the Arts in Philosophy in 1981, both in the same department. In 1985, he acquired a Doctorate in the Arts in Psycho-analysis in the University of Paris VIII. He started working as a research fellow at the Research Institute of Sociology and Philosophy (renamed as the Research Institute of Social Sciences, College of Social Sciences, University of Ljubljana in 1992) at the University of Ljubljana beginning in 1979. In the 1980s, he was actively engaged in the choice movement in Slovenia. He became a presidential candidate in the first multi-party elections held in the Republic of Slovenia in 1990. In 1991, he was appointed Ambassador of Sciences, but he resigned very soon after and returned to the university to teach. He has delivered numerous lectures in Europe, America and many other parts of the world. He is a vigorous researcher and has published more than 40 books and considerable theses, which have influenced contemporary academia, especially the wave of radicalism. His works include: *The Sublime Object of Ideology* (1998); *The Parallax View* (1991); *The Metastases of Enjoyment* (1994); *The Fragile Absolute* (2000); *Repeating Lenin* (2001) Zagreb: Arkzin D.O.O. which is noted by the author of this book in the second edition.

37   Edited by Zizek: *Illustrations Ideology*, p.13.

This might be the theory of ideology that starts with Marx and extends through until the early period of Althusser. While, according to Zizek in his 1969 text, Althusser's research object and criticisms of ideology changes markedly. Furthermore, his theory of ideology transits from the theory-in-itself to the theory-for-itself. This second mode of ideology is also "ideology in objective forms", i.e. "the theory of ideological state apparatuses". Zizek summarizes it as "otherness – externalized ideology: the externalization refers to the ideological material existence in the ideological practices, rituals and organizations."[38]

Besides Zizek argues that there is a third stage in the recent development of ideology; that is, the ideology both in-itself and for-itself, or which we can call "Cynic ideology", in which the involuntariness of ideology vanishes, and the state of being involuntarily changes into a clever trick. It is no longer something beautiful, out-of-reach, and beyond our understanding, but rather it is something residual that is excluded from the conscious level to unconscious level. In the past "they are doing it without knowing it" (Marx); now "they are doing it even if they are highly conscious of what they do."[39] They (the people) regard this involuntariness of ideology as a distant landscape: they depict it meticulously, but they do not tear it down. People perceive that "an ideology-for-itself functions in the factuality-in-itself of a super-ideology". At this stage, they are both sober analysts and sensible conspirators.

Here, Althusser takes another perspective in order to approach the issue. This new perspective is Marx's theory on **reproduction by men themselves**. He agrees with Marx that in order to exist, every social formation must reproduce its production conditions during this reproduction (of men). The production conditions include the reproduction of productive forces and production relations, and Althusser is concerned about the issue of the reproduction of productive forces (men) in the capitalist society. In contrast to the reproduction of productive forces, which Marx considers in the context of the economics of the past, Althusser holds that under capitalist conditions, the reproduction of productive forces (men/labor force) differ from their counterparts in the traditional society in that they are no longer produced from the **interior** of the production mechanism (to

---

38   Ibid., p.16.
39   Ibid., p.11. See also Zizek: *Sublime Object of Ideology*, translated by Ji Guangmao, Central Compilation & Translation Press, 2002, p. 39; p. 45.

inherit directly from the experienced apprentices), but from the **exterior**. This is accomplished through the capitalist educational system and its established institutions. Besides the material production and life-sustaining productive force, this is also an **indirect constructive process of knowledge (ration)**. Althusser makes a pointed remark that the nature of this type of reproduction is:

> *(T)he reproduction of labor power requires not only a reproduction of its skills, but also, at the same time, a reproduction of its submission to the rules of the established order, i.e. a reproduction of submission to the ruling ideology for the workers, and a reproduction of the ability to manipulate the ruling ideology correctly for the agents of exploitation and repression, so that they, too, will provide for the domination of the ruling class "in words".* [40]

Althusser believes that it is an absolute and necessary condition for the ruling class that labor is **consciously obedient** to the ideology of the ruling class, which can also be called as the reproduction of ideological practice. Now he seems to be more interested in how the "conscious obedience" takes place.

Unlike his previous arguments about ideology, Althusser no longer makes general discussions about the ideology of the system of ideas, which are related to the social reproduction and which are in opposition with science. He does, however, inquire into the ideology related to the state apparatuses, which are employed as tools of ruling. This is also what Zizek evaluates as the transformation from the ideology-in-itself (system of unconscious ideas) to the ideology-for-itself (autonomous will of a nation). If we can say the former is concerned more with the voluntary mechanism of ideology, then we can say the latter cares more about the microcosmic mechanism of ideology that a state uses to subtly and voluntarily (with their consent) govern its people. We can conclude from Althusser's relevant research that this is more focused upon the interpretation of the capitalist Ideological State Apparatuses (or ISAs). I can see that he is rather satisfied with his ability to add something else to the "Marxist theory of the state." [41] This is because although Marx and Engels had realized the complexity of state issues, they did not provide a timely theoretical explanation.

---

40   Althusser, Louis. *Lenin and Philosophy*, pp.155-156.
41   Ibid., p.163.

First of all, Althusser agrees with Marx's metaphor on the concepts of base and superstructure in his historical materialism. This is similar to Althusser's theory: "It is easy to see that this representation of the structure of every society as an edifice containing a base (infrastructure) on which are erected the two 'floors' of the superstructure, is a metaphor, to be quite precise, a spatial metaphor: the metaphor of a topography (topique)."[42]

Jameson and other scholars have later expanded this metaphor in such as way that it becomes profoundly significant: it even gives rise to a spatial mapping philosophy in the context of today's globalization. What different connotations do the two layers of architecture have, respectively? The first layer is political laws and their affiliation (the government, administrative organization, military forces, police, court and prison, etc.), which are generally considered as state apparatuses in certain social governance; the second layer is ideology in the form of ideas. Althusser's aim is to distinguish that the latter is not merely a form of ideas as evaluated in traditional studies, but that it is also a state apparatus, which differs from the former in that the former is the repressive state apparatus while the latter is the **ideological** state apparatus. Each has its own special characteristics. This is different from Althusser's previous thought in that ideology cannot simply be taken as a system of ideas; instead it is at the same time a special **optional** state apparatus embodied as a realistic being. This special ideological state apparatus is "a certain number of realities which present themselves to the immediate observer in the form of distinct and specialized institutions."[43]

However, this is not the crux of the issue. Althusser argues that the nature of ideological state apparatuses achieves that the ruling class successfully conceals their ruling purpose. They make the ruled believe that those who rule are not enslavers but rather, that they are the representatives of legitimate democracy and freedom! And believe that this democracy and freedom are realized through laws. "One of the characteristics of the ruling bourgeois ideology is that it covers up the class exploitation in such an unusual way that **any traces of the ruling by any class vanish into thin air systematically from**

---

42   Ibid., p.157.
43   Ibid., p.164.

its discourse. And the fact is the circumstances for its existence do not allow any ideology to emerge as the ideology of class rule."[44] This is the declaration of a new historical judgment. It rips away the legitimacy of the rule of law in capitalist society, which has existed since Weber.

> *The ISAs include: religious ISA (various church systems), educational ISA (public and private "school" systems), family ISA, legal ISA, political ISA (political system consisting of various parties), labor unions ISA, communications ISA (publications, broadcast and television, etc.), and cultural ISA (literature, art and sports). There is something different between the ISAs and the suppressive state apparatuses: the latter is singular, but the former is numerous, plural; the latter belongs to the public sphere, but the former is dispersed amongst the private spheres; what is more important, however, is that "the Repressive State Apparatus functions 'by violence', whereas the ISAs* **function 'by ideology'.**"[45] *This is a difference in capabilities, and Althusser mainly deals with how the capabilities of the ISAs operate. I agree that the ISAs function mostly in the form of ideology, but they are also sometimes accompanied by repression, which is not the same as the violence as directly imposed by the state apparatuses. The ISAs "function ... by repression ... only ultimately, this is very attenuated and concealed, even symbolic (There is no such thing as purely ideological)."*[46]

For example, as schools and churches employ means of punishment, such as expulsion, and as they select to "regulate" their shepherds and flocks, cultural ideology fulfills this function through the censorship of books and newspapers. It is interesting that Althusser's discussion can be directly connected to Gramsci's theory of **cultural hegemony**, which regards the functioning structure of the ISA as the cultural hegemony that the ruling class employs to safeguard the legitimacy of their governance. Barrett proposes that cultural hegemony and ideology are a kindred pair of terms.[47] He emphasizes that: **"no class can hold State power over a long period without at the same time exercising its hegemony over and in the State**

44 Poulantzas, Nicos. *Political Power and Social Classes*, p. 235.
45 Althusser, Louis. *Lenin and Philosophy*, p.165.
46 Ibid., p.166.
47 Edited by Zizek: *Illustrations Ideology*, p.313.

Ideological Apparatuses."[48] Althusser has not specifically discussed the relationship between ideology and cultural hegemony, but the way that he handles this pair leaves me with the impression that ideology is important to the construction and support of cultural hegemony.

Different historical periods witness different forms and mechanisms in which the ISA functions. In traditional societies, the number of ISAs is limited, such as in the feudal society where the ISAs are mainly churches and families. As capitalist society develops, the former ideological functions of churches and families are transferred to many other newly emerging ideological forms. For instance, the major **dominant** capitalist ISAs are educational ideological apparatuses.

> (B)ehind the scenes of its political Ideological State Apparatus, which occupies the front of the stage, what the bourgeoisie has installed as its number-one, i.e. as its dominant ideological State apparatus, is the educational apparatus, which has in fact replaced in its functions the previously dominant ideological State apparatus, the Church. One might even add: the School-Family couple has replaced the Church-Family couple.[49]

What are the causes? In a capitalist society, all of the ISAs, regardless of their identities, are meant for one purpose: **the reproduction of production relations (they are the relations of capitalist exploitation)**. This is where the goal of the capitalist ISA is set. However, every type of ISA fulfills this aim in its own way, such as the political ISAs, which are realized through direct elections (referendums) or indirect (representative systems) means for the people to identify themselves with the ruling class, or the broadcasting machines used to inculcate in people certain forms of ideas through publications and broadcast programs delivered in "regular doses" so as to control them. The occurrence of this ideology is like a concert

---

48   Althusser: *Lenin and Philosophy*, p.167. Althusser admits that Gramsci is the only one who went any distance in the road he is taking. He had the 'remarkable' idea that the State could not be reduced to the (Repressive) State Apparatus, but included, as he put it, a certain number of institutions from 'civil society': the Church, the Schools, the trade unions, etc. Unfortunately, Gramsci did not systematize his institutions, which remained in the state of acute but fragmentary notes" from the same book, p. 204, footnote 7.

49   Althusser, Louis. *Lenin and Philosophy*, p.173.

designed and staged by the bourgeoisie, "This concert is dominated by a single score, occasionally disturbed by contradictions (those of the remnants of former ruling classes, those of the proletarians and their organizations): the score of the Ideology of the current ruling class."[50]

That is to say the **score** and **theme** of bourgeois ideology establishes the fundamental key for the entire cultural and musical concert. Althusser believes that certain ISAs inevitably undertake the commanding role, though hardly anyone would lend an ear to the music: it is so silent! This is what school is. Education has become the backbone of the capitalist ISAs, which is a new social and historical fact. Ideology is, a strategy as well as a disguise, an intermediate between illusion and reality, and a dubious conspiracy between oneself and society.

Althusser remarks that schools have taken charge of the ideological capabilities that the churches once had occupied in feudal societies. Similar to the reproductive process in the capitalist industrial system, education is the most important workshop in which the "subject" of the capitalist reproduction is constructed, because various kinds of professional knowledge are subtly instilled with the ideology of the ruling class, and the apprenticeship system for the instruction of the professional knowledge ensures that the reproduction of the various capitalist modes of production are broadly conducted. Starting with kindergartens, people have been imbued with a certain amount of 'know-how' wrapped in the ruling ideology (French, arithmetic, natural history, the sciences, literature) or the ruling ideology in its pure state (ethics, civic instruction, philosophy). Althusser says with some exaggeration that there may not be a kind of ISA, like school, which trains all pupils to listen for eight hours a day! When they become adults, a huge mass of them are ejected "into production": these are the workers or small peasants. Another portion of scholastically adapted youth carries on: and, for better or worse, it goes somewhat further, until it falls by the wayside and fills the posts of small and middle technicians, white-collar workers, small and middle executives, and petty bourgeoisie of all kinds. A final segment of the population reaches the summit, either to fall into intellectual

---

50   Ibid., pp.173-174.

semi-employment, or to become the agents of exploitation (becoming capitalists, managers), or becoming the agents of repression (soldiers, policemen, politicians, administrators, etc.) and the professional ideologists.

Althusser also gives an example for philosophy teachers.

> *Philosophy teachers are teachers, i.e. intellectuals employed in a given education system and subject to that system, performing, as a mass, the social function of inculcating the "values of the ruling ideology". The fact that there may be a certain amount of "play" in schools and other institutions, which enables individual teachers to turn their teaching and reflection against these established "values" does not change the **mass** effect of the philosophical teaching function.*[51]

Such a sharp and penetrating remark sends chills to "philosophy teachers" who carry on the so-called "game."

4 IDEOLOGY HAS NO HISTORY BUT IS EVERLASTING

Althusser tried to rewrite some important theories, that is, to prove the theory of ideology **in general**. He fully supported Marx's idea that "ideology has no history", and in his book *For Marx*, he notes, "once it has been grasped that ideological history can only be understood through the real history which explains its formations, its deformations and their restructurations, and which emerges in it, then it is essential to ask, what survives of this **ideological history** itself as a **history**, and admit that the answer is nothing."[52]

However, Althusser bluntly criticizes the negative theory of ideology in *The German Ideology*. According to Althusser, Marx is correct about the notion that "ideology has no history". But when Marx established his theory on the basis of "positivism" and "historicism", "ideology was conceived as a pure illusion, a pure dream, i.e. as nothingness."[53] Ideology seems to be the construction of fantasies, like the dream, according to Freud. Therefore, "Ideology…is…an

---

51 Ibid., p.174.
52 Althusser, Louis. *For Marx*, p. 63, Note 1. The Chinese version has been modified. The translator has mistaken the key word "emerge" for "growth" which changes the author's intention.
53 Althusser, Louis. *Lenin and Philosophy*, p.178.

imaginary assemblage (bricolage), a pure dream, empty and vain, constituted by the 'day's residues' from the only full and positive reality, that of the concrete history of concrete material individuals materially producing their existence."[54]

Marx was inclined to see ideology as negative: firstly, as regard to the conviction that ideology is a pure dream, ideology becomes something futile; secondly, by saying that there is no history of ideology, Marx does not mean that it is not historical (the truth is quite the contrary, as ideology is merely the pale, illusory and inverted reflection of real history), but he meant that it does not possess **its own** history. While Althusser admits his agreement with this statement "ideology has no history," he concurs with Marx's statement in his argument that ideology is "absolutely and certainly" present.

Althusser thinks that "ideology has no history", can and must be related directly to Freud's proposition that the **unconscious is eternal**."[55] I can say this is a highly controversial theoretical resetting. The ideology we see in Marx's negative theory, which only exists under certain historical conditions, has turned into an eternally present image in Althusser's theory. He writes: "If eternal means, not transcendent to all (temporal) history, but omnipresent, transhistorical and therefore immutable in form throughout the extent of history, I shall adopt Freud's expression word for word, and write **ideology is eternal**, exactly like the unconscious."[56] It is crucial to clearly position this ubiquitous and pervasive theory of which its form never changes. Althusser's ideology is evidently not based on the historical contexts of Marx or Mannheim; it relies more on Freud and Lacan.

Well, why should ideology last forever? Althusser explains this using two theoretical essentials: the first one is **"Ideology is a 'Representation' of the Imaginary Relationship of Individuals to their Real Conditions of Existence."**[57]

---

54 Ibid., p.179.
55 Ibid., p.180. The Chinese translator has mistakenly translated the"unconscious" into "ideology".
56 Ibid., p.180.
57 Ibid., p.180.

This is a passive argument, like the belief in God, like the idea of vocation in religious theology, or like the idea about the primitive society, which is evaluated as not alienated by the humanistic philosophy, I can say these are certainly not the reflection of real relations. Most of these beliefs are only imaginary.

He argues in another way:

> *Men represent to themselves in ideology, but above all it is their relation to those conditions of existence which is represented to them there. It is this relation which is at the centre of every ideological, i.e. imaginary, representation of the real world.*[58]

That is to say, certain ideology does not embody a system of those real relations, which control the existence of individuals, like the production relationship and all of the social relations that exist as a result of that production relationship, but it shows a distorted imaginary relationship between individuals within real social relation networks. "It is the imaginary nature of this relation which underlies all the imaginary distortion that we can observe (if we do not live in its truth) in all ideology."[59] Althusser has already approached this issue.

Secondly, ideology is a kind of material existence. "An ideology always exists in an apparatus, and its practice, or practices. This existence is material."[60] This is a fresh perspective. Surely, Althusser does not mean that ideology turns into an object, but that its existence is secured by the highly repetitive objective practices of individuals or the practices of the entire society. This is similar to a believer's maintenance of a religious routine, such as performing Mass in a church, worshiping on bended knees, praying, repenting and confessing, and other such continuous theological activities used for maintaining his imaginary relationship with the theological world. Therefore Althusser states that:

> *The ideological representation of ideology is itself forced to recognize that every "subject" endowed with a "consciousness" and believing in the "ideas" that his "consciousness" inspires in him and freely accepts, must "**act** according to his ideas", must therefore inscribe his own ideas as a free subject in the actions of his material practice.*[61]

---

58   Ibid., pp.180-183.
59   Ibid., p.183.
60   Ibid., p.184.
61   Ibid., p.186.

Just like every Mass, wedding ceremony, political class or speech at an election, the practices, which are among the material practices of the ISA, are controlled by all kinds of rituals and are instilled with those practices, even if those rituals are only a small part of the ISA. As for every individual subject in the ideology, "**his ideas are his material actions inserted into material practices governed by material rituals which are themselves defined by the material ideological apparatus from which derive the ideas of that subject.**"[62]

Pecheux later remarks, "ideology is not made up of 'ideas' but of practices!"[63] Althusser believes that an important transposition occurs here: a transposition of the sequence of matters. This is exactly like what Pascal says: "Bend on your knees and pray, then you will believe it." Althusser calls our attention to the events that take place in this confused relationship: some terms have disappeared but others are strengthened. The lost term is "**view**"; the terms that are still present are **subject, consciousness, faith, action**, etc. The newly emerging terms are **practice**, **ritual**, and **ideological apparatus**. The views are hidden away; the "subject" that is clearly governed by the ideological system is transposed and presented as the autonomous form of the subject. "Ideology existing in a material ideological apparatus, prescribing material practices governed by a material ritual, which practices exist in the material actions of a subject acting in all consciousness according to his belief."[64] Here, Zizek takes it as the "way" for ideology to be "inserted in the object",[65] or in Bourdieu's terms, the memorization process of "humanization".[66]

Althusser observes that this analysis helps us to find that the key concept of ideology is the false concept related to **subject**. Hence he puts forward his famous assertion: "1. There is no practice except by and in an ideology; 2. There is no ideology except by the subject and for subjects."[67] That is to say, ideology could attain its end with the

---

62   Ibid., p.187.
63   Edited by Zizek: *Illustrations Ideology*, p.185.
64   Althusser, Louis. *Lenin and Philosophy*, p.188.
65   Edited by Zizek: *Illustrations Ideology*, p.11.
66   Bourdieu, Pierre. *Practice and Reflection*, translated by Li Meng and Li Kang, Central Compilation & Translation Press, 1998, p. 26.
67   Althusser, Louis. *Lenin and Philosophy*, p.188.

assistance of the subject and its functions, and without the strenuous performance of the subject. The splendid stage of ideology is just a void and frigid structure. Therefore, here lies a dialectical idea by Althusser: "ideology is produced by the subject, but it in turn, molds the individual into a subject."[68] The former is a false quasi-subject, and the latter is the fake subject. This is the subject **fabricated in two ways**. For Althusser, the way in which ideology constructs a subject inevitably becomes the central issue. As Eagleton comments on the Althusser's "challenge" to the theory of ideology, he concludes: "Ideology has nothing to do with falseness; it is more involuntary than it is voluntary; it is the intermediate of subjectivity; it is an issue about ceremonial practices, not ideological dogma; it is 'perpetual' in time and invariable in structure."[69] This is a very accurate definition. Its main parts are the issues that we have also talked about in this chapter. There is only one exception: if we say ideology is the "intermediate of subjectivity," in fact , when we aim to define it in a more precise manner, this becomes Althusser's tool for regarding ideology as the construction of the false subjectivity, that is, the inquiry of ideology and the mirror copy. These are the key issues for the next chapter, and they are directly related to Althusser's theoretical quotations from Lacanian philosophy.

68   Wolff: *The Social Production of Art*, translated by Dong Xuewen and Wang Kui, Beijing: Xuaxia Press, 1990, p. 170.
69   Eagleton: *History of Political, Philosophical, Eros*, translated by Ma Hailiang, Beijing: China Social Sciences Press, 1999, p. 94.

CHAPTER VII

THEORY OF IDEOLOGY AND LACANIAN PSYCHOANALYSIS

After the 1960s, Lacan's structuralist psychoanalysis began to have a significant impact on European academia and immediately became the major theoretical source of post-modernism regarding the resolution of the subject. Althusser was among the earliest scholars who were influenced by Lacanian philosophy, and it is under the conceptional governance of Lacan's pseudo individualism that Althusser rejected the philosophy of the subject and humanism by an ontological perspective. In 1969, he follows Levinas and Lacan to propose the well-known theory of **individual subject interpellation** and the mechanism of ideological mirror reflection and automatic obedience in his theoretical construction of the Ideological State Apparatuses. Amongst all of Althusser's philosophical ideas this has influenced post-modernist culture the most and deepest. However, his theory of ideology has been branded as "aristocratic".[1]

---

1   Edited by Zizek: *Illustrations Ideology*, p.352.

1 ALTHUSSER AND LACANIAN PHILOSOPHY

Let us continue our discussion. Althusser clearly asserts: "the category of the subject (which may function under other names: e.g., as the soul in Plato, as God, etc.) is the constitutive category of all ideology, whatever its determination (regional or class) and whatever its historical date – since ideology has no history."[2] This paragraph implies that **pseudo subject** is the key in the constructing of ideology; needless to say, I agree strongly that this is a new interpretation, and it is constructed upon the basis of Lacanian thoughts.[3] In order to understand his views, we need to probe into the essence of Lacanian philosophy.

Lacanian philosophy is an insightful theory of subject criticism, which integrates both psychoanalysis and structuralism. It is highly philosophical, critical and profound. Lacan's ideas have a direct influence on Foucault, Althusser and Deleuze and have become one of the important bases of post-modernistic thoughts. According to Althusser, Lacan – in practice – has initiated both the labor of ideological criticism and the epistemological elucidation.[4] We will focus on one of Lacan's arguments: **the subject has always been a kind of self-deception.**

We can safely conclude that Lacan is the first person, who announces the death of the **individual** subject "self" in the modern era. It is Lacan that mercilessly murders Stirner's "the Ego" and poses a dilemma for the **ontological origin of neo-humanism**, which is initiated by Kierkegaard.

Stirner pronounced the death of the quasi man in the Enlightenment, and Kierkegaard establishes the individual oriented philosophy of the neo-humanistic subject on the debris of this quasi concept (absolute idea, totality and nature). Nietzsche's superman and Heidegger's

---

2   Althusser, Louis. *Lenin and Philosophy*, p.189.
3   Jacques Marie Émile Lacan (1901-1981): the celebrated contemporary French structuralistic psychoanalyst and philosopher. His works include: *On Paranoiac Psychosis in its Relations to the Personality* / Orig. *De la psychose paranoïaque dans ses rapports avec la personnalité* (Doctoral Thesis 1932); *Au-delà du principe de réalité* (thesis 1953); *Le Séminaire de la lettre volée* (1955); *Les formations de l'inconscient* (thesis 1958); *Ecrits: A Selection* (1966) etc. See above.
4   Althusser, Louis. *Lenin and Philosophy*, p.212.

Dasein only come after. Lacan's argument happens to run counter to Piaget's;[5] because Lacan does not want to illustrate the construction of individual subject in positive terms. Instead, he negatively explicates the falseness of the individual subject as **being constructed**.[6] Lacan might believe that the "self" of the individual is formed by the forcefully alienated self-identity.

Firstly, it is the alienated identification of the mirror image that is also the initial (babyhood) image of the "self." He notices that a person's original understanding generally occurs when he is a baby between six and eight months. This is a process known as the **noumenon construction** of the "self" – the pseudo self-center.[7] When the baby, who is still in a non-uniformed state where he cannot define himself in the real world, sees a relatively stable image of himself, baby naturally mistakes this "other" (a) for the "self," which is a narcissistically false identification as "this leads to the creation" of the world "where there are only a body and some organs but no phenomenological center," and the individual is at most a kind of "overlapping of images and the self."[8]

Here, the self is reflected through its projection upon an object (image) or upon another human: "the subject is enchanted by his own image in the mirror!"[9] The "self" has thus become an alienated identity living without its own existence, and the "true self" as a true existence is outlawed as **a nameless mirror image of the other** (a').

Therefore, the subject is **nothing** from the very beginning; subject is a mistake. Lacan notes that the image is the "threshold to a seeable world," but the door opens to the path of alienation because after it, the individual and the self will be forever traveling on different life paths of alienation.[10]

---

5   For more information about Piaget, please refer to my book *Piaget and the Research on Marxist Epistemology* and *Selected Works of Zhang Yibing*, Guilin: Guangxi Normal University Press, 1999, p. 130.

6   Lacan: *Ecrits: A Selection*, translated by Zhu Xiaoquan, Shanghai: Shanghai Joint Publishing, 2001, p. 40.

7   Ibid., p. 90.

8   Jameson: *The Cultural Logic of Late Capitalism*, translated by Chen Qingqiao, Joint Publishing, 1997, pp. 212-213.

9   Ibid., p.216.

10   Lacan: *Ecrits*, p. 91.

Secondly, it is the naming or the fact that an individual is forced (slave-like) to identify himself with a symbol (the object that the elder family members call). As soon as you are born, the family says, "you are Jack". Naming is the starting point of your destiny; from that moment on, the "self", which has already been alienated as the subject of the mirror image, continues to transform into a symbol, a symbol to be called every minute and every day. Lacan believes that the symbol is the contempt that the signifier shows for the signified, the exploitation that the abstract performs upon the copious, and the oppression that death exerts on life; it is the agent for matter and death (absent).

As for the subject, naming is the alienation being alienated, or talking by Lacan's complex and over-elaborated terms, this is the nothing (symbol – existent corpse), which labels the nothing (the self lost in the "other's" mirror image) as the subject. Labeled by names, men never care about the "true self," which has been overshadowed by the "other" (which is the reflection of the "other" at the beginning and now "true self," has become the slave of the "Other" being called), and has never been truly present. People have too many expectations for "Jack", such as "Jack" should attend Tsinghua University, "Jack" should get his doctoral degree at Harvard, "Jack" should become a renowned jurist like his father... You are called "Jack" in people's eyes, and this is a **transcendental expectation**.

We can see that when people start to learn languages, they are driven by a compelling force, which is also a new, deeper, and more alienating beginning: to learn one's own name is a form of alienation – the "self" becomes a symbol. F. Jameson says: "in receiving a name, the subject transforms into a representation of oneself; this process of being oppressed and alienated is exactly the reality of the subject."[11] Althusser later extends this, claiming that even "(w)hen a young science branch is born, the family circle is always ready for astonishment, jubilation and baptism."[12] The "self" is not an entity; it is only exterior interpellation in which the "self" is constructed as a Gestalt topological field. To be interpellated is like the eager stares of your parents, teachers and classmates and the public; it is,

11 Jameson: *The Cultural Logic*, p.223.
12 Althusser, Louis. *Lenin and Philosophy*, p.214.

in others' aspiration, formed as the desire of the aspiration of the "self." As we are in pursuit of another pursuit, the fantasy of the reality vanishes because what we desire is actually the aspiration of the other – in fact, the desire is false, above all it is a fake.

Thirdly, it is the alienation of real society. This is a further step, as when men enter society (culture and history) and accept general education. They are officially on a path which has no return. This is easier to understand. It is also the theme of Freud's *Civilization and Its Discontents*. Althusser states that this is the miserable path where people are controlled by "cultural rules."[13] We can safely say for Lacan, alienation of the "true self" takes place when the "self of mirror image" (self) becomes skewed as the social self (super ego).

As I see it, the most critical logical formula of Lacan's theory is the inner contradiction between the **true self** – the ever flowing signifier of desire (generative existence) and the **subject** – the stagnate signified of symbols (ideas and knowledge). Lacan believes that the history of the subject or men's destiny of being alienated is associated with **three kinds of unification** (idealized recognition). According to Jameson's generalization, people's "thoughts of action and experience of a mature subject suggests a structural coordination among something fantastic, something symbolic and something real."[14] Here, below we can analyze the argument more rationally and systematically.

Firstly, it is the unification of the "true self" with the phantom (realm of imagination) that controls the self. According to Lacan, the construction of the "self" by an individual subject is nothing other than a formal freeze-framing (it starts with the image in the mirror!), as the mirror image contributes to the consistent and continuous whole of the many fragments of the self. And this is the agreement of an alienated "fact" of an everlasting identity with a real object. And the enslavement and alienation of the true self occurs in the process of this agreeing.[15] Hence, the mirror image becomes the most intimate core of the self, and the self can never perceive any break because if he did perceive any break he would be forever deceived by this

---

13   Ibid., p.226.
14   Jameson: *The Cultural Logic*, p.207.
15   Lacan: *Ecrits*, p. 188.

fabricated self-portrait. The live "true self" (the signifier of desire) becomes a shadow of the Other; therefore **the unconsciousness of the subject is the language of the Other.**[16] Lacan's unconsciousness no longer means the libido-like ontological origin espoused by Freud. Instead, it has become the groaning of an individual subject being transformed into the other. Therefore, Lacan notes, in this negative context, that "unconsciousness is a chapter that is intentionally blank or filled with lies in my history: it is banned."[17] Evidently, this is also an important extension and rewriting of the relation between Freud's civilization and the id.

Besides, it is the unification of the "true self" with the **symbols** (realm of imagination) of **human beings**. The self becomes a subject in the interpellation with languages (the Other). However, as soon as the self is identified in the **interpellation with languages**, the true self loses its existence in the language.[18] Lacan thinks that human beings maintain a general knowledge structure, which is eternal and static, and they put themselves at a strategic or intentional disadvantage, by following the absolute beliefs. In a kingdom which is supported by **symbolic orders**, people are governed by force, and with converging attacks from their own self-punishment, masking their personalities, and under various forms of abnormal disguise, this false subject is established, while the yearning individual is dead. Below Lacan vividly described this:

> *The symbolic signs surround a man's life like a perfect web… when he is born, they bring him gifts of the zodiac, or presents from the fairies, or even the outline of his destiny; they send him words for him to obey or disobey; they stipulate rules of action for him to follow through to the future where he has not been, or to his death; and also with these symbolic signs his ending gains its significance in the final trial, where languages are employed to pardon or punish his existence, unless he has existed for being dead.*[19]

---

16   Ibid., p. 275.
17   Ibid., p. 269.
18   Ibid., p. 364.
19   Ibid., p. 290.

The life of the subject is forever not speaking but being spoken! This idea later becomes a well-known saying within post-structuralism. "Be spoken" is like those buzzwords "be learned", "be educated", "be worked", "be employed", etc. All of these events and spectacles, that appear one after the other, refer to one characteristic of the subject: that subject is being abandoned. "Be" is a sad word, since it is the ultimate code to a symbolic sign, but it is also the only connection between the self and the other, and the only passage between the self and society. The order of symbols is the further alienation of the subject.

Thirdly, it is the unification of the "self" with the real and material **automatic machine of the world**. Lacan holds that the seeable world simply starts from the mirror that projects the "self;" hence it is inevitably a fictional world. The "self" and the "world" in the metaphysical sense are the kingdom of "Being" which was once proposed by Heidegger. Moreover, For Lacan the nature of the world, similar to the social relations in the concentration camp, and similar to the "self" in society, which plays a certain role in this world, is the corpse of the true self which has been murdered.[20] Following this logic, society is turned into an unnerving execution ground for the living dead.

Therefore, Lacan needs to rewrite Descartes's "*Cogito ergo sum* (I think therefore I am)." This is because the "self" is a false subject, and the "thinking" is the demon of ideas. For that reason, when the "self" (false subject) is "thinking" (logos), the true self is not **present** (Heidegger); the self thinks about his concerns where he is not **thinking** (Heidegger). "I am absent from the place where thinking is a plaything, I am where I am not thinking."[21] This is rather subversive when evaluated in the context of the traditional philosophy of the subject. And this theory of false subject is an important basis for Althusser's theory of ideology critique.

In Jameson's words, "the fact that Lacan regards science as a concept of the form of historical origin of the subject being decentralized – instead of being where the 'truth' is – is very inspirational for those Marxists who are still cooped up in the outdated idea of ideology versus science."[22] Here Jameson aims directly at Althusser. In 1964,

---

20   Ibid., p. 95.
21   Ibid., p. 449. The Chinese version has been modified.
22   Jameson: *The Cultural Logic*, p.254.

Althusser wrote his book on *Freud and Lacan*, but we seldo*m see Lacan's appearance in the two books For Marx and* Reading Capital, which were both written in 1965. In 1969, Lacan suddenly comes back in Althusser's "Ideology and Ideological State Apparatuses". But this time, Lacan had become the foundation of the Western Marxist critical theory. Lacanian philosophy expects the presence of the true self even if it dissolves the philosophy of abstract subject, but I can say it is still a (true self) covert humanism. Althusser employs Lacan in order to exterminate any subject (including Lacan's "true self"). Laclau says that in Althusser's theories, Lacan's psychoanalysis "encompasses an idea of the subject which is in complete accordance with historical materialism."[23] Therefore, Althusser joins the camp of critical theory for the first time. Wolff is right that Althusser quotes Lacan in a very limited and selected manner,"[24] while Eagleton discovers that Althusser has misread Lacan.[25]

2 IDEOLOGY INTERPELLATES THE INDIVIDUAL AS A SUBJECT

I find that the understanding that ideology **interpellates** the individual as a subject is a pivotal theoretical component of Althusser's re-assertion of ideology. At first glance, the interpellation resembles what Heidegger describes in his later years as the human forcefully **interpellating** the matter to be **present**, but we know that it is, in fact, Althusser's direct rewriting of Lacan. Because the symbolic, which is once a sign of the signal station, is replaced by ideology.

Zizek states:

> *(T)he category of the subject is only constitutive of all ideology insofar as all ideology has the function (which defines it) of "constituting" concrete individuals as subjects. In the interaction of this double constitution exists the functioning of all ideology, ideology being nothing but its functioning in the material forms of existence of that functioning.*[26]

---

23 Quoted from Zizek: *The Sublime Object of Ideology*, translated by Ji Guangmao, Central Compilation & Translation Press, 2002, p. 3 (preface).
24 Wolff: *The Social Production of Art*, translated by Dong Xuewen and Wang Kui, Beijing: Xuaxia Press, 1990, p. 172.
25 Edited by Zizek: *Illustrations Ideology*, pp. 282-286.
26 Ibid., pp. 282-286.

He retorts that the Althusser, who writes all these words, and the readers who read the text are all the subjects, or even, the ideological subjects, like you and I, no one can escape ideology 'voluntarily' or 'naturally' ." Regarding this issue, Eagleton explains: "Ideology can include actions like going to the church, voting act or letting the ladies go first; it also comprises not only the conscious preference like the deep love one has for monarchy, but also the way I dress or the type of car I drive, that is, the concept of the deep sub-consciousness that I have for others and myself."[27] Ideology is as thin as the air, but it is pervasive! And because of this, Althusser asserts that the man is an ideological animal by nature. What a pushy assertion this is!

There is a kind of "initial obviousness" regarding the view that you and I are **both subjects**. This obviousness is also a form of self-evidence in an average man's life and needs no introspection, and it is because the self-evidence "commandeers the obviousness" that a "basic ideological effect"[28] is shown. **This is it!** In identifying each other (the material ritual of ideology), you and I are executing a natural and ideological **co-referential capability**.

Althusser remarks: "The writing I am currently executing and the reading you are currently performing are also in this respect rituals of ideological recognition, including the "obviousness" with which the "truth" or "error" of my reflections may impose itself on you."[29] Ideology is thus generalized ever more fiercely by him.

> *(To) recognize that we are subjects and that we function in the practical rituals of the most elementary everyday life (the hand-shake, the fact of calling you by your name, the fact of knowing, even if I do not know what it is, that you "have" a name of your own, which means that you are recognized as a unique subject, etc.) – this recognition only gives us the "consciousness" of our incessant (eternal) practice of ideological recognition – its con-sciousness, i.e. its recognition – but in no sense does it give us the (scientific) knowledge of the mechanism of this recognition.[30]*

---

27   Eagleton: *Literary Theory: An Introduction*, translated by Wu Xiaoming, Xi'an: Shanxi Normal University Press, 1987, p. 189.
28   Althusser, Louis. *Lenin and Philosophy*, p.190.
29   Ibid., p.191. Althusser notes here: "this double 'currently' is one more proof of the fact that ideology is 'eternal', since these two 'currentlies' are separated by an indefinite interval; I am writing these lines on 6 April 1969, you may read them at any subsequent time."
30   Althusser, Louis. *Lenin and Philosophy*, p.191.

Althusser believes **"all ideology hails or interpellates concrete individuals as concrete subjects**, by the functioning of the category of the subject."[31] Interpellation is what Althusser has said about the practice of the material rituals of ideological understanding in the everyday life. He further explicates:

> *Ideology "acts" or "functions" in such a way that it "recruits" subjects among the individuals (it recruits them all), or "transforms" the individuals into subjects (it transforms them all) by that very precise operation which I have called interpellation or hailing, and which can be imagined along the lines of the most commonplace everyday police (or other) hailing: "Hey, you there!"*[32]

As we penetrate into the "clouds" of theoretical confusion, I find that Althusser's interpellation has gone beyond the boundary of Lacan's theory and has misappropriated the French philosopher Lévinas's theory. Lévinas proposes the famous non-violent power of the "other's" image in his book *Totalité et Infini: essai sur l'extériorité*, which was written in 1961. The core idea in this book centers on how the faceless other interpellates the "self" (individual self) everywhere, how the faceless other pulls the "self" into certain relations and forces it to respond. Althusser uses the faceless "other" as ideology, that is, the "Other" placed in a new social and political context. We might still remember that in Lacan's symbolic kingdom, the individual self is interpellates in languages, and the parents, teachers and classmates are looking. Here, the interpellator is the faceless" other": ideology.

Althusser further explains that someday we meet a friend on the street, we greet him, shaking hands and talking, and in this moment, we realize the ideological interpellation. The self-evidence here refers to the understanding that you and I have **always** been subjects and continually practiced the rituals of ideological recognition. This kind of ritual proves that we are truly specific and individual subjects can recognize each other but cannot be replaced.

It is fair in this sense that Althusser will write as follows: "The existence of ideology and the hailing or interpellation of individuals as subjects are one and the same thing."[33] Eagleton criticizes

---

31 Ibid., p.191.
32 Ibid., 1990, pp. 191-192. The Chinese version has been modified.
33 Ibid., p.192.

Althusser's idea of daily interpellation as over-centralized because he does not notice the variety of social interactions.[34] Althusser's argument may seem a bit assertive. At first glance, it is difficult to decipher Althusser's interpretation of ideology. But when we return to Lacan's context, the interpretation reflects a kind of profoundness. Lacan once said that human beings' understanding, in the field of the social dialectics, is decided by the "little reality;" namely, the basic facts of their daily life, or the things that people use to make claims and the tasks that they influence. Althusser's focus is also the little reality of ideology. This critical view by Lacan is also the foundation of Lefebvre's "critique of everyday life."

M. Poster has also commented on Althusser's view in his book *The Second Media Age*. He holds that Althusser is the first one to introduce the concept of "interpellation" into the theory of social criticism.[35] We can actually go back on this understanding. Althusser's theory of the Ideological State Apparatuses (ISAs) enables the concept of interpellation to enter the circle of social critical theory. Poster remarks that on the microscopic level of everyday life, the subject man is formed with language and culture: "it is formed because of the continuous re-structuring of interpellation or 'hailing.' An established linguistic behavior might trigger an elucidating gesture, the way that the gesture functions conceals the position or the gesture itself."[36] In effect, "interpellation is the social invasion of individuals."[37]

It is ironic that ideology (I deem that it is just bourgeois ideology) often does not exist within the ideology. What always functions is the external everyday life. Therefore Althusser writes:

> One of the effects of ideology is the practical de-negation of the ideological character of ideology by ideology: ideology never says, "I am ideological". It is necessary to be outside ideology, i.e. in scientific knowledge, to be able to say: I am in ideology (a quite exceptional case) or (the general case): I was in ideology.[38]

It is needless to say that this discussion is too circuitous and complicated.

---

34   Edited by Zizek: *Illustrations Ideology*, p.283.
35   Poster: The Second Media Age, translated by Fan Jinghua, Nanjing: Nanjing University Press, 2000, p. 130, Note 4.
36   Ibid., p. 113.
37   Ibid., p. 114.
38   Althusser, Louis. *Lenin and Philosophy*, pp.192-193.

3 MIRROR DUPLICATION AND SELF-OBEDIENCE

Althusser thinks that the reason why ideology has a self-evident governing effect is that **the individual always remains the subject**. "That an individual is always-already a subject, even before he is born."[39] This argument is also clearly influenced by Lacan. Here we should recall a paragraph about Lacan's subject recognition that we discussed earlier on. Althusser simply paraphrased it. He said, the birth of a child is an ideological ritual: the child is **expected** in this ideological form (the expectation would be repeatedly interpellated to be present in his life); he would accept the family name and experience the process of recognition and become a unique person. It is like the fictional example of Jack. The child is therefore always-already a subject, appointed as a subject in and by the specific familial ideological configuration in which he is "expected" once he has been conceived.[40]

Althusser raises a famous example here: the mirror copying of the interpellating subject of the Christian ideology. He mentions that Christianity not only speaks through the Bible or the mouth of a preacher, but it also interpellates the subject through religious practices, religious ritual and "sacrament." The God that claims "I am that I am" (the Subject) says through the mouths of the Bible and the preachers: Hey! You are Nikon. It is your name. You were born, and it is your origin, you were created by God. The fact that you were born in the year 2001 does not matter, for it is only your position in this world. Throughout your life from birth until death, if you believe, you will be saved and become part of the mortal body of Jesus. Here, every individual in the ideological framework of Christianity is interpellated as a subject with a body and with a name. In every prayer, every religious service and devout confession, they are told and confirmed: "God is thus the Subject, and Moses and the innumerable subjects of God's people, the Subject's interlocutors-interpellates: his **mirrors**, his **reflections**."[41] This is a marvelous process of ideological configuration in which the Subject* duplicates the subjects and duplicates

---

39   Ibid., p.193.
40   Ibid., pp.193-194.
41   Ibid., p.197. The Chinese version has been modified.
*)   Please notice the big S.

itself as a subject. We should note that Althusser differs from Lacan, since he substituted Lacan's Other (A) with the Subject. In Lacan's theory, the God is the Other in the theological context.

And the matter that Althusser's Subject is dealing with is the job of the previous Other.

Althusser continues to reason: "the structure of all ideology, interpellating individuals as subjects in the name of a Unique and Absolute Subject is **speculary**, i.e. a mirror-structure, and **doubly** speculary: this mirror duplication is constitutive of ideology and ensures its functioning."[42]

This is a strange form of rewriting of Lacan. But the mirror effect, which occurs only in the initial (babyhood)structuring of individual subjects in Lacan's theory, has been transformed into an interior mechanism of the entire operation of ideology. It turns out that Lacan believes that the self = the mirror projection of the other (a' = the mirror image of a), the subject = the remaining trace left behind when the self is restyled into the Other in the process of symbolization (S = A). Instead Althusser changes it so that the Other – which has been transformed by him from a symbolic sign into ideology – directly duplicates the individual subject. This could be both: a misreading or dishonest misappropriation. Althusser holds that the subject is God and various quasi natures (absolute views, existence, human, totality, and doctrines, etc.), and the individuals, which exist in reality, are only the mirror duplications of the master. For him this is the secret of ideology. This is an invisible rotation, in which the mirror duplication – voluntarily or involuntarily – governs the many levels of our life. Barthes once wrote: "All of the social public institutions are duplicated machines: schools, sports, ads, public works, songs, news, are repeating the same structures, meanings, and generally in the same tone: these clichés are political facts and the major image of ideology."[43] Here, Barthes refers to the bourgeois ideology. He also said the self-duplication of the bourgeois ideology always "naturalizes" itself in everyday life, and gradually, but unobtrusively, becomes the "anonymous ideology."[44]

42   Ibid., p.197.
43   Barthes. *The Pleasure of the Text*, p. 51.
44   Barthes: *Mythe–interprétation de la culture populaire*, translated by Xu Qiangqiang & Xu Qiling, Shanghai: Shanghai People's Publishing House, 1999, p. 200.

Althusser thinks that the "duplicate mirror-structure of ideology simultaneously ensures: 1. the interpellation of 'individuals' as subjects; 2. their subordination to the Subject; 3. the mutual recognition between subjects and the Subject*, and also the subjects' recognition of each other, and finally the subject's recognition of himself; 4. the absolute guarantee that everything really is so."[45] This is a rather rough statement because if we follow these clues, we will find that the process of individuals interpellated as subjects is very complex: the interpellation of the parents, teachers and classmates, society, ideology, and in this generation, the most important might be the interpellation of the illusion of media.

Currently in China, the illusionary circumstances of tabloids, TV series and movies have become the model for numerous duplications of individual subjects. However, Althusser only points out the mutual structuring of the individual subject and the ideology (the Self), unless the ideology that we talk about here covers everything. Evidently, Althusser's notions are not flawless in their respective theological logics. Zizek notes that Althusser's theory of interpellation is crude; firstly because he did not explain the relationship between the interpellation and the ISA and secondly, because Althusser did not correctly understand the essence of Lacan's false subject, that, the illusion of subject is the supporter of "reality."[46]

The characteristics of the subject duplicated by the mirror structure are: "1. a free subjectivity, a subject as the center of initiative spirit, a self-controllable and responsible person; 2. an obedient person that subordinates himself to a more superior authority, therefore besides freely accepting the position of being a subject, he is literally deprived of all his freedom." This is the sharp contradiction between the exterior "which looks as if it is true" and its contrast the objective reality. It is worth mentioning here that the moment people fall into the quadruple system of being interpellated as a subject, an obedient subject, mutually recognizable, and absolute guaranteeing, the subject begins to "work," and generally they "work by themselves".

---

45 Althusser, Louis. *Lenin and Philosophy*, p.198. The Chinese version has been modified.
46 Zizek: *The Sublime Object of Ideology*, pp. 61-63.

This idea, subject "working by itself or themselves" is critical, as it uncovers the governing nature of ideology. **"The individual is interpellated as a (free) subject in order that he shall submit freely to the commandments of the Subject, i.e. in order that he shall (freely) accept his subjection, i.e. in order that he shall make the gestures and actions of his subjection 'all by himself'."**[47] Althusser remarks that except for some callous subjects (hostile elements and persons of critical reflection) who might induce the intervention of repressive state apparatuses, the majority of good subjects are free-standing: "they are inserted into practices governed by the rituals of the ISAs. They 'recognize' the existing state of affairs (Germ.: das Bestehende), that 'it really is true that it is so and not otherwise', and that they must be obedient to God, to their conscience, to the priest, to president de Gaulle, to the boss, to the engineer, that thou shalt 'love thy neighbour as thyself', etc."[48] The subjects are merged consciously, voluntarily and willingly into the body of ideological governance. Therefore, "if there is no obedience, there is no subject." The nature of subject is its unconscious self-obedience. Zima, once made a very classical statement, he argued that the value judgment of ideology and the ideology that varies in its degree decide that individuals can act as **subjects**. They **unconsciously** agree with the values and norms that make them the subjects that feel responsible for some behaviors. These theories are of course helpful to understand Althusser's quote: "Ideology interpellates the individual subject."[49] As a matter of fact, I think that Althusser's research on the automatic mechanism of ideology duplicating subjects has unconsciously solved an important problem, that is, the cultural hegemony theory of Gramsci and the critical ideological foundation for a one-dimensional man as proposed by Herbert Marcuse. This is an important issue that needs further discussion.

Consequently, Althusser does raise one concern: what is the most important ideological mechanism for the interpellation of the individual subject?

---

47 Althusser, Louis. *Lenin and Philosophy*, p.199. The Chinese version has been modified.
48 Ibid., pp.198-199. The Chinese version has been modified.
49 Zima. *Manuel de sociocritique*, p.16.

Indeed, what is really in question in this mechanism of the mirror recognition of the Subject and of the individuals interpellated as subjects, and of the guarantee given by the Subject to the subjects if they freely accept their subjection to the Subject's 'commandments'? The reality in question in this mechanism, the reality which is necessarily ignored (méconnue) in the very forms of recognition (ideology = misrecognition/ignorance) is indeed, in the last resort, the reproduction of the relations of production and of the relations deriving from them.[50]

This is the real nature of ideology – the reproduction of certain social production relations. However, this kind of reproduction is no longer repressive, but instead it is automatic and people aspire to it. I see it as the reality behind the bourgeois kingdom of our day.

---

50   Althusser, Louis. *Lenin and Philosophy*, pp.199-200. The Chinese version has been modified.

PART TWO
RE-DIAGNOSE THE HISTORY OF
MARX'S PHILOSOPHICAL THOUGHTS

CHAPTER VIII

NEW INTERPRETATION BY ALTHUSSER:
HIS INNOVATION ON THE METHODOLOGY OF RESEARCH
INTO MARX AND CRITIQUE

CHAPTER IX

THE NEW TEXTUAL RESEARCH INTO THE DEVELOPMENT
OF MARXIST PHILOSOPHICAL THOUGHTS

CHAPTER X

THE MOST IMPORTANT PRINCIPLE OF MARXISM

CHAPTER XI

MARXIST HISTORICAL SCIENCE

CONCLUSION

RAIN OF DECONSTRUCTION:
THE END OF ALEATORY MATERIALISM

CHAPTER VIII

NEW INTERPRETATION BY ALTHUSSER: HIS INNOVATION ON THE METHODOLOGY OF RESEARCH INTO MARX AND CRITIQUE

In part I of this book, we conducted various studies of the several most important core paradigms of Althusser's methodology. In part II, we will naturally turn to Althusser's reflection on Marxist theoretical formations on the basis of methodological innovation. I have mentioned that in the theoretical logic of Western Marxism there exist two major theoretical themes: one is to reinterpret Marx and the other is critique of capitalism.[1] For Althusser, direct critique of capitalism is not the issue which he tends to focus on. Instead, he hopes to construct a brand new theoretical structure and method of inquiry to expose the truth of Marxist philosophy, which is veiled by anthropological ideology. His most significant achievement is renewed research into Marxist philosophy. In his research, Althusser regards the interpretation of the history of philosophy as the "key issue" facing historical research. He is not satisfied with

---

1   See: In-Depth Interpretation: Western Marxism and Lukacs, *Journal of Philosophical Trends*, 1999(8).

traditional interpretations of Marxist philosophical history because, in these interpretations, "we had been made to treat science, a status claimed by every page of Marx, as merely the first-comer among ideologies."[2] In Althusser's opinion, a new interpretation must be established if we want to alter past situations. "I stress this as a crucial point for contemporary interpretations of Marxist philosophy, by which I mean serious, systematic interpretations, based on real philosophical, epistemological and historical knowledge, and on rigorous reading methods."[3] In this chapter, we are going to discuss the new interpretation of Marxist philosophical history that Althusser posed during the mid-1960s.

1 THE WORKS OF YOUNG MARX AS THE SUBJECT OF POLITICAL DISCUSSION

In his *For Marx*, Althusser made a direct attack on the well-known discussion on the nature of the works of Young Marx. He comments that this is a serious "political discussion," but the two sides involved both take the same nonscientific, argumentative positions.

It is well known that for a long time after Marx's death, what most scholars discussed regarding traditional Marxist intellectual history was the published "mature works" of Marx and Engels. The fundamental ideas embodied in *The Holy Family*, *Manifesto of the Communist Party* and *Capital* are the basic principles of Marxism. I once classified these texts as "Text III" of Marxism.[4] This appears to be an incontrovertible assumption. However, between the end of the 1920s and the beginning of the 1930s, this theoretical stereotype was broken. Many of Marx's works, previously almost unknown, were published, including *The German Ideology* and *Economic and Philosophical Manuscripts of 1844*, which I once classified as "Text II." The resulting new works stimulated a new line of thinking, especially *Manuscripts of 1844*, which was published in 1932 garnered the attention of Western academia. In this book, people were surprised to find that the Young Marx turned out to be a philosopher of **anthropology**. This undoubtedly attracted the interest of a great

---

2 Althusser, Louis. *For Marx*, p. 22.

3 Ibid., p. 37.

4 Zhang Yibing. *Back to Marx: The Change of Philosophical Discourse in the Context of Economics*. p. 14. English version published by Göttingen University Press, in 2013.

many Western scholars who first initiated political discussions on the nature of the Young Marx's works.

For these scholars, only the early philosophical works of Marx, especially *Manuscripts of 1844*, can stand for the truth of Marxist anthropological ethics. The later works, such as Marx's *Capital*, only objectify anthropology in concrete forms. This is the so-called, but well-known incident of "the advent of new Marx" launched by Western scholars. More precisely, this viewpoint is merely the explanation given by the Western Marxist anthropology, namely "the second interpretation" that I have identified. But Althusser does not focus on criticizing Western Marxism, which contrasted the Young Marx with the old Marx; in other words, "the first interpretation."[5] Therefore, he writes: "*Capital* is an **ethical** theory, the silent philosophy of which is openly spoken in Marx's Early Works".[6] Obviously, in the eyes of Western scholars, only anthropology can be seen as the authentic logical structure of Marxist philosophy. Althusser once quoted them saying, "a slight alteration in the first sentence of the *Communist Manifesto* would give us: the history of all hitherto existing society is the history of the self-alienation of man".[7] The essence of this issue is as follows:

> *They let Marx be restored to his source, and let him admit at last that in him, the mature man is merely the young man in disguise. Or if he stubbornly insists on his age, let him admit the sins of his maturity, let him recognize that he sacrificed philosophy to economics, ethics to science, man to history. Let him consent to this or refuse it, his truth, everything that will survive him, everything which helps the men that we are to live and think, is contained in these few **Early Works**.*[8]

During this period, Western bourgeois scholars and most Western Marxists and European Leftist thinkers held the following view: Engels, was one of the theorists of the Second International, Lenin by his *Materialism and Empirio-criticism* and Stalin's philosophical interventions had deviated from Marx's original philosophical thinking, and changed the **anthropological** philosophy of Marxism

---

5   Ibid., pp. 3-6.
6   Althusser, Louis. *For Marx*, p. 52.
7   Ibid., p. 52.
8   Ibid., p. 52.

into an abstract **nonhuman** dogma. Therefore, they declared that the so-called "orthodox Marxism," which came into being after Engels, had betrayed Marxist anthropology, and Stalin completely erased the necessity of anthropological Marxism and instead, turned it into a tool of state politics. Thus, Marxism itself became ideology: 'the opium of the people' and a morbid joke.[9] These philosophers of Western Marxism claimed to restore the totality of Marxist philosophy; which – more specifically – was to fundamentally revise Marxist philosophy by means of the logic of anthropology. The most outstanding assertion was E. Fromm's "anthropological Marx" (*Marx's Concept of Man*) and Sartre's "anthropological dialectics" (*Critique of Dialectical Reason*).[10] Faced with this theoretical discussion, Althusser clearly sees that "this is the **location** of the discussion: the Young Marx. Really at stake in it is Marxism itself. The **terms of the discussion**: whether the Young Marx was already and wholly Marx."[11] In truth, a similar dispute also happened in Chinese academia at the end of the 1970s, but the discussion at that time did not reflect back into its own academic research. As I mentioned in the introduction of this book, the emergence of Anthropological Marx during the 1980s was mainly a cultural phenomenon based on emotions exhibited after the Cultural Revolution of China. The end of sub-feudal autocracy of the Cultural Revolution turned humanism into a theory, a theory of humanized Marx, and upheld *Manuscripts of 1844* as its banner. All of sudden, the issue of humanism and alienation became the focus of the academia. However, it is a shame that as the discussion began, the intervention of political ideology constrained such an important discussion and for no reason, but still the problem remained unsolved, and now it is emerging in facets and in different theoretical fields.

In those days of Western Europe faced with this sudden theoretical challenge, Marxists became defensive, including some scholars from the former Soviet Union and European Communist Parties.

---

9   Lefebvre, Henri. *The Survival of Capitalism & Western Marxism*. Published by Beijing: The Central Party School of the Communist Party of China, 1988. p. 296.
10   Fromm, Eric. *Marx's Concept of Man & Western Scholars on Economic and Philosophical Manuscripts of 1844*. Shanghai: Fudan University Press, 1983. Sartre, Jean-Paul. *Critique of Dialectical Reason*. Beijing: The Commercial Press, 1963; Hefei: Anhui Literature and Art Publishing House, 1998.
11   Althusser, Louis. *For Marx*, p. 53.

They represented the antagonists in the ensuing dispute. However, Althusser thinks that since "young Marxists were caught out, ill-prepared for a struggle they had not foreseen. They reacted as best they could. There is some of this surprise left in the present defense, in its reflex movement, its confusion, its awkwardness. I should also add: **in its bad conscience**. For this attack surprised Marxists on their own ground: that of Marx".[12] In Althusser's words, Marxists were ambushed on the battlefield of ideology. Yet in their "counterattack," they still remained within the circle of bourgeois ideology.

What is more disappointing is that, while fighting back, scholars of the former Soviet Union adopted an unscientific position. In taking a **position exactly opposite to bourgeois scholars**, they mistakenly confused Marx with the Young Marx, compared the opinions of Western scholars, and the **logical order** of Marx's works was inversed in their interpretation . Capital was no longer read as *On the Jewish Question*, but *On the Jewish Question* was being read as *Capital*. The shadow of the Young Marx was no longer projected on to Marx, but rather, the shadow of Marx was projected on to the Young Marx. The primary reason for this was that, in traditional research, people only discussed the outstanding Marx with his **published works** (Text of III). Yet when suddenly faced with the numerous and complicated texts of the Young Marx, they panicked and were unable to accept the presence of another **non-Marxist Marx**. I think this represents the biggest drawback of the research problematic in traditional philosophical history researches. We must abandon this inertia and sluggishness of thinking. Thus, due to "a devout fear of a blow to Marx's **integrity** inspires as its reflex a resolute acceptance of **the whole Marx**: Marx is declared to be a whole, '*the Young Marx is part of Marxism*.'"[13] It seems that if we admit the existence of the Young Marx, we will immediately lose the whole Marx. Simply put, people are afraid to turn the Young Marx into an historical object which can be critically assessed. In Chinese academia, we also encountered a similar situation in the ideological beating ("the clearance of ideological contamination") and the embarrassing break in academic discussion at the beginning of 1980s.

---

12   Ibid., p. 53.
13   Ibid., pp. 54-55.

According to Althusser, the "defense" for the whole Marx was a total failure because although it appears opposite to bourgeois humanism; but in essence, the two fighting parties of the dispute were the same. They are the two sides of **one Marx**. Aiming at this point, Althusser begins his own **scientific** defense of Marx.

2 FUTURE ANTERIOR OF TELEOLOGICAL: THE METHODOLOGICAL DEFECTS OF THE RESEARCH ON THE HISTORY OF MARXIST PHILOSOPHY

Althusser points out that the reason why the Soviet scholars' defense of the 'whole Marx' is wrong does not lie in the opinion itself but rather, in the **fundamental paradigm** of traditional Marxist philosophical history. "A pseudo-theory of the history of philosophy in the '**future anterior**' is erected to justify this counter-position, without realizing that this pseudo-theory is quite simply Hegelian."[14] I ask myself is this view by Althusser exaggerated? What is "future anterior" and why does this pseudo-theory wear the hat of Hegelian "pseudo-theory"? Now let us look at Althusser's analysis.

Althusser first quotes the words of Schaff, a famous Polish Marxist philosopher, who clearly objects to Western scholars' taking Marx's early works as the yardstick for evaluation:

> *Marx's work as a whole cannot be seriously understood, nor Marxism itself as thought and as action, on the basis of the conception of his early works he happened to have when he was working them out. Only the opposite approach is valuable, that is, the approach which understands the significance and appreciates the value of these first fruits (?) and enters those creative laboratories of Marxist thought represented by writings such as the* **Kreuznach Notebooks** *and* **Manuscripts of 1844** *via Marxism as we have inherited it from Marx and also – it must be plainly stated – as it has been enriched by a century in the heat of historical practice. In default of this there is nothing to prevent an evaluation of Marx by criteria taken from Hegelianism if not from Thomism.* **The history of philosophy is written in the future anterior: ultimately, a refusal to admit this is a denial of this history and the erection of oneself as its founder in the manner of Hegel.**[15]

---

14 Ibid., p. 54.
15 Ibid., p. 54.

Althusser deliberately used **italics** in this quote, but obviously it is not he who labeled Schaff as "future anterior". Indeed, Althusser makes a very detailed analysis on this interpretation. Althusser wrote:

First and foremost, the key of this interpretation is **theory of sources starting from the origin and the other is the theory of anticipation based on elements theory**. In traditional research related to the history of Marxist philosophy, "only too often the form of the **reading** of Marx's early writings adopted depends more on free association of ideas or on a simple comparison of terms than on a historical critique".[16]

Just like some contemporary readers of today, while reading Marx's *Dissertation* of 1841 they contrast terms ("self-consciousness", "subject") with similar viewpoints espoused by Hegel. While reading *Critique of Hegel's Philosophy of Right*, they compare those viewpoints ("inversion of subject and predicate", "Man is the supreme essence of man") to those of Feuerbach. While reading *Manuscripts of 1844*, they conduct similar studies of its theoretical objects (economic relations and phenomenological criticism) and compare them to *Capital*. However, they ignore the different meanings embedded within each of these terms according to their respective historical contexts. This has been the common problem of theoretical research, but it does not arouse much attention. If classified according to Althusser's theories of reading, this is **Reading I**. People make comparisons for the sole purpose of seeing what the Young Marx has said compared to Hegel and Feuerbach regarding a certain idea, and search in what ways is *Capital* more profound than *Manuscripts of 1844*. In Althusser's opinion, this method of reading is also indispensable for research because it can produce something preliminary that serves as the **guide** for truly understanding the original works. Nevertheless, if people only make simple and superficial comparisons, and regard the piecing together of theoretical **elements** as the ultimate academic achievement, the situation will develop in another direction. This is the so-called "old opinion" within academic research which is popular in orthodox bourgeois colleges. Undoubtedly, Althusser's actions

---

16   Ibid., p. 55.

and words were a heavy blow both against the origin theory view and the cognitive model. Althusser proceeds:

> *Indeed, to stick to spontaneous or even enlightened associa-tion of theoretical elements is to run the risk of remaining the prisoner of an implicit conception only too close to the current academic conception of the comparison, opposition and approxi-mation of elements that culminates in a theory of* **sources** *– or, what comes to the same thing, in a theory of anticipation. A so-phisticated reading of Hegel "thinks of Hegel" when it reads the* **1841 Dissertation** *or even* **Manuscripts of 1844**. *A sophisticated reading of Marx "thinks of Marx" when it reads the* **Critique of the Philosophy of Right**.[17]

These are two historical logics that interact with each other. Althusser explains that **the theory of sources** advocates measuring things or measures the development process of thoughts by the source of an origin, whereas other party **the theory of anticipation** holds that what is at the final point determines the meaning at every stage and the meaning of the whole process. These two methodological logics are the same in nature, namely they are **teleological** only in different forms. The "source" of teleological logic (teleological factors like Marxism and historical materialism as the orientation) actually re-fers to an inversed inference of existing things in reality. The Young Althusser also explored this in *On Content in the Thought of G.W.F. Hegel*. As identified by Yimamura Hitoshi, the concept of "source", the imagined "departure point", starts from the already existent spe-cific explanation and goes back to the past. Therefore, in the sense of things conceived later, source is the product of thinking. Originating from specific purposes and dating back to the past, source is an in-vented imaginary beginning. Both the purpose and origin of source are a fantasy separated from reality.[18]

Secondly, in these two historical research logics there exist three invisible theoretical presuppositions that "function quietly". **The first presupposition is analytic.** According to this **analytic** presup-position, any theoretical system or any constituted thought **can be reducible to its elements.** Under this condition, people are able to make an independent study of some element in a theoretical system

---

17 Ibid., p. 56.
18 Hitoshi, Yimamura. *Althusser: Epistemological Rupture*, p.56.

and compare it with **another** similar element belonging to **another** theoretical **system**. Just like the mistaken division of Marxist philosophy into materialism, dialectics and epistemology in the traditional philosophical framework of interpretation, people separate elements of both contradiction and unity out of its theoretical system, and compare this isolated element with the concept of paradox in Hegel's dialectics in order to find the difference. People also isolate the element of materialist view and compare it with Feuerbach's thoughts.

Althusser says that this is formalism tainted with reductionism and under this reductionism "it seems as if writing the history of Marx's early theoretical development entailed the reduction of his thought into its '**elements**', which is grouped in general under two rubrics: the materialist elements and the idealist elements".[19]

So when trying to understand Marx's philosophical thoughts, people are content to look for these two different elements in Marx's texts. For instance, in the papers of the Young Marx published in *Rheinische Zeitung*, we see the elements of materialism in addition to the idealism of Hegelian philosophy. In the book of *Critique of Hegel's Philosophy of Right*, although we still saw the influence of Feuerbach on Young Marx's views, these views had also contained the element of historical materialism (such as the civil society determines the state and law). Ultimately, "as this procedure enables us to find some **materialist elements** in all Marx's early texts, including even his famous letter to his father in which he refuses to separate the ideal from the real".[20] I think Althusser's analysis corresponds with the traditional research on the history of Marxist philosophy.

Consistency theory, which is similar to reductionism, claims that Marx's views are not consistent in his texts. For example, inconsistency theory claims that the Young Marx established historical materialism in 1843, but argues that he showed inconsistency on some important views such as labor, production and social relations. Additionally, it claims that in *Manuscripts of 1844* the Young Marx had successfully reformed Hegel's idealist dialectics and established materialist dialectics, but he did not consistently apply them to the realm of society and history.

19   Althusser, Louis. *For Marx*, p. 57.
20   Ibid., p. 59.

In Althusser's opinion, "this inconsistency-consistency theory which haunts many a Marxist in ideological history is a little wonder of ideology, constructed for their personal use by the Philosophers of the Enlightenment. Feuerbach inherited and, alas, made good use of it! It deserves a short treatise all to itself, for it is the quintessence of historical idealism."[21] Why is that? Here Althusser quotes the words of N. Lapine, the former Soviet philosopher, an expert in the history of Marxist philosophy, in order to demonstrate:

> This decomposition of a text into what is **already materialist** and what is **still idealist** does not preserve **its unity**, and that this decomposition is induced precisely by reading the early texts through the content of the mature texts. Fully developed Marxism, the Goal are the members of the tribunal which pronounces and executes this judgement, separating the body of an earlier text into its **elements**, thereby destroying its unity.[22]

The **presupposition in the second sentence above is teleological**: it establishes a secret tribunal of history that **judges** the ideas submitted to it, or even dissolves different systems into their elements, then institutes these elements as elements in order to measure them according to its own norms of truth. For example, it uses the theory of surplus value in Marx's *Capital* to measure the maturity of the whole Marx which t is always moving towards the science of political economy. In Althusser's opinion, the most important reason why Marx's thoughts are reduced and dissolved into independent elements is because the implicit logic of this analysis is Hegelian **"theoretical teleological and self-knowledge of ideas."** Moreover, discriminating between elements that are detached from the internal context of thought expressed and conceived in isolation is only possible when the reading of these texts is **slanted**, or **teleological**. Similar to the phenomenon and essence, which is studied and exist independently in Hegelian philosophy and this is only transiting absolute ideas to the ultimate goal, the self-realization of absolute ideas is distributed to every concrete historical formation that it undergoes. Part turns into the whole **pre-suppositionally**. Things that appear under certain conditions are the necessary part of the next emergence. Fundamentally, this exhibits the following characteristic:

---

21 Ibid., p. 72.
22 Ibid., p. 58.

God (reason) realizes its divinity by means of everything that has happened in reality. The traditional interpretation on the history of Marxist ideology is the same. Historical materialism seems to be a presupposed goal. On the way to historical materialism, the Young Marx keeps accumulating the right elements in order to achieve this goal of historical materialism. This is a total presupposition of subjective ideas, which is the Gestalt of the history of **implicit materialist** philosophy. So it appears that Althusser's above labeling is not too excessive.

Thirdly , Althusser indicates that "these two presuppositions depend on a third, which regards the history of ideas as its own element, maintains that nothing happens there which is not a product of the history of ideas itself and that the world of ideology is **its own principle of intelligibility**".[23] The Young Marx's texts in the Gestalt of traditional research on Marxist philosophical history are actually governed by criteria outside the real intellectual history. People always assume that the Young Marx should inevitably evolve into Marxism, and only when the elements included in these works are absorbed into the whole of Marxism can the meaning of these works be grasped. In this "analytico-teleological", a presupposed idea precedes analysis. Althusser clearly points out:

> *The analytico-teleological way merely **judges itself, recognizes itself behind the objects it considers**, that it **never moves outside itself**, that the development it hopes to think it cannot definitively think other than as a **development of itself within itself**? And to anyone whose response to the ultimate logic that I have drawn from this method is to say **that is precisely what makes it dialectical** – my answer is **Dialectical, yes, but Hegelian**![24]*

After negating the analytico-teleological that divides theoretical texts into different parts, Althusser requires us to pay careful attention to the **unity** shown in the development of Marxist thoughts, especially the constructed theoretical framework of the internal unity of text and the internal essence of thought, which is the **problematic** we have elaborated in Part I.

---

23   Ibid., p. 57.
24   Ibid., p. 60.

It should be said that in contrast to the traditional interpretation of the history of Marxist philosophical thoughts, the key to Althusser's new interpretation requires us to find the **implicit theoretical Gestalt used by thinkers to pose, analyze and solve questions**. In traditional research, people tend to focus more on the theoretical goal of writers rather than **how they achieve** this goal. For instance, when they are faced with Feuerbach's philosophy, people like to approve his definition of man. They roam in Feuerbach's texts, and from time to time pick up some dazzling "pearls or jewels" of "man", "subject", "alienation of species being" and so on. However, although they take great pains to extract these important concepts from Feuerbach's text, they do not and cannot ask how these concepts are constructed. The bright spots of these "pearls or jewels" of "man", "subject", "alienation of species being" are left behind while significant intellectual exploration is neglected. Instead, there is a focus on the trifles and a complete disregard of the essentials. "It arises because they do not succeed in conceiving what it is that constitutes the basic unity of a text, the internal essence of an ideological thought, that is, its **problematic**."[25] In fact, the most important part of a thinker's thoughts or a classical text is not the divided elements, but the **internal mode of thinking** that can govern theoretical viewpoints, integrate intellectual elements, and construct the whole of thoughts. Althusser comments:

> *This modification in the modality of a reflection, this restructuration of the problematic of an ideology can proceed by many other routes than that of the simple immediate relation of object and reflection! So anyone who still wants to pose the problem of elements in this perspective must recognize that everything depends on a question which must have priority over them: the question of* ***the nature of the problematic which is the starting-point for actually thinking them****, in a given text.*[26]

We are familiar with this discussion and critical thinking surrounding problematic, argued by Althusser. We also know that if we want to achieve this, only symptomatic reading can penetrate the words on the surface so that we may grasp important blanks and gaps concealed within the text. And only in this way can the deep theoretical

---

25 Ibid., p. 66.
26 Ibid., p. 68.

production mode, namely problematic, be presented. It can be said that Althusser directly identifies the symptomatic reading of problematic as the "new interpretation" for him to reconstruct the understanding of Marxist philosophical thoughts. In Althusser's opinion, only a new theoretical paradigm can grasp the authentic process of development of Marx's thoughts because "the deeper unity of the thought (its problematic) casts light on their theoretical elements, and the acquisitions of Marx's actual experience (his history; his discoveries) illuminate the development of this problematic".[27]

If we grasp this point, all the three mistaken theories based on element choosing, teleology and the presupposition of ideas will completely be dissolved, and this will become the "fourth interpretation"[28] on Marxism represented by Althusser.

3 MARX IS NOT AN INBORN MARXIST

Althusser lays bare the truth by saying that "the application of Marxist theory to Marx himself appears to be the absolute precondition of an understanding of Marx and at the same time as the precondition even of the constitution and development of Marxist philosophy".[29] This is undoubtedly true. Actually, taking the unorthodox position of Western Marxism, Althusser claims that "Marxism is not the *truth of* in the Hegelian and Feuerbachian sense, but a discipline of scientific investigation, Marxism need be no more embarrassed by its own genesis than by the historical movement it has marked by its intervention".[30] To be honest, Marxism is not absolute truth and Marx is not an inborn Marxist. This should have been a common sense viewpoint in the research of history of Marxism. However, in traditional Gestalt of research on Marxism, this common sense is usually not accepted.

If we can get rid of the presupposition of the teleological, the historical truth can only be: **there was a time when Marx was not a Marxist**. Besides, we can say **Marx has also written non-Marxist texts**. In class, I often mention that in the book, titled **Karl Marx**

27   Ibid., p. 84.
28   Zhang Yibing. *Back to Marx*, pp. 3-6. , pp. 7-8.
29   Althusser, Louis. *For Marx*, p. 38.
30   Ibid., p. 63.

and Frederick Engels, there is also non-Marxist content, and even a content of idealist mistakes. But after hearing what I say, the students, whose minds have long been poisoned by ideological dogmas, feel very shocked. Objectively speaking, before 1845, Marx had never thought about establishing a theory called Marxism, or becoming a Marxist in the future. And among the numerous texts written before 1845, he also did not expect that they included the Marxist "element" which we identify later. I regard this as a very correct and important viewpoint.

Regarding this issue, Althusser quotes from Hoeppner: "Hoeppner calmly brings this into perspective in his article ('*A propos du passage de Hegel à Marx*', *Recherches*, p. 180): 'History must not be studied from the front backwards, searching from the heights of Marxist knowledge its ideal germs in the past. The evolution of philosophical thought must be traced on the basis of the real evolution of society.'"[31] This is indeed a sharp warning that can awaken us.

In truth, if we can escape from the ideological realm of the traditional interpretative framework of philosophy, this will become common sense. "**Even philosophers** are young men for a time. They must be born somewhere, some time, and begin to think and write."[32]

When those great thinkers were born, their first cry was not necessarily different from ordinary people. Before they become giants, they were young and then had to grow up. They were once childish, made mistakes, or did not write very outstanding works at the beginning. According to Althusser, some people think that we should never publish the works written in our youth, or even write them in the first place. However, in the preface of this book, we have observed that Althusser himself is a double-minded man because he successfully suspends the works of his youth and also does not publish those works finished in his later years. This is rather ridiculous. How do we know we can be great minds in future? Everything has its beginning. Should we deny the gloom of the beginning for the brightness at the top? Sun Bokui once told me not to publish immature works. He also said that philosophers had better not publish their works until they are in their forties. Otherwise, after reading what you wrote

31 Ibid., p. 54.
32 Ibid., pp. 63-64.

earlier people might say, "Oh, he is terrible!" However, I am a diso-
bedient student and have published quite a few of my "bad" things.

"People are unable to choose their beginnings!" This is exactly
the viewpoint of Marxist historical materialism. The original meaning of this sentence is that people are unable to choose their productive forces.[33] Therefore, "Marx did not choose to be born into the
thought German history had given to him in his university education, nor to think its ideological world: German Ideology. He grew
up in this world, in it he learned to live and move, with them he
'settled accounts', from them he liberated himself."[34] In Heidegger's
words, Marx was thrown into German ideology during the first half
of the 19th century. Thus, "it is impossible to think the unity of an
individual's thought while ignoring its ideological field, if this field
is itself to be thought it requires the thought of this **unity**.[35] This
makes good sense.

> *Understanding an ideological argument implies, at the level of
> the ideology itself, simultaneous, conjoint knowledge of the **ide-
> ological field** in which a thought emerges and grows; and the
> exposure of the internal unity of this thought: its **problematic**.
> Knowledge of the ideological field itself presupposes knowledge
> of the problematics compounded or opposed in it. This interrela-
> tion of the particular problematic of the thought of the individ-
> ual under consideration with the particular problematics of the
> thoughts belonging to the ideological field allows of a decision
> as to its author's specific difference.[36]*

Similarly, if we want to study the ideological development of Marx,
we must locate ourselves in the **ideological world** of the Young
Marx, think deeply, and seize the intellectual movement of Marx at
the moment he begins communicating with the prevalent thoughts in
that era. This is the vertical mode often used in structuralism.

Meanwhile, Althusser indicates that when focusing on an ideological movement we must be aware of the following question: "it is as if
the authors of these thoughts were themselves **absent**. The concrete

---

33   See: *Karl Marx and Frederick Engels*. Beijing: People's Publishing House, 1972.
pp. 477-478.
34   Althusser, Louis. *For Marx*, p. 64.
35   Ibid., p. 66.
36   Ibid., p. 70.

individual who expresses himself in his thoughts and his writings is absent, so is the actual history expressed in the existing ideological field."[37] Here we see the nothingness of subject favored by Althusser appears again. This is a **double absence**. Why? Under any historical condition thinkers are masked by their works. It is only through their works that people are able to observe the rigorous thoughts of thinkers. Besides, the history is also veiled by the ideology of the time. People are only able to observe the ideological system. For a thinker, what people see are his dazzling works. Most of these works have been repeatedly embellished. Some of them are even created in order to cater to the times. As a result, the primary authenticity of the work disappeared very early on. Similarly, the true history will never be displayed directly. It is always disguised and veiled consciously or unconsciously by specific ideological presentational relations.

Thinking further on the Young Marx who could not be an inborn Marxist, Althusser indicates that every thinker will start thinking and writing in a given world, which is the **ideological** world of the time. Marx is not an exception. For Marx, this world was the world of German ideology during the 1830s and 1840s. The core ideological structure at that time was the philosophical problematic of German idealism. In Althusser's opinion, the world of the German ideology was the world most crushed by its own ideology, the ideological world farthest from historical reality, the most mystified, and the most alienated world that ever existed in European ideological worlds. This claim makes sense to some extent. The Young Marx was **aleatorily** born in this world and took up thinking.

> We tend too easily to project Marx's later consciousness on to this epoch and, as has been said, to write this history in the 'future anterior', when it is not a matter of projecting a consciousness of self on to another consciousness of self, but of applying to the content of an enslaved consciousness the scientific principles of historical intelligibility (not the content of another consciousness of self) later acquired by a liberated consciousness.[38]

This paragraph still criticizes the traditional research method on the history of Marxist philosophy. In Althusser's eyes, when he was born, the Young Marx was **beneath an enormous layer of ideology,**

---

37   Ibid., p. 64.
38   Ibid., p. 75.

and he succeeded in **breaking through this crushing layer**.[39] The historical liberation and rebirth of Marx was of great significance. According to Althusser's analysis, Marx once declared that the French had political minds, the English economic minds, while the Germans had **theoretical** minds. "The counterpart to Germany's **historical underdevelopment was an ideological and theoretical 'over-development'** incomparable with anything offered by other European nations. But the crucial point is that this theoretical development was an **alienated ideological** development, without concrete relation to the real problems and the real objects which were **reflected in it**."[40] In particular, the Hegelian philosophy, which was the encyclopedia of knowledges of the 18th century, embodied this "developed" ideology. During the second half of the 18th century and the mid-19th century, the whole of German academia was almost governed by this idealist, philosophical ideology. The precondition of liberation was to rediscover real history and real objects, beyond this enormous layer of ideology which had hemmed them in, distorted them, and reduced them to their shades. Thus, "Marx was inevitably obliged to realize that Germany's **ideological overdevelopment** was at the same time in fact an expression of her **historical underdevelopment**, and that therefore it was necessary to retreat **from** this ideological flight forwards in order to reach the things themselves, to touch real history and at last come face to face with the beings that haunted the mists of German consciousness."[41]

Thus, a new meaning comes into being by Althusser.

4 "SUPERSESSION", "INVERSION" OR "RETREAT" OF ALTHUSSER?

We have seen that Althusser adopts the eye-catching word **"retreat"** and he emphasizes that it is used only "after consideration." I find that the "theory of retreat" criticizes two famous arguments in the traditional research methodology on the history of Marxist philosophy: One is transcendentalism (supersession) and the other is inversion. After careful deliberation, this idea really enlightens those who are benighted.

---

39   Ibid., p. 74.
40   Ibid., pp. 75-76.
41   Ibid., p. 76.

First of all, Althusser clearly objects to **supersession**. In previous research into Marxist philosophical history, people usually mentioned that Marx surpasses Hegel and Feuerbach; for example, Marx crafted dialectics to gain the materialist basis to transcend Hegel's idealist materialism, and additionally, Marx combined materialism with dialectics to transcend Feuerbach's old materialism. This supersession logic "tends to suggest some **continuous** pattern of development, or at least a development whose discontinuities themselves should be thought within the same **element of continuity** sustained by the **temporality** of history itself (the story of Marx and his time)."[42] Based on the above discussion of epistemology, we know about the concept that Althusser has learned from Bachelard, namely his idea to **focus on the rupture in a continuous process**.

Naturally, Althusser begins to clearly reject the transcendental **evolutionary** development mode of ideological history. He thinks that in the revolutionary leap of Young Marx's thoughts, the essence of this incident is not the internal continuity in the history of his ideas but its achievement of epistemological rupture. This is because Marx returns to the real from the ideal rather than try to advance concepts (like "dialectics" or "materialism").

This rupture theory is the core of Althusser's "fourth interpretation". Not eager to become a good philosopher, Althusser intends to call on the proletariat to revolutionize **from reality**. Therefore, Althusser comments that without this **retreat**, the story of the Young Marx's liberation is incomprehensible; without this **retreat**, Marx's relationship to German ideology, and especially to Hegel, is incomprehensible; without this return to real history (which was also a retreat to some extent) the Young Marx's relationship to the labor movement will remain a mystery.

Apparently, we can say that Althusser evaluates **the transcendental development within the history of ideas and secondly the rupture from ideas to reality** as extremely important methodological issues in the research of philosophical history. For this, Althusser gives two examples.

---

42   Ibid., pp. 76-77.

First, in his preliminary economic research, Marx retreats to the pre-Hegelian. Althusser comments that one of Hegel's secrets lies in that he draws nourishment from English economics and French politics, namely the English market economy after the Industrial Revolution as well as the French Revolution. Hegel mystifies Idea into the internal essence of these two historical reforms. Lukacs is the first to identify this crucial theoretical fact, which is analyzed further in the book *Back to Marx: The Philosophical Discourse in the Economic Context*.[43] Althusser has a very important viewpoint here. He thinks that the essence of the problematic of German ideology was its distorting true historical problems into **philosophical** problems. Thus Marx's falsification of ideology is characterized by retreating from philosophy to real history. In *The German Ideology*, Marx repeatedly emphasizes that German ideology answers all theoretical questions except **the relationship between theory and real history**. In Althusser's opinion, in 1843 the Young Marx began reading historical works about the French Revolution and works on economics in order to discover the reality of those objects as studied by Hegel. So to a very great extent, "Marx's return to the theoretical products of the English and French eighteenth century was a real **return to the pre-Hegelian**, to the **objects themselves** in their reality".[44]

Here there does not exist the supersession of Marx over Hegel. If "supersession" is used, "**it was not a supersession of error towards its truth, on the contrary, it was a supersession of illusion towards its truth, or better to say, rather than a 'supersession' of illusion towards truth, in fact it was a dissipation of illusion and a retreat from the dissipated illusion back towards reality**: the term 'supersession' is thus robbed of all meaning".[45]

This is an important definition. According to Althusser, there does not exist the supersession of error towards its truth within the history of ideas regarding the relationship between Marx and Hegel and Feuerbach's philosophy because Marx does not intend to amend the Ideas but rather, he tries to enable the illusion that exists beyond idealist ideology return to reality from idealism. Althusser gives us

---

43   Zhang Yibing. *Back to Marx: The Change of Philosophical Discourse in the Context of Economics*, p. 69, English version published by Göttingen University Press, 2014.
44   Althusser, Louis. *For Marx*, p. 77.
45   Ibid., p. 78.

the following opinion on this matter:

> *Even within his ideological consciousness the Young Marx dem-*
> *onstrated an exemplary critical insistence: an insistence on con-*
> *sulting the **originals** which Hegel had discussed. But with Marx*
> *himself, this 'retreat' ultimately lost the retrospective aspect of*
> *a search for the **original** in the form of an **origin**, as soon as*
> *he returned to German history itself and destroyed the illusion*
> *of its "backwardness", that is, thought it in its reality without*
> *measuring it against an external model as its norm. This **retreat***
> *was therefore really the current **restoration, recuperation and***
> ***restitution** of a reality which had been stolen and made unrecog-*
> *nizable by ideology.*[46]

Secondly, Marx discovers the **working class** while retreating from
the ideal to the historical reality. Althusser says that Marx's retreat
from ideology towards reality came to coincide with the discovery
of a radically new reality. The radically new reality refers to the discovery of developed capitalism and an organized working class. He
thinks that "Marx's double discovery played a decisive part in the
Young Marx's intellectual evolution: the discovery beneath the ideology which had deformed itself from **the reality it referred to** –
and the discovery beyond contemporary ideology, **which knew it
not, of a new reality**".[47] Discovery beyond contemporary ideology
is the developed capitalism and an organized working class

I think that Althusser's analysis has significant rationality. However,
there is also an arbitrary metaphysics embedded within his analysis. The
revolution of Marxism is the return to reality from idealism (no matter,
it contained the Young Hegel Movement's theory of self-consciousness
and/or it contained the anthropological, transcendental, logic in the
Manuscripts of 1844) to historical reality, but for him it will not directly
contradict with the materialist philosophy that develops in the thought
course of Marx. If we remove Althusser's structural arbitrariness in his
above analysis, then the truth of the development of Marxism will be
the dialectical unity of discontinuity (revolution) and continuity. I guess
this is the most crucial and the most fundamental difference between
Althusser's structural problematic and that of Sun* and myself.

---

46   Ibid., p. 79.
47   Ibid., p. 81.
*)   Sun Bokui, is the tutor of the author whom he dedicated this book. He is a bright
member of second generation of Marxist philosophers in China.

Secondly, Althusser contests another important idea of historical Marxist methodology, which is the well-known **theory of inversion**. In truth, the Young Althusser has explored this in *On Content in the Thought of G.W.F. Hegel*. He clearly points out that the methodology of inversion is impossible to really change the old philosophy, such as Hegelian philosophy[48] In traditional Marxist historical research, especially in the historical study of development of materialist dialectics, people usually regard the establishment of Marxist materialist dialectics as the inversion of Hegelian dialectics. This is according to the famous statement made in the second edition of *Capital*. To be specific, people often invert Hegel's idealist dialectics as materialist dialectics, invert absolute idea as substance, and replace his rational trick (cunning of the rational by Hegel) with objective laws. It seems for them that in this way Hegel will naturally be transformed into Marx.

According to Althusser's analysis, in the understanding of the "inversion" of Hegel's dialectics as claimed by Marx, in fact what actually changes is **only the concept itself**. What Hegel referred to as absolute spirit and rational logic are now respectively called "substance" and "objective laws". The essence of Hegelian philosophy has not really changed. It seems that a confusing merry-go-round is occurring, but actually the confusion is just the interchange of terms with terms. He comments on this issue:

> *This is the basic logic implied by the famous theme of the "inversion", the "setting back on to its feet" of the Hegelian philosophy (dialectic), for if it were really a matter merely of an inversion, a restoration of what had been upside down, it is clear that to turn an object right round changes neither its nature nor its content by virtue merely of a rotation! A man on his head is the same man when he is finally walking on his feet. And a philosophy inverted in this way cannot be regarded as anything more than the philosophy reversed except in theoretical metaphor: in fact, its structure, its problems and the meaning of these problems are still haunted by the same problematic.[49]*

---

48   Hitoshi, *Althusser*, pp. 86-87.
49   Althusser, Louis. *For Marx*, p. 73.

Although this inversion methodology inverts the speculative philosophy of idealism, the problematic used by Hegel to pose and analyze questions is unchanged. Thus whatever it is called, it is still the speculative philosophy of idealism, it is the changed visible idealism into the **invisible** idealism. Here, "inversion" seems to be an inversion of the sense of the dialectic, but it does not touch the dialectic itself. Althusser says that the "inversion" here is not a real inversion, but this term is used as a form of metaphor to describe the real transformation to materialist dialectic.[50] While writing the preface of *Capital*, Marx used an inappropriate metaphor that could cause misunderstanding.

> So I think that, in its approximation, this metaphorical expression – the "inversion" of the dialectic – does not pose the problem of **the nature of the objects** to which a **single method** should be applied (the world of the Idea for Hegel – the real world for Marx), but rather the problem of the **nature of the dialectic** considered itself; that is, the problem of its **specific structures**; not the problem of the inversion of the "sense" of the dialectic, but that of the **transformation of its structures**.[51]

In Althusser's opinion, Marx does not completely accept some of the basic structures of Hegelian dialectics. Even on the basis of his materialism, Marx's dialectics still **has a structure different from Hegel's**. This shocking affirmation includes all the characteristics of Althusser's thinking. He thinks that, after tremendous effort, he has proved the authentic context of questions and in the process, reformed the whole system instead of just transforming a concept. The inversion as discussed by Marx actually includes the revolution of problematic.[52]

Or said in the words of Hoeppner: "Marx did not reach his solution by resorting to the manipulation of the Hegelian dialectic, but essentially on the basis of very concrete investigations into history, sociology and political economy . . . the Marxist dialectic was in its essentials born of the new lands which Marx cleared and opened up

---

50   Althusser, Louis. *Soutenance d'Amiens*. Cited from *Research Material on Marxism and Leninism*. People's Publishing Press, 1986. p. 303.
51   Althusser, Louis. *For Marx*, p. 93.
52   Althusser, Louis. *Reading Capital*, p.69.

for theory . . . Hegel and Marx did not drink from the same source."[53] The source refers to the problematic. Marx did not turn around and drink from Hegel's source. Instead, he established a new source in the fertile lands of the humanities. This metaphor by Hoeppner is really quite unique.

By understanding this issue, Althusser shows his profundity. He clings to the symptom of the traditional research on history of Marxist philosophy, namely the **simple inversion of concepts**. Nevertheless, Althusser denies Marx's comments that his dialectics is an **ontological** inversion of Hegel's idealist dialectics. Althusser considers Marx's comments as irrational arguments that ignore facts. Inversion does exist, but it is the inversion of theoretical logic rather than a simple inversion of ideas Here, Lenin's understanding of this point is both right and precise.[54]

---

53   Althusser, Louis. *For Marx*, p. 77.
54   See: *The Selected Works of Zhang Yibing*. Ningxia: Guangxi People's Publishing House, 1999. pp. 24-25, and Lenin Revisited (English version) pp. 121-122, published by Canut International, London-Berlin, 2012.

CHAPTER IX

THE NEW TEXTUAL RESEARCH INTO THE DEVELOPMENT OF MARX'S PHILOSOPHICAL THOUGHTS

The new historical research and interpretations of the development of Marx's philosophy occupy an important part in Althusser's monograph, *For Marx*, and this work marks his debut into European academia.[1] Due to Althusser's new cognitive style and methodology on problematic and Lecture Symptomale, research into Marx's thoughts has been significantly deepened. The division between ideology and science constitutes Althusser's criteria regarding the division of the different stages in the development of Marxist philosophy. For the first time in research into the development history of Marxist philosophy, Althusser explicitly proposes that there exists a shift from the period before history to the scientific period. More specifically, this represents a shift from the humanistic ideology to

---

1   Yimamura Hitoshi once said "Heidegger acknowledges the contribution that Nietzsche made in western metaphysics and completed the re-interpretation of the works of Heidegger. Althusser has made similar contributions to Marxism." This comment is quite sensible. See: Yimamura Hitoshi: *Althusser: Epistemological Rupture*, pp. 43-44.

the science of Marxism (historical materialism). The completion of the shift is realized via the "epistemological rupture" of Young Marx, which occurred in 1845. The significance of Althusser's division is that *Manuscripts of 1844*, though highly praised by Western humanist Marxism, is still a work of ideology which was edited and composed before Althusser shifted toward the science of Marxism. However, the establishment of the science of Marxism is based on the total abandonment of the humanistic framework presented in *Manuscripts of 1844*. To some degree, Althusser's argument shakes the very foundation on which humanistic theory is based. This accounts for the significance of his theory.[2]

I, however, must point out that Althussser's interpretation of the development of Marxism seems to be both metaphysical and dogmatic. The flaws inherent in structuralist logic, corrupt the accuracy and objectivity of Althusser's academic research.

1 THE NEW DIVISION ON THE HISTORY OF MARX'S THOUGHTS

According to Althusser, the establishment of Marxism begins with *Theses on Feuerbach* (Hereinafter referred to as "*Theses*") and this work marks ideology's detachment from the science of Marxism. However, Althusser is not the first to find that this is the case. Engels has already regarded Theses as the origin of the new outlook of historical materialism. However, the division that Engels made between humanistic ideology and Marxism is both vague and generally unknown because the logical framework of evolutionary teleology in research becomes dominant after the period of the Second International. The founding of Marxism was artificially moved to 1843. This is particularly true for research that originated in the Soviet Union and countries in Eastern Europe because they were constrained by Lenin's framework of the history of Marxism (Lenin did never get access to the later published monographs written by Young Marx). So these scholars insisted on a theory that was not well grounded. They regarded Marx (at the time when *Pariser Hefte*

---

2 Yimamura Hitoshi once said that the publishing of *For Marx* and *Reading Capital* are the two important books that re-write and re-interpret the history of Marxism. There is nothing exaggerated in this comment. See: Yimamura Hitoshi: *Althusser: Epistemological Rupture*, pp. 43-44.

(*Paris Notes*) was not yet composed) as Young Marx, and Young Marx was still under the influence of Hegel. They also believed that Marx began to shift towards neo-materialism and communism (they could not be certain whether it was a shift towards Marxism) during the summer of 1843. This shift continued up until *Theses* and did not stop until it reached *The German Ideology* in the autumn of 1845. In this way, the founding of Marxism was a **progressive** process for them.. Here, the method, or "human anatomy is the key to monkey anatomy", as Marx put it, is distorted as "human anatomy is monkey anatomy". In this way, the significance of Marx's 1845 methodological revolution was greatly weakened. As a result, Althusser's division becomes significant. It should also be pointed out that there exists a general imbalance in Althusser's research into Marxist philosophy. He always had a penetrative insight into methodology, but he never practiced what he preached; he made right-to-the-point criticisms on texts and history but he never bothered to find first-hand texts. As a result of this imbalance, we should explore the theoretical background, historical context and additional text identification. Of course, this also reflects the basic difference between his research and ours.[3]

Althusser believes that there is an unequivocal "epistemological rupture" in Marx's work. In fact, this rupture occurs at the point where Marx himself locates it. More specifically, it is noted in the book, *The German Ideology*, which remained unpublished during his lifetime and is a critique of his erstwhile philosophical conscience. In fact, the two texts, *The German Ideology* and *Theses on Feuerbach*, are essentially the same. The Theses was written in the spring (April) of 1845, while *The German Ideology* was begun to be written in the autumn of the same year. Though there are some differences in the content of the two texts, the differences are not fundamental. Therefore, according to Althusser, this "epistemological rupture" divides Marx's thought into two long but very distinct periods: the **"ideological" period** and the **scientific** period. Two points must be made explicit here. First, this new division suggests that Althusser has come up with a new division criterion: **the empirical logic (be) versus the critical logic (should be)**. According

---

3   Zhang Yibing. *Back to Marx*, pp.7-8.

to the empirical logic, facts should be faithfully followed; but facts are the target of criticism according to critical logic. To put it simply, Althusser sees the two logics as science and ideology, respectively. Therefore, Althusser rejects the subject (agent) in his analysis of Marx's thoughts. Instead, he focuses on the problematic of "be" or "should be" in the condition of existence. In previous sections, I have already identified this logic as a flawed one. Second, Althusser regards Marx's pre-1845 thoughts as ideology. Althusser's insight here stands as a great theoretical innovation. This argument can be likened to a powerful bomb, which shocks humanists devoted to Young Marx's *1844 Manuscript*. It smashes the illusion, which Soviet scholars tried to maintain, that Marx's thoughts are unified from beginning to end. I think Althusser's division makes sense to some degree, but it is again a metaphysical division. The fact is that before 1845, ideology is not the whole story. In the following sections, we will make a clear examination of this issue.

Althusser's arguments are as follows:

Firstly, "there is an unequivocal 'epistemological rupture' in Marx's work which does in fact occur at the point where Marx himself locates it: in the book, unpublished in his lifetime, which stands as a critique of his erstwhile philosophical conscience: *The German Ideology*."[4] By saying "Marx himself locates it in the book: *The German Ideology*," Althusser is referring to the fact that Marx once said, "it is clearing of his past belief" referring to *The German Ideology. The Theses on Feuerbach*, which is only several sentences long, marks the advent of this rupture. Strangely, Althusser always underestimates *The Theses* without providing any particular reasons as to why. In previous discussions, we have talked about the meaning of "epistemological rupture" in Bachelard's original context. Therefore, it is easy for us to understand that, here, Althusser simply wants to exaggerate the significance of the methodological revolution in 1845. Of course, the theory of rupture directly negates the notion of a "unified Marxism" (from *1844 Manuscripts* to *Capital*) held by Humanists. The theory of rupture is also different from the traditional argument that Marxism is **a "great theoretical revolution" in continuity**. It is a **rupture** of two thoughts that are different

---

4 Althusser, Louis. *For Marx*, p.33.

in nature. To put it simply, it is a Gestalt shift between two problematics. Althusser's argument on this point makes sense except for the adoption of the term "rupture."

Secondly, this "rupture." leads to two different results: "by founding the theory of history (historical materialism), Marx simultaneously broke with his erstwhile philosophy and established a new philosophy (dialectical materialism)."[5] Althusser always divides Marxism into two parts: philosophy, namely dialectical materialism and science, namely historical materialism. However, I find that Althusser never clearly stated the relationships and differences between the two parts despite his elaborations on the issue.

Thirdly, Marx's thoughts can be divided into two periods: "the 'ideological' period before, and the scientific period after the rupture in 1845."[6] If we go into detail, these two periods can be divided into four stages.

Stage One (1840-1845) is the period of **Young Marx**. Althusser claims that all the works that are written during this period are "ideological works". The ideological works involve everything that Marx wrote from his Doctoral *Dissertation* to *Manuscripts of 1844* and *The Holy Family*. Althusser treats these ideological works as **unscientific** works. At that time, this judgment was quite sensational. He also further divided this stage into several periods, which will be mentioned in our later discussions.

Stage Two (1845) is the so-called **rupture period**. In The Theses and *The German Ideology*, Marx ruptures with the theory in which history and politics are all reduced to the essence of man. This is one of the most important "epistemological ruptures" in Marx's thought, and this is the rupture to which Althusser wants to call our attention. **It is the rupture of scientific problematic from ideological problematic**. Althusser says: "In fact, The German Ideology is a commentary, usually a negative and critical one, on the different forms of the ideological problematic Marx had rejected."[7] This argument is, without a doubt, accurate.

---

5   Ibid., p.33.
6   Ibid., p.34.
7   Ibid., p.34.

Stage Three (1845-1857) is the **transitional period**. During this period, Marx wrote a series of works including the first draft of *Capital*, *The Poverty of Philosophy* and the *Manifesto*. At this stage, Marx devoted himself to theoretical innovation. "But from *The Poverty of Philosophy*, this clearing takes place in the realm of science. Proudhon used to be regarded as the great proletarian theorist, but now his false scientific ideas became the target of this 'clearing'."[8]

In our research into the history of Marx's thoughts, we call this the transitional period. Transitional, to some degree, means **immature**. The reason why Althusser renders *Manifesto* and *Capital* as immature is that they still bear a Hegelian influence, but I disagree with him in this aspect, and I will elaborate on this later.

The Fourth stage (1857-1883) is the **mature period**. Works in this period include all the works after 1857. Among them, Althusser prefers *Critique of the Gotha Program* and *A Comment on A. Wagner's Textbook of Political Economics* and he even regards them as representational of Marx's scientific framework. He never offers a convincing explanation for this strange comment, though.

In general, Althusser is correct in his division of the different periods of the establishment and development of Marx's thoughts. He focuses on the three stages of the establishment and development of Marxism and its internal logic. This represents significant theoretical progress for both traditional research into Marxism and the Western studies on the history of Marxism. However, there are also some flaws in his analysis.

Firstly, he regards the establishment of Marxism as a kind of rupture, which is a type of metaphysical thinking, that I have mentioned before. It is true that Marxism does go through a fundamental revolution in 1845, but it is the result of the development of history. The new world outlook is nothing like Sister Lin who comes from heaven and who suddenly appears as a new family member in *A Dream in Red Mansions* by Cao Xueqing. Professor Sun Bokui once discussed this with me. There existed two heterogeneous logics (two opposite theoretical frameworks) in Young Marx's thoughts. One is the alienated historical thought of humanism, and the other is the

---

8   Ibid., p.223.

scientific thought originating from reality. Before 1845, the former was dominant but the later was also active though to a lesser extent. The contrast between the two logics reached its peak around 1844. Then in 1845, the Gestalt shifted from the former to the latter. From the above analysis, we can see that Althusser's own analysis ignores the complex process of waxing and waning of the two internal logics. This can serve as proof to the fact that Althusser's research model is the **"mono-logic linear logic"**, which is criticized by Bakhtin. In the theory of "epistemological rupture", Althusser only replaces one mono-logic discourse with another discourse. Obviously, Althusser, who is influenced by structuralism, cannot understand the **"polytonality"** in the development of a theory. The music of the Aeolian bells is made by the mixture of the polytonal tic sounds of different bells.[9] Secondly, there is a deadly flaw in Althusser's division of the history of Marxist thoughts. He ignores the fact that Marx's thoughts were put forward to serve practices. The development of Marxism is not only a theoretical development, but it is also the reflection of the proletariat revolution. Thirdly, we can find traces of methodological imperialism in Althusser's rupture theory. He rejects the subject philosophy and limits himself from subject and blocks his road with the contrast between "be" and "should be". Since Althussser's reading of historical materials is **methodology-oriented**, he only reads to find those that support his arguments, and he ignores other materials.[10] Materials are selected according to the requirements of supporting his arguments. Therefore, those texts that oppose his arguments are neglected and those that agree with his arguments are over-used.[11] Mr. Hu Wanfu's explanation on this point is both accurate and proper. I believe that Althusser has never read Marx's books carefully in spite of the fact that he has developed Symptomatic Reading. Lastly, Althusser did not examine Marx and Engels' later literature very carefully. The later literature refers to the parts which are added to *The Complete Works of Marx and Engels (MEGA)*. It is true that *MEGA2* only appeared from 1975 onward,

---

9   See: Sun Bokui. *Research into the Path of the Pioneers*. Hefei: Anhui People's Publishing House, 1985. Zhang Yibing. *Subjective Dimension of Marxist Historical Dialectics*, English version by Canut Intl. London 2010.

10   Hu Wanfu. *On the Young Marx*, P.45.

11   Ibid., p.56.

but *MEGA1*, was published before 1930,[12] and already offered some new materials even before the publishing of *MEGA2*. These four points are exactly where our study goes beyond that of Althusser's.

In the following section, we will examine some key issues in Althusser's research into the history of Marx's thoughts. The focus will be on the transitional period and the so-called "Epistemological Rupture" period.

2 THE IDEOLOGICAL PERIOD BEFORE THE "EPISTEMOLOGICAL RUPTURE"

Althusser regards all the works written by Young Marx from 1840-1845 as ideological texts. During this period, the ideological problematic (theoretical framework) is dominant, but besides it, there also exists a kind of theoretical alternative. This period can thus be divided into two moments.

The liberal-rationalist moment (1840-1842). During the first moment, Althusser prefers to put the humanistic theory together with the liberal-rationalism. If we dig deeper, "the presupposition of the first moment is a problematic of Kantian-Fichtean type".[13] Althusser believes that Marx's articles, such as *On the Prussian Censorship* and *On the Theft of Wood*, are dominated by a liberal-rationalist humanism. This kind of problematic is closer to that of Kant and Fichte rather than that of Hegel. His understanding here makes some sense. However, Young Marx only refers to Kant and Fichte during the earlier periods. In his doctoral dissertation and the articles in *Rheinische Zeitung*, this influence can only be found in the form of subjective initiative of rationalism. Without any doubt, his basic theoretical basis is early Hegelianism, which highlights self-consciousness theory. This Jacobin humanism is indeed quite different from the late Hegelianism though it is closer to Kant and Fichte. However, it is still an exaggeration to say that, during this time, there exists a problematic of the Kantian-Fichtean type in Young Marx's thoughts. Althusser writes that Marx's brain was filled with

---

12   The details about *The Complete Works of Marx and Engels (MEGA)* can be found in my book. Zhang Yibing. *Back to Marx, The Change of Philosophical Discourse in the Context of Economics*. English version published by Göttingen University Press, in 2014. See Part appendix 2

13   Althusser, Louis. *For Marx*, p. 35.

bourgeoisie ideologies, such as freedom and philanthropy, which were so pervasive at the time. He says:

> *Marx's political struggle and the theory of history sustaining it were based theoretically on a philosophy of men. Only the essence of man makes history, and this essence is freedom and reason. Freedom: it is the essence of man just as weight is the essence of the bodies. Man is destined to freedom, it is his very being.*[14]

Althusser thinks that, at this time, Marx is still a radical humanist, so he adopts the bourgeoisie liberalism to refute feudalism. He believes that Marx, in his struggles against Prussian despotism, built his thought on the philosophy of man. Althusser finds that Young Marx believes that history can only be understood by way of the essence of man, which is freedom and reason. This can explain why Marx demands that Prussia should embark upon a democratic reform process.

It should be clear, however, that Althusser never admits that Hegelian influence does not exist in the development of Young Marx's thoughts. On the contrary he said that, except in *Manuscripts of 1844*, the belief of Young Marx was a Hegelian, though widely acknowledged today, was in general a myth. He also said, "the Young Marx was never strictly speaking a Hegelian, except in the last text of his ideologico-philosophical period (he means *Manuscripts of 1844*); instead, he was first a Kantian Fichtean, then a Feuerbachian."[15] This corresponds with what we have previously discussed. What Althusser means is that although Marx has read Hegel's works, he is not influenced by him; rather he goes further against him. Marx only goes back to Hegel in the book, *Manuscripts of 1844*, and the result is explosive.

I want to point out that Althusser's interpretation of Marx's texts may seem careful and profound at first glance, but his interpretation will seem both vague and rough with further examination. The flaws in his interpretation are as follows. First, there are two alienated problematics (**sub-problematic**) in the ideological framework of Young Marx as evaluated by him. The first is the liberal-rationalism of Kant

---

14   Ibid., p.224.
15   Ibid., p.35.

258 ALTHUSSER REVISITED: PROBLEMATIC, SYMPTOMATIC READING

and Fichte and the second is Feuerbachian humanistic theory, about which we will discuss later. Althusser provides no illustration on whether **the shift of the problematic** is through a rupture or through a natural shift. Second, there is no text supporting the view that Marx is only influenced by Kant and Fichte. In an earlier period, Marx, in his study of the philosophy of law, is close to Hegel and Fichte. During this period, however, early Hegelianism is the primary influence on Young Marx. But since he does not support Hegel's idea of anti-human philosophy, **the idea of subject** siding by the German Bourgeoisie thus stands out. This subject philosophy of him, which is seemingly similar to the thoughts expressed by Kant and Fichte, is in fact part of Hegel's philosophy. Althusser, who only knows the meta-theoretical structure, namely the **macro problematic**, cannot understand this. This leads to the third flaw in Althusser's argument. Althusser tries his best to eliminate the fact that Marx was been influenced by Hegel. He cannot accept the fact Marx used to be a follower of Hegelianism during the writing of his doctoral dissertation. Yet the fact is that Marx is, indeed, a defender of humanism on **Hegel's** side from this period until *A Comment on Censhorship* and in those articles he contributed to *Rheinische Zeitung*. Althusser once said "Feuerbach was witness to the theoretical crisis of young Hegel". However, is the early Hegelianism, which seeks after reason and freedom, a Kant-Fichtean Problematic? What kind of change is Marx's shift to Feuerbach? All of these are questions that Althusser fails to make explicit.

Second, the communist-rationalist moment (1842-1844). During this period, Marx openly shifted towards Feuerbachian humanism (leaving back Kant and Fichte). Feuerbach's "communalist" humanism is dominant during this period. Althusser, consciously or unconsciously, hides the real reason behind this shift. Furthermore, he weakens the **significance of the establishment of the basic principles of materialism by Marx**. This is because he avoids **ontology** and **subject philosophy** and also he never carefully examined The Kreuznach Notes, he mentioned in his text.

The Kreuznach Notes and the first shift in Marx's thoughts

Marx started to rupture with the idealism of Hegelian philosophy. Before long, he was still dominated by the self-consciousness philosophy of young Hegelianism But starting from his text, **Kreuznach Notes** *a change occured. This text (Kreuznach Notes) prepared the main content of the* **Critique of Hegel's Philosophy of Law***. Obviously, Marx did not change his mind the moment he encountered Feuerbach. The first reason behind this change had to do with his poor living conditions. Second, he only supported Feuerbach's materialism after he had validated it in his own research. As far as I am concerned, this Marxian text should not be overvalued. Then, of course, it cannot be said that Marx initiates* **Marxism** *based on this text. Compared to the thoughts put forward by other pioneers of early Hegelianism, who shifted towards materialism during this time, Marx's thoughts were not the most profound. The shift in his political standpoint is also similar because Marx did not transit from humanism to communism until the* **Introduction to The Critique of Hegel's Philosophy of Law***.*[16]

Althusser also explicitly comments on Marx's systematic criticism of Hegelian philosophy. According to Althusser, Marx's criticism of Hegel is as follows:

*But **the theoretical principles** on which this critique of Hegel was based are **merely** a reprise, a commentary or a development and extension of the admirable critique of Hegel repeatedly formulated by Feuerbach. It is a critique of Hegelian philosophy as **speculative and abstract**, a critique appealing to the concrete-materialist against the abstract-speculative, i.e. a critique which remains a prisoner of the idealist problematic it hoped to free itself from, and therefore a critique which belongs by right to the theoretical problematic with which Marx broke in 1845.*[17]

In other words, Marx's criticism of Hegelianism was significant because he adopted the Feuerbach problematic. In this way, he changes from the Kant-Fichtean problematic to the Feuerbach problematic, as Althusser puts it, although this contrasts with historical facts. Althusser said that Marx, at this time, tried and hoped to be free from the ideological problematic that enslaved him. At first glance, this

---

16   Zhang Yibing. *Back to Marx: The Change of Philosophical Discourse in the Context of Economics*, pp.152-153. English version published by Göttingen University Press, in 2013. pp. 152-153.
17   Althusser, Louis. *For Marx*, p.37.

comment appears to be quite clever, but Althusser did not point out to the progress that Young Marx had made in the shift to Feuerbach's general materialism from early Hegelian subjective idealism. Instead we regard this as the first important shift in Young Marx's philosophical thoughts. Since Althusser cannot detect this progress, he thus cannot further figure out the hidden idealism behind the general materialism. Althusser has, as he himself puts it, "simplified" the **sub-forms** and **variations** of the theoretical problematic.

On the other hand, Marx has turned towards the proletariat position in politics. This is why Althusser says "so it is a **political** and **theoretical** reading of the writings of Marx's youth".[18] Although the problematic of Marx is still one of ideology during this time, he has by this time become a radical communist. But the point here is "it is possible to be 'communist' without being 'Marxist'".[19] Althusser points out that Marx has devoted himself to a whole-new type of political practice. He no longer resorts to the rationality of the state, nor praises the rationalist critique. Rather, he advocates and also practices to restore the essence of man through the practice of man. Marx begins to pursue communism. This communism aims at returning the essence of men to men. Men's essence used to be alienated as money, power and God. The aim is a trail of barriers, an act of breaking the emptiness. It can only be completed by the alliance between philosophical criticism and the proletariats. As a result, his philosophical critique based on humanism began to appear in abundance, and they join each other to form a general force. In this way, the philosophy of humanism becomes the theoretical basis of the proletarian revolution. The flaw in Althusser's analysis here is that he has ignored both the Young Engels and Hess' influence on Marx at this time.

> *Young Marx, Hess and Young Engels: Hess and Young Engels are two key figures who enter into the general materialism framework together with Marx. They had a profound influence on him. It should be pointed out that their thoughts were much more insightful than that of Marx in 1844 (before Marx conducted his research on economics). The traditional research related to the history of Marxism gives serious consideration to Young Engels'*

18 Ibid., 160.
19 Ibid., 160.

*role, in particular. However, scholars prefer to believe that it is Marx who exerted influence on Engels, and they ignore the fact that Engels' text **An Outline of the Science of Political Economy** greatly affects Marx during this particular period. It should also be noticed that this text Outline is one of the key factors that leads Marx to study economics. Another figure who influenced Marx is Hess, who is generally ignored in the study of the history of Marx's thoughts. Compared with Hegel, he is neglected or hidden both consciously and unconsciously. The first reason for this is that Marx, in his Thesis on Feuerbach, mainly comments on Hegel and Feuerbach. The second reason is the Lenin's Formula (Karl Marx and The Three Sources and Components of Marxism), which was developed without reference to Marx and Engels' earlier works. In fact, the real historical fact is that Hess was the only person who was on the same path with Young Marx and Engels. This kind of cooperation lasts until the writing of **The German Ideology** (Hess composed two chapters of the book: the chapter which criticizes Bauer in the first volume and the chapter which criticizes Kuhlmann in the second volume). Both of the two chapters were published in newspapers. It was not until February of 1848 that Hess split with Marx and Engels due to the contrast between the hidden humanism in Hess' thoughts and the internal logic of Marx's scientific world outlook. Therefore, it is inappropriate to treat Hess in the same way that traditional researchers generally do. Hess' socialist theory, which is based on economics, primarily focuses on criticizing capitalist society. I think it is important for us to identify how Hess' theory influenced both Young Marx and Engels at this time so as to truly understand the essence of the philosophical revolution made by Marx and Engels in 1845.[20]*

Althusser believes that "not only Marx's terminology from 1842 to 1845 is Feuerbachian (alienation, species being, total being, 'inversion' of subject and predicate, etc.) but, what is probably more important, so is the basic **philosophical problematic**".[21] Why would he say this? The reason is because Young Marx does not simply or only adopt the terminology of humanism. The terms are not borrowed one by one, but were borrowed as a whole, this whole which was exactly the Feuerbachian problematic. If we review our discussion of problematic by Althusser in Chapter One, we will know that the problematic, which Althusser sets, is that "it brings out within

20 Zhang Yibing. *Back to Marx*, pp.114-115.
21 Althusser, Louis. *For Marx*, p.45.

the thought **the objective internal reference system of its particular** themes, the system of **questions** commanding the **answers** given by the ideology."[22] Besides, Althusser wrote:

> *When real mutations take place in the theoretical problematic: the **object** of the theory then suffers a corresponding mutation, which now does not only affect 'aspects' of the object, details of its structure, but this structure itself. What is then made visible is a new structure of the object, often so different from the old that it is legitimate to speak of **a new object**.*[23]

However, due to his poor theoretical accomplishments, Althusser cannot make clear distinctions between the two: the premise of general philosophical materialism and the logic of humanism. Therefore, according to Althusser, Feuerbach's theory is humanism. I have to say that this is a very big mistake. As far as Althusser is concerned, Marx is adopting the Feuerbachian problematic, i.e. I can certainly say the overall logic of the value advocated suspense in humanism when dealing with the world. Marx also starts from men and regards the true ideal men as the standard for reality. Ideal ("should be") is defined as true labor (as the general essence of man) the reality (the "be") is the alienated capitalist society, measured by true man. As a result, the proletarian revolution and their act of pursuing communism is more or less representative of their ethical demands.

> *That is why Althusser says: He is no more than **an avant-garde Feuerbachian applying an ethical problematic to the understanding of human history**. In other words, we can say that at this time Marx was merely applying the theory of alienation, that is, Feuerbach's theory of "human nature", to politics and the concrete activity of men, before extending it (in large part) to political community in the **Manuscripts**.*[24]

As Hu Wanfu puts it, Marx is saying **what Feuerbach wants to say but cannot finish**. Also, he is dominated by Feuerbach's philosophy in the above works. "His views are only extension inside the Feuerbachian framework of humanism."[25] I believe that Althusser's analysis of the Young Marx's internal theoretical framework is

---

22   Ibid., p. 67 footnote.
23   Althusser, Louis. *Reading Capital.* Trans. Ben Brewster. London: Verso. 1970. p.156.
24   Althusser, Louis. *For Marx*, p. 46.
25   Hu Wanfu. *On Young Marx*, p.52.

basically correct. This accounts for why *Manuscripts of 1844* is the key part of Althusser's theory, which is also his most important contribution to the 'political debate' surrounding Young Marx.

3 DISTINCTLY DIFFERENT EVALUATIONS ON 1844 MANUSCRIPTS

In Althusser's point of view, *Manuscripts of 1844* "is the text which has for thirty years been in the front line of the problematic between defenders of Marx and his opponents."[26] For Althusser, this text only exerts a negative influence on the researches into Marxist thoughts because, since the 1930s, the text has become an important means of proving the **humanistic** or **unscientific** tendency in Marx's philosophy. In the Western academic field, the Marxist-Humanist side in particular, the terminology of "**alienation, humanism** and **the social essence of men**" has become their basis for misinterpreting Marx from the humanistic point of view.

In contrast to Western scholars who overestimate the value of *Manuscripts of 1844*, Althusser offers a distinctly different evaluation. More specifically, Western scholars overestimate the theoretical significance of *1844 Manuscript* and believe that *Manuscripts of 1844* bears the core content of Marx's philosophy. They also hold that *Capital* merely serves as a further illustration of *Manuscripts of 1844*. Althusser disagree with these scholars. In the meantime, he also rejects the views of the "Orthodox Marxists," who use several arguments in *Capital* when interpreting the *Manuscripts of 1844* and who believe that *Manuscripts of 1844* was a mixture of both old and new thoughts. Althusser prefers to treat *Manuscripts of 1844* as a whole, suggesting that instead of mechanically finding elements of materialism or idealism (the remains of Hegel and Feuerbach's thoughts), the overall idea can be taken from the text's internal problematic. Althusser's argument here makes some sense.

Althusser believes "the text of the last hours of the night is, theoretically speaking, the text the furthest removed from the day that is about to dawn".[27] The reason for this is that the deep theoretical framework of *Manuscripts of 1844* is the philosophical problematic

---

26   Althusser, Louis. *For Marx*, p.155.
27   Ibid., p. 36.

that Marx abandoned in *German Ideology*. This problematic abandoned here is the Feuerbachian "ideology which does not fructify."

For the first time, Althusser asks if there is anything new in *Manuscripts of 1844* compared to other works. In contrast to all of the other researchers who only focus on the concepts of "men" and "alienation" in *Manuscripts of 1844*, Althusser insightfully finds that *Manuscripts of 1844* is a reflection of Marx's studies on **political economy**. This is indeed a new perspective. Unfortunately, Althusser could not get access to Marx's *Pariser Hefte (Paris Notebooks)* and this failure exerts a negative influence on the quality of his research.

> ***Pariser Hefte, (Paris Notebooks) by Young Marx****: Pariser Hefte gives the true record of how Marx studies economics for the first time. It was written from October 1843 to January 1845. In the broad sense, there are ten notebooks in total. Seven of them make extracts of economics and the other three of them are only manuscripts, which record some of Marx's preliminary thoughts. The three manuscripts and the seven notebooks can be regarded as written during the same period. Strictly speaking, we cannot separate the ten notebooks from one another. However, in a narrow sense, we can also regard the seven notebooks as **Pariser Hefte** and the three manuscripts as Manuscripts of 1844 (to put it more specifically, the composition of Manuscripts of 1844 was accomplished before the writing of the sixth notebook in August of 1844). Based on the latest research conducted by scholars from Amsterdam Archive and the Soviet Union in the 1980s, **there exists no independent Manuscripts of 1844**.28 Therefore, it is impossible to get the correct insight into **Manuscripts of 1844** if neglecting the **Pariser Hefte**.[29]*

According to Althusser, the writing of *Manuscripts of 1844* marks Marx's **initial** investigations into political economy. Marx commented on economic issues before that, such as his condemnation of the feudal land property in his *On the Theft of Wood* in 1842. However, at that period of time he only considered the economic issues which he encounters in his research or discussions on politics. More importantly, before 1844, Young Marx still remains as a democrat, but during his composing of *Manuscripts of 1844* text he already started serving the proletariat. Beginning by and in 1844,

28   Marx, Karl. *Parise Hefte (MEGA 2)*, Section 4, volume 2, pp.283-589.
29   See: *Materials for Marxism-Leninism*, 2nd issue, Beijing: People's Press, 1988..

Marx begins to carefully study political economy in order to find a theoretical basis for the proletarian revolution. Marx is convinced that economic sphere is the decisive factor in social life and that generally speaking, economic sphere should also provide the basis for revolution. But what greatly disappoints Marx is the following:

> *But while recognizing it, he states that this fact **rests on nothing**, at least in the economics he has read, it is ungrounded and lacks its own **principle**. So, in one and the same movement, the encounter with political economy is **a critical reaction** to political economy and a thorough investigation of its **foundations**.*[30]

What causes Marx to believe that political economy is unfounded? He answers: "The **contradiction** it states and registers, or even accepts and traduces: and before all else, the major contradiction opposing the increasing **pauperization** of the workers and remarkable wealth whose arrival in the modern world is celebrated by political economy."[31] As a "science", it is really disgraceful for political economy to lack principles. Therefore, Marx wants to restore this "principle" in *Manuscripts of 1844*.

I am certain that Althusser makes his judgment without reading the *Pariser Hefte*.[32] Despite this, his analysis is basically right, although perhaps it is too broad. This also reflects his great talent for theoretical studies.

How to restore the "principle" which is lacking in political economy? Althusser says that we should come to the other aspect of the *Manuscripts*: philosophy. "Marx's encounter with political economy is also the encounter of **philosophy** and political economy."[33] Of course, the philosophy here is still the problematic of idealism.

> *Naturally, not of any philosophy: of the philosophy erected by Marx through all his practico-theoretical experiments (Bottigelli sketches out the essential moments: the idealism of the very first writings, closer to Kant and Fichte than to Hegel; Feuerbach's*

---

30   Althusser, Louis. *For Marx*, p. 157.
31   Ibid., p.157.
32   Ibid., p.157.
33   About detailed information about *Pariser Hefte* by Young Marx, and the complex change in Marx's thought when he first encountered political economy, references can be made to my book: Zhang Yibing. *Back to Marx*. English version published by Göttingen University Press, in 2014.

anthropology), modified, corrected and amplified by this encounter itself.[34]

The key concept of this philosophy is **alienated labor**. Marx tries to solve the basic contradiction in the capitalist society via this humanistic category. Marx does not fully get rid of the influence of the alienated historical view of humanism. Why? The reason is that the premise of alienated labor is certainly **non-alienated** labor, which is the direct origin of the generic essence of true men. To put it simply, it is still the story of the decaying of God. The ancients living in God's grace are easily tempted by the seduction of the serpent. On this, Althusser offers very insightful comment. He says, in the eyes of Marx, men are still the decaying (degeneration, original sin) myth of the ancients. The existence of "Eden" and "innocence" is the prerequisite for this "decay" just like non-alienated labor is the prerequisite of alienated labor. This decaying is alienation. "Innocence" is the essence of human life. Eating the "forbidden fruit" is the split and ruin of human life. In this way, there exists the hope and need to turn the ruined human life back to "innocence".[35] This alienated historical view, which starts from the innocent **non-alienated labor (true labor)**, belongs to idealism. "This is the philosophy which resolves the contradiction of political economy by **thinking** it, and through it, by thinking the whole of political economy and all its categories, with a key-concept as starting point, the concept of alienated labor."[36] In Althusser's point of view, this is a kind of theoretical impasse.

Young Marx solves the contradiction in political economy by way of humanist philosophy, but he also sets a trap for himself in the meantime. In this humanist philosophy, we can identify categories like private property, capital, money, and division of labor, the alienation of the laborer, laborer's emancipation and humanism. "These are all, or nearly all, **categories** we shall meet again in *Capital*, and on this basis we might accept them as **anticipations** of *Capital*, or better, as a project for *Capital*, or even as *Capital* crayoned, already outlined, but only as a sketch."[37] However, the overall connections between

---

34   Althusser, Louis. *For Marx*, pp.157-158.
35   See: Yimamura Hitoshi: *Althusser: Epistemological Rupture*. p.57.
36   Althusser, Louis. *For Marx*, p.158.
37   Ibid., p.158.

these concepts, or the particular problematic, are not a scientific theoretical framework, but rather they are a transcendental abstract philosophical logic. Althusser holds that "there is also the conviction, the meaning conferred by this logic and rigor on the concepts we recognize in it, and therefore the very meaning of this logic and rigor: a meaning which is still philosophical."[38] The logical core of this way of questioning by Marx is still the alienated labor, and it is still to build an alienated historical view. If Marx, at this time, has already made up his mind to be a follower of communism, he receives it **as a mandate** and commission from a whole conception of Man, which is derived from **the essence of Man**, the necessity and content of the familiar **economic concepts**.

We have already seen Marx's criticism of capitalist economy and the reality in capitalist society, but what about the effect of his criticism? In other words, what is the reality that Marx encounters in terms of economics – the economy itself? Or more likely, an economic ideology inseparable from the "economic" theories? The value suspense in the philosophy of Feuerbach still holds its dominance in *Manuscripts of 1844*. Therefore, as Althusser comments, confronting economics with philosophical humanism is premised on such a fact: "Marx accepts political economy precisely as it presents itself without questioning the content of its concepts or their systematicity."[39] As a result, here Althusser delivers quite a confusing sentence: "the Marx furthest from Marx is this Marx, the Marx on the brink, on the eve, on the threshold."[40] According to Althusser, Young Marx adopts the philosophical problematic of humanism for the last time in *Manuscripts of 1844*. "In order to achieve it, he had to give philosophy every chance, its last, this absolute empire over its opposite, this boundless theoretical triumph, that is, its **defeat**."[41] I believe his analysis on this point is profound.

Secondly, Althusser wants us to know that, at this time, Young Marx was dominated by the Feuerbachian philosophical problematic of humanism. According to this logic, man is first of all the generic subject. Man is first of all a 'communal being.' It can only

38   Ibid., p.158.
39   Ibid., p.159.
40   Ibid., p.159.
41   Ibid., p.159.

be consummated theoretically (science) and practically (politics) in universal human relations. This universal human relationship involves relations with men and with his objects. Here the essence of man is also the basis for history and politics. Althusser holds that this alienated historical view of humanism is ideological. He explains:

> *History is the alienation and production of reason in unreason, of the true man in the alienated man. Without knowing it, man realizes the essence of man in the alienated products of his labour (commodities, State, religion). The loss of man that produces history and man must presuppose a definite pre-existing essence. At the end of history, this man, having become inhuman objectivity, has merely to re-grasp as subject his own essence alienated in property, religion and the State to become total man, true man.*[42]

The communism based on this is a new type of political action: the politics of practical re-appropriation. The revolution is no longer merely political (rational and liberal reform of the State), but it is also "human" (communist). Only in this way can men be restored to his nature, who used to be alienated as money, power and gods. Althusser says that revolution is the very practice of the logic immanent in alienation-istic view on revolution. Callinicos offers a very precise comment on this: "There exists the dialectic structure of teleology in *Manuscripts of 1844*. Men are alienated in the capitalist society and are united in the communist society."[43]

In 1968, Althusser went back to comment on *Manuscripts of 1844* once again, but his basic arguments did not change by much. He said it was a text that Marx never published and never referred to, and it was a text bearing a lot of "crisis".

> *Politically, Marx wrote the **Manuscripts** as a Communist, and thus made the impossible theoretical gamble of attempting to use, in the service of his convictions, the notions, analyses and contradictions of the bourgeois economists, putting in the forefront what he calls "alienated labor", which he could not yet grasp as capitalist exploitation. Theoretically, he wrote these manuscripts on the basis of petty-bourgeois philosophical positions, making the impossible political gamble of **introducing** Hegel into Feuerbach, so as to be able to **speak of** labour in alienation, and of History in Man.*[44]

---

42   Ibid., p.226.
43   Callinicos, Alex. *Althusser's Marxism*, p.84.
44   Althusser, Louis. *Essays in Self-criticism*. Trans. Grahame Lock. New York & London: Verso, 1976. p. 15.

If Althusser is judging the dominant discourse in Young Marx's thoughts, then I can say his argument is well founded; but when he believes that this is what *Manuscripts of 1844* contains, he appears subjective and lacks textual support. In fact, the structure of *Manuscripts of 1844* is extremely complex. Regarding this aspect, Professor Sun Bokui's theories of "double logic" and my theory of "three discourses" offer the latest research results on this point.[45] We have reflected on Althusser's incorrect way of rejecting subject philosophy (his totally ignoring of **the theoretical logic starting from the social practice in classical economic analysis**). Otherwise, the establishment of historical materialism would be like creating something from nothing – just like the notion that God creates everything.

4 1845: THE RUPTURE OF NEW FROM THE OLD PROBLEMATIC

According to Althusser, there exists an important "epistemological rupture" in Marx's thoughts when he writes *Theses on Feuerbach* and *The German Ideology*. The rupture is **a rupture (one) from the ideological problematic to the scientific problematic**. Marx's famous "'settling of accounts with our erstwhile philosophical conscience,' implied his adoption of **a new problematic**, which even if it did integrate a certain number of the old concepts, did so into a whole which confers on them a radically new significance."[46] We have become quite familiar with this idea.

Specifically speaking, Marx negates his past ideological problematic and tries to get out of various ideologies and builds a new problematic with a theoretical revolution. This is a wholly new theoretical basis. Mr Hu Wanfu comments on this issue: "Marx's theoretical revolution was precisely to base his theory on **a new element** after liberating it from its **old element**: the element of Hegelian and Feuerbachian philosophy."[47] Here, we should take note of the issue of the absoluteness of rupture. Hu Wanfu continues: "What Althusser means by 'rupture' is to **abandon everything**, not only

---

45   See: Sun Bokui. *Research into the Path of the Pioneers*. Hefei: Anhui People's Publishing House, 2002. Zhang Yibing. *The Subjective Dimension of Marxist Historical Dialectics*, Chapter 3. English version published by Canut Publishers Intl. London 2011.
46   Althusser, Louis. *For Marx*, p.47.
47   Ibid., p.47.

the **old theoretical whole** (like Hegel and Feuerbach) but also any **elements contained in this whole**."[48] Hu Wanfu insightfully points out that Althusser's theory of "epistemological rupture" exhibits an anti-dialectic tendency, which is reflected by two gaps: first being the gap between theoretical practice and reality and the second being the gap between science and ideology.[49] The criticism makes some sense.

Althusser claims:

> So something **irreversible** really does start in 1845: the "epistemological rupture" is *a point of no return*. Something begins which will have no end.[28] A "continuing rupture", I wrote, the beginning of a long period of work, as in every other science. And although the way ahead is open, it is difficult and sometimes even dramatic, marked by events – theoretical events (additions, rectifications, corrections) – an end, by its very nature, like science in general. (The Collapse of the Second International) which concern the scientific knowledge of a particular object: the conditions, the mechanisms and the forms of the class struggle.[50]

The implied meanings are as follows. First, the shift from ideology to science is irreversible. That is why Althusser feels so angry when the scientific thoughts of Marx are incorrectly interpreted as humanistic ideology again. Second, the rupture does not happen in a single moment. It is not the qualitative change that is accomplished immediately, but rather it is the beginning of a scientific activity.

> Obviously this epistemological rupture is not an instantaneous event. It is even possible that one might, by recurrence and where some of its **details** are concerned, assign it a sort of premonition of a past. At any rate, this rupture becomes **visible** in its first sight, but these signs only inaugurate the beginning of an endless history. Like every rupture, this rupture is actually a sustained one within which complex reorganizations can be observed.[51]

He even claims that "we are still inscribed in the theoretical space marked and opened by this rupture today".[52] The reason why he

---

48   Hu Wanfu. *On Young Marx*, p.68. note 1.
49   Ibid., pp.69-70.
50   Althusser, Louis. *Essays on Self-Criticism*, pp.66-67.
51   Althusser, Louis. *Lenin and Philosophy and Other Essays*. Trans. Ben Brewster. New York; London: Verso.1971. p. 39.
52   Ibid., p.40.

believes so lies in the fact that the rupture that Marx establishes the science of history in 1845 is a rupture that "inaugurates a history which will never come to an end"[53]. Althusser later adds this argument.

According to Althusser, this unique rupture contains three non-seperable elements: 1. Humanism is regarded as an **ideology**; 2. The **theoretical pretentions** of philosophical humanism are severely and radically criticized 3. The theory of history and politics based on radically new concepts is formed.

The first element is a judgment on the theoretical logic. Marx explicitly negates his alienated logic of humanism, which reflects his self-retrospection regarding the theoretical problematic. The second element reflects his refusal of the ideologic problematic. The third element demonstrates his thinking after he changed to a new problematic. The first two elements are revolutionary negation, declaring the death of the old problematic. The last element is the revolutionary affirmation, marking the birth of a new problematic, i.e. the establishment of Marx's science of history. We can observe that Althusser is only able to perceive the theoretical changes related to humanism but not perceive the changes **related to historical materialism whose revolutionary significance is more important than** that of general materialism. In Althusser's theoretical construction, many historical facts are consciously or unconsciously ignored, and his science misinterprets the complex theoretical development as a linear replacement of ideology.

Althusser holds that this marks the appearance of Marx's new problematic, i.e. the new scientific theoretical framework. This new world outlook emerges in the critique of the old ideology (humanism). This is an in-depth argument. By 1845, Marx had indeed developed a new world outlook, but it was not displayed **in a scientific way**. Marx's rupture with every philosophical anthropology or humanism is coherent with Marx's scientific discovery. "It means that Marx rejected the problematic of the earlier philosophy and adopted a new problematic in one and the same act."[54]

---

53   Ibid., p.40.
54   Althusser, Louis. *For Marx*, p.227.

Of course, as the text, which bears the "epistemological rupture," *Theses on Feuerbach* is weighed differently from *The German Ideology*. He comments: "What was announced in the *Theses on Feuerbach* was, in the necessarily philosophical language of a declaration of rupture with all 'interpretative' philosophy, something quite different from a new philosophy: a new science, the science of history, whose first, still infinitively fragile foundation Marx was to lay in *German Ideology*."[55] Althusser believes that *Theses on Feuerbach* is only a **theoretical flash** in the rupture of the old and new problematic.

> *The Theses on Feuerbach were written in haste after a crucial theoretical event: the **introduction of Hegel into Feuerbach** (it took place in the **Manuscripts of 1844**). The **Manuscripts** are **an explosive text**. Hegel, re-introduced by force into Feuerbach, induces a prodigious acting out of the Young Marx's theoretical contradiction, in which is achieved the rupture with Theoretical Humanism.*[56]

In contrast to the conventional comments made about Theses, Althusser does not give much credit to the theoretical significance of it. He says "as is well known, a spark dazzles rather than illuminates: nothing is more difficult than the point of light which breaks it."[57]

What he means by this is that *Theses* is no more than a small part of what ignited the new problematic. The *Theses* declares the death of all the old philosophies, but it only bears the significance of a declaration.

However, I believe that Althusser's understanding of the *Theses* is an irresponsible misinterpretation. He is angry at the fact that humanists build their humanistic theory based on Marx's words of "starting from subject". He is also angry that Marx is still talking about the essence of man. What he cannot understand is that man is and will always be the object of Marx's thoughts, which, however, is different from the humanists' point of view. Since his understandings are different from those of the humanists, Marx is able to **scientifically**

---

55 Althusser, Louis. *Lenin and Philosophy and Other Essays*, p.37.
56 Althusser, Louis. *Politics and History*. Trans. Ben Brewster. New York; London, Verso, 1967. p.178.
57 Althusser, Louis. *For Marx*, p.36.

understand man and its essence.[58] There exist problematic meta-physical remains in Althusser's methodology, which prevents him from moving further in the right direction. We have already made a very careful examination into Marx's *Theses on Feuerbach*.[59]

Althusser does not give much credit to *German Ideology*, which many researchers believe to be the origin of historical material-ism. Firstly, according to Althusser, this text only demonstrates how Marx breaks with his past theories, namely the abandonment of the ideological philosophy. He comments:

The German Ideology bases this suppression of philosophy on a theory of philosophy as a hallucination and mystification, or to go further, as a dream, manufactured from what I shall call the days' residue of the real history of concrete men, day's residue endowed with a purely imaginary existence in which the order of things is inverted.[60]

There are traces of Freud's psychoanalysis in this. The old philoso-phy is a hallucination of ideology. *The German Ideology* is the text, which abandons the old philosophy.

He continues: Secondly,

the philosophical emptiness which followed the proclamation of **Thesis IX** was the fullness of science, the fullness of the intense, arduous and protracted labor which put an unprecedented sci-ence on to the stocks, a science to which Marx was to devote all his life, down to the last drafts of **Capital**, which he was never able to complete.[61]

In the long history of philosophy, the old philosophy is dead, but the new one (dialectical materialism) is not immediately established. That is why Althusser says that after the *The German Ideology* there exists philosophical emptiness. The emptiness is most likely to emerge during the shift between the old and new problematic.

---

58   See: Zhang Yibing. *Back to Marx*, Section 4, Chapter 4 for reference on the under-standing of *Theses on Feuerbach*.
59   See: Zhang Yibing. *Back to Marx*, pp.353-369. Zhang Yibing. *Subjective Dimension of Marx's Historical Dialectics*, Chapter 3. English version published by Canut Publishers Intl. London 2010, pp.91-98.
60   Althusser, Louis. *Lenin and Philosophy and Other Essays*, pp.37-38.
61   Ibid., p.38.

"Peace in Mind helps understand everything and emptiness can hold everything." In this way, the philosophical emptiness also holds a thriving new start in it. The German Ideology is not in Marx's philosophical scheme but rather it is an important part of his **working** toward science (historical materialism). Of course, Marx and Engels want to establish this new thought in *The German Ideology*, but this new thought, so unyielding and precise in its criticism of the ideological error, cannot define itself without both difficulty and ambiguity. This suggests that historical materialism only works in the critical negation but not in the positive description. In fact, there is something wrong with this argument. *The German Ideology* is first of all a critical work, but, in it, Marx and Engels, also directly talk about the new world outlook, especially historical materialism.[62] Though, further examinations were needed to be made on what this new world outlook really is.

Therefore, Althusser reminds us to notice two points. First, *The German Ideology* does mark the shift from the old problematic to the new one, but this shift did not happen immediately. It cannot inaugurate the new problematic once and for all in the theory of history, as well as in that of philosophy. The new problematic could only achieve its **final** theoretical project, gradually. "Long years of positive study and elaborations were necessary before Marx could produce fashion and establish a conceptual terminology and systematic that was adequate to his theoretical revolution project."[63] This is quite an insightful argument. Compared to traditional researchers, who list all of the concepts in Marx's texts, this is a necessary classification. Second, "*The German Ideology* is a commentary, usually a negative and critical one, on the different forms of the ideological problematic Marx had rejected."[64] Or, it is a negation or critique of the old philosophy. This is of course a process of rejecting the old concepts and systems, i.e. ideology, but "it is processed in a very general and abstract way."[65] The reason for this is that the remains of the framework of the old philosophy still exist even when Marx is criticizing the old problematic.

62 See: Zhang Yibing. *Back to Marx*, Section 4, Chapter 6 for details about researches into German Ideology.
63 Althusser, Louis. *For Marx*, p. 34.
64 Ibid., p. 34.
65 Ibid., p. 233.

*In 1845 Marx **began** to lay down the foundation of a science which did not exist before he came along: the science of history. And in order to do that he set out a number of new concepts which cannot be found elsewhere in his humanist works of youth:* **mode of production, productive forces, relations of production, infrastructure-superstructure, ideologies,** *etc.*[66]

However, another problem emerges, "often the old words are charged with the conduct of the rupture throughout the period of the search for new ones."[67] This judgment makes sense. Marx also adopts words and phrases like 'acquaintanceship' and 'division of labor,' which are remains of the old philosophy.

The battle between thought and language is still going on, and the remains of the old language will eventually die out. However, during the battle the fire of the old language still damages some of the old thoughts. This is sure to happen in the transition and period of the break before the founding of a new problematic. In *The German Ideology*, it is true that Marx no longer adopts theoretical concepts like the concepts of man or humanism; instead, he adopts other, quite new concepts, the concept of the modes of production, forces of production, relations of production, relations of communication, superstructure, ideology, etc. But these **practical concepts** are sometimes **internally conflicting**. We know that, for Althusser, the practical category is negative. The adoption of the **'theoretical concept'** is still related to the battle with the old ideology. In one way they belong to the old ideological universe, which serves as their 'theoretical' reference (the humanism); but in the other they relate to a new domain, pointing out the displacement to be put into effect to get to it. The efforts toward a new theory suggest a transcendence of the ideological domain, but the signpost is still standing there. Many of Marx's thoughts are still written in **the language of ideology**, even if he does use new words. "Even the rejection of ideology is written in ideological language".[68] This is what happens during the shift from one ideology to another. Yimamura Hitoshi once said that, according to Althusser, rupture does not mean the damage of the old problematic, but the direct abandonment of it and a shift to a new

---

66   Althusser, Louis. *Essays for Self-Criticism*, p.66.
67   Althusser, Louis. *For Marx*, p.36.
68   Ibid., p.244.

one. However,

> *The old problematic still exists even after the appearance of the new one and the two compete with each other. In this process, the power of the old problematic gets restricted. Therefore, the rupture does not result in a new thought immediately. There is a long process of progressing after the emergence of the rupture. This process of progressing is the process toward maturation.*[69]

Althusser once offers such an example: "Or again, it is possible to be taken in by the ambiguous role of **the division of labor**, which, in this book (*The German Ideology*), plays a principal part taken by alienation in the writings of his youth, and commands the whole theory of ideology and the whole theory of science."[70] I really admire Althusser's insights on this point. He never carefully examined Marx's economic manuscripts, but he is sensitive enough to find the theoretical logic in Marx's philosophical texts. Besides, Althusser identifies that Marx's own expressions in *The German Ideology* speak of the concrete, the real, of 'real' concrete men. This suggests that "the works of the rupture themselves are still trapped in the ambiguity of a negation which still cling to the universe of the concepts it rejects, without having succeeded in adequately formulating the new and positive concepts it brings with it."[71]. But this argument of him is biased because it again refuses to take men as the "object." This is typical of structuralism.

Strangely, Althusser argues that the development of Marxism after *Theses* and *The German Ideology* is very disappointing, and he even adopts the word **'barren'** to describe this period. He says that people can find many reasons to defend this like Marx's lacking of time, Engels' extemporization in philosophy, and Lenin's involvement in the ideological struggles, in which he is forced to turn his enemies' own weapons against them. However, these are not the key issues for Althusser: "The ultimate reason is that the times were not ripe, that dusk had yet not fallen, and that neither Marx himself, nor Engels, nor Lenin could yet write the great work of philosophy

---

69   Yimamura Hitoshi. *Althusser: Epistemological Rupture*, p.30.
70   Althusser, Louis. *For Marx*, p. 37.
71   Althusser, Louis. *Reading Capital*. Trans. Ben Brewster. London: Verso. 1970. p. 39, note 18.

which Marxism-Leninism lacks."[72] Therefore, "the Marxist theoretical practice of **epistemology**, of the history of science, of the history of ideology, of the history of philosophy, of the history of art, has yet in **large part to be constituted**."[73]

Then, who is the one to explore this "barren" and "virgin" land? Althusser himself? Obviously, this is an ignorant and pretentious self-approbation. The reason why he is not the one is that wherever it is necessary for him to offer some new thoughts, he always provides something quite vague and ambiguous.

---

72   Althusser, Louis. *Lenin and Philosophy and Other Essays*, p.44.
73   Althusser, Louis. *For Marx*, p.169.

CHAPTER X

THE MOST IMPORTANT PRINCIPLE OF MARXISM

On the last page of his monograph, *The Order of Things: An Archeology of the Human Sciences*, Michael Foucault wrote down this famous sentence: "Man would be erased, like a face drawn in sand at the edge of sea."[1] The sentence suggests that the concept of man has only recently been established (the discourse of modernity, the sand), and is weakly constructed. Thus, any flows of water could wash him (the ideology, the face) away. In fact, in the 1960s, Althusser, who was also a student of Bachelard, put forward the same logic in his own theory. What was different between Althusser and Foucault was that Foucault had crossed from problematic of structuralism into post-structuralism, which opposed the subject philosophy. Althusser, however, progressed into the reconstruction of the scientific Marxism by his problematic theory, which also went against subject philosophy. From this it can be observed that the most important principle of Marxism is to reject any theoretical or logical humanism and to oppose any form of subject philosophy. Marxism is the "theoretical anti-humanism," which was both an enlightening and inspiring slogan of the epoch.

---

1   Foucault, Michael. *The Order of Things: An Archeology of the Human Sciences.* London & New York: Routledge, 2001. p.422.

1 MARXISM: THE THEORETICAL "ANTI-HUMANISM"

Althusser proposes the famous notion that "Marxism is the theoretical anti-humanism," which is based on his division of the developmental stages of Marxism. The so-called theoretical humanism argues that "in the logical sense, man, center of the world, is the essence and purpose of the world".[2] Althusser explicitly stated the following:

> I say **theoretical**, for Man is not just for Feuerbach an Idea in the Kantian sense, but the theoretical foundation for **all** his "philosophy", as the Cogito was for Descartes, the Transcendental Subject for Kant and the Idea for Hegel. It is this Theoretical Humanism that we find in so many words in **Manuscripts of 1844**.[3]

If what Althusser means is that the dominant **discourse** in *Manuscripts of 1844* is "theoretical humanism," then his argument is quite sensible. However, what he actually intends to do here is to prove that everything in *Manuscripts of 1844* represents theoretical humanism. In this way, Althusser fails to detect the objective historical logic budding in Young Marx's thoughts.

> *The polyphonic structure of Manuscripts of 1844: I have made it explicit that the dominant logic of this text is as follows: to break down the established political premise of classical economics so as to confirm the position of the proletariat; overturn the idealist dialectics (phenomenology of spirits) of Hegel; extend Feuerbach's humanist theory of alienation (humanistic phenomenology); and negate the method of empirical criticism of both Proudhon and the young Engels, in particular, and upgrade and systematize Hess' theory of Economic Alienation. In Feuerbach's humanist theory of alienation, humanism is the secret to theology and man's essence is the secret to God; man's relationship is the secret to trinity. In Hess' theory of economic alienation, man is the essence of national economy and man's generic essence, namely man's relationship is the essence of currency. Therefore, in Marx's alienated labor theory, **humanism is the secret to national economy; labor is the secret to capital (alienated labor**

---

2   Althusser, Louis. *Soutenance d'Amiens*. Cited from collections of *Issue 3-Issue 4, Research Material on Marxism and Leninism*, Beijing: People's Education Press, 1986. pp.304-306.
3   Althusser, Louis. *Politics and History*, p.180.

is the secret to private property and social beings are the secret to currency. Due to the fact that his understanding of the reality of economics has gone deeper compared to that of others, Marx actually develops a way of thinking that starts from the reality of economics. This way of thinking is, however, unconscious and invisible in **Manuscripts of 1844** *(mainly in the third draft of* **Manuscripts of 1844***). In contrast to the understanding commonly found in Soviet Union, I hold that this is not an argument consciously proposed by Marx; rather, it is Marx's unconscious reflection when he encountered economics. Thus* **two kinds of alienated logics and discourses can be found in the same text***, and they both display a fancy polyphonic structure. Of course, we should also bear in mind that the logic of humanism possesses the dominant discourse. Althusser, however, cannot figure out the complexity of this polyphonic structure.*[4]

In fact, as Althusser holds "this idea of 'man' as a starting-point, an absolute point of departure, is the basis of all bourgeois ideology; it is the soul of the great Classical Political Economy itself. 'Man' is a myth of bourgeois ideology: Marxism-Leninism cannot start from 'man.'"[5] This seems to be a natural and reasonable conclusion. It is in every sense that Man is the basis of Enlightenment and that Marxism does not start from man. However, Althusser never indicates that Marxism must confront man, which consists the theoretical task of illustrating man in theory, both historically and scientifically.

As previously stated, "theory" here refers to some systematic and holistic worldview: the integral structure of a particular theoretical framework (problematic), as Althusser has proposed. Therefore, Young Marx's theory can be viewed as "theoretical humanism," which suggests that the basis of Marx's theory (mainly philosophy) is still the humanistic problematic of bourgeois ideology. In *Manuscript 1844*, the significance of "man" lies in the fact that it has not only become an ethical weapon to denounce the exploitative and enslaving nature of capitalist society, but it also becomes the logical standpoint and the basis for all of Young Marx's historical and world views. Moreover, "the generic essence of man" (some transcendental subject that exists prior to man and history) is the

---

4 Zhang Yibing. *Back to Marx*, English version published by Göttingen University Press, in 2014. pp. 218-219.
5 Althusser, Louis. *Essays in Self-criticism*. p.52.

basis for all of Marx's theories here. It is on the basis of this logical essence that the complete theory of logical deduction is established. The historical view of humanistic alienation works like this: authentic labor (the generic essence of man) → alienated labor → proletariat revolution (discarding alienation) → emancipation of mankind (reversion of human essence). This humanistic philosophy cannot belong to Marxist science. If the bourgeois ideology attempts to reconstruct Marxist philosophy based on the humanistic ideology, it will be nothing but counterfeit. I think that Althusser's judgment here is sensible.

Althusser says that the problematic of humanism is "constituted by a coherent system of precise concepts tightly articulated together." It contains two very important theoretical postulates: "1. that there is a universal essence of man; 2. that this essence is the attribute of "**each single individual** who is real subject".[6] The two postulates are interrelated and complementary. He comments:

> *If the essence of man is to be a universal attribute, it is essential that **concrete subjects** exist as absolute givens; this implies **empiricism of the subject**. If these empirical individuals are to be men, it is essential that each carries in himself the whole human essence, if not in fact, at least in principle; this implies an **idealism of the essence**.[7]*

If the essence of man is to be a universal attribute, it is essential that concrete subjects exist as absolute givens: if the empirical individuals are to be men, it is inevitable that each carry within himself the whole human essence. It is a kind of empiricism and idealism that **regards man as the central subject**. This can be easily understood in the context of Lacan and Althusser's Ideological State Apparatuses. Subject duplicates the individual as the subject through the interpellation of ideology, and it treats the automatic submission of the conditions of production, which are essential to reproduction, as the terminus. Man, as the subject of philosophy, whether he is the generic essence of man as in the classical humanism of Enlightenment or the individual as subject in neo-humanism since Kierkegaard, is the **pseudo-subject** constructed by ideology. "Man at the centre of his world, in the philosophical sense of the term, the originating

6   Althusser, Louis. *For Marx*, p.227.
7   Ibid., p.228.

essence and the end of his world – that is what we can call a theo-retical humanism in the strong sense."[8] We can conclude from his analysis that the two key concepts of the problematic of humanism are subject **(man)** and the abstract ideal essence. Althusser says that the problematic of humanism exists in some form throughout the modern intellectual history of the bourgeoisie in the principle of theories of society (from Hobbes to Rousseau), of political economy (from Petty to Ricardo), and in ethics (from Descartes to Kant) or the principle of the "theory of knowledge" (from Locke to Feuerbach). This argument still appears even if Althusser had put forward more theories and thoughts into this category.

Althusser proclaims that the fundamental mark of the emergence of Marxism is as follows: "By rejecting the essence of men as his theoretical basis, Marx rejected the whole of this organic system of postulates. He drove the philosophical categories of the subject, of **empiricism**, of the **ideal essence**, etc., from all the domains in which they had been supreme."[9] He means, as soon as Marx ceas-es to regard the essence of the transcendental man as the logical standpoint of all his theories, he is eliminating the philosophical cat-egories such as subject, value suspense and essence from his dis-course. This implies that Marx has abandoned the old philosophical framework of humanism once for all. Therefore, "Marx's theoreti-cal anti-humanism is above all a philosophical anti-humanism"[10], which is precisely the essence of historical materialism according to Althusser's point of view.

> *Marx's theoretical anti-humanism, as it operates within histori-cal materialism, thus means a refusal to root the explanation of social formations and their history in a concept of man with theo-retical pretensions, that is, a concept of man as an **originating subject**, one in whom originate his needs (**homo economicus**), his thoughts (**homo rationalis**), and his acts and struggles (**homo moralis, juridicus and politicus**).*[11]

---

8   Althusser, Louis. *Essays in Self-criticism*, p.198.
9   Althusser, Louis. *For Marx*, p.228.
10 Althusser, Louis. *Essays in Self-criticism*, p.200.
11 Ibid., p.205.

According to Althusser, the most important premise of Marx's establishment of the science of historical materialism is that he ceases to
regard Subject (pseudo-subject) as the historical ontology. He abol-
ishes the materialization myth of "homo oeconomicus" advocated in
political economy, and he also eliminates the "homo rationalis" in
epistemology, "social atomism" in history and "juridicus" in political
jurisprudence etc. According to Althusser, it at this time that Marx
proclaims theoretical humanism is an ideology, and the essence of
this ideology is a deceptive pretext. In fact, the bourgeoisie adopts
the illusionary relation of freedom and human value to cover up the
real social structure of the capitalist society. "The word Humanism
is exploited by an ideology which uses it to fight, i.e. to kill, another,
true, word, and one vital to the proletariat: **the class struggle**."[12]
Marx ceases to start from man because he refuses to draw conclusions on the process of history from man's point of view. In opposition to the bourgeoisie ideology, which starts from man, Marx starts
from the present social formation, capitalist society. In so doing, he
reveals the historically inevitable emergence and development of
capitalism and the objective law that the proletariat shall overthrow
the capitalists. These are essentially different from previous ethical
criticism, and Althusser's verdict on this point still stands.

Finally, in 1845, Marx ruptured radically with every theory, which
concludes that everything in history and politics is an essence
of man, namely, "theoretical humanism." Marx broke with his
Feuerbachian beliefs and regarded humanism, which used to be his
whole theoretical framework, as ideology. Then he abandoned it.
Therefore, Marxism in its maturity is "theoretical anti-humanism."
It is widely known that Marx rejected the old concepts and replaced
them with new ones through a complete theoretical revolution. "In
fact Marx established a new problematic, a new systematic way of
asking questions of the world, new principles and a new method."[13]
Delving deeper into this issue, Marx actually adopts a new theoretical framework, a new systematic way of asking questions for the
world, which represents a "new theory" constituted by new principles. Here, Marx replaces the old "couples" like human and his

---

12   Althusser, Louis. *Lenin and Philosophy and Other Essays*, p.22.
13   Althusser, Louis. *For Marx*, p.229.

essence, subject and alienation, with new categories (forces of pro-duction, relations of production, superstructure, ideology, economy playing the decisive role and other special determining factors). In this way, the science of historical materialism, or the **Historical Science** of Marx, is founded.

In reference to the fact that some people attempt to establish sys-tematic humanism based on the works of Young Marx, Althusser insists that in respect to theory, one should and must speak openly for **Marx's theoretical anti-humanism**. In our society, where vari-ous thoughts and theories exist, "it is impossible to know anything of man except on the absolute precondition that the philosophical (theoretical) myth of man is reduced to ashes. So any thought that appeals to Marx for any kind of restoration of a theoretical anthro-pology or humanism is no more than ashes."[14] I hold that this critical division is still significant today. However, it should not be denied that Althusser simplifies the issue in his fight against humanism. The fact is that man can be the object of study by historiography even after Marx established historical materialism. The fact that Marx re-jects the discourse logic of humanism does not lead to the exclusion of man as the object of study in histography. The reality is that Marx is probing into the issue of man (including alienation) even during the later stage of his thinking on economical-philosophy. Therefore, this is different from Althusser's claim that concepts like "man", "subject" and "alienation" disappear from Marx's thoughts ever since the establishment of historical materialism.[15]

It should be pointed out that Althusser believes that the existence of humanism is necessary although he refuses to regard Marxism as theoretical humanism. This has something to do with the fact that a particular ideology serves a particular class in the society. He com-ments: "The slogan of humanism has no theoretical value, but it does have value as a practical index."[16] In poverty-stricken areas and de-veloping countries in particular, humanism can be the banner, which calls on people to rise against their oppressors.

---

14   Ibid., p.229.
15   Zhang Yibing. *Back to Marx*, pp.656-663.
16   Althusser, Louis. *For Marx*, p.247.

Even today, this "humanism" and "historicism" find genuine-
ly revolutionary echoes in the political struggles waged by the
people of the Third World to conquer and defend their political
independence and set out on the socialist road. But these ideo-
logical and political advantages themselves, as Lenin admirably
*discerned, are offset by certain effects of the **logic** that they set*
in motion, which eventually and inevitably produce idealist and
empiricist temptations in economic and political conceptions
and practice – if they do not, given a favorable conjuncture, in-
duce, by a paradoxical but still necessary inversion, conceptions
which are tainted with reformism and opportunism, or quite sim-
ply revisionist.[17]

Have we traveled on the same path? Has the October revolution exerted a negative influence on the construction of the Soviet Union
and Eastern Europe? Has Mao Zedong's slogan of "never forget
class struggle" caused the prevailing idealism seen in China's socialist practices? Is it true or not that these "ideological and political
advantages", as proposed by Althusser, are offset by certain effects
of the **logic**? Historical facts will prove all of these points.

2 PSEUDO-SUBJECT: HISTORY IS A PROCESS WITHOUT A SUBJECT

Althusser says, considering the fact that the philosophical premise
of humanism is subject, it is natural that the historical view of it is
to regard history as a process **with a subject**. This means that "history is **a process of alienation which has a subject**, and that subject is man".[18] In the logical framework of this Subject Philosophy,
"history then becomes the transformation of a human nature, which
remains the subject of the history which transforms it."[19] He points
out in particular that Marx admitted this transcendental subject in
his *Manuscripts of 1844*. He argues: "the untenable thesis upheld by
Marx in the *Manuscripts of 1844* was that History is the History of
the process of alienation of a Subject, the Generic Essence of Man
alienated in 'alienated labor'."[20] Here, Althusser is basically correct.

---

17   Althusser, Louis. *Reading Capital*, p.141.
18   Althusser, Louis. *Politics and History*, p.182.
19   Althusser, Louis. *Reading Capital*, p.140.
20   Althusser, Louis. *Lenin and Philosophy and Other Essays*, p.121.

It has become clear to us that subject philosophy is the representation of bourgeoisie ideology. On this, Yimamura Hitoshi explains
as follows: according to Althusser, "modern philosophy, since
Descartes and Bacon, regards the basis of epistemology and being
as 'man, the subject'. Based on this, 'God' in the medieval theology
is disregarded as the basis. Man dominates the place of the basis
of the theories in knowing and understanding the world."[21] Man as
the subject is the replacement of the absence of God, which is a
very important identification of the essence of humanism following
Stirner and Nietzsche's theory of "anthropotheism". Nevertheless,
Althusser stresses its characteristics in political ideology.

> It is for precise ideological ends that bourgeois philosophy has
> taken the legal-ideological notion of the **subject**, made it into a
> philosophical category, its number one philosophical category,
> and posed **the question** of the Subject of knowledge (the ego of
> the cogito, the Kantian or Husserlian transcendental subject,
> etc.), of morality, etc., and of the Subject of history.... To be
> dialectical-materialist, Marxist philosophy must break with the
> idealist category of the **"Subject"** as Origin, Essence and Cause,
> responsible in its internality for all the determinations of the ex-
> ternal "Object", of which it is said to be the internal **"Subject"**...
> think real history (the process of the reproduction of social for-
> mations and their revolutionary transformation) as if it could be
> reduced to **an** Origin, **an** Essence, or **a** Cause (even Man), which
> would be its Subject – **a Subject**, a "being" or "essence", held
> to be **identifiable**, that is to say existing in the form of the unity
> of an **internality**, and (theoretically and practically **responsible**
> identity, internality and responsibility are constitutive, among
> other things, of every subject), thus accountable, thus capable of
> **accounting for** the whole of the "phenomena" of history.[22]

This is an important elaboration on subject philosophy. Similar to
that of Foucault, Althusser, whether as the descendant of structuralism or as the successor to Lacan, was to reject subject philosophy in his philosophical logic. Althusser directly rejected the notion of **individual as subject** in his research into Ideological State
Apparatuses, which we have previously discussed. At this point, he
is in fact attempting to logically falsify the **generic essence** notion in
the subject philosophy. What is different, however, is that he is not

---

21 Yimamura Hitoshi: *Althusser: Epistemological Rupture*, pp.115-116.
22 Althusser, Louis. *Essays in Self-criticism*, p.96.

simply falsifying subject philosophy but rather, he is directly trying to describe how Marx struggled out of it.

Althusser points out that it is in the *Manuscripts of 1844* in which the problematic of theoretical humanism still prevails and that these theses in it produce an **explosion**. This reminds us of Foucault's **grenade metaphor**. "But it was precisely this thesis that exploded. The result of this explosion was the evaporation of the notions of subject, human essence, and alienation, which disappear, that are completely atomized, and the liberation of the concept of **a process (prods or processus) without a subject**, which is the basics of all the analysis in *Capital*."[23] Why does subject philosophy explode? What is "a process without a subject"? These are issues that need to be discussed further.

According to Althusser, Marx introduces Hegel's philosophy into his own thoughts and the result is an explosion. "In Hegel, History is thought as a process of alienation **without a subject**, or a dialectical process **without a subject**."[24] As far as Althusser is concerned, there never exists a subject in Hegel's philosophy. "One cannot at any 'moment' assign a subject to the process of alienation any 'subject' whatsoever: neither some being (not even man) nor some nation, nor some 'moment' of the process. Therefore, 'a process without a subject or a purpose' is a category which can also be defined as 'a process without a subject or an object.'"[25] This is another paradox in Hegel's philosophy: process itself bears no subject but has a Subject which acts as the absolute Idea in the teleology of the process. **The only subject in the process of alienation is the process itself. According to Althusser**, the subject that is not the subject is only a theoretical logic developed by Hegel, namely, dialectic, or "the 'path' of the process as a process, the 'absolute method.'"[26]

The Hegel with this logic seems to be quite different from the Hegel with whom we are familiar. In Absolute Idea, the subject is of course an objective subject, rather than an **epistemological subject**, like Jehovah in the disguise of rationalism. The absolute Idea is no Being,

23 Althusser, Louis. *Lenin and Philosophy and Other Essays*, p.121.
24 Althusser, Louis. *Politics and History*, p.182.
25 Althusser, Louis. *Essays in Self-criticism*, p.119.
26 Althusser, Louis. *Politics and History*, p.184.

but it can dominate the Being behind it; absolute Idea is no common subject (individual as passion), but it can achieve its goal by way of "passion". Therefore, the process of its alienation and involution is its historical process of self-realization. The logic and concept are the dialectics. Here, there exist obvious discrepancies in Althusser's explanation.

Althusser says that there is, in Hegel, there is no **origin**, or (which is never anything but its phenomenon) any beginning. The origin, indispensable to the teleological nature of the process (since it is only the reflection of its End), has to be denied from the moment it is affirmed for the process of alienation to be a process without a subject. Being is immediately Non-being and affirmation is denial, and these are both right. However, is this for the sake of turning the process of alienation into a process without a subject? According to Althusser's point of view, the logical origin of a theory is its logical subject, and historical alienation describes the process of the decay and involution of the subject. However, Hegel starts from the theory that Being is Non-being. Personally, I hold that, in line with Althusser's elaboration, Hegel is post-structuralized.

> *The beginning of the Logic is the theory of the non-primordial nature of the origin. Hegel's Logic is the Origin affirmed-denied: the first form of a concept that Derrida has introduced into philosophical reflection, erasure (rapture)... But the Hegelian "erasure" constituted by the Logic from its first words is the negation of the negation, dialectical and hence teleological. It is in teleology that there lies the true Hegelian Subject. Take away the teleology; there remains the philosophical category that Marx inherited: **the category of a process without a subject.**[27]*

It is now time for Derrida to appear for the sake of deconstruction. Hegel proposes subject (Being), but he keeps erasing man. Although Althusser seems to be seriously examining Derrida's works, he cannot understand that Derrida actually belongs to a new theoretical era, as I have pointed in my first annotated text (Appendix I). Considering deconstruction's direct intention, the problematic of deconstruction must be Althusser's second target after he rejects the subject philosophy. By deducting the teleology in the above arguments, a historical truth will emerge: a process without a subject.

---

27   Ibid., pp.184-185.

That is why Althusser says "that is Marx's principal positive debt to Hegel: the concept of **a process without a subject**."[28] This is the biggest theoretical debt that connects Marx and Hegel. However, Althusser also implies that the concept of a process without a subject underpins the whole of Freud's work. More specifically, this idea can only stand if the subject category is replaced by **consciousness**. The reason lies in that, according to Freud, unconsciousness (libido and drives that are not repressed by civilization and education) is the essence of human existence and nature. In this sense, unconsciousness can be considered on par with the notion of "without a subject". On the other hand, "theoretical debt" represents one of Lacan's most important arguments: He thinks subject is overthrown by its image in the mirror stage and then is murdered by the replacement of symbols. In this voidness of subject, symbols are constantly adopted to fill in the gap. In this way, the debt, which can never be paid, accumulates. Obviously, this is not an appropriate metaphor.

According to Althusser, Marx borrows from the concept of **a process without a subject** from Hegel in order to eradicate teleology. He also takes the concept of "a process without a subject" as the key concept of historical materialism. He insists that "Marx was close to Hegel in his insistence on rejecting every philosophy of the Origin and of the Subject, whether rationalist, empiricist or transcendental; in his critique of the cogito, rejection of the sensualist-empiricist subject and the transcendental subject, thus in his critique of the idea of a theory of knowledge."[29] This explanation is basically acceptable.

For Marx, who establishes the science of history, "history is **a process without a subject**, that the dialectic at work in history is not the work of any Subject whatsoever, whether absolute (God) or merely human, but that the origin of history is always already thrust back before history, and therefore that there is neither a philosophical origin nor a philosophical Subject to History."[30] In historical materialism, there is no logical origin nor is there a logical subject. Neither individuals nor groups are subjects of history. "Men (plural), in the concrete sense, are necessarily subjects (plural) in history, because they act in history

---

28   Ibid., p 185.
29   Althusser, Louis. *Essays in Self-criticism*, p.178.
30   Althusser, Louis. *Lenin and Philosophy and Other Essays*, p.122.

as subjects (plural). But there is no Subject (singular) of history."[31] Alex Callinicos says that "the role that human individuals play in history as individuals is that of the embodiments of the process, not as its subjects."[32]

Obviously, he is correct. Men are subjects in history but not the subject of history, which is an issue difficult to be made explicit. "The question of the constitution of individuals as historical **subjects**, active in history, has nothing in principle to do with the question of the '**Subject** of history', or even with that of the '**subjects** of history'."[33] This explanation may seem awkward unless we relate it to the context of Lacan's subject criticism we dealt above. Subject is to be constituted (interpellation) and then falsely reproduced in the social and historical life. It regards itself as the subject of history, but it is merely a "trick" of ideology. In time, Althusser will unveil this cover.

> *History really is a "process without a Subject or Goal(s)", where the given circumstances in which "men" act as subjects under the determination of social **relations** are the product of the class **struggle**. History therefore does not have a **Subject**, in the philosophical sense of the term, but a motor: that very class struggle.*[34]

This corresponds to what Marx and Engels once said: the history of humanity is a history (process) of class struggle to the present day (and since the beginning of recorded history).

Althusser holds that, after 1845, Marx replaces subject with "process" in his science of history because "the concept process is scientific; the notion subject is ideological."[35] He argues "there is only one thing in the world which is absolute, and that is the method or the concept of the process."[36] I have pointed out that Althusser is a typical methodological imperialist, where methods are all that matters. Althusser says **process is without a subject**. "The word process which expresses a development considered **in the totality of its real conditions** has long been part of scientific language

31   Althusser, Louis. *Essays in Self-criticism*, p.94.
32   Callinicos, Alex. *Althusser's Marxism*, p.70.
33   Althusser, Louis. *Essays in Self-criticism*, p.95.
34   Ibid., p.100.
35   Althusser, Louis. *Politics and History*, p.185.
36   Althusser, Louis. *Lenin and Philosophy and Other Essays*, p.123.

throughout Europe."[37] Althusser does not clearly tell us how long this has been part of the scientific language, but I believe it has been since the Kant-Hegel period. Althusser emphasizes that process is a scientific term, and **"there is no such thing as a process except in relations**."[38] This "in relations" usage is typical in post-structuralist discourses. Althusser intends to promote the status of "process," but this process is not a historically linear progress.

3 PSEUDO HISTORICAL TIME AND ANTI-HISTORICISM

Althusser admits that Marx has established a new science of history, but he disagrees with traditional researchers' understandings of Marx's historical concepts; in particular, the **pseudo historical** time of historicism. The notion of pseudo historical time is "a conception of historical time as continuous and homogeneous and contemporaneous with itself,"[39] which Bachelard opposes. In fact, it corresponds with Bachelard's objection to subject philosophy, which regards history as a linear **continuum** with a subject. Therefore, on the one hand, Althusser advocates a process without a subject; on the other hand, he defines it as a diachronic process that is neither linear nor continuous. That is why Althusser specifically needs to give a description for **Historical time**.

Althusser claims that our understanding of Marx's historical concepts focuses on the proposition that Marx establishes his own historical descriptions based on his criticism of the non-historicity of classical economics (the whole bourgeoisie ideology). There is nothing wrong with this. Marx has an **ahistorical**, eternal, fixed and abstract conception of the classical economic categories. He historicizes these categories, regarding them as **relative, provisional** and **transitory**. In so doing, he breaks up the illusion that the capitalist mode of production is natural and eternal. This is significant, but what is interesting is that he believes that it is not **the last word of Marx's** critique since "it remains superficial and ambiguous, whereas his real critique is infinitely more profound."[40]

---

37 Ibid., p.121.
38 Ibid., p.186.
39 Althusser, Louis. *Reading Capital*, p.96.
40 Ibid., p.92.

Why? In Althusser's opinion, Marx's critique here has actually led to a crucial misunderstanding, Marx misunderstood historicism. In this case, Marx's relationship to classical economics can be represented as identical to that of Hegel's relationship to classical philosophy. Marx would then be Ricardo set in motion. In this case, Marx's whole achievement would once again be that he Hegelianizes Ricardo and makes him a follower of dialectic. Marx refuses to take Ricardo's categories as fixed, absolute or eternal but rather, he regards them as "relative, provisional and transitory, i.e., as categories subordinated in the last instance to the moment of their historical existence".[41] Obviously, Althusser is not satisfied with his elaboration and adds that "the two terms of the **eternity/history opposition** derive from a common problematic".[42] The origins of this misunderstanding may be in the conception of Hegel's historical time.

Hegel defines time as "**der daseiende Begriff**", i.e. as the concept in its immediate empirical existence and consciously proclaims that historical time is merely a reflection of the continuity of time and of the internal essence of historical totality. This historical totality personifies a moment in the development of the concept (in this case the Absolute Idea). At this moment, Althusser ignores his interpretation on "the process without a subject"; because the "essence of the historical totality" is nothing but the classical logical **subject**!

Althusser says there are essentially two characteristics of Hegel's historical time. The first is the homogeneous continuity of time, which is the reflection of the continuity of the dialectic development. In this sense, "the whole problem of the science of history would consist of the division of this continuum according to a *periodization* corresponding to the succession of one dialectical totality after another."[43] The moments of the Hegel's Idea exist in the number of historical periods into which the time continuum is accurately divided. According to Althusser, this is still the major trend in historiography studies.

---

41   Ibid., p.92.
42   Ibid., p.112.
43   Ibid., p.94.

The second characteristic is the contemporaneity of time or the category of the historical **present**, which suggests that Hegel's conception of historical time is the logical coexistence of the totality of
concepts. "The fact that the relation between the social totality and
its historical existence is a relation with an *immediate* existence, implies that this relation is in itself *immediate*."[44] In other words, "The
structure of historical existence is such that all the elements of the
whole always co-exist in one and the same time, one and the same
present, and therefore are contemporaneous with one another in one
and the same present."[45] In the logical subject, i.e. Hegel's absolute
idea, the structure of history is the logical process of the **'essential
section.'** "The structure of historical existence is such that all the
elements of the whole always co-exist in one and the same time, one
and the same present, and therefore are contemporaneous with one
another in one and the same present."[46] I believe this explanation to
be profound.

According to Althusser, this distinction of historical time is still popular today, as can be seen in the widely spread distinction between
synchrony and diachronic. In essence, this distinction is still based
on Hegel's historical time just like the claim that the synchronic is
just contemporaneity itself, the co-presence of the essence with its
determinations; the present being readable as a structure in an 'essential section' because the present is the very existence of the essential structure. From this, synchronic is identified as "the ideological
conception of a continuous-homogeneous time."[47] The synchronic
therefore presupposes the ideological conception of a continuous-
homogeneous time.

It follows that the diachronic is merely the development of this
"present" in the sequence of a temporal continuity in which the
"events" to which "history," in the strictest sense, can be reduced
and are merely successive contingent presents in the time continuum. Althusser holds that many contemporary historians like Lucien
Febvre, Braudel and many others are constrained by Hegel's time
continuum idea. In the ideological conception of the time continuum,

---

44   Ibid., p.94.
45   Ibid., p.94.
46   Ibid., p.94.
47   Ibid., p.96.

there are different times in history, varieties of time, long times, medium times and short times. Historians are only content to note their interferences as so many products of their intersection; "they do not therefore relate these varieties as so many variations to the structure of the whole although the latter directly governs the production of those variations."[48] These criticisms, nonetheless, make sense, but what is the relationship between Marx's historical time and all that Althusser has stated?

Here, what Althusser wants to propose is revealing: "the fact that **the structure of the social whole** must be strictly interrogated in order to find it in the secret of the conception of history in which the 'development' of this social whole is thought."[49] Althusser argues that the Marxist conception of the social totality can be constructed on the basis of **Marx's conception of social totality**. There is truth in Althusser's claim that history is a whole that is **being constituted**. The whole that is being constituted, if I do not take it wrong, it is the practical basis of the theoretical problematic, which he has mentioned. However, he does not extend his discussion on this historical whole in the same way that he does for problematic, and it never occurs to him to combine this research with that of problematic in order to fill a gap in his theory.

Althusser says the Marxist whole cannot possibly be confused with that of the Hegelian whole: it is a whole whose unity, far from being the spiritual unity, is constituted by a certain type of "**complexity, the unity of a structured whole**".[50] It is definitely alienated from the logical co-existence of the essential section.

> The structure of the whole is articulated as the structure of an **organic hierarchized whole**. The co-existence of limbs and their relations in the whole is governed by the order of the dominant structure which introduces a specific order into articulation (**Gliederung**) of the limbs and their relations.[51]

48   Ibid., p.96.
49   Ibid., p.97.
50   Ibid., p.97.
51   Ibid., p.98.

Pay attention! Althusser emphasizes that, in Marx's theory, the dominance of structure cannot be reduced to the primacy of a **centre**, any more than the relation between the elements and the structure can be reduced to the expressive unity of the essence contained in its phenomena. That is to say, the co-existence of the different structured levels, the economic, and the political, the ideological, etc., and therefore of the economic infrastructure, of the legal and political superstructure, of ideologies and theoretical formations (philosophy, sciences) can no longer be grasped as being co-existent with the Hegelian present. In other words, "it is no longer possible to think that the process of the development of the different levels of the whole **in the same historical time**, each of these different 'levels' does not have the same type of historical existence. On the contrary, we have to assign to each of these levels a particular time, relatively autonomous and hence relatively independent, even in its dependence of the times of the other levels."[52] This is one of Althusser's main arguments. This whole is not a homogeneous absolute whole, with each level possessing some degree of autonomy, which turns into the direct theoretical basis of Althusser's widely known multiple-determinism theory.

Althusser believes that, for each mode of production, there is a peculiar time and history, punctuated in a specific way by the development of the productive forces; and the relations of production have their peculiar time and history, punctuated in a specific way; also the political structure has its own history, etc.. What is more important is that "each of these peculiar histories is punctuated with peculiar rhythms and can only be known on condition that we have defined the concept of the specificity of their historical temporality and their punctuations (continuous development, revolutions, breaks, etc.)."[53] Althusser rejects the notion of the continuous and homogeneous historical temporality and also the alienated rhythm of history and time. These histories and times are **relatively autonomous**. Besides, this relative autonomy and independence are established with a certain type of dependence with respect to the whole. Therefore, "the mode of independence and degree of **independence** of each time

---

52   Ibid., p.99.
53   Ibid., p.100.

and history is therefore necessarily determined by the mode and degree of **independence** of each level within the set of articulations of the whole."[54]

It is in this context that Althusser offers an interesting proposal of two modes of time-existence, one being the **visible** and measurable time and the other being invisible time. This is also an issue of the invisible rhythms and punctuations concealed beneath the surface of the visible time. He even cites an example:

> *It shows, for example, that the time of economic production is a specific time (differing according to the mode of production), but also that, as a specific time, it is a complex and non-linear time – a time of times, a complex time that cannot be **read** in the continuity of the time of life or clocks, but has to be **constructed** out of the peculiar structure of production.*[55]

"The time of economic production" constructed by the capitalist mode of production has nothing to do with everyday ideological time. In daily life, ideology can always construct a continuous and homogeneous time which moves smoothly. But the time of economic production is different in that "it is a time that can be **read immediately** in the flow of any given process. It is an invisible time, essentially illegible, as invisible and as opaque as the reality of the total capitalist production process itself."[56] "The labor time under different productivities is alienated, thus labor time forms contradictory relation. This is further developed in Anthony Giddens' time-space deviation theory."[57] In addition, Althusser calls our attention to "the unconsciousness time," which has appeared since Freud. He also says that if we read Michel Foucault's remarkable studies in the *History of Madness* or the *Birth of Clinical Medicine*, we will understand the meaning of this concept. The so-called "unconsciousness time" is **time deleted by the official chronicles**, "in which a discipline or a society merely reflect its good conscience, i.e., the mask of its bad conscience".[58] Here, the complex historical time is actually a linear time of "good conscience", a trick played by the ideological historical time.

---

54 Ibid., p.100.
55 Ibid., p.101.
56 Ibid., p. 101.
57 Giddens, Anthony. *Modernity and Self-identity*, p.113.
58 Althusser, Louis. *Reading Capital*, p.103.

Althusser says, Marx's concept of historical time "can only be based on the complex and differentially articulated structure which is in dominance of the social totality that constitutes the social formation arising from a determinate mode of production".[59] This is an in-depth analysis. The concept of historical time is dominating the whole structure of the social totality.

> *It needs to be said that, just as there is no production in general, there is no history in general, but only specific structures of historicity, based in the last resort on the specific structures of the different modes of production, specific structures of historicity which, since they are merely the existence of determinate social formations (arising from specific modes of production), articulated as social wholes, have no meaning except as a function the essence of these totalities, i.e. of the essence of their peculiar complexity.*[60]

On this, Schmidt once commented that, the historical view of Althusser is "a theory that is dedicated to the transformation of social structures, which gives methodological priority to synchrony".[61]

To conclude, Althusser says:

> *From the theoretical standpoint, Marxist is no more a historicism than it is a humanism; that in many respects both historicism and humanism depend on the same ideological problematic; and that, "**theoretically speaking**, Marxism is, in a single movement and by virtue of the unique epistemological rupture which established it, an anti-humanism and an anti-historicism.*[62]

Schmidt says Althusser's point that there exists no "dogmatism, anthropologic or abstract humanism" is correct. Schmidt continues: however, "when they reject radically the construction effect of Hegel's logic on Marx's economic monographs, and maintain 'theoretical anti-humanism and anti-historicism', an inconsistency appears, for there is no evidence for this in Marx's texts."[63] I agree with Schmidt on this point. We may observe that in the discussion of historical temporality, Althusser does not focus purely on the general principles of Marx, but instead he has come to the historical reality.

---

59 Ibid., p.108.
60 Ibid., p.108.
61 Schmidt, Alfred. *History and Structure.* p.6.
62 Althusser, Louis. *Reading Capital*, p.119.
63 Schmidt. *History and Structure*, p.66.

If we are to further our understanding of his views, we need to probe into Althusser's detailed research on the science of the historical dialectic.

CHAPTER XI

MARXIST HISTORICAL SCIENCE

As has been stated, Althusser holds firmly that "Marxist-Leninism includes a **science** (historical materialism) and a **philosophy** (dialectical materialism)."[1] Since philosophy is not science, dialectical materialism is alienated to historical materialism. This is a very weird conclusion. What is even stranger, however, is that Althusser believes that philosophy always lags behind science, so it is science that determines the existence and development of philosophy. Philosophy is merely the class struggle in theory, while historical science (historical materialism) is the quintessence of Marxism. To be frank, I think this is the most awkward part of Althusser's academic research. Using the ideas of structuralism, Althusser reevaluates the effects of the mode of production on the society and history. This is also the core part of his statement on Marx and Marxism. He then proposes structural causality and his over-determination concept.

---

1   Althusser, Louis. *Lenin and Philosophy and Other Essays*, p.13.

1 PHILOSOPHY IS NOT SCIENCE

In 1968, Althusser's theories have changed. He confessed that the argument he made in *For Marx* – that the "epistemological break" took place in *Grundrisse* and *The German Ideology* – now seemed quite awkward. The critical theoretical revolution did, in fact, take place in 1845. However, there has to be a time-consuming process before Marx' scientific theoretical system was established. The break still existed, but in spite of this, science was not completely established. On the other hand, Althusser admitted, he was not attentive enough to the unscientific philosophical category, which still existed after the "epistemological **(scientific)** break" because "I did not separate Marx's philosophical revolution from the 'epistemological break'."[2] At first glance, this seems to be a profound self-criticism. However, he is not reflecting any word on his theory of rejecting subject. He only acknowledged that philosophy is not science, therefore, necessarily Marx's philosophical revolution does not lead to the scientific epistemological break.

> *I therefore talked about philosophy as if it were science, and quite logically wrote that in 1845 Marx made a **double** break, scientific **and** philosophical. ...It is impossible to reduce philosophy to science, and (it is impossible to reduce Marx's philosophical revolution to the "epistemological break". Marx's philosophical revolution preceded Marx's "epistemological break". **It made the break possible.**[3]*

The reasoning behind this line of thinking is related to Althusser's re-dividing science and philosophy.

Firstly, Althusser endows philosophy with a narrow connotative: "1. Philosophy is not a science, and it has no object, in that sense in which a science has an object. 2. Philosophy is a practice of political intervention carried out in theoretical form."[4] Let us further the argument. One reason why philosophy is not science is that it has no object while a science has an object. Furthermore, science deals with facts while philosophy deals with ideals. In this context, Althusser seems to possess a derogatory attitude towards philosophy in his

---

2   Althusser, Louis. *Essays in Self-criticism*, p.67.
3   Ibid., pp.67-68.
4   Althusser, Louis. *Lenin and Philosophy and Other Essays*, p.68.

comparison. Philosophy bears no object, so it is displayed as a practice, "a practice of political intervention carried out in theoretical
form." Compared with theory, practice is always in an inferior place.

He writes: "World outlooks are **represented** in the domain of **theory**
(science + the 'theoretical' ideologies which surround science and
scientists) by **philosophy**. Philosophy represents the class struggle
in theory."[5] **Philosophy is only the particular theoretical operation of science**. Althusser even goes further and adds that "philosophy, in its last instance, is the class struggle in theory,"[6] but this is
actually an exaggerated point.

If we set our discussion in the context in which Althusser studies Marxism, the result will be like this: historical materialism is
a historical science with object while dialectical materialism, as a
philosophy without object, only represents "class struggle" as one
of the scientific theories of historical materialism. To put it simply,
Althusser's arguments appear like this: Marx established the science
of historical materialism (historical science); however, in Engels and
Lenin's defense for this historical science, there emerges the theoretical mode, which opposes to all ideologies, but displays itself in
the form of ideology which fights on the same battle ground; and
this theoretical mode is the philosophy of dialectical materialism.
Obviously, this is a vulgar and untenable deduction.

In Althusser's point of view, every great scientific discovery induces a great transformation in philosophy in the history of human
development:

> *Every great scientific discovery induces a great transformation
> in philosophy. The scientific discoveries which open up the great
> scientific continents constitute the major dates in the periodiza-
> tion of the history of philosophy: 1st continent (Mathematics):
> birth of philosophy. Plato. 2nd continent (Physics): profound
> transformation of philosophy. Descartes. 3rd great continent
> (History, Marx): revolution in philosophy, announced in the 11th
> Thesis on Feuerbach.*[7]

---

5   Ibid., p.18.
6   Ibid., p.18.
7   Althusser, Louis. *Politics and History*, p.167.

We have mentioned this thesis above. Althusser says that "Marxist philosophy or dialectical materialism **cannot but be behind the science of history**."[8] This is because:

Philosophy only exists by virtue of the distance it lags behind its scientific inducement. Marxist philosophy should therefore lag behind the Marxist science of history. This does indeed seem to be the case. The thirty-year desert between the *Theses on Feuerbach* and *Anti-Dühring* is the evidence of this.[9]

This is by no means a responsible attitude toward history.

I, however, believe that Althusser's division between science and philosophy is meaningless. The origins of this division lay in Stalin's binary system. To make this binary system of philosophical framework more reasonable, Althusser creates the following groundless notion: according to this binary system, dialectical materialism, as class struggle in theory, becomes something like ideology while on the other side historical materialism is regarded as profound scientific theory. This notion is obviously untenable. His argument that "science has no object" is, in particular, groundless. He himself once had pointed out that the object of philosophy is problematic. It is common sense that the object of philosophy is the whole world, and philosophy transcends specific knowledge (with an object that can be felt by us). Besides, it is always the case that science induces philosophy. Both the existence and development of philosophy precede the establishment of science. Even in modern times, the relationship between philosophy and science is not the mechanical causality of determining and being determined. There is always unevenness in history.

According to the development of Marx's theory, his philosophical methodology agrees with his scientific discoveries. Sometimes, the philosophical methodology is the scientific discoveries. In his historical and philosophical thinking, there is no such philosophy of class struggle and no specific science of Marxism. It is just a fact that Marx has applied his new world outlook to the fields of politics, economics, historical science, etc. Marx's philosophical thoughts are in a constant active development after 1845. From 1847 to 1858, research into the historical materialism of economics reaches

---

8   Ibid., p.167.
9   Althusser, Louis. *Lenin and Philosophy and Other Essays*, p.43.

its third important theoretical peak.[10] However, due to the fact that Althusser's understanding on philosophy is still metaphysical and he still bears the prejudice of rejecting subject, he cannot get insight into real history, especially Marx's philosophical thinking following his rupture with metaphysics. In truth, this is rather pitiable.

2 THE NEW CONTINENT OF HISTORICAL SCIENCE

We mentioned above that Althusser claims that Marx establishes the third new continent of science, the new continent of historical science, after the ideological rupture of 1845. However, Althusser changes his point of view once again because he argues that the discovery of this new continent is not in *The German Ideology* but in *Capital*. "*Capital*, a mighty work, contains what is simply one of the three great scientific discoveries of the whole of human history: the discovery of the system of concepts (and therefore of the **scientific theory**) which opens up to scientific knowledge what can be called the 'Continent of History'."[11] Although this remark can be regarded as a self-criticism, it is also an identification of monism. However, the construction of history is also a process. The Marxist science of history did not progress in a simple straight line, according to the classic **rationalist scheme**, without problems or internal conflicts, or under its own power, from the moment of the "point of no return" – the "epistemological break".[12] It seems that, once again, Althusser is going to create something new.

According to Althusser, the famous Preface of 1859 (to *A Contribution to the Critique of Political Economy*) is still profoundly Hegelian-evolutionist. The *Grundrisse* of Marx, which date from the years 1857-59, are themselves profoundly marked by Hegel. When *Capital, Volume One* appeared (1867), traces of Hegelian influence still remained: "Marx (*Capital*) is the product of the work of Hegel (German Philosophy) on English Political Economy + French Socialism, in other words, the Hegelian dialectic on: **Labor theory of value (R) + the class struggle (FS).**"[13]

---

10   Zhang Yibing. See Chapters 6-9 of *Back to Marx: The Change of Philosophical Discourse in the Context of Economics.*
11   Althusser, Louis. *Lenin and Philosophy and Other Essays*, p.72.
12   Althusser, Louis. *Essays in Self-criticism*, p.71.
13   Althusser, Louis. *Politics and History*, p.173.

It seems that Althusser's old habit of monism was to come to life once again. Whenever the concepts of man, subject or anything else that the classical philosophy has ever touched upon appear, Althusser regards them as the remainings of old philosophy. However, Marx has never abandoned this kind of philosophy, which Althusser is opposing. Indeed, economic works like *1857-1858 Economic Manuscripts* and *The Poverty of Philosophy* are both excellent philosophical texts. In his studies on economics, the science of history and his political practice, Marx can always detect the real essence underneath the surface. If Althusser decides to treat all of these important philosophical criticisms as unscientific, he is sure to lose the essence of Marx's historical and dialectical materialism.

Althusser proposes an example of the word "value" to prove Marx's Hegelian influence. According to Althusser, the use of the term "value" can simply be replaced by the term of "social usefulness of products." He also argues that Marx has adopted Hegel's "negation of negation" to describe "expropriation of expropriation". He adds that the most obvious influence can be seen in the chapter of *"The Fetishism of Commodities and the Secret Thereof."* According to Althusser, "this time a flagrant and extremely harmful one, all the theoreticians of "reification" and "alienation" have found a base in it, a "foundation" for their idealist interpretation of Marxist's thought."[14] It is well known that the theory of surplus value is the most important basis of Marx's economic discoveries and the fetishism of commodity is the key part of Marx's historical phenomenology. If these theories are negated, we can imagine what is left for Althusser.

When does Marx eventually rid himself of Hegel? According to Althusser, *"The Critique of the Gotha Programme* (1875) as well as the Marginal Notes on Wagner's *"Lehrbuch der Politischen Ökonomie"* (Text book of Wagner in short) (1882) totally and definitely are exempt from any trace of Hegelian influence."[15]

It is at this time that Marx abandons the influence of subject theory and regards history as "a process without a history," thus the science of history is established. In accordance with Althusser's logic, as long as there exist concepts like subject and alienation in Marx's

---

14 Althusser, Louis. *Lenin and Philosophy and Other Essays*, p.95.
15 Ibid., p.95.

works and as long as Marx adopts the theoretical descriptive way of speculative philosophy, the old philosophy remains. According to Althusser, thoughts and language are closely related to each other: language is the announcer of the appearance of new thoughts and will accompany thoughts along the new road. The construction of Marx's historical science is not completely finished until the adoption of new terms in positive science.

To be frank, Althusser's analysis on this point is groundless and illogic because in the development of Marx's theory, Marx never reaches such phase.

In Althusser's point of view, it is only after the 1870s that Marx completely rejects the basic system of classical philosophical categories. The old philosophical system which argues "(Origin = ((Subject = Object) = Truth) = End = Foundation)" is circular. The most important logical base of the old philosophical system is the fact that "the adequation of subject and object is the teleological origin of all truth."[16] To demonstrate his opposition toward Hegelian philosophy, Althusser says that essentially we find in Marx a non-Hegelian conception of history, a non-Hegelian **conception of the social structure** (a structured whole in dominance) and "a non-Hegelian **dialectics**."[17]

Please pay attention to the notion of "a non-Hegelian **conception of history**". Here, Althusser presumes that all of these thoughts are not philosophy, especially not historical philosophy, but rather they are historical science. This implies that Marx no longer **uses philosophy to describe history**. "He elaborates a system of new scientific concepts where previously there had prevailed only the manipulation of ideological notions. Marx founds the science of history where there were previously only philosophies of history."[18] It is something that has been mentioned by Althusser before "it is the effect of a new theory, which is the system for posing problems in a correct form – the effect of a new problematic. Hence every theory is in its essence a problematic, i.e., the theoretical-systematic matrix for posing every problem concerning the object of the theory."[19] The reason is that

16   Ibid., p.173.
17   Ibid., p.173.
18   Ibid., p.38.
19   Althusser, Louis. *Reading Capital*, p.155.

"every revolution (new aspect of a science) in its object necessarily leads to a revolution in terminology."[20] This notion by him is, however, quite profound.

What Althusser actually implies here is that when Marx actually establishes historical materialism, he adopts a scientific conception, like mode of production, forces of production, relation of production, base and superstructure rather than the categories of classical philosophy like man, subject and alienation. "He (Marx) substituted others, only distantly related terms for them. Furthermore, he overhauled the connection which had previously ruled over these terms. For Marx, **both terms and relation** changed in nature and sense."[21] On this point, Althusser gets it right. "The basic concepts exist in the form of a system, and that is what makes them a theory. A theory is indeed a rigorous system of basic scientific concepts."[22] A new production mode which belongs to scientific theory, namely the problematic of historical materialism, needed to be established. In the meantime, "every terminology is linked to a definite circle of ideas, and we can translate this by saying: every terminology is a function of the theoretical system that provides its bases, every terminology brings with it a determinate and limited theoretical system."[23] However, there is nothing novel about Althusser's argument here.

In the theoretical system, there are a series of scientific conceptions. These concepts are abstract notions, basic tools. However, scientific abstraction is not at all "abstract." On the contrary, "what makes any abstraction scientific is precisely the fact that it designates a concrete reality which certainly exists but it is impossible to 'touch with one's hands' or 'see with one's eyes'."[24] This object is terribly concrete in that it is infinitely more tangible, more effective than the objects one can "touch with one's hands" or "see with one's eyes". One example is the production relation. It is the natural quality, the natural attribute of a substance or a subject that cannot be felt or touched. When you interpret the production relationship from the point of actual existence, you are under the illusion of fetishism,

20   Ibid., p.148.
21   Althusser, Louis. *For Marx*, p.109.
22   Althusser, Louis. *Lenin and Philosophy and Other Essays*, p.76.
23   Althusser, Louis. *Reading Capital*, p.148.
24   Althusser, Louis. *Lenin and Philosophy and Other Essays*, p.76.

which appears thanks to the special mechanisms of bourgeoisie society.[25] Although Althusser gets to the very core of it, it is actually metaphysical thinking.

Now, let us move to an important example, i.e., study on the mode of production, which is Althusser's key paradigm in his concept of historical science.

3 PRODUCTION MODE: THE BASIC COMPONENT OF MARX'S SCIENTIFIC PROBLEMATIC

According to Althusser, the most important concept in Marx's historical science is the mode of production. I notice that Althusser's argument here is still firmly adhered to by some other Marxists (Jameson and Eagleton). "By producing his key concept of **the mode of production**, Marx was indeed able to express the differential degree of material attack on nature by production, the differential mode of unity existing between 'men and nature' and the degree of variation in that unity."[26] The differential mode of unity existing between men and nature is **productive forces**, which Althusser nevertheless fails to consider and adopt. He says, "the men-nature unity expressed in the degree of variation in that unity is at the same time both the unity of men-nature relationship and the unity of **social relations** in which production takes place. The concept of the mode of production therefore contains the concept of the unity of this double unity."[27] Interestingly, to avoid using the concept of "man", Althusser adopts the notion of social relations in production rather than the relationship between men (man and man), which Marx originally used in describing the relations of production. This is really awkward. Besides this, Althusser provides further statements on the relations of production and the relationship between men and men:

> *The social relations of production are on no account reducible to mere relations between men, to relations which only involve men, and therefore to variations in a universal matrix, to inter-subjectivity (recognition, prestige, struggle, master-slave relationship, etc.)*[28]

25 Althusser, Louis. *Essays in Self-criticism*, p.52.
26 Althusser, Louis. *Reading Capital*, p.174.
27 Ibid., p.174.
28 Ibid., p.174.

Althusser stresses almost every word (using italics in the original version). He stresses that the social relations of production do not bring men alone onto the stage, but also the agents of the production process and the material conditions of the production process, in "specific combinations." This is a key concept put forward by Althusser, and this concept argues that in the economic process, men are mere "**agents** of the production" and agents of specific functions, i.e., the hypostatization of labor and capital, but are not subject or "man." This reflects Althusser's rejection of anthropological philosophy.

Obviously, Althusser does it on purpose when he defines notion of the relation of production because he never ignores the subject philosophy of anthropological philosophy. If we can grasp the relations of production as a regional structure, the mirage of the theoretical anthropology then dissolves. This is because:

> *The fact that the structure of the relations of production determines the **places** and functions occupied and adopted by the agents of the production, who are never anything more than the occupants of these places, insofar as they are the "supports" of these functions. The true "subjects" (in the sense of constitutive subjects of the process) are therefore not these occupants or functionaries, are not, despite all appearances, the "obviousness" of the "given" of naïve anthropology, "concrete individuals", "real men" – but the **definition and distribution of these places and functions. The true "subjects" are these definers and distributers: the relations of production** (and political and ideological social relations).[29]*

This is a very famous elaboration as well as a powerful bomb in Althusser's opposing to subject philosophy and anthropological philosophy. He explicitly points out that since the relations of production are object, they cannot be thought of as within the category **subject**. And if by chance anyone proposes to reduce these relations of production to relations between men, i.e., "**human relations**", he will be violating Marx's thought. In fact, Althusser himself realizes that the reason why Marx comes up with such a thought in the first place is that men are reduced to this function in economic contexts, function of production and exploitation in the relations of production

---

29   Ibid., p.180.

in bourgeoisie society. This is the unique nature of the relations of production in bourgeoisie society.

Indeed, it is only when the producers are in the bourgeoisie mode of production, suggesting that the producer is anonymous, replaceable, a mere "relation bearer" and "function carrier" that they can be regarded as agents of the production. Because if they are workers, they can be fired and if they are capitalists, they can achieve prosperity as well as bankruptcy.[30]

Here, I have to provide another theoretical marginal note. I discovered that the basic logic of Althusser's historical view is to adopt the **inverted Lacan** philosophy so as to interpret Marx's historical materialism. Why would I say this? Firstly, it can be observed that Althusser focuses on the phenomenon of materialization that Marx exclusively used to describe bourgeoisie society, and he then extends it to the whole process of history. By him **history in particular is extended to history in general**. It never persuaded Marx that personalized capital and materialized labor would be a perpetual historical phenomenon. In contrast, this is, however, the notion of the bourgeoisie ideology. This incorrect way of thinking resembles that of classical philosophy when it tries to interpret the framework of philosophy.[31]

Secondly, the existence of subject as a posthumous "agent" corresponds to the process in which the oblique-lined S disappears and the S1 (signifier) replaces it. However, in the social context, subject functions as the agent, as in work's productive tyranny and the crystallization of materialized relations is the biggest challenge to subject.[32] Lacan's argument – that absence of subject is then falsified as a "scientific" identification – is promoted by Althusser as the essence of Marx's historical materialism. It is a question that should draw our attention: who is actually violating Marx?

---

30   Althusser, Louis. *"Soutenance d'Amiens"*. Cited from *Collections of Issue 3 and Issue 4, Serial Book of Research Material on Marxism and Leninism*. Beijing: People's Education Press, 1986. p. 304-306.
31   Zhang Yibing. *The Subjective Dimension of Marxist Historical Dialectics*, Canut Intl. Publishers, London 2011. p. 5.
32   Lacan, Jacques. *Lacan's Seminars*. Trans. Chu Xiaoquan. Shanghai: SDX Joint Publishing Company, Verso. 2001. p.118.

In Althusser's point of view,

> *Marx shows in the greatest depth that the relations of production (and political and ideological social relations) are irreducible to any anthropological inter-subjectivity – since they only combine agents and objects in a specific structure of the distribution of relations, places and functions, occupied and "supported" by objects and agents of production.*[33]

For example, surplus-value is not a measurable reality for it is not a thing, but rather it is a kind of relationship, namely the existing social structure of production. When Adam Smith and others are confronted with the fact of surplus value in capitalist production, they remain in the dark, not realizing what they have produced. The reason for this is that bourgeoisie ideology is too far removed to imagine that "the fact might be the existence of a relation of 'combination', a relation of complexity, consubstantial with the entire mode of production".[34] This analysis by Althusser is quite acceptable; if we ignore that the premise of analysis is still "without a subject".

According to Althusser's point of view, the determining factor in identifying the social form is not the abstract conception, but the structure of the relations of production constructed on a particular economic basis under certain historical conditions. Therefore, the real subject of the historical process is not the individuals who are the bearers of the relations of production, but rather the real subject is the relations of production. Man as the subject is not the essence of his social relations. Instead, the status and effect of man is determined by the overall structure of relations of production. It is in this sense that history is a process without a subject. He asserts:

> *What Marx studies in **Capital** is the mechanism which makes the result of a history's production exist as a **society**; it is therefore the mechanism which gives this product of history, that is precisely society-product he is studying, the property of producing the "**society effect**" which makes this result exist as a society, and not as a heap of sand, an ant-hill, a workshop or mere collection of men.*[35]

---

33 Althusser, Louis. *Reading Capital*, p.180.
34 Ibid., p.181.
35 Ibid., p.65.

Althusser holds that Marx accepts the existence of subject when he is composing *Capital*. The subject is not the transcendental subject, but rather the process of objective social relations and structures. "No human, i.e. social individual can be the agent of a practice if he does not have the **form of a subject**. The 'subject-form' is actually the form of historical existence of every individual, of every agent of social practices."[36] Marx says that, in his economics, Ricardo's regards men as their caps. But Althusser says that a cap without man is real "man", but for me this is no more than a vivid fairy tale. Let us cite a comment from a normal man, L. Goldmann to illustrate this point:

> *It seems that Althusser has forgot there is no relationship be-*
> *tween human and non-human, ideology of non-human, or non-*
> *human quality (the productivity produced by proletariat, or the*
> *real estate like apparatus, raw materials and other products of*
> *human existence which only exists when they are used by men*
> *and which generate productivity). As to the concepts of super-*
> *structure and mode of production, they are important concepts in*
> *ordinary level. They consist of those more peculiar relations that*
> *we have mentioned above and they pointed out some aspects of*
> *the essence of the human activities.*[37]

Goldmann's criticism of Althusser here is quite a sobering one. Although Goldmann knows nothing about Lacan, he clearly understands that Althusser's relation of production is another form of the implicit discourse structure, which puts man and subject to death in the context of structural linguistics.

4 STRUCTURAL CAUSALITY OF HISTORICAL DEVELOPMENT AND OVER-DETERMINATION

What should also be mentioned here is that in the chapter of *"Marx's Immense Theoretical Revolution"*, Althusser has proposed a new idea of methodology, namely **structural** causality. According to Althusser, there are two distinctly different causalities in Marx's philosophy before science: **linear** and expressive causality. But Marx establishes his own structural causality based on the negation of these two false causalities.

---

36   Althusser, Louis. *Essays in Self-criticism*, p.95.
37   Goldmann, Lucien. *Marxism and Humanism*. Trans. Luo Guoxiang, p.180.

The linear causality is also a kind of **mechanical** causality. It originates from the mechanical philosophy of Descartes, which concludes that causality is a transitive and analytical function. This function usually occurs in planar space.

> *That a determinate effect could be related to an object cause, a different phenomenon; such that the necessity of its immanence could be grasped completely in the sequence of a given. The homogeneity of this space, its planar character, its property of giveness, its type of linear causality; these are so many theoretical determinations which, as a system, constitute a structure of a theoretical problematic.[38]*

Althusser believes, this is an empirical problematic, and Marx's (new) theory is radically opposed to this conception. Marx does not present his economic phenomena in the infinity of a homogeneous planar space, but rather he does it in a space determined by a regional structure itself inscribed in a site defined by a global structure: as a complex and deep space. To define economic phenomena by their concepts is to define them, he defines it below:

> *By the concept of the **(global) structure** of the mode of production, insofar as it determines the (regional) **structure** which constitutes as economic objects and determines the phenomena of this refined region, located in a defined site in the structure of the whole.[39]*

"But this place is no longer a point, nor is it fixed – it is an articulated system of positions governed by the determination in the last instance."[40]

Expressive causality, which began by Leibniz, is brought to its apex by Althusser and is accepted by Lukacs, Korsch and many others. In this expressive causality, every phenomenon can be analyzed as having a nature and all the elements are only expressive of the entire whole. Althusser asserts: In Hegel's logic, when approaching to any phenomenon, **"it presupposed that the whole had a certain nature, precisely the nature of a 'spiritual' whole in which each element was expressive of the entire totality as a 'pars totalis'."**[41]

---

38 Althusser, Louis. *Reading Capital*, p.181.
39 Ibid., p.182.
40 Althusser, Louis. *Essays in Self-criticism*, pp.183-184.
41 Althusser, Louis. *Reading Capital*, p.180.

Althusser believes that the key reason why Marx could discover the new continent of historical science is that he has fully abandoned the above linear and expressive causality and creates a new causality, namely the structural causality. In this new causality, structure stands above the elements rather than as part of the effects of the whole. The structure of the relations of production defines the economy. Therefore, the description of the proactive relations in a particular mode can only be set in the whole society. Obviously, the real constraint on history roots from prescriptions related to the whole of the object structure. Therefore, Marx's structural causality can correctly describe the influence of (the whole of the object structure's impact) overall impact on local (regional) structure and the relative independence of local structure.

Althusser later restates it as "Hegel thought of society as a **totality**, while Marx thought of it as a complex whole, structured in dominance."[42] Hegel's totality is **expressive** while the concept of totality in Marx's scientific theory is a complex whole, structured in dominance.

> *In the Marxist conception of a social formation everything holds together, that the independence of an element is only ever the form of its independence, and that the interplay of the differences is regulated by the unity of a determination in the last instance.*[43]

This paragraph suggests that, in his arguments on social formation, Althusser carefully distinguishes totality from whole. The former is the **overall logical paradigm** of Hegel's idea-tional teleology while the latter is the **actual analysis** of the social complex whole, which is structured in dominance. He analyzes:

> *As to Hegel, society and history is circle in circle and ball in ball. The dominant concept in this ideal is totality: all the elements are part of the totality and are expressive of the totality's internal unity. The internal unity, however complex, is always the objectification and alienation of the basic principles. In Marxist theory of social formation, the whole is dominant of everything and the independence of any element is only expressive of its identification. The differences of the dominant elements are regulated by the determinant factors in the last stage.*[44]

---

42   Althusser, Louis. *Essays in Self-criticism*, p.180.
43   Ibid., p.183.
44   Althusser, Louis. *"Soutenance d'Amiens"*. Cited from *Collections of Issue 3 and Issue 4, Serial Book of Research Material on Marxism and Leninism*. Beijing: People's Education Press, 1986.304-306.

Althusser says that the reason why he does not adopt the concept of totality to describe Marxist theory of social formation is that the actual social structure is complex and imbalanced and thus cannot be grasped by using Hegel's logical paradigm. If I do not get it wrong, Althusser's distinction between totality and whole aims to falsify the anthropological description, which starts from the young Lukács and is succeeded by Lefebvre and Sartre. Of course, his negation of totality is not the more general and deeper negation made by Adorno regarding totality. What is more, Althusser adds:

> *I tried to show this in connection with the question of contradiction, by pointing out that if you take seriously the nature of the Marxist whole and its unevenness, you must come to the conclusion that this unevenness is necessarily reflected in the form of the* **overdetermination** *or of the* **underdetermination** *of contraction.*[45]

This leads to another of Althusser's methodologies: **over-determination**. If history is a process without a subject, there remains another key issue that needs to be made explicit, because that the basis and developmental process of history is the **over-determination** of various historical elements. Althusser himself says that the word over-determination "is borrowed from two existing disciplines: especially from linguistics and psychoanalysis".[46] As I have already mentioned the word "over-determination" is mainly borrowed from Freud. According to Freud, it is the mixture of unconscious impulses and ideas that occur when men are in a situation of abundant fantasies. Althusser then holds that we are all elements in the system of over-determination.

It can be concluded that everyman's acts are the result of "over-determination". Obviously, over-determination originally refers to a kind of mental illness, posited by Freud, and is caused by the collective influence of many factors. However, Althusser adopts this term to represent the ultimate formation of social bases and to explain a vast accumulation of contradictions in the development of society according to his interpretation of Marxist historical view.

---

45   Althusser, Louis. *Essays in Self-criticism*, p.184.
46   Althusser, Louis. *For Marx*, p.155.

Althusser points out that the Marxist historical view is not a simple, linear development. The existence of social contradiction does not work alone and the contradiction is reduced to **the purest form** (the contradiction between capital and labor). "The Capital-Labor contraction is never simple, but always specified by the historically concrete forms and circumstances in which it is exercised."[47] Therefore, the causes of the existence and the structure of the social entity consists of a vast accumulation of contradictions. "A vast accumulation of 'contradictions' comes into play **in the same court**, some of which are radically heterogeneous – coming from different origins, different sense, different **levels** and **points** of application – but all of which nevertheless merge into a ruptural unity."[48] Althusser opposes the idea which regards historical materialism as economic-determinism. He says, "the idea of a 'pure and simple' non-overdetermined contradiction is, as Engels said of is the economist turn of phrase 'meaningless, abstract, and senseless'."[49]

This explanation of him may be of pedagogical convenience, but it is not the true reflection of the essence of history. This is because all of the contradictions appear as the over-determined contradiction in real historical practice. We cannot reduce the causes for the development of history to a unique internal principle, like economy. The reduction of all the elements that make up the concrete life of any historical epoch (economic, social, political and legal institutions, customs, ethics, art, religion, philosophy, and even historical events: wars, battles, defeats, and so on) to one principle of internal unity, is itself only possible in the ideology of Hegel's idea-tional idealism. As Althusser sees it, the contradiction in social life "is radically **affected by them**, determining, but also determined in one and the same movement, and determined by the various **levels** and **instances** of the social formation it animates; it might be called **overdetermined in its principle**".[50]

Then, what is "over-determination", as the way Althusser puts it? In his point of view, the existence of the contradiction is not linear, nor is it in chaos, but rather it displays a context in which one

47   Ibid., p.106.
48   Ibid., p.100.
49   Ibid., p.113.
50   Ibid., p.101.

contradiction is **in the dominant position**. Social contradiction is a complex whole. **"The complex whole has the unity of a structure articulated in dominance."**[51] On this, Poulantzas offers the following interpretation:

> *This relation is not linear causality nor an expressive mediated relation or analogical correlation. It is only a kind of relation in which the dominant structure determines the system (property) of other branch structures so that all these structures can play their own parts. Therefore, the relations in each levels are not simple and **overdetermined** by relations of other levels.*[52]

Therefore, according to Althusser, economy only becomes the decisive factor in social and historical development **in the last instance** and only as the dominant contradiction among other contradictions. In certain circumstances, other contradictions may also be the dominant part of the whole. This idea contributes to the concept of overdetermination, which possesses the characteristic of "variability of dominant structure and the invariability of the totality". In so doing, he defends "the notion of economic determination and does not reduce it to a static and one-way process".[53] Althusser says that it is economism (mechanism) and not true Marxist theory that sets up the hierarchy of instances once and for all, assigns each its essence, its role and defines the universal meaning of their relations; instead it is economism that that identifies roles and actors eternally, not realizing that the necessity of the process lies in an exchange of roles "according to circumstances", "whereas in real history determination in the last instance by the economy is exercised precisely in the permutations of the principal role between the economy, politics, theory, etc."[54]

> *Only overdetermination enables us to understand the concrete variations and mutations of a structured complexity such as a social formation (the only one that has really been dealt with by Marxist practice up to now), not as the accidental variations and mutations produced by external conditions in a fixed structured whole, in its categories and their fixed order (this is precisely mechanism) – but as so many concrete restructuration inscribed*

---

51   Ibid., p.202.
52   Poulantzas, Nicos. *Political Power and Social Class*, p.4.
53   Woolf, Janet. *The Social Production of Art*. p.107.
54   Althusser, Louis. *For Marx*, p.213.

in the essence, the "play" of each category, in the essence, the "play" of each contradiction, in the essence the "play" of the articulations of the complex structure in dominance which is reflected in them.[55]

Althusser himself claims that his theory of over-detemination finds its origin in Mao Zedong's Contradiction theory.[56]

It seems that Althusser's theory has accidentally won universal praise from both Oriental and Western scholars in the research field of Marxist philosophy. For example, Schmidt holds that Althusser's arguments and "polemic against the all-too-smooth linearity of a naïve, evolutionist understanding of history, a view that was not at all alien to the Marxism of the Second International, contains moments of truth".[57] The scholar David McLellan says that Althusser comes up with the theory of over-determination, "thus Althusser rejected the idea that there was only one simple contradiction between productive forces and relations of production, between base and structure".[58] Even in the more orthodox academic field, in the Soviet Union, Althusser's ideas were accepted.[59] Time passes by, and many outstanding theories fade into the flow of history. However, echoes of this theory can still be captured even in a post-Marxist context.[60]

---

55   Althusser, Louis. *For Marx*, p.210.
56   Ibid., p.100.
57   Schmidt, Alfred. *History and Structure*, p.7.
58   McLellan, David. *Marxism after Marx*, p.331.
59   *Contemporary Marxist Review*. Beijing: Social Sciences Academic Press, 1986. pp.419-421.
60   Graham, Gibson. *The End of Capitalism*. Trans. by Chen Dong. Beijing: Social Sciences Academic Press, Verso.2002. pp. 33-37.

CONCLUSION:

RAIN OF DECONSTRUCTION:
THE END OF ALEATORY MATERIALISM

In 1982, Althusser, who was recently discharged from hospital, wrote a new philosophical essay called *Aleatory Materialism*. During those ten years before he passed away, a new philosophical concept of "aleatory materialism" became his last theoretical situating. In some papers concerning "the Althusser in his late years", aleatory materialism is regarded as a new phase in the development of his thoughts. It seems that Althusser is still developing his philosophical ideas. For instance, Antonio Negri considers aleatory materialism as a real turning point in Althusser's theoretical works. At every philosophical turn, continuity and creativity are intertwined but creativity finally gains the dominant position.[1]

Regarding this, my judgment is contrary to Antonio's. In my opinion, the aleatory materialism is just the inevitable outcome of Althusser's philosophical, logical situating. But it is a tragic final. In the shadow of death, the originally solid logical structure is completely deconstructed. Like the aleatorily falling rain, the exploded fragments of logic fall from the sky. The last drop of rain is Man's ideological

---

1   See, article of Morfino, Vittorio. *The Later Works of Althusser.* Journal Article from Theories Abroad. Beijing 2008 (3).

tear. In truth, the philosophy of rain is metaphysics of tears. This is Althusser's last ideological outcry.

In 1966, Adorno's *Negative Dialectics* was published. Since then, Adorno has transformed from the blind worship of Enlightenment to the negation of the metaphysical Gestalt, which symbolized the end of the theoretical logic in Western Marxism that criticized modern capitalism.[2]

Also in 1966, *Écrits of Lacan* was published, which was a death sentence for Freudian pseudo-ego, also for the individual pseudo-subject of new anthropology and all violent rule of language structure.[3]

In 1967, Derrida, Althusser's student, published three works: *Writing and Difference*, *Speech and Phenomena*, and *Of Grammatology*, which firstly tolled the funeral bell for the ideological trend of structuralism, the theoretical basis of his teacher.

In that same year, Guy Debord's *The Society of the Spectacle*[4] and Vaneigem's *Revolution of Everyday Life*[5] were published. The replacement of the commodity kingdom by the spectacle world (referring to the society of the spectacle), and the revolution "turning everyday life into art" have started the conceptual rebellion of the post-Marxist ideological trend.

In May 1968, the "Red Storm," which started in Paris, swept through France and spread rapidly across European countries. The walls at universities were covered with slogans such as "useless Althusser" and "structure can't go to streets". The year 1968 tolls the funeral bell for the ideological trend of structuralism. A. Badiou, the previous team member of Althusser, was fanatically involved in this red storm.

---

2 See: *Deep Plough Unscrambling Major Post-Marxist Texts, from Adorno to Zizek*, published in 2011 by Canut Intl. Publishers, London and *Atonal Dialectic Imagination: The Textual Interpretation of Adorno's Negation of Dialectics* by Joint Publishing, 2001, China.
3 See: *The Impossible Truth of Existence-Mirror Image of Lacanian Philosophy*. Beijing: The Commercial Press, 2006.
4 Debord, Guy. *The Society of the Spectacle*. Trans. Wang Zhaofeng. Nanjing: Nanjing University Press, 2005. See: *Deep Plough Unscrambling Major Post-Marxist Texts, from Adorno to Zizek*, published in 2011 by Canut Intl. Publishers, London.
5 Vaneigem, Raoul. The Revolution of Everyday Life. Trans. Zhang Xinmu et al. Nanjing: Nanjing University Press, 2008.

In 1969, Foucault gave up his *Episteme* advocated in *The Archaeology of Knowledge* and turned to discourse practice. In 1970, he changed from archaeology to Nietzschean Carnival Genealogy.

In 1969, Althusser published *Ideology and Ideological State Apparatus*, which was written under the influence of Lacan. In this essay, Althusser criticizes the construction of individual pseudo-subject by ideology (devil), but he did not critically ponder over the otherness of **logic of scientific knowledge**.

In 1970, Barthes' *S/Z* was published, which symbolized his shift from structuralist semiotics to post-modern textology.

Up to now, people found that the "Four Musketeers" of French structuralism (Lacan, Althusser, Barthes, and Foucault) revolted together and aimed their guns directly at structuralism. Lacan was not a practitioner in this team of structuralism but a lurking killer that "kills someone with a borrowed knife." Both Barthes and Foucault rejected structuralism. Althusser fails to find the exit of the defect, and he finally points the gun at himself.

In 1974, Althusser's *Essays in Self-Criticism* was published.

In 1974, Jacques Ranciere, the student of Althusser, published his first book *Althusser's Lesson*. In this book, Ranciere claims that Althusser died on the roadblock of "European May 1968".

In October 1979, Poulantzas, who was Althusser's follower, killed himself.

In 1980, Lacan declared his dismission of EPT*. In August 1980, Althusser confessed to Balibar, the only student who did not betray him: I would not kill myself. I would deal with worse matters. I would destroy all I have created and all that I have displayed to myself and others.

On November 16th in 1980, Althusser killed his wife as a result of his mental disorder.

In 1985, Michelle, Althusser's disciple, committed suicide.

---

*) Ego Psychology Theory (EPT). The development of EPT was inspired by Freud's (1923) structural theory, which defined the ego as one of three psychic structures that have separate, but interrelated functions that play an essential role in personality development, along with the id (e.g. basic instincts) and the superego (e.g. conscience and external influences), (Turner, 1996).

This is a tragic historical clue. The most tragic is that Althusser chooses passive theoretical retreat when faced with the significant historical turn from modernity to post-modernity in European ideological history.

In 1974, while writing the preface for *Philosophy and the Spontaneous Philosophy of the Scientists*, Althusser said that philosophy does not have any **object** but only **enjeu** and philosophy does not produce knowledge but only states *theses*.[6]

Please note that the *enjeu* here is not the firm **enjeu of faith** as advocated by Pascal and Goldmann but the retreating to *enjeu* of luck which weakens absolute idea in ideological system to incidents. It also means that when Althusser assumed philosophy instead of having object, has *enjeu* and science does not produce instead it states theses, the problematic theory that he constructed, determines every thinker's inquiring method, and producing his/her theoretical thoughts becomes an *enjeu* without firm faith. Althusser once told the following story: when confronted with the crisis, collapsing of a theoretical building, there are three groups of scientists that react differently. The first group ignores the crisis and continues to work. The second group turns to philosophical speculation without object after finding that everything collapses. The third group admits that the crisis awakens them from "dogmatism". It appears that Althusser belongs to the third group. He now wakes up from the "dogmatism" of "theoreticism", but fails to quickly fit in the post-modern ideological trend of deconstruction like Barthes and Foucault. His attitude is self-dissolving.

During the year of 1975, Althusser began to modify the manuscript of *Machiavelli and Us*.[7]

---

6   Ego Psychology Theory (EPT). The development of EPT was inspired by Freud's (1923) structural theory, which defined the ego as one of three psychic structures that have separate, but interrelated functions that play an essential role in personality development, along with the id (e.g. basic instincts) and the superego (e.g. conscience and external influences), (Turner, 1996). Althusser, Louis. *Philosophy and Politics: The Works of Althusser*. Changchun: Jilin People's Publishing House, 2003. p. 5.
7   Althusser, *Philosophy and Politics*, pp. 376-504.

In 1978, Althusser regressed from his original position and transited to position *Crisis of Marxism* evaluation, thus started to doubt his previous faith in Marxism. He evaluated Marx's view of successive progress of social formations to communist society as stated in Capital as a "transparent" fantasy. Besides, he considered the progress from the realm of necessity towards the realm of freedom as an "idealist statement".[8] He described Marx's works after 1845 as full of "blanks, paradoxes, and fantasy". Therefore, he loudly declared "crisis of Marxism". In Greek diaspora's Hellenic Journal N. Poulantzas wrote in 1979, "On the crisis of Marxism its opponents proclaim. On that point, in spite of all the disagreements between us as to the nature of the crisis, I agree with [Louis) Althusser, who recently spoke of a *creative and hopeful crisis* in Marxism."

In 1982, the completely mad Althusser wrote the book *About Aleatory Materialism* during his lucid intervals. According to my understanding, this was not a "new phase" of Althusser's theoretical development, **but the killing of his own theoretical logic**. The strong scientific problematic was broken into the aleatory situating of thinking. In this inevitable self-explosion, all structuralist Gestalts were crushed into fragments and **fell from the sky down to earth**, which is momentous rain of deconstruction. In this delightful rain, Althusser feels sorrowful and embarrassed rather than happy and excited as Barthes was after his liberation.

So we find that in the manuscript of *Machiavelli and Us* which is modified for the second time after 1985, "aléatoire" and "fragment" have become the key words in Althusser's thinking. Apparently, it was the result of the trend of post-modernism. Aléatoire is the powerful weapon used to fight against grand narrative, and fragment is the sharp sword used to dissolve the logos of modernity. In Althusser's eyes, Machiavelli has constructed economy, geography, language and culture into an "aleatory space". The formation of a people is merely the aleatory generation of a specific existing element.[9] Political subject is just a temptation of "vacancy" and an aleatory filling under inquiry.[10] Man is "complete emptiness" and

---

8   Althusser, *Philosophy and Politics*, p. 254.
9   Ibid., p. 387.
10   Ibid., p. 414.

can only obtain their identities aleatorily in a specific context. The "allocation" of theories appears more fun, and Althusser even advocates to mobilize theoretical fragments in a vacuum because it is never possible to find the center that connects all things.

He assumes: the theory exists in a strange form of fragments which of an "unfinished" whole. However, these fragments are rather parts of seemingly absent whole than an unfinished whole. They are arranged in a strange deformed space. With such structure, it is impossible to include or gather these fragments into a perfect unity.[11]

Obviously, Machiavelli is fried in the hot oil of Althusser's postmodern logic because the "new monarch" of the past centuries should have thought with the concept of aleatory and unique conjuncture.[12] Judging the manuscript, we see that Althusser refined this statement after 1986. Instead of being the simple addition of elements and the enumeration of all situations, this concept of "conjoncture" is their paradoxical system. It is the paradoxical system of these elements and situations. It is the situation, circumstance, and conjunction that are dynamically constructed in the **comparative relations of force** in the political fight.[13] Conjunction is the aleatory encounter and collision of elements. Thus, Althusser enables Machiavelli to think in a brand-new ideological experiment of "event and circumstance". How tired the ancients are! Althusser desperately modified the texts which he wrote ten years ago. And he wrote those concepts such as "aléatoire", "emptiness" and "encounter" on his old drafts.

In my opinion, the theory of **aleatory materialism** was a compromise to post-modernism. The scientific problematic (logical structure) and the material production mode (objective social structure) are liquefied into the rain of logic, and are violently beaten upon the beach by the waves of post-modern logic. Althusser's last book is the book about "ordinary rain". The philosophy of rain is the rain of logic that falls from the sky and disappears when upon the land. He quotes the story of Malebranche, and discusses the rain falling on the beach, falling on the road and into the ocean. The rain neither increases nor is it wasted. **It rains materialistically everywhere,**

---

11   Ibid., p. 392.
12   Ibid., p. 395.
13   Ibid., p. 396.

throughout the whole history of ideology, starting from Lucretius to Democritus and Epicurus, even to Spinoza, Machiavelli, Hobbes, Rousseau, Marx, Heidegger and Derrida.

Two questions need to be discussed here. People who are familiar with the ideological development of the Young Marx will ask the following questions: Wasn't the materialism of Democritus and atomism of Epicurus discussed in the dissertation of the Young Marx? And what kind of logical progress is there in Althusser's thinking? The Young Marx in Prussian influenced Germany during the 1840s was a radical bourgeois democratic fighter. He attempted to negate the inevitable straight line atomic declination idea* in Epicurus' atomism. The deflection made by Marx here represents the initiative of self-consciousness. And behind this aleatory deflection was the individual subject in German bourgeois revolution. However, what Althusser does is to eliminate the initiative of that deflection and restore the real aléatoire. The aleatorily constructed world is a huge emptiness, it is an abandoned and empty historical stage. Besides, the Young Marx turns materialist Epicurus into an self-conscious idealist militant for the bourgeois democratic revolution. But Althusser turns both the materialism of Epicurus and Marx into aléatoire which is **the basis of ontology**. Therefore, in this sense, Heidegger's **thrown** *Dasein* that rejects any fossilization and Derrida's negation of the **deconstruction** of Logocentrism are both **materialism**!

And it is in this sense that Althusser regards the new-style of materialist philosophers as "people who board a running train". He never knows the starting point, the first principle, and teleology. He always faces the empty and changeable world in an unexpected and aleatory way.[14] What is interesting is that this metaphor firstly makes people think of Bloch's ironical statement while criticizing the dogmatic historical teleological of the former Soviet Union, namely people

---

14 Althusser, *Aleatory Materialism*, p. 290.

*) Epicurus' original concept consisted in the notion of the declination of atoms from the straight line. The fall in a straight line, that is, the motion of gravity, reduces the atom to dependence upon the blind necessity of nature; its existence is purely material. The motion of declination from the straight line, therefore, constitutes the independence and freedom of the atom. In virtue of this deviation the atoms are purely autonomous bodies, or rather are bodies conceived in an absolute autonomy. In declination the real soul of the atom, the concept of abstract individuality, is represented.

can get to the beautiful future as long as they buy a ticket to communism from the authorities. Althusser also lets people board the train, but it is an aleatory journey with neither return nor direction. Actually, what is really happening here is a logical yielding, resembling the metaphor of "ideological surfing" posed by Deleuze in the post-modern context.[15] Althusser does not have a clue about what will happen to the ideological surfing on the torrents. Anyway, this may have been a blessing for Althusser who, by this time, had already gone out of his mind.

"It is raining."[16] This is a slightly sad poem. Rain symbolizes tears and the world does not have roofs. Althusser, who had already been mentally destroyed, is silently crying.

---

15   Deleuze, Gilles. *The Negation of Philosophy and Power*. Trans. Liu Han. Beijing: The Commercial Press, 2000. p. 206.
16   Althusser, *Aleatory Materialism*, p. 167.

POSTSCRIPT

In the term of textual theory, there are few scholars who are worth careful interpretation in Western Marxism philosophy. Yet, there do exist masters. However, because of the humanistic, transcendental logical setting, few of their works can withstand careful deliberation, or repeated consideration by later generations whose intent may be to open up new horizons for historical interpretation. Meanwhile, we cannot lose sight of the fact that some works stand out, such as the young Lukacs' *History and Class Consciousness*, Bloch's *The Principle of Hope*, Fromm's *Marx's Concept of Man*, Schmidt's *Marx's Concept of Nature*, Goldmann's *The Hidden God*, and Kosik's *Dialectics of the Concrete*. Following these works, Adorno, the initiator of the post-modern trend in ideology, who wrote the masterpiece *Negative Dialectics* (Based on this, I wrote *Atonal Dialectic Imagination-Textual Interpretation of Adorno's Negative Dialectics*). After post-modernism, the text itself is deconstructed. Among the representative figures of post-modern era, only the works of Deleuze, Baudrillard, and Zizek are worth careful interpretation. To some extent, works that belong to the humanistic Gestalt trend in Western Marxism display rationality and preciseness. Therefore, the majority of objects within textual research belong to the range of humanism. Certainly, there are exceptions, such as Althusser whom we have discussed in this book.

In contrast to humanistic trend, scientific Marxism trend pay more attention to methodology and rigorous theoretical logical structure, and they stick to return to empiricism. Thus, most of the scientific texts are "plain boiled water" in the interpretative sense. The principle remains on the surface of discourse, as we see by Della Volpe, Cohen, Elster, and Poulantzas. However, as the founder of scientific Marxism, Althusser is different from others. At first, his thinking stems from the super-organic God, though he purposefully intended to hide this cultural origin. Then he is educated and nurtured by masters like Spinoza, Hegel, and Machiavelli. His teacher Bachelard is both a poetic philosopher and an empirical scientist. Sometimes we are even unable to believe that the author of *Psychoanalysis of Fire and History of Science* is the same person.[1] Besides, Lacan is also another great thinker who has exerted significant influence on Althusser. The "post-structuralist" (Zizek objects to this theoretical orientation) psychological text of Lacan is a philosophical poetry. Yet, behind every line and every word of his poetry hides profound thinking. These complex, supporting foundations allow Althusser to successfully write the texts in ways that are even better than anthropological texts. He makes great effort to use scientific methodology, but he borrows many internal Gestalts from speculative philosophy. When constructing the non-ideological, scientific problematic, Althusser uses many elusive words.[2] This is a unique academic phenomenon. *For Marx* and *Reading Capital* are both poetic and empirical texts, but his *Ideology* and *Ideological State Apparatus* is more like a classic example of critical theory. Before the postmodern context emerges, these works can be called masterpieces of Western Marxism texts. In today's post-Marxist context, it is said that Althusser voice is heard once again,[3] but this was historically inevitable.

---

1   Hitoshi says that the relations of Althusser and Bachelard are not quite close. But this does not affect the significant academic influence exerted by Bachelard on Althusser. See: Yimamura Hitoshi: *Althusser: Epistemological Rupture*. Trans. Niu Jianke. Hebei Education Press, 2001. pp. 43-44.

2   Anderson, Perry. *Considerations on Western Marxism*.Trans. Gao Tian. Beijing: People's Publishing House, 1981. p. 71.

3   Graham, Gibson. *The End of Capitalism*, P. 33.

In fact, this book is a collection based on my lectures, I have given for my doctoral students. Since 1998, I started writing the book *Deep Plough. Unscrambling Post-marxist Texts* that systematically interprets the classic texts of Western Marxism. At the same time, I promote seminars in class and ask the students to take up selected readings of Western Marxism classics. For over two years, most of the texts of Western Marxism philosophy have been studied in these classes. In most cases, we spend one semester discussing only one book in order to gain a more profound understanding. Regarding my learning and teaching, I tend to follow Husserl's guidance when he said: "gentleman, small change is preferred to a large note." My exploration into Althusser's texts began during the first semester of 2001. After much discussion, students all felt that they had gained a great deal from the class, and they asked for my lecture notes. At first, I only printed part of the lecture notes, but later I provided them the electronic editions. After revising the notes four different times, the relatively complete manuscript finally came into being. Subsequently, with the help of Mr. Wang Jisheng from the Central Compilation and Translation House Press, we decided to publish a series of books that focus on Nanjing University's interpretation of Marxist classical texts. This book is the first one in this series. Without his support and hard work, this series and this book would never have come out. I express my heartfelt thanks to the Central Compilation and Translation House Press and to Mr. Wang.

At last, there are two points that I need to clarify. Firstly, this book is included in the research project of "Modern Chinese Literature" of Nanjing University. Additionally, this book came into being with the help of the Project for the Tenth Five-year Plan of Social Science in Jiangsu Province. Herein, I am grateful to all of the teachers at the Academic Council of "Modern Chinese Literature" of the Nanjing University and all of the teachers who are part of the Review Committee of the Project for the Tenth Five-year Plan of Social Science in Jiangsu Province. Secondly, this book is also my completed dissertation as part of the doctoral degree conferred by the Department of Philosophy at Zhongshan University. In the process of applying for the degree, my tutor Mr. Ye Ruxian has given me many suggestions to refine my dissertation. Professor Xu Junzhong at the Graduate School of Zhongshan University has also offered me both guidance and help. I am deeply thankful to both of them.

Mrs. Wu Yufang from the Department of Philosophy of Nanjing University devoted a lot of time to the material organization of this book. My students Wu Jing and Meng Mugui also contributed to edit the manuscripts. I am grateful for their hard work.

Finally, I would like to dedicate this book to my teacher, Mr. Sun Bokui. Without his efforts to pave the road of bold exploration, there would be far less possibility for younger Marxist philosophers at Nanjing University to grow and develop. Herein I express my sincere thanks to Mr. Sun. Three years ago, he was diagnosed with liver cancer, but he faced death with amazing courage and determination. During those three years, he insisted on continuing his lectures for doctoral candidates even while fighting against cancer. He edited *Approaching Marx* and wrote several significant academic papers. He never gave up thinking and practicing until the last moment of his life. In our hearts, Mr. Sun represents the most outstanding thinker in contemporary China. We will never forget his contribution and achievements.

Zhang Yibing
Longjiang, Nanjing
Aug 27th, 2004

BIBLIOGRAPHY

Adorno, Theodor. *Aesthetic Theory*. Trans. Wang Keping. Chengdu: Sichuan People's Publishing House, 1998.

Adorno, Theodor. *Negative Dialectics*. Trans. Zhang Feng. Chongqing: Chongqing Publishing House, 1993.

Agger, Ben. *Introduction to Western Marxism*. Trans. Shen Zhi. Beijing: China Renmin University Press, 1992.

Ai, Zhilai. Western Marxism and Althusser's Theory of Marxism. *Collections of Philosophical Translations*,1983(1).

Akari, Shinohara. *Deleuze*. Trans. Xu Jinfeng. Shijiazhuang: Hebei Education Press, 2001.

Althusser, Louis. *A Bibliography*. Joan Nordquist (Editor) Reference & Research Services, 1986.

Althusser, Louis. *Essays in Self-criticism (auxiliary volume)*.Trans. Lin Qiming&XuJunda. Taipei: Long Stream Publications, 1990.

Althusser, Louis. *Essays in Self-criticism*.Trans. Du Zhangzhi& Sheng Qiyu. Taipei: Long Stream Publications, 1990.

Althusser, Louis. *For Marx*. Trans. Gu Liang. Beijing: The Commercial Press, 1984.

Althusser, Louis. *For Marx*. Verso, 1996.

Althusser, Louis. *Ideology and Ideological State Apparatus*. Shanghai: Shanghai Literature and Art Publishing House, 1995.

Althusser, Louis. *Lenin and Philosophy and Other Essays*. Monthly Review Press, 1990.

Althusser, Louis. *Lenin and Philosophy*. Trans. Du Zhangzhi. Taipei: Long Stream Publications, 1990.

Althusser, Louis. *Machiavelli and Us*. Verso, 1999.

Althusser, Louis. *Montesquieu, Rousseau, and Marx: Politics and History*. Verso, 1982.

Althusser, Louis. *Philosophy of the Encounter: Later Writings, 1978-87*. Verso, 2006.

Althusser, Louis. *Reading Capital*. Trans. Li Qiqing. Beijing: The Central Compilation and Translation Press, 2001.

Althusser, Louis. *Reading Capital*. Verso, 1998.

Althusser, Louis. Soutenanced'Amiens. *Studies on Marxism-Leninism*. Beijing: People's Publishing Press, 1986.

Althusser, Louis. *The Future Lasts Forever: A Memoir*. New Press, 1993.

Althusser, Louis. *The Spectre of Hegel: Early Writings*. Verso, 1997.

Althusser, Louis. *Writings on Psychoanalysis: Freud and Lacan*. Columbia University Press, 1999.

Anderson, Perry. *Considerations on Western Marxism*. Trans. Gao Xian. Beijing: People's Publishing House, 1981.

Anderson, Perry. *Contemporary Western Marxism*. Trans. Yu Wenlie. Beijing: Oriental Press, 1989.

Assiter, Alison. *Althusser and Feminism*. Pluto Press, 1993.

Attali, Jacques. *Noise: Political Economy of Music*. Trans. Song Sufeng. Shanghai: Shanghai People's Publishing House, 2000.

Barthes, Roland. *A Lover's Discourse*. Trans. Wang Yaojin & Wu Peirong. Shanghai: Shanghai People's Publishing House, 1988.

Barthes, Roland. *Elements of Semiology*. Trans. Li Youzheng. The Joint Publishing Company, 1988.

Barthes, Roland. *Empire of Signs*. Trans. Sun Naixiu. Beijing: The Commercial Press, 1994.

Barthes, Roland. *S/Z*. Trans. Tu Youxiang. Shanghai: Shanghai People's Publishing House, 2000.

Barthes, Roland. *The Fashion System*. Shanghai: Shanghai People's Publishing House, 2000.

Barthes, Roland. *The Pleasure of the Text*. Trans. Tu Youxiang. Shanghai: Shanghai People's Publishing House, 2002.

Baudrillard, Jean. *The Consumer Society: Myths and Structures*. Trans. Liu Chengfu & QuanZhigang. Nangjing: Nanjing University Press, 2000.

Baudrillard, Jean. *The Perfect Crime*. Trans. Wang Weiming. Beijing: The Commercial Press, 2000.

Baudrillard, Jean. *The System of Objects*.Trans. Lin Zhiming. Shanghai: Shanghai Publishing Group, 2000.

Benjamin, Walter. *Experience and Poverty*. Trans. Wang Binjun & Yang Jin. Tianjin: Baihua Literature and Art Publishing House, 1999.

Benjamin, Walter. *A Lyric Poet in the Era of High Capitalism*. Trans. Zhang Xudong & Wei Wensheng. The Joint Publishing Company Ltd., 1989.

Benjamin, Walter. *The Work of Art in the Age of Mechanical Reproduction*. Trans. Wang Caiyong. Hangzhou: Zhejiang Photography Press, 1993.

Bennett, Tony. Science, Literature and Ideology-Althusser's Literary Theories. *Journal of Liaoning University*, 1994(4).

Benton, Ted & Giddens, Anthony (Editor). *The Rise and fall of Structural Marxism: Althusser and His Influence*. St. Martin's Press, Inc., 1984.

Bourdieu, Pierre. *Practice and Reflection*. Trans. Li Meng & Li Kang. Beijing: Central Compilation and Translation Press, 1998.

Buber, Martin. *You and I*. Trans. Chen Weigang. The Joint Publishing Company Ltd., 1988.

Cai Yingtian. Mao Zedong's Unbalanced Theory and Althusser's Multi-decisions. *Studies on Mao Zedong and Deng Xiaoping Theories*, 1998 (2).

Callari, Antonio & Ruccio, David. *Postmodern Materialism and the Future of Marxist Theory: Essays in the Althusserian Tradition*. University Press of New England, 1995.

Callinicos, Alex. *Althusser's Marxism*. Trans. Du Zhangzhi. Taipei: Long Stream Publications, 1990.

Central Party School of the Communist Party of China, *The Collected Essays of Western Marxism*, 1990.

Chen Binghui. Review of Althusser's "Ideological State Apparatus. *Journal of Xiamen University*, 1994 (4).

Chen Lixu. A Tentative Analysis of Althusser's Explanation about Marx's Historical Views. *Journal of Liaoning Normal University*, 1999 (1).

Chen Xueming. *Freudian Marxism*. Shenyang: Liaoning People's Publishing House, 1989.

Chen Xueming. *On Western Marxism*. Shenyang: Liaoning Education Press, 1991.

Chen Yongguo & Ma Hailiang. *Selected Works of Benjamin*. Beijing: China Social Sciences Press, 1990.

Chen Zhenming. Contemporary Western Marxism. Xiamen: Xiamen University Press, 1995.

Cohen, G. A. *Karl Marx's Theory of History*. Trans. DuanZhongqiao. Chongqing: Chongqing Publishing House, 1989.

Compilation and Translation Bureau of the CPC Central Committee. *Selected Works of Gramsci*. Beijing: People's Publishing House, 1992.

Cong Dachuan. Althusser's Distorted Critique of Marxist Philosophy. *Journal of Yanbian University*, 1996(4).

Contemporary Review of Philosophical Trends. Qiushi Press, 1984.

Derrida, Jacques. *Of Grammatology*. Trans. Wang Jiatang. Shanghai: Shanghai Translation Publishing House, 1999.

Derrida, Jacques. *Speech and Phenomena*. Trans. Du Xiaozhen. Beijing: The Commercial Press, 1999.

Derrida, Jacques. *The Specter of Marx*. Trans. He Yi. Beijing: China Renmin University Press, 1999.

Derrida, Jacques. *Writing and Difference*. Trans. Zhang Ning. The Joint Publishing Company, 2001.

Dilthey, Wilhelm. *Geisteswissenschaften*. Trans. Tong Qizhi & Wang Haiou. Beijing: China City Publishing House, 2002.

Dilthey, Wilhelm. *Meaning in History*.Trans. Ai Yan & Yi Fei. Beijing: China City Publishing House, 2002.

Du Zhangzhi. About Lukacs and Althusser's Critique of Engels. *Trends of Social Sciences Abroad*, 1985 (10).

Du Zhangzhi. *The Biography of Lukacs*. Beijing: Social Sciences Academic Press, 1986.

Duan Yi, Gong Jingcai. The Research on Young Marx by Althusser. *Journal of Hebei University*, 1997(2).

Duan Zhongqiao. Review of Althusser's Multi-decisions and the Process without a Subject. *Journal of Renmin University of China*, 1995 (3).

Eagleton, Terry. *Literary Theory*. Trans. Wu Xiaoming. Xi'an: Shanxi Normal University Press, 1986.

Eagleton, Terry. *Marxism and Literary Criticism*. Trans. Wen Bao. Beijing: People's Literature Publishing House, 1980.

Eagleton, Terry. *The Ideology of the Aesthetic*. Trans. Wang Jie. Guilin: Guangxi Normal University Press, 1997.

Elliott, Gregory. *Althusser: The Detour of Theory*. Verso, 1988.

Elliott, Gregory. *Althusser: A Critical Reader*. Blackwell Publishers, 1994.

Erikson, Luke. Althusser and Reviewing of Revolutionary Marxism. *Trends of Social Science Abroad*, 1983 (11).

Finn, Geraldine. *Why Althusser Killed His Wife: Essays on Discourse and Violence*. Brill Academic Publishers, Incorporated, 1996.

Fiori, Giuseppe. *The Biography of Gramsci*. Trans. Wu Gao. Beijing: People's Publishing House, 1983.

Foucault, Michel. *Discipline and Punish*. Trans. Liu Beicheng & Yang Yuanying. The Joint Publishing Company, 1999.

Foucault, Michel. *Madness and Civilization*. Trans. Sun Shuqiang & Jin Zhuyun. Hangzhou: Zhejiang People's Publishing House, 1990.

Foucault, Michel. *The History of Sexuality*. Trans. Ji Xusheng. Shanghai: Shanghai Science and Technology Publishing House, 1989.

Foucault, Michel. *Words and Object*s. Trans. Mo Weimin. Shanghai: The Joint Publishing Company, 2001.

Fromm, Erich. *Beyond the Chains of Illusion*. Trans. Zhang Yan. Changsha: Hunan People's Publishing House, 1986.

Fromm, Erich. *Escape from Freedom*. Trans. Chen Xueming. Beijing: Workers' Press, 1987.

Fromm, Erich. *Man For Himself*. Trans. Sun Yiyi. The Joint Publishing Company, 1988.

Fromm, Erich. *Marx's Concept of Man*. Shanghai: Fudan University Press, 1983.

Fromm, Erich. *The Art of Loving*. Trans. Chen Weigang et al. Chengdu: Sichuan People's Publishing House, 1986.

Fromm, Erich. *The Heart of Man*. Trans. Sun Yuecai. Beijing: The Commercial Press, 1989.

Fromm, Erich. *The Sane Society*. Trans. Sun Kaixiang. Beijing: China Federation of Literary and Art Circles Publishing Corporation, 1995.

Fromm, Erich. *To Have or to Be?* Trans. Guan Shan. The Joint Publishing Company Ltd., 1986.

Gerratana, Valentine. Althusser and Stalinism. *Trends of Social Science Abroad*, 1990 (2).

Gibson & Graham. *The End of Capitalism-The Feminist Critique of Political Economy*. Trans. Chen Dongsheng. Beijing: Social Sciences Academic Press, 2002.

Giddens, Anthony. *Modernity and Self-Identity*. Trans. Zhao Xudong & Fang Wen. The Joint Publishing Company, 1998.

Giddens, Anthony. *Modernity*. Trans. Yin Hongyi. Beijing: Xinhua Publishing House, 2001.

Giddens, Anthony. *The Consequences of Modernity*. Trans. Tian He. Nanjing: Yilin Press, 2000.

Gilles, Deleuze. *Foucault*. Trans. Yang Jie et al. Changsha: Hunan Literature and Art Publishing House, 2001.

Gilles, Deleuze. *Negotiations*. Trans. Liu Hanquan. Beijing: The Commercial Press, 2000.

Goldmann, Lucien. *Essays on Method in the Sociology of Literature*. Trans. Duan Yi & Niu Hongbao. Beijing: Workers' Press, 1989.

Goldmann, Lucien. *Marxism and Humanities*. Trans. LuoGuoxiang. Hefei: Anhui Literature and Art Publishing House, 1989.

Goldmann, Lucien. *The Hidden God*. Trans. Cai Hongbin. Tianjin: Baihua Literature and Art Publishing House,   1998.

Gorman R. A *Biographical Dictionary of New Marxism*. Trans. Zhao Peijie. Chongqing: Chongqing Press, 1990.

Gramsci, Antonio. *The Practical Philosophy*. Trans. Xu Chongwen. Chongqing: Chongqing Publishing House, 1990.

Gramsci, Antonio. *The Prison Notebooks*. Trans. Bao Xu. Beijing: People's Publishing House, 1983.

Gray, John. *Berlin*. Trans. Ma Junfeng et al. Beijing: Kunlun Press, 1999.

Gu Liang. About Althusser's Soutenanced'Amiens. *Studies on Marxism-Leninism*, Beijing: People's Publishing Press, 1998.

Habermas, Jürgen. *Communication and the Evolution of Society*. Trans. Zhang Boshu. Chongqing: Chongqing Publishing House, 1990.

Habermas, Jürgen. *Knowledge and Human Interests*. Trans. Guo Guanyi & Li Li. Shanghai: Xuelin Publishing House, 1999.

Habermas, Jürgen. *Legitimation Crisis*. Trans. Chen Xueming. Shanghai: Shanghai People's Publishing House, 2000.

Habermas, Jürgen. *Reconstruct Historical Materialism*. Trans. GuoGuanyi. Beijing: Social Sciences Academic Press, 2000.

Habermas, Jürgen. *Technology and Science as Ideology*. Trans. Li Li & Guo Guanyi. Shanghai: Xuelin Publishing House, 1999.

Habermas, Jürgen. *The Structural Transformation of the Public Sphere*. Trans. Cao Weidong. Shanghai: Xuelin Publishing House, 1999.

Habermas, Jürgen. *The Theory of Communicative Action*. Trans. Jiang Peiyu et al. Chongqing: Chongqing Publishing House, 1994.

Hakuo, Yuasa. *The Withering of Bataille*.Trans. Zhao Hanying. Shijiazhuang: Hebei Education Press, 2001.

Hegel, Friedrich. *Elements of the Philosophy of Right*. Trans Fan Yang & Zhang Qitai. Beijing: The Commercial Press, 1961.

Hegel, Friedrich. *Science of Logic*.Trans.YangYizhi. Beijing: The Commercial Press, 1966.

Hegel, Friedrich. *The Early Works of Hegel*. Trans. He Lin et al. Beijing: The Commercial Press, 1997.

Hegel, Friedrich.*Lectures on the Philosophy of History*.Trans He Lin & Wang Taiqing. Beijing: The Commercial Press, 1959/1978.

Hegel, Friedrich.*Phenomenology of Spirit*. Trans. He Lin& Wang Jiuxing. Beijing: The Commercial Press, 1961.

Heidegger, Martin. *Being and Time*. Trans. Chen Jiaying& Wang Qingjie. Beijing: The Joint Publishing Company, 1999.

Heidegger, Martin. *Being and Time*. Trans. Sun Zhouxing. Shanghai: The Joint Publishing Company, 1996.

Heidegger, Martin. *Discourse on Thinking*. Trans. Chen Xiaowen & Sun Zhouxing. Beijing: The Commercial Press, 1996.

Hirsch, Joachim. Althusser and Structuralist Marxism. *Studies on Marxism-Leninism*. Beijing: People's Publishing House, 1983 (5).

Hitoshi, Yimamura. *Althusser: Epistemological Rupture*. Trans. Niu Jianke. Shijiazhuang: Hebei Education Press, 2001.

Hoffman, John. *Theory of Praxis Group and Marxism*. Trans. Zhou Yuchang & Du Zhangzhi. Beijing: China Social Sciences Press, 1988.

Hokori, Tsiwai. Althusser: Philosophy and Politics. *Trends of Social Science Abroad*, 1980 (2).

Horkheimer & Adorno. *Dialectic of Enlightenment*. Trans. Hong Peiyu & Lin Yuefeng. Chongqing: Chongqing Publishing House, 1990.

Horkheimer, Max. *Traditional and Critical Theory*. Trans. Li Xiaobing. Chongqing: Chongqing Publishing House, 1990.

Hu Wanfu. The Structuralist Nature of Althusser's Theories. *Journal of Central China Normal University*, 1987 (6).

Huang Jifeng. Althusser's "Anti-historicism". *Journal of Nanjing University*, 1988 (3).

Huang Xiaoming. Review of Althusser's Theory of Ideology. *Fujian Academic Journal*, 1993 (1).

Huang Zhongjin. Philosophy, Science, Humanism-The Ideological Basis of Althusser's "Rupture". *Social Science*, 1994 (3).

Huang Zhongjing. *Biography of Sartre*. Nanchang: Baihuazhou Art and Publishing House, 1995.

Husserl, Edmund. *Logical Investigations*. Trans. Li Liangkang. Shanghai: Shanghai Translation Publishing House, 1999.

Institute of Philosophy, China Academy of Social Science. *Yugoslavia Philosophical Papers*. The Joint Publishing Company, 1979.

Institute of Philosophy, Former Soviet Academy of Science. *Contemporary Overseas Philosophy of Marxism-Leninism*, Beijing: China Social Science Press, 1986.

Institute of Philosophy, Shanghai Academy of Social Science. *Selected Works of Frankfurt School*. Beijing: The Commercial Press, 1998.

Israel, J. *Language of Dialectics and Dialectics of Language*. Trans. Wang Lu & Ye Xiang. Beijing: The Commercial Press, 1990.

Jameson, Fredric. *Cultural Logic of Late Capitalism*. Trans. Zhang Xudong. The Joint Publishing Company, 1998.

Jameson, Fredric. *Culture and Politics*. Trans. Wang Fengzhen. Beijing: China Social Sciences Press, 1998.

Jameson, Fredric. *Late Marxism*. Verso, 1990.

Jameson, Fredric. *Marxism and Form*. Trans. Zhou Yao. Nanchang: Baihuazhou Literature and Art Publishing House, 1996.

Jameson, Fredric. *Postmodernism and Cultural Theories*. Trans. Tang Xiaobin. Xi'an: Shanxi Normal University Press, 1986.

Jameson, Fredric. *The Cultural Turn*. Trans. Hu Yamin et al. China Social Sciences Press, 2000.

Jameson, Fredric. *The Prison-House of Language*. Trans. Qian Jiaoru. Nanchang: Baihuazhou Literature and Art Publishing House, 1996.

Jameson, Fredric. *The Seeds of Time*. Trans. Wang Fengzhen. Guilin: Lijiang Publishing House, 1997.

Jay, Martin. *A History of the Frankfurt School*. Trans. Shan Shilian. Guangzhou: Guangdong People's Publishing House, 1996.

Jay, Martin. *Adorno*. Trans. Zhai Tiepeng et al. China Social Sciences Press, 1992.

Jin Hongming. Althusser and Western Marxism. *Journal of Social Sciences Abroad*, 1990 (2).

Kant, Immanuel. *Critique of Judgement*. Trans. Han Shuifa. Beijing: The Commercial Press, 1990.

Kant, Immanuel. *Critique of Practical Reason*.Trans. Han Shuifa. Beijing: The Commercial Press, 1999.

Kant, Immanuel. *Critique of Pure Reason*. Trans. Wei Zhuomin. Wuhan: Central China Normal University Press, 1991.

Karl Marx and Frederick Engels (first edition). Beijing: People's Publishing House, 1965/1985.

Karl Marx and Frederick Engels (second edition). Beijing: People's Publishing House, 1965/1985.

Lukacs, George. *History and Class Consciousness*. Trans. Du Zhangzhi et al. Beijing: The Commercial Press, 1995.

Kierkegaard, Soren. *Fear and Trembling*.Trans.WenShaojun& Lu Xinghua. The Joint Publishing Company, 1994.

Kierkegaard,Soren. *Fear and Trembling*.Trans. Liu Ji.Guiyang: Guizhou People's Publishing House, 1994.

Korsch, Karl. *Karl Marx*. Trans. Xiong Ziyun & Weng Yanzhen. Chongqing: Chongqing Publishing House, 1993.

Korsch, Karl. *Marxism and Philosophy*. Trans. Wang Nanshi & RongXinhai. Chongqing: Chongqing Publishing House, 1989.

Kosik, Karel. *Dialectics of the Concrete*. Trans. Fu Xiaoping. Beijing: China Social Science Press, 1989.

Kristeva, Julia. *Powers of Horror: An Essay on Abjection*. Trans. Zhang Xinmu. The Joint Publishing Company, 2001.

Lacan, Jacques. *A Selection*. Trans. Chu Xiaoquan. Shanghai: Shanghai Translation Publishing House, 2000.

Launde, Akira. Jarorty and Althusser's Discussion of Humanism. *Trends of Social Science Abroad*, 1993 (4).

Lefebvre, Henry. *On Countries*. Trans. Li Qingyi et al. Chongqing: Chongqing Publishing House, 1988.

Lefebvre, Henry. *The Basis of Dialectic Materialism &On Economic and Philosophical Manuscripts of 1844 by Western Scholars*. Shanghai: Fudan University Press, 1983.

Lefebvre, Henry. *The Crisis of Marxism*. The Joint Publishing Company, 1966.

Leiss, William. *The Domination of Nature*. Trans. Yue Changling & Li Jianhua. Chongqing: Chongqing Publishing House, 1993.

Levinas, Emmanuel. *Existence and Existent*. Trans. Gu Jianguang & Zhang Letian. Hangzhou: Zhejiang People's Publishing House, 1987.

Levinas, Emmanuel. *God, Death and Time*. Trans. Yu Zhongxian. The Joint Publishing Company, 1997.

Lezra, Jacques. *Depositions: Althusser, Balibar, Macherey, and the Labor of Reading*. Yale University Press, 1995.

Li Anyang. Althusser's Understanding of Marxist Dialectics. *Modern Philosophy*, 1987 (2).

Li Liangkang ed. *Selected Works of Husserl*. Shanghai: The Joint Publishing Company, 1997.

Li Qingyi. *Althusser and "Structuralist Marxism"*. Shengyang: Liaoning People's Publishing House, 1986.

Li Qingyi. Althusser's Autobiography and Biography. *Trend of Social Science Abroad*, 1995 (5).

Li Qingyi. *Contemporary Imperialism of Western Marxism*. Beijing: Xinhua Publishing House, 1990.

Li Shuhua. Althusser's Critique of the Humanization of Marxism. *Journal of Nankai University*, 1992 (4).

Li Zhongshang. *Analysis of New Marxism*. Beijing: China Renmin University Press, 1987.

Li Zhongshang. *The Third Road*. Academy Press, 1994.

Lichtheim, George. *Lukacs*. Trans. Wang Shaojun& Xiao Sha. Beijing: China Social Sciences Press, 1989.

Liu Beicheng. *The Ideological Portrait of Benjamin*. Shanghai: Shanghai People's Publishing House, 1998.

Liu Beicheng. *The Ideological Portrait of Foucault*. Beijing: Beijing Normal University Press, 1995.

Liu Shen. Philosophy and Science. *Journal of Chongqing Normal College,* 1987 (1).

Liu Xiaofeng. *Selected Works of Scheler*. Shanghai: The Joint Publishing Company, 1997.

Lu Hailin. *The Collected Essays of Western Marxist Aesthetics*. Guiling: Lijiang Publishing House, 1988.

Lu Meilin. Althusser's Artistic Thoughts. *Foreign Literature*

Review, 1989 (4).

Lukacs, George. *Existentialism or Marxism?* Trans. Han Runtang. Beijing: The Commercial Press, 1962.

Lukacs, George. *The Destruction of Reason*. Trans. Wang Jiuxing et al. Jinan: Shandong People's Publishing House, 1988.

Lukacs, George. *The Ontology of Social Being*. Trans. Li Qiuling et al. Chongqing: Chongqing Publishing House, 1993.

Lukacs, George. *The Young Hegel*. Trans. Wang Jiuxing. Beijing: The Commercial Press, 1963.

Luo Gang & Liu Xiangyu. *Cultural Studies Reader*. Beijing: China Social Sciences Press, 2000.

Lyotard, Jean-Francois. *The Postmodern Condition*. Trans. Dao Zi. Changsha: Hunan Fine Arts Publishing House, 1996.

MacIntyre, Alasdair. *Marcuse*. Trans. Shao Yidan. Beijing: China Social Sciences Press, 1989.

Mannheim, Karl. *Ideology and Utopia*.Trans Li Ming & Li Shuchong. Beijing: The Commercial Press, 2000.

Marcuse, Herbert. *Eros and Civilization*. Trans. Huang Yong & Xue Min. Shanghai: Shanghai Translation Publishing House, 1987.

Marcuse, Herbert. *Industrial Society and New Leftists*. Trans. Ren Li. Beijing: The Commercial Press, 1982.

Marcuse, Herbert. *One-Dimensional Man*. Trans. Zhang Feng. Shanghai: Shanghai Translation Publishing House, 1989.

Marcuse, Herbert. *The Aesthetic Dimension*. Trans. Li Xiaobing. The Joint Publishing Company, 1989.

McLellan, David. *Marxism after Marx*. Trans. Lin Chun et al. Beijing: Oriental Press, 1986.

McRobbie, Angela. *Postmodernism and Popular Culture*. Trans. Tian Xiaofei. Beijing: Central Compilation and Translation Press, 2001.

Merleau-Ponty, Maurice. In Praise of Philosophy.Trans. Yang Dachun. Beijing: The Commercial Press, 2000.

Merleau-Ponty, Maurice. *Phenomenology of Perception*. Trans. Jiang Zhihui. Beijing: The Commercial Press, 2001.

Michitaka. *Levinas*. Trans. Zhang Jie& Li Yong. Shijiazhuang: Hebei Education Press, 2001.

Mihailo, Marković. *History and Theory of Yugoslavia Praxis Group*. Trans. Zhen Yiming & Qu Yuehou. Chongqing: Chongqing Press, 1993.

Mo Weimin. *Fate of Subjects*. Shanghai: Shanghai People's Publishing House, 1995.

Mou Jianjun. Reevaluation of Althusser. *Theoretical Trends Abroad*, 1999 (10).

Majumdar, A. *Margaret; Althusser and the End of Leninism*, Pluto Press, 1995.

Nishikawa, Naoko. *Kristeva*. Trans. Wang Qing & Chen Hu. Shijiazhuang: Hebei Education Press, 2002.

O'Neill, John. *For Marx against Althusser: And Other Essays*. University Press of America, 1983.

Ouyang Qian. *Subjectivity and Liberation of Man*. Jinan: Shandong Literature and Art Publishing House, 1986.

Payne, Michael. *Reading Knowledge: An Introduction to Foucault Barthes and Althusser*. Blackwell Publishers, 1997.

Peng Yun. Althusser's Extreme Thinking of Marxist Theories and Humanistic Relations. *Studies on Marxism*, 1996 (3).

Poster, Mark. *Existential Marxism in Postwar France: From Sartre to Althusser*. Princeton University Press, 1977.

Poster, Mark. *The Mode of Information*. Trans. Fan Jinghua. Beijing: The Commercial Press, 2000.

Poster, Mark. *The Second Media Age*. Trans. Fan Jinghua. Nanjing: Nanjing University Press, 2000.

Poulantzas, Nicos. *Political Power and Social Classes*. Trans. Ye Lin et al. Beijing: China Social Sciences Press, 1982.

Predrag, Vranicki. *History of Marxism*. Trans. Li Jiaen et al. Beijing: People's Publishing House, 1986-1990.

Rakowski, Mieczysław. *Eastern European Marxism*. Trans. Zhong Changan. The Joint Publishing Company, 1984.

Rickman, H. P. *Dilthey*. Trans. Yin Xiaorong & Wu Xiaoming. Beijing: China Social Science Press, 1989.

Resch, Robert. *Althusser and the Renewal of Marxist Social Theory*. University of California Press, 1992.

Safranski, Rüdiger. *The Biography of Heidegger*.Trans. Jin Xiping. Beijing: The Commercial Press, 1999.

Sartre, Jean-Paul. *Being and Nothingness*. Trans. Chen Xuanliang. The Joint Publishing Company, 1987.

Sartre, Jean-Paul. *Critique of Dialectical Reason*. Trans. Lin Xianghua. Hefei: Anhui Literature and Art Publishing House, 1998.

Sartre, Jean-Paul. *Existentialism is a Humanism*. Trans. Zhou Xuliang& Tang Yongkuan. Shanghai: Shanghai People's Publishing House, 1988.

Sartre, Jean-Paul. *The Imagination*. Trans. Wei Jinsheng. Beijing: China People's Publishing House, 1986.

Schaff, Adam. *A Philosophy of Man*. Trans. Cheng Menghui. Nanjing: Jiangsu People's Publishing House, 1988.

Scheler, Max. *The Future of Capitalism*. Trans. Luo Tilun. Shanghai: The Joint Publishing Company, 1997.

Scheler, Max. *The Subversion of Value*. Trans. Luo Tilun et al. Shanghai: The Joint Publishing Company, 1997.

Scheuerman. William E. *Scientific Civilization and Man's Future*. Trans. Li Xiaobing. Beijing: The Oriental Press, 1995.

Schiller, Friedrich. *Aesthetic Education Letters*. Trans. Xu Hengchun. Beijing: China Federation of Literary and Art Circles Publishing Corporation, 1984.

Schmidt, Alfred. *History and Structure*. Trans. Zhang Wei. Chongqing: Chongqing Publishing House, 1993.

Schmidt, Alfred. *Marx's Concept of Nature*. Trans. Ou Litong & Wu Zhong. Beijing: The Commercial Press, 1988.

Shan Feng. Introduction to Althusser's Two Posthumous Works. *Marxism and Reality*, 1996 (2).

Shaw, William. *Marx's Theory of History*. Trans. Ruan Renhui et al. Chongqing: Chongqing Publishing House, 1989.

Shi Chaoyi. Whether Althusser is a Structuralist or not. *Modern Philosophy*, 1988 (2).

Simmel, George. *Money, Gender and Modern Living Style*.Trans. Liu Xiaofeng. Shanghai: Academia Press, 2000.

Sombart,Werner. *Modern Capitalism*. Trans. Li Ji. Beijing: The Commercial Press, 1958.

Song Gewen. About Country. Trends of Social Science Abroad, 1980 (2).

Steven B. Smith. *Reading Althusser: An Essay on Structural Marxism*. Cornell University Press, 1984.

Stevenson, Nick. *Knowledge of Media Culture*. Trans. Wang Wenbin. Beijing: The Commercial Press, 2001.

Stiegler, B. *Technology and Time*. Trans. Pei Cheng. Nanjing: Yilin Press, 2000.

Storey, John. *Cultural Theory and Popular Culture*. Trans. Yang Zhushan. Nanjing: Nanjing University Press, 2001.

Strinati, Dominic. *Theoretical Introduction of Popular Culture*. Trans. Yan Jia. Beijing: The Commercial Press, 2001.

Research Material on Marxism-Leninism, 1983 (5).

Research Material on Marxism-Leninism, 1983 (6).

Research Material on Marxism-Leninism, 1984 (3).

Research Material on Marxism-Leninism, 1984 (5).

Research Material on Marxism-Leninism, 1986 (4)-(5).

Research Material on Marxism-Leninism, 1989 (3).

Sun Bokui et al. *Western Marxology*. Nanjing: Jiangsu People's Publishing House, 1992.

Sun Bokui, Zhang Yibing. *Approaching Marx*. Nanjing: Jiangsu People's Publishing House, 2001.

Suzuki, Kazunari. *Barthes: The Pleasure of the Text*. Trans. Qi Yinping & Huang Weidong. Shijiazhuang: Hebei Education Press, 2001.

Ta Seiichi. *Maurice Merleau-Ponty: Reversibility*. Trans. Liu Jisheng. Shijiazhuang: Hebei Education Press, 2001.

Tang Zhengdong. Lukacs and Althusser's Interpretation of Marxist Philosophical Views: Coexistence of Profundity and Shallowness. *Nanjing Social Sciences*, 1997 (8).

Volpe, D. G. *Critique of Taste*. Trans. Wang Keping & Tian Shigang. Guangming Daily Press, 1990.

Volpe, D. G. *Rousseau and Marx*. Trans. Zhao Peijie. Chongqing: Chongqing Publishing House, 1993.

Wakole. *Adorno: Philosophy of Non-identity*. Trans. Xie Haijing & Li Haoyuan. Shijiazhuang: Hebei Education Press, 2001.

Wang Jie. Art and Ideology: Althusser's Aesthetic Thoughts. *Social Sciences Abroad*, 1996(5).

Wang Jie. The Horizon and Limits of Althusser's Literary Critique. *Journal of Guangxi Normal University*, 1996 (3).

Wang Luxiang (trans). *Western Modern Aesthetics in the Eyes of Western Scholars*. Beijing: Beijing University Press, 1987.

Wang Mingan, Chen Yongguo, Ma Hailiang. *The Postmodern Philosophical Discourse*. Hangzhou: Zhejiang People's Publishing House, 2001.

Wang Yuchen. Althusser's Discussion on the Relations between Marx and Hegel. *Qinghai Social Sciences*, 1997(3).

Wang Yuchen. *On Althusser's Understanding of Marxist Philosophy*. Hubei Social Sciences, 1996(9).

Wang Zhenlin. Althusser's Interpretation of Marxist History. *The Journal of Humanities*, 1994 (2).

Wang Zuo. Ideological Critique and Its Ontological Meaning-Enlightenments of Althusser's Ideological Critical Theories. *Journal of Baoding Teachers College*, 2000 (1).

Weber, Max. *Economy and Society*.Trans. Lin Rongyuan. Beijing: The Commercial Press, 1997.

Weber, Max. *Economy, Society and Religion*. Shanghai: Shanghai Academy of Social Science Press, 1997.

Weber, Max. *Politics as a Vocation*. Trans. Feng Keli. The Joint Publishing Company, 1998.

Weber, Max. *The Protestant Ethic and the Spirit of Capitalism*. Trans. Yu Xiao & Chen Weigang. The Joint Publishing Company, 1987.

William C. C. Dowling. *Jameson, Althusser, and Marx: An Introduction to the Political Unconscious*. Cornell University Press, 1990.

Wolff, Janet. *Social Production of Art*. Trans. Dong Xuewen & Wang Kui. Beijing: Huaxia Press, 1990.

Wolin, Richard. *The Terms of Cultural Criticism*. Trans. Zhang Guoqing. Beijing: The Commercial Press, 2000.

Wright, Mills. *Marxist*. Beijing: The Commercial Press, 1965.

Wu Wanfu. *On the Young Marx*. Wuhan: Central Normal China University Press, 1988.

Xi Guangqing. *Dictionary of Western Marxism*. Beijing: China Economic Press, 1992.

Xu Bi. Ideology and Symptomatic Reading-Althusser and Macule's Critique of Literary Ideology. *Literary Review*, 1995 (1).

Xu Chongwen. Althusser's Anti-empiricist Knowledge and Marxism. *China Social Sciences*, 1997(3).

Xu Chongwen. Althusser's Multi-decisiveness and Marxism. *The Journal of Chinese Academy of Social Sciences*, 1997(3).

Xu Chongwen. Althusser's Theoretical Anti-humanism and Marxism. *Studies on Marxism*, 1997(1).

Xu Chongwen. *Essays of Western Marxism*. Chongqing: Chongqing Publishing House, 1989.

Xu Chongwen. *Western Marxism*, Tianjin: Tianjin People's Publishing House, 1982.

Xu Junda. Review of Althusser's Structuralist Research Methodology of Marxism. *Jinyang Academic Journal*, 1985.

Xue Ming. Althusser's Theories of Anti-humanism. *Journal of Fudan University*, 1983 (3).

Yasichitaika, Fukuhara. *Lacan: Mirror Stage*. Shijiangzhuang: Hebei Education Press, 2001.

Yi Chen. Althusser and Structuralism. *Red Flag*, 1983 (9).

Yi Kexin. Lewis' View of Marxism-His criticism of Althusser. *Trends of Social Science Abroad*, 1994 (1).

Yu Keping. Marxism in the Age of Globalization. Beijing: The Central Compilation and Translation Press, 1998.

Yu Wenlie. *Introduction to "Analytical Marxism"*. Chongqing: Chongqing Publishing House, 1993.

Yu Wujin, Chen Xueming. *Foreign Schools of Marxism*. Shanghai: Fudan University Press, 1990.

Yu Wujin. Althusser's Theory of Ideology. *Jiangsu Social Sciences*, 1992 (6).

Zhang Jinpeng. *Althusser toward Structuralist Marxism-Studiees, On the Young Althusser*. Thesis stored in the archive of Nanjing University.

Zhang Jinpeng. Theoretical Meaning and Limitations of Althusser's View of Non-subject. *Nanjing Social Sciences*, 2001 (12).

Zhang Kangzhi. Totality of History and Structure-Comparison of Lukacs and Althusser. *Social Science of Beijing*, 1995 (5).

Zhang Pinggong. On Saussure's Influence on Barthes and Althusser. *Journal of Foshan Institute of Science and Technology*, 2000 (4).

Zhang Wenxi. Dissolving Ego: Althusser's Interpretation of Marx. *Journal of the Communist Party School of Zhejiang Provincial Committee*, 2001 (3).

Zhang Yibing. *Atonic Dialectical Imagination-The Textual Interpretation of Ardono's Negative Dialectics*.

Zhang Yibing. *A Deep Plough: Unscrambling Major Texts From Adorno to Zizek*. Canut Intl. Publishers London 2011. The Joint Publishing Company, 2001.

Zhang Yibing. *Back to Marx: The Philosophical Discourse in the Context of Economics*.Nanjing: Jiangsu People's Publishing House, 1999. English version published by Göttingen University Press, in 2014.

Zhang Yibing. *Selected Works of Zhang Yibing*. Guilin: Guangxi Normal University Press, 1999.

Zhang Yibing. *Subjective Dimension of Marxist Historical Dialectics*. Nanjing: Nanjing University Press, 2002, English version by Canut Intl. Publishers London 2011.

Zhang Yibing. *The Broken Wing of Reason-Philosophical Critique of Western Marxism*. Nanjing: Nanjing Publishing House, 1990.

Zhang Yibing. *The Past and Present of Marxist Philosophy*. Nanjing: Nanjing University Press, 1992.

Zhao Xingliang. Althusser's Discussion about the Research Methods of the Young Marx. *Zhengmin*, 1988 (1).

Zhong Liqian. Deception, Enlightenment, Individual Practice. *Journal of Guangxi Normal University*, 1996 (3).

Zhou Hui. Althusser's View of Ideology. *Open Times*, 2001 (8).

Zima, Pierre. *Introduction to Sociology Critique*. Trans. Wu Yuetian. Nanning: Guangxi Normal University Press, 1993.

Zizek, Slavoj. *Drated Ideology*. Trans. Fang Jie. Nanjing: Nanjing University Press, 2002.

Zizek, Slavoj. *The Sublime Object of Ideology*. Trans. Ji Guangmao. Beijing: Central Compilation and Translation Press, 2002.

TRANSLATORS' NOTES

Ten years ago when I was a doctoral candidate in Nanjing University, I first encountered this book by Professor Zhang Yibing. My research area was translation theories and aesthetics. Because of the strong interest in the relationship between translation and ideology, I read a number of philosophical works. At that time, Professor Zhang was a well-known professor and philosopher and was admired by so many students that it is no surprise that his books were among my favorites. My Ph.D. dissertation even cited his incisive arguments about the research on ideology. Moreover, while supervising the graduate students, I recommended that they read this book. Ten years later, when I returned to Nanjing University and became a professor and a Ph.D. supervisor of translation studies, I found that Professor Zhang had revised this book. It appealed to me as a supervisor of doctoral candidates in translation studies, translation philosophy and translation aesthetics. I also believe that this book can bring uniquely enlightened research in other relevant disciplines. Naturally, when the head of our department recommended that I translate one of his works, I chose this book without hesitation.

Nevertheless, Professor Zhang's book was a big test for us. This is not only because of his profound academic thoughts, his multi-faceted research object, but it is also because of Professor Zhang's creation of the "situating" method and his courage to name new philosophical words. How hard it is to interpret the deep meanings of these artistic philosophical words and translate them into an English academic work with literary taste! Many times, we felt that we were struggling in the philosophical net that Professor Zhang and Althusser co-woved. Besides, beyond their own wide horizon, we needed to comprehend the dialogues between numerous great minds. Undoubtedly, this was a huge challenge for us translators whose area of expertise is not philosophy.

Fortunately, though, Professor Zhang helped us in our difficulties of philosophy and supported us when exploring the "mysteries" in this book. He clearly answered our questions and spared no efforts in finding relevant books and data for our references. Mr. Zhou Jiaxin also answered hundreds of questions for us. Mr. Tang Zhengdong, Mr. Zhang Liang, Mr. Li Yuehua and Mr. Li Qiankun have also helped us to find needed materials and books. I am deeply grateful to Proessor Zhang, his colleagues and his students.

As translators and proofreaders, our team members' contributions are also very touching. In fact, shortly after I accepted the translation of this book, I fell ill. In order to finish the task in time, I invited my friends and students, Zhan Chongyang, Yi Diandian and Wang Yan to join in. Lacey Bradley, my American friend and expert in political science readily agreed to help us for proofreading of all the translations. I am impressed by her carefulness and rigorous academic spirit. I am also thankful for the timely help that my friends have extended to me.

Yang Liu
Institute for International Students
School of International Studies
Nanjing University, China
March 26th, 2012

ABOUT THE AUTHOR

Dr. Zhang Yibin, whose pen name is Zhang Yibing, was born in 1956 in Nanjing, a main city in Jiangsu Province, China. He graduated from the Department of Philosophy at Nanjing University in China in 1981. He is now the Vice Chancellor of Nanjing University; one of the prominent leaders of Association of Dialectical Materialism of China; dean of the Academy of Marxism and director of the Research Center of Social History of Marxism at Nanjing University, works as professor and doctoral tutor in the Department of Philosophy. He is one of rare scholars in China focusing on textological research He has written numerous articles for Chinese academic journals. His main books include: *The Broken Wing of Reason-Philosophical Critique of Western Marxism*. Nanjing: Nanjing Publishing House, 1990; *The Past and Present of Marxist Philosophy*. Nanjing: Nanjing University Press, 1992; Selected Works of Zhang Yibing. Guilin: Guangxi Normal University Press, 1999 and 2009; *Back to Marx: The Change of Philosophical Discourse in the Context of Economics*, Nanjing: Jiangsu People's Publishing House, 1999; Co-authored by Sun Bokui and Zhang Yibing. *Approaching Marx*. Nanjing: Jiangsu People's Publishing House, 2001; *Atonal Dialectical Imagination: A Textological Reading of Adorno's "Negative Dialectic"*. The Joint Publishing Company, 2001; *A Textological Reading of Althusser. Problematic, Symptomatic Reading and Ideology*. Central Compilation and Translation Press, 2003; *Deep Plough: Unscrambling Major Texts of Western Marxism*. Volume I and II published by China Renmin University Press, 2004-2008; *Contra Baudrillard*. Nanjing Publishing House, 2008; *The Subjective Dimension of Marxist Historical Dialectics*. Nanjing: Nanjing University Press, 2002; *The Impossible Real of Being: Imago of Lacanian Philosophy*. The Commercial Press, 2006; *Back to Lenin: A Post-textological Reading of His "Philosophical Notes"*. Jiangsu People's Press, 2008; *The History of the Understanding of Capitalism*, 5 volumes (Co authored with Zhang Liang, Hu Daping). Nanjing: Jiangsu Renmin Press, 2009.

His following books were later translated into English and Turkish by Canut Intl. Publishers and Kalkedon Publishing, *A Deep Plough: Unscrambling Major Texts of Western Marxism, Volume II- From Adorno to Zizek*, 2010; *The Subjective Dimension of Marxist Historical Dialectics*, English version by Canut Intl. London, 2010; *Lenin Revisited: His Entire Thinking Process on Marxist Philosophy: A Post-textological Reading on Philosophical Notes*, Canut Intl. London 2011; *Back to Marx: The Change of Philosophical Discourse in the Context of Economics*. English version published by Göttingen University Press, 2014; *A Marxist Reading of Young Baudrillard Throughout His Ordered Masks*, English version published by Canut Intl. Publishers London, 2014.

INDEX

CANUT SERIES

Books in English

Defense for Marx
A New Interpretation of Marxist Philosophy
Yang Geng

A Marxist Reading of Young Baudrillard
Throughout His Ordered Masks
Zhang Yibing

A Deep Plough: Unscrambling Major Post-Marxist Texts
From Adorno to Žižek
Zhang Yibing

Problematic, Symptomatic Reading and Ideology
A Textological Interpretation of Althusser
Zhang Yibing

Lenin Revisited
A Post-textological Reading on Philosophical Notes
Zhang Yibing

The Subjective Dimension of Marxist Historical Dialectics
Zhang Yibing

Back to Marx.
The Change of Philosophical Discourse in the Context of Economics
Zhang Yibing

Into the Depths of History
Research on Marx's Historical Materialism
Chen Xianda

New Research into the New Edition of The German Ideology
Han Lixin

Marxist Theory of Economic Cycles and Crises
Liu Mingyuan

New Monistic Living Labor Theory of Value
The Normative and Positive Research of Labor Value
Cheng Enfu

A Review on Marxist and Left Debates
Post-marxism, Eco-marxism, Post-modernism, Market Socialism,
New Imperialism, Post-modern Feminism, Socialist Feminism,
Radical Democracy, Baudrillard's Political Economy, Future Socialism
Zeng Zhisheng

Marx's Practical Materialism
The Horizon of Post-Subjectivity Philosophy
Wang Nanshi, Xie Yongkang

Between Surging Ideas and Real Changes:
Contemporary Interpretation on Marx's Practice View
Ouyang Kang, Zhang Mingchang

History of Marxist Thought on Literature, Art, Aesthetics
Ideas of Major Critics and Political Thinkers
Zhou Houzhong

Books in German:

Verteidigung für Marx
Eine Neue Auslegung der Marxistischen Philosophie
Yang Geng

Ein Tiefer Pflug: Entschlüsselung der postmarxistischen Hauptwerke
von Adorno bis Žižek
Zhang Yibing

Zurück zu Lenin.
Eine post-textologische Lektüre seiner Philosophischen Hefte
Zhang Yibing